BUILDING
AMERICAN
Cities

BUILDING AMERICAN
Cities

The Urban Real Estate Game

SECOND EDITION

JOE R. FEAGIN & ROBERT E. PARKER

BeardBooks
Washington, D.C.

Library of Congress Cataloging-in-Publication Data

Feagin, Joe R.
    Building American cities : the urban real estate game / by Joe R. Feagin and Robert
Parker.--2nd ed.
        p. cm.
    Originally published: Englewood Cliffs, N.J. : Prentice Hall, c1990.
    Includes bibliographical references and index.
    ISBN 1-58798-148-3 (alk. paper)
    1. Land use, Urban--United States. 2. Real estate development--United States. 3. City
planning--United States. 4. Urbanization--United States. 5. Urban renewal--United
States. 6. Housing--United States. 7. Urban policy--United States. I. Parker, Robert,
1957-II. Title.

HG257 .F43 2002
307.1'46'0973--dc21

                                                                    2002071167

Printed in the United States of America

*To our parents, Hanna and Frank Feagin
and Elizabeth and Charles Parker,
and to the memory of Neva Sharp.*

CONTENTS

PREFACE

Building American Cities is about people like Jimmy White, a 72 year-old Chicagoan living a mile from the Loop who survived the winter of 1988-89 in one of the nation's coldest cities in a ramshackle shanty. Before moving there, White had slept in cheap boarding houses, on the sidewalks and in a crude assemblage of mattresses and wood covered by sheets of plastic. A proud, persevering man, Jimmy has not applied for Federal welfare assistance or food stamps. The former car wash and auto shop worker explains, "I'm so busy I don't have time to get it." In a city with an estimated 25,000–40,000 homeless—and only 2,800 beds available—White has not taken the trouble to seek protection from the weather in one of his city's scattered and inadequate shelters. His explanation echoes the sentiments of many homeless people when he calls the shelters "too crowded." White's dilemma symbolizes the *affordable* housing crisis in the United States.[1]

This book is also about our local and federal governments—about our political leaders and their often deficient housing perspectives and policies, policies that after decades of an affordable housing crisis and a decade of visible homelessness have done little to solve our underlying housing dilemmas. One recent example of a governmental leader who ignored those Americans with affordable housing problems is former President Ronald Reagan. After the 1988 election in which then-Vice-President George Bush was elected the next President, President Reagan was interviewed by ABC's David Brinkley. In spite of regular reports documenting the problem, this was one of the few occasions during his eight-year administration in which he addressed the homeless issue. When asked, then President Reagan replied that many of the homeless people "make it their own choice" not to seek out shelter and that a "large percentage" of the homeless are "retarded" people who have "walked away from those institutions." The highest official in the land then blamed the increase in numbers of homeless people primarily on the American Civil Liberties Union for promoting changes in the law that allowed "mentally impaired" people to leave institutions. Mr. Reagan was not only ill-informed about the reasons for the closing of many inadequate and unsafe mental institutions, but he was also oblivious to the fact that two-thirds of the homeless do not fall into this category. And in spite of the severe shortage of beds available at private and public shelters, Reagan emphasized that "there are shelters in virtually every city and shelters here [Washington, D.C.] and those people still prefer out there [sic] on the grates or the lawn to going into one of those shelters."[2]

Building American Cities is also about people like Robert Moses, perhaps the most powerful public developer the United States has ever known, and like Donald Trump, a major private developer who exemplifies the high-profile breed of private real-estate capitalist. Consider the legacy of Robert Moses, a man who at one point held a dozen New York City and New York state offices simultaneously. Utilizing government capital from the 1920s to his retirement in the late 1960s, Moses built many governmental projects in the New York area, so many that he has been called the greatest public builder since the pharaohs of ancient Egypt. Moses supervised the building of the Verrazano-Narrows, Triborough, Westside, Bronx-Whitestone and Henry Hudson Bridges, the Queens Midtown and Brooklyn-Battery Tunnels, highways (the Northern and Southern State Parkways, the Long Island Expressway), power stations, the New York Coliseum, housing projects, the Lincoln Center for the Performing Arts, the United Nations headquarters, and many beaches, playgrounds, and parks. While many have lauded Moses' public accomplishments, there was a seamy underside to his usually autocratic approach and to his ignoring of the negative impact his projects had on ordinary citizens. Critic Paul Goldberger, reflecting on the 100th anniversary of Moses' birth, made these observations:

> *It all changed in the years after World War II, when Moses' tactics, which had always been highhanded, became more arrogant still; he pushed through projects...and the bulldoze-and-rebuild philosophy of urban renewal became his stock-in-trade. No public official was more closely identified with the banal red-brick towers of postwar public housing than Moses, or with the insistence that highways took priority over existing neighborhoods. Moses had no patience with those who argued that demolishing stable neighborhoods for urban expressways was a grievous error; he talked frequently about not being able to make an omelet without breaking eggs, and that was all the justification he believed he needed.[3]*

Then there is another famous New York developer—Donald Trump. Since Trump's activities are detailed in Chapter 3, we will cite here a *Fortune* business writer, who gives an unflattering portrait of this powerful developer:

> *Born in 1946, Trump is undoubtedly the finest example we have of materialism, ambition, and self-love among the baby-boomers. His book [The Art of the Deal, 1988], written with Tony Schwartz, will no doubt someday be on the required reading lists at great universities for history courses with names like "The Roaring Eighties: The Age of Excess." It will not be of much use in business schools or to anyone with a real job. What it delivers is everything you always suspected about*

*the makeup of Donald Trump: The pomposity, the shallowness, and above all, the
need for more money, more toys, and more attention.*[4]

What this rather harsh picture does not detail are the facts of Trump's
widespread development activities. Trump's real estate holdings in North
America have been estimated to be nearly $4 billion. His development
firm, like other development firms, has played a major role in reshaping
our cities. Trump's company has been involved in numerous large-scale
New York projects, including Trump Tower, a retail-office-apartment complex next to Tiffany's on Fifth Avenue. In the late 1980s Trump ranked 27th
among major developers in the United States.

   This book is also about the courageous actors who are resisting the
actions and decisions of the Moses, Reagans, and Trumps and have been
defending the likes of Jimmy White. One recent case of citizen protest in
San Francisco took place at the Alexander Residence, a hotel subsidized
by a federal housing program. The owner illegally raised the furniture
rental rate, and the tenants organized and applied pressure to hotel owners
and federal officials. After months of protest the group succeeded in
rolling back rents and in getting rebates for overcharges. A leader of the
group perceptively commented that

> *I thought that when you're down like this, way below the poverty level, you're
> powerless. But I realized that you can make the big shots stand up and listen. It was
> amazing to me to learn that if you work together you can do something.*[5]

In the next chapter we will discuss a very successful movement of tenants,
in Santa Monica, who forced developers to make major "linkage" concessions to citizen demands.

   A professional group supportive of such citizen actors is the group
of planners who identify themselves as "advocacy planners." These urban
planners are working to integrate the interests of low-income families,
members of minority groups, and less powerful urbanites into the urban
decisionmaking process that shapes modern cities. Expressing a widely
shared view, advocacy planner Lewis Lubka has noted that

> *...there are still some radical planners around—or progressive, or whatever you
> want to call them. True, I see a lot of "privatizing"—a lot of fine planning minds
> spending their time figuring out how to keep business profitable. But I'm still
> fighting, I'm still involved. My state, through the efforts of some of the planners,
> voted for nuclear freeze and against money for phony nuclear relocation plans. It's
> clear that there are still people who are looking for alternatives.*[6]

   Building American Cities is not only about people, about urban actors
in various class, race, and gender groups, but also about the processes,
structures, and social texture of urban America. People make their own

history, but they make that history within the context of structures and institutions. This book presents the story of the often concealed struggle underlying our diverse and complicated urban landscapes. It is an account of how American cities emerge, transform, contract, die, and become resurrected. It is a book that demonstrates the need for a critical examination of urban social processes, such as population migration to suburbia, patterns of corporate location decisions, and cycles of foreign capital investments in U.S. real estate. It attempts to explain the specific mechanics involved in the assembling, organizing, and construction of development projects in urban areas. It examines the patterns in the location, development, financing, and construction decisions of small and large corporations, as well as the patterns of relationships between industrial and development corporations and various levels of government. This book pays particular attention to the patterns and consequences of the social costs—such as pollution, wasted energy, and congestion—of unbridled urban growth (and of decline) in a capitalistic context.

An important central theme running through *Building American Cities* is that our urban society is characterized by ongoing, often volatile, social conflict. This citywide conflict takes many specific forms and is acted out by diverse groups of actors: small business owners and large capitalists; profit-oriented industrial and development firms and ordinary workers, consumers, and homeowners; the better-off, tax-generating whites who fled to the suburbs and poorer inner city minority Americans who became saddled with substandard services as a consequence; public officials who attempt to shift urban decisionmaking in the direction of business interests and progressive community groups pressing for greater democratization of this decisionmaking process. It is this social dynamic, this perennial conflict, that fundamentally gives shape to our urban centers. While we see the pitched battle over the shape and character of urban landscapes as favoring large developers and their corporate and governmental allies, we argue here that the contest over urban form, structure, and process has by no means been resolved. As long as the resistance efforts of groups such as the Alexander Residence protestors, the Santa Monicans for Renters Rights, the Municipal Art Society of New York City, and the advocacy planners persist and have a progressive impact, the urban struggle for more liveable cities will doubtless continue.

OVERVIEW OF BUILDING AMERICAN CITIES

We begin our examination of U.S. urban society, past and present, by analyzing in Chapter 1, "Building American Cities," the traditional market-oriented social science perspectives on cities and the newer critical urban perspectives. We lay out the advantages of the new critical perspectives, advantages documented fully in the chapters that follow. We detail who the major and minor urban development actors are, in both the governmental and private spheres, and we examine the complex web of institutions and structures, such as capital investment circuits and state bureaucracies, that surround and limit these actors. We briefly discuss the significance of the powerful development actors, such as developers and bankers, as well as the citizens' protest movements.

Chapter 2, "Corporate Location Decisions," examines the impact of corporate location determinations, those actions that often set urban real estate development processes into motion. We pay attention to capital mobility and detail the numbers of Americans involved in plant closings and employee cutbacks. We examine the role of government subsidies for industrial and commercial corporations seeking new city locations. And we note the importance of the global corporate search for "good business climates."

Chapter 3, "Developers, Bankers, and Speculators: Shapers of American Cities," describes the different types of actors involved in urban development. We identify the specific actors involved in transforming cities. Our emphasis on particular agents is designed to counter the argument that cities emerge and grow "naturally" as the result of some "invisible hand." We also trace the institutional frameworks, such as finance capital institutions, through which these powerful development actors work. We analyze the recent increases in foreign capital investments in U.S. real estate.

Chapter 4, "Skyscrapers and Multiple-Use Projects," begins a series of chapters on specific features of our urban environments. We demonstrate how high-rise commercial developments have transformed urban America. We describe and explain the oscillating market in office space nationwide. And we conclude with a detailed examination of the emergence and rapid growth of multiple-use developments, those mega-projects that incorporate such features as office buildings, shopping facilities, residential facilities, and selected urban amenities.

Chapter 5, "Gentrification and Redevelopment in Central Cities," discusses one of the most controversial issues in urban America today—gentrification. By describing and analyzing gentrification and other urban displacement scenarios we uncover the uneven investment patterns that are characteristic of contemporary patterns of urban real estate investment.

Chapter 6, "Autos, Highways, and City Decentralization," details the emergence and impact of the automobile on urban form. We describe the forces lying behind the decline of mass transit, the impact of highways, and the role of the key public and private actors involved in the construction of metropolitan beltways, parkways, and highways. We scrutinize traffic congestion as a key social cost involved in unregulated and poorly planned urban growth. And we study city decentralization and outline its influence on the growing mismatch between jobs and housing in U.S. cities.

Chapter 7, "Shopping Centers and Business Parks: Decentralized Urban Growth," describes two major dimensions of the decentralized structure of our urban settings: shopping malls and industrial/business parks. We delineate several types of malls, identify major owners and developers, and show how large malls can have a deleterious impact on surrounding environments. We also include a discussion about the private versus public nature of malls and consider the oft-celebrated "village square" imagery surrounding shopping centers. And we conclude with a discussion of the decentralization of business parks.

Chapter 8, "Suburbs and Central Cities: Residential Housing Development," is a key chapter dealing with housing in America. We examine the growing problem of the lack of affordable housing, the major developers of housing, the role of the government in housing trends, the emergence and patterning of suburban housing developments, the low rate of public housing construction, rates of homeownership, and problems facing those who must rent their housing.

Chapter 9, "Governments and the Urban Development Process," takes an in-depth look at the role of government in shaping the structure of our cities. It offers specific examples and discusses both older and recent forms of developmental subsidies provided by all levels of government. It traces the history of zoning in the U.S. and reveals the conflicting interests that produce fiscal crises in cities.

Chapter 10, "Citizen Protest: Democratizing Urban Investment and Development," discusses the efforts of individuals and groups active in resisting powerful industrial and real estate capitalists. Many peoples' movements envision an alternative to the present elitist, private-profit-centered decision making about our cities. A survey of these citizens' movements suggests the possibility of a more democratically organized decisionmaking system. The role of a variety of movements, including tenant struggles, in urban change and the emergence of advocacy planners are also examined in some detail in this final chapter.

ACKNOWLEDGMENTS

We would like to thank the following people for their insightful reading of various drafts of this book and/or for their encouragement and support: Terry Sullivan, Mark Gottdiener, Michael Peter Smith, Peter Dreier, Tony Orum, Bennett Harrison, John Gilderbloom, Arnold Fleischmann, Jerry Jacobs, Richard Walker, Steve Worden, Stella Capek, Claire McAdams, Walter Firey, Gideon Sjoberg, Manuel Castells, Carrolyn and Rosie, David Derosset, Ernest Cantrell, Chelsea and Ashley Parker, Sue Boland, Harriet and Dick Mears, David Byrne, and Robert Zimmerman. We would like to thank Pat Thomas for editing assistance and Janice Campbell, Clairece Booher Feagin, and Barbara Phillips for word processing aid. And we are indebted to our editors at Prentice Hall, Bill Webber and Nancy Roberts, for their continuing support for this book.

NOTES

1. James Barron, "Cold Forces Reluctant Homeless Into Sometimes Dangerous Shelters," *The New York Times*, December 13, 1988, p 1; Isabel Wilkerson, "In Chicago, a Shanty Shelters an Aging Man and His Pride," *The New York Times*, December 20, 1988, p 1.
2. "Reagan: Homeless Choose Streets," *St. Louis Post Dispatch*, December 23, 1988, p 7A.
3. Paul Goldberger, "Robert Moses: Patron Saint of Public Places," *The New York Times*, December 18, 1988, p 45.
4. Gary Belis, "Donald Trump Explained," *Fortune* 117 (January 4, 1988): p 92.
5. Barbara Goldoftas, "Organizing in a Gray Ghetto," *Dollars and Sense* No. 133 (January/February 1988), p 18-19.
6. Ruth Knack and James Peters, "There Have All the Radicals Gone?" *Planning* 51 (October 1985): 14.

BUILDING AMERICAN CITIES

1

BUILDING AMERICAN CITIES
Traditional and Critical Perspectives

One rainy morning Dorothy Lykes, not knowing where else to turn, telephoned the Gray Panther office in New York City....Mrs. Lykes was 78, terminally ill with cancer and weighed 70 pounds. Her husband was in the hospital, also terminally ill. Most of their Social Security was going for his hospital bills. The city had taken possession of their Bronx home, which they bought in the 1950s, because they could not pay the property taxes. Nor could they pay the $300 a month rent the city was asking from them for living in their own home. Mrs. Lykes asked: "Is the next step for me to move to Penn Station?"[1]

...the Times Square area is changing its character. At the north edge is Edward Larrabee Barnes's huge, just-completed Equitable Tower. To the south, at 42nd and Broadway, two hotly debated towers by Philip Johnson and John Burgee are set to rise. In between, sites have been assembled for new hotels and office buildings. Further west, the lure of the new Convention Center has spurred proposals for new megacomplexes in an area once dominated by manufacturing. Caught in the middle is the old working class neighborhood of Clinton (once known as "Hell's Kitchen"), which is experiencing powerful gentrification pressures despite the special zoning meant to protect the area.[2]

INTRODUCTION

Locating new factories. Relocating offices. Buying hotels. Building office towers. Mortgaging whole streets of houses. Buying and selling utility companies. Bulldozing apartment buildings for office construction. Purchasing large blocks of urban land to secure a land monopoly. Going bankrupt because of overextension in real estate. These actions are part of the real estate game played in every American city. The only place most Americans are able to play anything analogous to this is on the *Monopoly* game board in living-room encounters with their friends. The board game mimics the real world of real estate buying, selling, and development, but the parallels between playing *Monopoly* on the board and playing the real estate game in cities are limited, for in the everyday world of urban development and decline there are real winners and real losers.

In U.S. cities the powerful elites controlling much development—
the industrial executives, developers, bankers, and their political allies—
have built major development projects, not just the hotels and houses of
the *Monopoly* game, but also shopping malls, office towers, and the like.
They typically build with little input from local community residents.
Executives heading industrial firms and real estate developers have
frequently been able to win a string of favorable concessions from city
officials: cheap land, industrial parks, tax decreases, and utility services
subsidized by rank-and-file taxpayers. In many cities these industrial
executives and developers threaten to go elsewhere if these governmental subsidies are not provided. Yet in the 1970s and 1980s some citizen
groups have tried to change this way of doing city business. Periodically, the voters in cities, from Santa Monica and Berkeley on the West
Coast, to Cleveland in the Midwest, to Burlington and Hartford on the
East Coast, vote out pro-development political officials in favor of
candidates more tuned to slow growth and enhancing the local quality of life. For instance, in the 1980s the residents of Santa Monica,
California, voted out a city council allied with landlords, developers, and
bankers. They elected in their place a progressive council determined
to break with the developer-oriented dominance of city politics. The
new council has rejected policies favoring developers and has used a
policy called "linked development" to force those developers building
new office complexes and shopping centers to take action to meet important local needs. One Santa Monica city council agreement with a
developer building a million-square-foot hotel-office complex specified that he must include landscaped park areas, a day-care center,
energy conservation measures, and a positive plan for hiring minority
workers.[3]

Who Decides on Development?   Some powerful developers, bankers, and
other development decision makers are becoming known to the public.
There is, for example, Gerald D. Hines, a Houston mechanical engineer
whose $200 million estimated net worth was just under the amount
necessary to be listed among the nation's 400 richest people by *Forbes* in
1987.[4] Still, Gerald D. Hines Interests of Houston, one of the largest U.S.
development firms, controlled buildings worth more than $4.5 billion. In
the early 1980s Hines celebrated the laying of the foundation of a Republic
Bank office complex in Houston with a lavish $35,000 reception for top
business and government leaders; it included a brass ensemble playing
fanfares, fine wine and cheeses, and other culinary delights. The massive
building itself, red granite in a neo-Gothic style, is just one of more than
360 such office buildings, shopping malls, and other urban projects that
have been built by Hines' company in cities from New York to San
Francisco.

Residential developers have also shaped U.S. cities in fundamental ways. The famous firm Levitt and Sons is among the 2 percent of developer-builders that have constructed the lion's share of U.S. residential housing since World War II. Using nonunion labor, Levitt and Sons pulled together in one corporation the various aspects of the house manufacturing and marketing process, from controlling the source of nails and lumber to marketing the finished houses. After World War II, Levittowns—names now synonymous with suburbs—were built in cities on the East Coast. One subdivision, Levittown, New Jersey, was carefully planned so that the acreage was within one political jurisdiction. According to Herbert Gans, the company executives had the boundaries of a nearby township changed so that it was not part of the area in which this Levittown would be built, thus giving Levitt and Sons more political control. William Levitt was the key figure in this development firm for decades, and he reportedly built his suburbs with little concern for the expressed tastes of his potential customers; Levitt was not especially "concerned about how to satisfy buyers and meet their aspirations. As the most successful builder in the East...he felt he knew what they wanted."[5] Profitability was the basic standard; community-oriented features were accepted when they enhanced profit. No surveys of potential buyers were made to determine consumer preferences, but a great deal of attention was given to advertising, marketing, and selling the houses to consumers. Friendly salespeople were selected and trained by a professional speech teacher. Buyers who were viewed as "disreputable" were excluded; and blacks were excluded until the state government began to enforce a desegregation law.[6]

Developers such as Hines and Levitt and Sons have been a major force in making and remaking the face of American cities. They are key figures in shaping city diversity and decentralization. Since World War II, U.S. cities have exploded horizontally and vertically with thousands of large-scale developments—shopping centers, office towers, business parks, multiple-use projects, convention centers, and residential subdivisions. The "built environments" of our cities have expanded to the point that their growing, and dying, pains have become serious national problems. Trillions of dollars have been invested in tearing down, constructing, and servicing the many and diverse physical structures scattered across hundreds of urban landscapes. For large development projects to be completed in downtown or outlying areas of cities, older buildings are often leveled, even when local citizens oppose such development. The major U.S. developers often see their projects as the "cutting-edge of western civilization." Yet these massive expenditures of capital for large-scale urban development, for lavish towers and the parties celebrating them, are made in cities with severe urban problems—extreme poverty, housing shortages, severe pollution—for whose solution little money allegedly can be found.[7]

Cities are not chance creations; rather, they are human developments. They reflect human choices and decisions. But exactly who decides that our cities should be developed the way they are? Who chooses corporate locations? Who calculates that sprawling suburbs are the best way to house urbanites? Who decides to put workers in glassed-in office towers? Who determines that shopping is best done in centralized shopping centers? Who creates the complex mazes of buildings, highways, and open spaces? There is an old saying that "God made the country, but man made the town." Cities are indeed human-engineered environments. But which men and women made the cities? And what determines how they shape our cities?

GROWTH AND DECLINE OF CITIES: TRADITIONAL SOCIAL SCIENCE PERSPECTIVES

The Traditional Approach: The Market Knows Best Examination of urban development and decline has been dominated by a conflict between the market-centered approaches of traditional social scientists and the newer critical analyses developed in recent decades. Traditional social scientists have dominated research and writing about American cities. Beginning in the 1920s and 1930s, there was a major spurt of activity in urban sociology and ecology at the University of Chicago, where researchers such as Robert Park and Ernest W. Burgess drew on the nineteenth century social philosopher Herbert Spencer to develop their concept of city life, organization, and development; they viewed the individual and group competition in markets in metropolitan areas as resulting in "natural" regularities in land-use patterns and population distributions—and thus in an urban ecological or geographical map of concentric zones of land use, moving out from a central business district zone, with its office buildings, to an outlying commuter zone, with residential subdivisions.[8]

Much urban research between the 1940s and the 1970s established the dominance of the traditional market-centered paradigm in urban sociology, geography, economics, political science, and other social science disciplines. Largely abandoning the concern of the earlier social scientists with urban space and land-use zones, sociological, economic, and geographical researchers have for the most part accented demographic analysis and have typically focused on population trends such as migration flows, suburbanization, and other deconcentration, and on statistical distributions of urban and rural populations in examining modern urban development. Writing in the *Handbook of Sociology*, the urban analysts Kasarda and Frisbie review mainstream research and a small portion of the newer critical research, but they explicitly regard the ecological approach in sociology, geography, and economics as the "dominant (and arguably, the only) general theory of urban form" that has been tested by empirical verification.[9] Books such as Berry and Kasarda's *Contemporary Urban Ecology*, Micklin and Choldin's *Sociological Human Ecology*, and textbooks like Choldin's *Cities and Suburbs* have been influential in establishing a conventional perspective accenting the role of a competitive market in urban development and emphasizing market-centered city growth as beneficial to all urban interest groups. The political scientists in this tradition have also given attention to capitalism-generated growth and the role of the market in city development; they alone have given much attention to the importance of government in urban development. However, their view of government typically accents a pluralism of competing interest groups and an array of government officials acting for the general welfare, a perspective that, as we will discuss, is rather limited.[10]

Consumers and Workers as Dominant Conventional social scientists have accepted uncritically the workings of the dominant market and the processes of capital accumulation. This perspective on competitive urban markets is grounded in neoclassical economic theory; it sees urban society as the "algebraic sum of the individuals...the sum of the interests of individuals."[11] In this view, given a "free-market" system, urban consumers and business firms will freely buy and sell. "If consumers want certain goods they will demand them. Businessmen will sense this demand through the marketplace and seek to satisfy the consumers' wishes. Everyone is happy."[12] Urban sociologist John Kasarda has written of profit-seeking entrepreneurs operating in self-regulating markets as a wise guiding force in city development.[13] Similarly, economists Bradbury, Downs, and Small, reviewing problems of city decline, argue that "market forces are extremely powerful; so it would be folly to try [governmental] policies that ignored their constructive roles in guiding the form and structure of economic change."[14] From this perspective capitalists follow the profit logic of capital investments that seeks out "good business climates" (low taxes and pro-business governments) in certain cities, such as those in the South. This conventional view implies that whatever exists as the economics and geography of the urban landscape today is fundamentally good for all concerned, if it has resulted from competitive market activity. The rather utopian competitive market idea, Lewis Mumford has suggested, was taken over from earlier theologians: "the belief that a divine providence ruled over economic activity and ensured, so long as man did not presumptuously interfere, the maximum public good through the dispersed and unregulated efforts of every private, self-seeking individual."[15]

Imbedded in this common market assumption is the idea that individual workers and consumers are often more important than corporate decision makers in shaping urban patterns, because the capitalists mostly react to the demands of consumers. A study of the U.S. business creed accented this point: "One way of shedding awkward responsibility is to believe that the consumer is the real boss."[16] Such analysts accept the business view of individual consumers and workers as "voting" in the marketplace with their consumer choices: Cities are viewed as having been created by average Americans whose demands for such things as autos and single-family houses have forced developers, builders, and industrial executives to respond. Consumers are often termed "kings" and "queens" when it comes to urban development. For decades not only urban scholars but also business leaders have argued that through their consumption choices "the masses of Americans have elected Henry Ford. They have elected General Motors. They have elected the General Electric Company, and Woolworth's and all the other great industrial and business leaders of the day."[17]

One assumption in much traditional urban research is that no one individual or small group of individuals has a determinate influence on patterns of urban land uses, building, and development. Mainstream sociologists and land economists such as William Alonso and Richard Muth have argued that urban commercial and residential land markets are determined by free competitive bidding. According to these theories, thousands of consumers, and thousands of firms, are pictured as autonomous atoms competing in a market system, largely without noneconomic (for example, political) relations and conventions, atoms that have a "taste" for commodities such as more space and housing. As their incomes grow, they will seek more space. Conventional analysts offer this as an explanation of why cities grow, expand, or die. Actors in this competitive bidding are recognized as having different interests, even different incomes, which affect the bidding process. However, the fact that a small group of the most powerful decision makers (such as major developers) can do far more to shape the land and building markets than simply outbid their competitors is not seriously analyzed. And the negative consequences of market-generated growth (for example, water pollution from sewer crises) in these same cities are seldom discussed.[18]

David L. Birch, Director of the Massachusetts Institute of Technology's Program on Neighborhood and Regional Change, has offered a worker-driven theory in explaining why many cities have had too much office space. Birch argues that the story of the current high vacancy rates in office buildings in many U.S. cities began decades ago when the "war babies" began to enter the labor force. This movement into the labor force caused a huge increase in employment. Birch argues that both sexes decided they did not want to work in factories. Rather, they "wanted to work in offices. They wanted to join the service economy, wear white shirts, and become managers or clerks."[19] According to this line of reasoning, there was only one thing for developers and builders to do; in order to satisfy this new generation of workers and consumers, "we built them offices." Yet the power of workers and consumers in shaping the urban office landscape has never been as profound as Birch and others describe.

Indeed, it is the industrialists, investors, developers, bankers, and their associates who have the capital to invest in job creation and to build office buildings and other workplaces—in places they decide upon and in terms of their corporate restructuring and profit needs.

Accenting Technology and Downplaying Inequality Traditional social scientists often view the complexity of cities as largely determined by historical changes in transportation and communication technologies, whose economic contexts, histories, and alternatives are not reviewed. Changes in urban form are explained in terms of technological transformation, including shifts in water, rail, and automotive transport systems, without reference to the decisions of powerful decision makers such as investors and top government officials. Water-borne commerce favors port and river cities, while auto, train, and truck technologies facilitate the location of cities apart from water systems. In an opening essay for a 1985 book *The New Urban Reality*, Paul Peterson views technological innovations as independent forces giving "urban development its rate and direction."[20] And in the influential book *Urban Society*, mainstream ecological researcher Amos Hawley looked at the relocation of industry from the industrial heartland to outlying areas and explained this decentralization substantially in terms of technological changes in transport and in communication.[21] Transport and communication technologies are certainly important in urban centralization and decentralization. But the corporate history and capitalistic decision-making *context* that led to the dominance of, for example, automobiles—and not mass transit—in the U.S. transport system should be more carefully examined (see Chapter 6).

Some Major Omissions Missing from most traditional research on cities is a major discussion of such major factors in urban development as capital investment decisions, power and resource inequality, class and class conflict, and government subsidy programs. The aforementioned collection, *The New Urban Reality*, has important essays by prominent geographers, economists, political scientists, and sociologists on urban racial demography and the black underclass, but there is no significant discussion of capital investment decisions made by investors and developers and the consequences of these decisions for urban development. Moreover, in the recent summary volume *Sociological Human Ecology*, prominent ecologists and demographers have reviewed the question of how humans survive in changing social environments, including cities, but without discussing inequality, power, conflict, or the role of governments.[22] Traditional urban scholars such as the geographer Berry and the sociologist Kasarda briefly note that in market-directed societies the role of government has been primarily "limited to combating crises that threaten the societal mainstream," that government involvement tends to be incremental, and that state government dealing with the "social consequences of laissez-faire urbanization" are "ineffective in most cases."[23] In his influential urban textbook, *Urban Society,* sociologist Amos Hawley has devoted little space to the government role in city growth and decline. This neglect of the role of government has been most common among mainstream urban sociologists, geographers, and economists. As we will see, the mainstream political scientists among contemporary urban researchers have given more attention to government, but generally with a pluralistic emphasis.[24]

An Important Government Report   However, the federal government has used this traditional urban research for policy purposes. In the 1980s a major federal government report, *Urban America in the Eighties,* publicly articulated the traditional urban perspective for the general public. Prepared by the President's Commission for a National Agenda for the Eighties, this report called on the federal government to refrain from assisting the troubled northern cities. Free-enterprise markets are viewed as driving the basically healthy changes in urban development. And these markets know best. The *Urban America* report's strong conclusions were publicly debated—particularly those suggesting that the federal government should neglect dying northern cities and should, at most, assist workers in leaving Frostbelt cities for the then-booming cities of the Sunbelt. Some northern mayors protested the report's conclusions, but many Sunbelt mayors were enthusiastic. While northern officials were concerned about the report's conclusions, few publicly disputed the report's basic assumptions about how cities grow or die.[25]

This market-knows-best view of the Frostbelt-Sunbelt shift in capital investment and of urban growth more generally drew on the work of traditional urban researchers. Prepared under the direction of prominent business leaders, this report conveys the view of cities found in mainstream urban research: that cities are "less conscious creations" than "accumulations—the products of ongoing change." Again, choices by hundreds of thousands of individual consumers and workers are emphasized as the fundamental determinants of urban landscapes. Changes in cities, such as the then-increasing prosperity of many Sunbelt cities, reflect "nothing more than an aggregate of countless choices by and actions of individuals, families, and firms."[26] The urban land and building market is again viewed as self-regulating; according to this theory the market efficiently allocates land uses and maximizes the benefits for everyone living in the cities. The hidden hand of the market receives heavy emphasis in this conventional accounting. In the policy-oriented conclusions, the authors of *Urban America* pursued this market logic to its obvious conclusion: Those impersonal individuals and firms actively working in cities and shaping urban space know best, and government officials should thus not intervene when impersonal decisions lead to the decline of cities in the North. Growth in, and migration to, booming cities such as those in the Sunbelt should simply be recognized, and, at most, governments should encourage workers to move from dying cities to booming cities.

GROWTH AND DECLINE OF CITIES: THE CRITICAL URBAN PERSPECTIVE

Basic Themes in the New Approach   Since the 1970s the dominance of the mainstream urban research in the United States has been challenged by a critical urban perspective, called by some the "new urban sociology." Both European and American researchers have developed a critical urban paradigm grounded in concepts of capital investment flows, class and inequality, activist governments, and powerful business elites. European researchers such as Henri Lefebvre, Manuel Castells, and David Harvey had developed critiques of the traditional urban approaches by the late 1960s and early 1970s.[27] This European influence was soon felt in U.S. urban studies. By the late 1970s critical urban studies were pursued and published by Michael Peter Smith, Mark Gottdiener, Allen Scott, John Mollenkopf, Norman and Susan Fainstein, Richard Child Hill, Ed Soja, Michael Dear, Richard Walker, Allen Whitt, Todd Swanstrom, and Harvey Molotch, to mention just a few of the growing number of critical social scientists in the United States.[28] The critical urban approach accents issues neglected in most traditional sociological, economic, and political science analysis. While there is still much ferment and debate among contributors to the critical urban perspective, there is some consensus on three fundamental themes.

The first major theme is that city growth and decline, internal city patterns, and city centralization and decentralization are shaped by both *economic* factors and *political* factors. Although some critical scholars accent the economic over the political, and others the political over the economic, in this book we will focus on both the economic and political factors. In Figure 1.1 we show the economic and political influences on cities, as well as the interaction between these economic and political influences. Most Western cities are shaped by capitalistic investments in production, workers, workplaces, land, and buildings. These urban societies are organized along class (also race and gender) lines; and their social institutions are substantially shaped by the commodity production and capital investment processes. Capital investment is centered in corporations calculating profit at the firm level; this can result in major urban social costs associated with the rapid inflow of capital investment and accompanying growth and also with capital

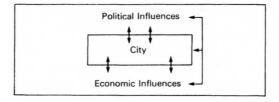

Figure 1.1

outflow (disinvestment) and accompanying urban decline. But Figure 1.1 indicates that there are governmental (state) factors in urban growth, structuring, and decline as well. Governments protect the right to own and dispose of privately held property as owners see fit. Moreover, governments in capitalistic societies are often linked to business elites and the investment process; various levels of government play a part in fostering corporate profit making. But government officials also react to citizen protests, to class, race, and community-based struggles; as a result, they often try to cope with the costs of capitalist-generated growth and decline. In addition, in cities with relatively independent political organizations (for example, "machines"), politicians may develop interests of their own and work *independently* of individual capitalists and citizen groups to shape and alter cities. In the urban worlds there is much interaction between the political and economic structures and political and economic decision makers.

A second important theme to be found in many critical urban arguments has to do with the central role of *space*. Some critical scholars only implicitly touch on spatial issues, while others feature the spatial dimension at the center of their city analysis. As Figure 1.2 is designed to illustrate, we human beings live not only economic and political lives as workers affected by investments in markets and voters affected by political advertising, but also lives as occupiers of space, in households and families living in the home and neighborhood spaces of our cities. On the one side, we have the group of profit-oriented industrialists, developers, bankers, and landowners who buy, sell, and develop land and buildings just as they do with other for-profit commodities. *Exchange value*, the value (price) of commodities exchanged in markets, is usually the dominant concern in their decisions about buying and selling land and buildings. The investment actions of developers and others seeking to profit off the sale of, and construction on, land are centered in exchange-value considerations. On the other side, we have the group of American tenants and homeowners, low-income and middle-income, black and white, who are usually much more concerned with the *use value* of space, of home and neighborhood, than with the exchange value.

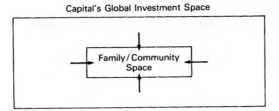

Figure 1.2 Capital's global investment space

Corporate exchange-value decisions frequently come into conflict with the use-value concerns of many Americans. A concern with use value can mean that the utility of space, land, and building for everyday life, for family life, and for neighborhood life is much more important than land or building profitability. Such use-value concerns are behind the actions of neighborhood residents who have fought against numerous office buildings, malls, and redevelopment projects in order to keep them from intruding on their home and neighborhood spaces. Some zoning and other government land-use controls have thrown up barriers to the unrestrained expansion of capitalistic investment. Historically, much pressure for land-use regulation has come from worker-homeowners concerned with protecting family spaces and neighborhoods against industrial and commercial encroachment.[29]

Capitalist investors operate today in a worldwide investment space, so they may move factory and office jobs (or real estate capital) quickly from one city or country to another. However, workers and consumers generally spend their lives in more constricted family and home spaces. They often invest their lives in particular communities and cities and cannot move so easily to a city in another region or country, so they suffer when investors relocate quickly to other areas on the globe. Capital accumulation, capital investment, and the capitalistic class structure interact with space to generate urban and rural spatial patterns of production, distribution, and consumption. The aforementioned competition of local urban politicians for capital investments by corporate actors has not only job and construction effects, but also effects on the livability of local urban space. Uneven economic development also means uneven spatial development. Some places, homes and neighborhoods, stay viable and livable, while other urban communities become difficult to live in because of capital flight to other places across the nation or the globe.

A third basic theme in the new critical perspective is that of *structure* and *agency*, which is suggested in Figure 1.3. While most critical scholars tend to accent either structure (for example, institutions) or agency (for example, decision makers) in research on urban development, a number of scholars such as Lefebvre, Gottdiener, and Giddens, have called for

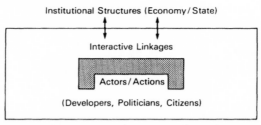

Figure 1.3 Institutional structures (economy/state)

research giving more attention to *both* dimensions. Some focus on the concrete actors involved in making cities, such as developers and business elites or citizens protesting development, while others prefer to emphasize the complex web of institutions and structures, such as state bureaucracies and capital investment circuits. In this book we will give attention not only to the decision makers themselves but also to the institutions that shape, and are shaped by, their concrete actions. Economic systems and governments do not develop out of an inevitable and unalterable structural necessity, but rather in a contingent manner; they result from the conscious actions taken by individual decision makers in various class, race, gender, and community-based groups, acting under particular historical circumstances. The most powerful actors have the most influence on how our economic and political institutions develop. Yet they, in turn, are shaped by those institutions.[30]

A Structural Dimension: Private Property The U.S. legal system, a critical part of our governmental structure, institutionalizes and protects the right to private property. Yet this legal system is critical to the perpetuation of great inequalities in real estate ownership and control. Most Americans own or control little property, other than their homes. Essential to the maintenance of inequality in land decision making is the legal protection of individualized property ownership. The rights of private property give owners, especially the large property owners, a great deal of control over land and buildings. Within broad limits land can be developed, and buildings constructed, as owners desire. This unbridled use of private property has not always been the case in the United States. The early Puritans, for example, had highly planned towns from Maine to Long Island. For two generations Puritan towns were designed by pioneers whose strong religious values influenced the layout of urban areas. The private ownership and control of property were not central; more important communal and collective goals often overrode private property interests. But the Puritan group-centered town planning soon gave way to intensified private landholding, even in New England. Fee-simple (unrestricted transfer) ownership of land became central to the expanding capitalistic system of eighteenth-century America. Early immigrants from

Europe were generally hostile to landlords and vigorously sought to own their own land. Ownership of even a small piece of property was a sign of independence from landlords; many immigrants had come to the colonies to escape oppressive European landlords. Land was seen as a civil right by the many small farmers.[31]

Yet this early and heavy commitment to the sacredness of privately held property had a major negative effect on development once the United States was no longer primarily a country of small farmers. By the early decades of the nineteenth century, there were fewer land-holders and ever more tenants without land. In many cases, the growing number of Americans with little or no real estate property were seen as unworthy. Yet the strong commitment to private property, on the part of both propertied and landless Americans, has continued to legitimate the private disposal of property by the powerful landowning and development decision makers. As a result, over the last two centuries control over urban land development has become more concentrated in the hands of executives of banks, insurance firms, development corporations, and industrial companies.[32] In addition, there are major social costs for a private property system that gives owners of large amounts of land the right to use the land more or less as they wish. Those who build and develop large projects on central-city land have shown that they can transfer certain social costs onto other people nearby. A good example is the modern skyscraper with its mirrored glass walls, which often generate heat problems for nearby buildings, and with its thousands of workers whose exit in the evenings can create massive traffic jams. Such social costs of skyscraper development are generally not paid for by the developers and owners of the buildings.

A Structural Dimension: Capital Investment Circuits Particular human agents and decision makers have a profound influence on urban development and decline. But as we have just noted all human actors, even the most powerful, are constrained by the social, economic, and political rules, roles, and institutions in which they find themselves. For example, some of the critical urban analysts accent the historical emergence and current character of capital investment circuits. Capital investment across the world is important to urban and metropolitan development. Several circuits of capital have been identified and discussed. The "primary circuit" of capital encompasses the ebb and flow of money and credit capital into raw materials, manufacturing equipment, labor power (workers), and transport vehicles to distribute manufactured goods around the world. This primary circuit can be discussed in terms of its rules and dominant organizations, such as the large national and multinational corporations that make crucial manufacturing investments in the United States and around the globe. The exploitation of workers' labor in this primary circuit is a foundation of capitalistic profit. And the acceleration, or decline, in profitability of investments in particular manufacturing industries—such as the auto and steel industries—has resulted in a greater velocity of capital movement into and out of specific cities such as Detroit or Youngstown. Capital flight often increases the problems of worker and community adjustment. The actions of particular capitalists and workers are shaped by the institutionalized rules and roles of this primary capital circuit. And the industrialized primary circuit of capital is not static, for there is a circulation of capital through industrial investments over time. There are recurring periods of capital turnover. Time, as well as space, is an important dimension of capital circuits, as we will document in Chapter 2.

The "secondary circuit" (or "second circuit") of capital encompasses the flow of capital into undeveloped land and into the "built environment," which includes factories, office buildings, shopping malls, houses, and government-built water systems.* One critical scholar, Henri Lefebvre, has argued that this built environment of cities is important not only as the general precondition for actual manufacturing and other production, but also as a place for the investment of *surplus* private capital, for there is often a surplus in the hands of capitalists who have done well in primary circuit investments. David Harvey has drawn on the work of Lefebvre and has written about the secondary circuit; from his viewpoint there must be a surplus of capital in the primary circuit of production for capital to flow into the built environment, the secondary circuit. However, critics of Harvey suggest that the secondary circuit has its own dynamic, sometimes independent of surpluses in the first circuit. An activist government commonly gets involved, because individual capitalists have difficulty in switching capital from one circuit to another without government-backed banking institutions, such as the U.S. Federal Deposit Insurance Corporation and the Federal Reserve banking system. Note too that the secondary circuit of capital involves the circulation of capital through both productive fixed capital investments, such as factory and office buildings, as well as through what some call reproduction investments, such as workers' housing. Critical analysts argue for a dynamic conception: that the circulation of capital through fixed capital and reproduction investments takes place over succeeding periods of capital turnover. Both time and space are important dimensions of the secondary circuit.[33]

Uneven Urban Development and Multinucleated Cities   The movement of capital into and out of the primary and secondary circuits creates distinc-

---

*A tertiary circuit of capital can be seen as including investments in science, technology, and government-funded education.

tive patterns of urban development and decline. Gottdiener has used capital circuit analysis to interpret the shift in U.S. cities from the bounded industrial city form to a sprawling, multicentered urban form. The highly deconcentrated growth is distinctive from that in Europe; the multinucleated city has been generated by relentless investment in the secondary circuit; real estate investment has been central there to profit making. Subsidized by governmental home loan guarantees, preferential tax laws, and defense expenditures in suburban and Sunbelt areas, "this second circuit of capital is so active that real estate investment, speculation and development comprise a major economic sector that rivals the industrialized first circuit of capital."[34]

Oscillations of capital movement into both the primary industrial circuit and the secondary real estate circuit account for the uneven development within and across U.S. cities. The multicentered city of Houston boomed from the 1940s to the early 1980s, with much capital flowing into its petrochemical plants, ship channel facilities, and large real estate projects, while in the 1970s both Detroit and Newark suffered serious disinvestment, with corporate investors pulling capital out of the cities. The results have included capital flight and capital shortages. *Uneven development* is a term sometimes used to describe this oscillating process of mostly private investment decisions.

And the human-related inefficiencies of a private market system can be seen in this uneven development. Take the example of the state of Maine's urban and rural areas in the 1980s. In some areas of the state, all the signs of "revitalization" have been present:

> *...southern and coastal regions and other places handy to Interstate 95, are in the midst of an economic boom. Visible signs of growth are everywhere: beachfront condos, Main Street boutiques, shopping malls in cow pastures, industrial parks carved from forests, new office buildings crowding Portland's horizon—and plenty of "help wanted" ads in the local papers.[35]*

However, at the same time that some of the state's regions were experiencing a boom in investment and thus in trade and construction, there was another Maine: There was both "the booming southern and coastal region; and the depressed northern and interior section."[36] The north and the interior have endured heavy losses in manufacturing, particularly in the paper industry. Capital flight has characterized these urban and rural areas. Moreover, even in the reviving areas, vacation homes and marinas have pushed fishing people out, the low- and middle- income workers have endured a housing crisis as neighborhoods are "gentrified," and developers have driven land and housing prices up through speculation. Uneven urban development is substantially shaped by those who control capital.

POWERFUL AGENTS OF URBAN CHANGE:
PRIVATE PRODUCERS

Neglecting Powerful Agents   The primary and secondary circuits of capital, and the urban land and building markets, are important features of our capitalistic urban system. Their operations shape the land and built environments of cities. Mainstream scholars often portray these land and building markets as "natural" markets guided by an invisible hand. But they are not natural. In reality, these markets are the creation of the most powerful players on the urban scene—the array of visible real estate decision makers in industry, finance, development, and construction. Over decades of urban development these powerful decision makers have both shaped, and been shaped by, the structures and institutions of urban real estate capitalism. Not only some of the critical analyses, such as the research of Harvey, but also traditional urban analyses, such as Berry and Kasarda's *Contemporary Urban Ecology* and Micklin and Choldin's *Sociological Human Ecology,* have largely ignored the central role of specific capitalistic and political actors in basic decisions about shaping urban land and built environments, the complex array of residential subdivisions, shopping malls, factories, warehouses, and office buildings.[37]

Among the primary decision makers in the urban real estate game are the capitalistic producers. Today real estate capitalism is organized around a complicated network of entrepreneurs and executives heading corporations of varying size. The size and complexity of the urban development industry can be seen in Table 1.1, which lists major real estate and development decision makers. The categories refer to sets of major decisions that are critical to urban development.[38]

Looking at the private sector, we see that category 1 encompasses those corporate executives whose location decisions (for example, the choice of locating a factory in a northern city or a Sunbelt city) often set the other decision makers into motion. Category 2 covers the developers, land speculators, and landowners who buy, package, and develop land for use by industrial corporations and others.* Category 3 encompasses, among others, those bankers and financial corporations that make the loans for land purchase, construction, and related development. Category 4 includes the various design and construction actors who actually construct urban projects. And category 5 covers a variety of supporting actors, including real estate brokers and chamber of commerce executives.

---

*The term "corporation" is used in this book for the various organizational arrangements, including partnerships, that capitalists utilize in profit making, whether or not legally incorporated.

Table 1.1 Urban development: Decision categories
and selected decision makers

1. Industrial and commercial location decisions
    Executives of industrial companies
    Executives of commercial companies

2. Development decisions
    Executives of development companies (developers)
    Land speculators and landowners
    Apartment owners and landlords

3. Financial decisions
    Commercial bankers
    Executives of savings and loan associations ("thrifts")
    Executives of insurance companies
    Executives of mortgage companies
    Executives of real estate investment trusts

4. Construction decisions
    Builders and developer-builders
    Executives of architectural and engineering firms
    Construction subcontractors

5. Support decisions
    Chamber of commerce executives
    Real estate brokers
    Executives of leasing companies
    Apartment management firms

Today a single corporation may include subsidiaries and other organizational units involved in a variety of decisions across several categories. Within one firm there may be a development subdivision, which not only develops projects but also engages in land speculation; a real estate brokerage subsidiary; and an architectural subsidiary. A major insurance company may have a lending department, as well as its own urban land development subsidiary. Large integrated real estate development companies are often involved in major decisions in more than one category. Frequently, local developers, realtors, and bankers are the major decision makers in local development projects; studies of community decision makers show clearly the role and power of local business people in all types of cities in the North and South.[39] However, major real estate decisions are made not only by local individuals and real estate companies but also by powerful regional and national firms, such as the Hines and Levitt firms cited earlier. There are complex interconnections between influential interests external to cities and those that are part of the internal power structure of a particular city. An example would be a major insurance company, such as the Prudential Life Insurance Company, which, in connection with other local and national companies, finances and owns real estate and development projects in cities across the United States.

Local Growth Coalitions   Those interested in urban growth and development often organize themselves. Some of these organizations are formal and national, such as the Urban Land Institute, a prominent developers' think tank. Other organizations are local. The term local "growth coalitions" has been used by scholars such as John Mollenkopf and Harvey Molotch for those local business elites working to boost local economic and population growth. Molotch, for example, has suggested that virtually all U.S. cities are dominated by a "small, parochial elite whose members have business or professional interests that are linked to local development and growth.(40) This elite is usually centered around local developers, bankers, and industrialists interested in a city's economic growth; the latter are assisted by others, including real estate agents and lawyers. The cast of characters in a particular city's growth coalition can vary significantly depending on where the city fits in the regional, national, and global economic contexts. In some cities (for example, Houston in the 1950s and 1960s) most members of the coalition are local bankers, developers, industrialists, and other localized business people, whereas in other cities (for example, Dallas) the coalition has included business people in local firms and top executives in major multinational corporations. With the emergence of the large national and multinational development, banking, and industrial corporations, it is not surprising to find complex growth coalitions including both small-business leaders ("immobile capital") and the locally based executives of the larger national and multinational corporations ("mobile capital"). Whatever their composition, however, these growth coalitions typically work hard to make their cities into "growth machines," into commodified urban spaces maximizing returns on industrial and real estate investments.

Some Examples of Individual Decision Makers   Powerful decision makers such as D. M. Carothers, retired head of Allright Auto Parks, frequently seek what they call the "higher and better uses" for urban land, sometimes losing sight of the older traditions of urban neighborhoods or the needs of smaller-business tenants. For many landowners and developers, the most important tradition to uphold is profit making in an "efficient and rational" way. As Carothers said to journalist Elizabeth Ashton: "In the growth of the city, you can't take care of old traditions." Long-term homeowners, small-business people, or renters are all only temporary occupants in this view. "They like to think of it as a heritage that has been passed on to them, but they're living in another century."[41] The city block Carothers had in mind is the site for one of the tallest office buildings west of the Mississippi, the Texas Commerce Tower in Houston. Smaller businesses were moved out in order to build the tower. Small businesses are common casualties in the private urban redevelopment engineered by landowners, developers, and their associates.

Allright Auto Parks has made money directly from fees off parking lots on cleared central-city land. In the mid-1980s it had 1,600 parking lots in 70 cities; and it owned 2.3 million square feet in 39 downtown areas. But parking-lot revenue is not its only source of profit. "Banking" the land for "higher" uses is the goal, as Carothers has explained it:

> We were figuring how the property could, in effect, buy itself. If we could get the old buildings off it and begin to park the cars...would income be sufficient to meet the payments? And in the back of my mind was always this extra—this icing: the eventual control of real valuable property that could be turned for a higher and better use.[42]

Selling land has accounted for much of this parking lot company's income, as the parking lots are sold at good prices to developers and bankers who recycle the land. Older buildings are cleared off, and the land is "banked" in the form of parking lots until a more profitable use is found for it. In central-city areas the more profitable use is usually an office tower, a shopping mall, or a high-rise parking garage.

A few hundred developers and financial institutions now construct and finance most major and many smaller urban development projects, from office parks and shopping malls to suburban housing projects, in most American cities. Among the nation's dozen largest developers is Century Development Corporation, which, like Gerald D. Hines Interests mentioned previously, builds large metropolitan projects. For example, Greenway Plaza, a major multiple-use development, involved the purchase of several hundred single-family houses in several large residential subdivisions not far from downtown Houston. Century had real estate agents buy houses from the local residents. Once the homes had been acquired, the houses were moved or razed. Despite the fact that the city had a serious housing shortage, there was no organized protest of this destruction of residential neighborhoods. Greenway Plaza is of such a scale that it required financing from large insurance companies. The scale of modern city developments is frequently staggering.[43]

Citizen Preferences and Limited Choices   Corporations such as Allright Auto Parks, Century Development Corporation, Gerald Hines Interests, and Levitt and Sons are among the most important urban decision makers; they have the power to shape the spread and decline of cities in funda- mental ways. The choices made by top executives in these and other powerful land-oriented companies dominate the urban landscape, but these development decisions are not necessarily efficient or desirable from the point of view of most city dwellers, including those displaced by development projects. Other Americans more or less have to accept what is in fact built and available. James Lorimer has noted that in today's corporate cities "people may *feel* free to make their own decisions about how they will live, but in fact they are restricted by the limited number [of] choices offered by developers and planners."[44]

People are not, of course, coerced into growing cities or into using the shopping centers, office towers, business parks, suburbs, and high-rise apartment complexes that constitute much of the growth, but so much of daily life is centered in these urban places that it is hard for Americans not to live out some, or much, of their lives in them. Often these urban developments provide the only realistic working, housing, and shopping options. Other choices have vanished (for example, many downtown shops run by small-business people) or are allowed to decay and disappear (many small towns and much row-type housing in central cities). A major assumption of conventional theories is that the "most frequently chosen location is that which is most preferred." But what if workers and their families have very limited choices? If there is only one adequate option, or a limited range of options, no strong consumer preference is truly revealed. If only a few adequate housing or working facilities are available, the lack of availability makes individual preferences less relevant to individual choices.

The absence of alternatives for some Americans has even been extended to encompass a fundamental lack of choice about the region of the country in which they may live. Consider, for example, the Amish and Mennonite residents of Lancaster County, Pennsylvania, an increasingly urbanized area. For 250 years a fertile valley in East Lancaster has been the homeland of the Amish and Mennonites, strong communities with their own distinctive family- and religion-centered subcultures. But recently Lancaster County, 50 miles west of Philadelphia, has undergone a tremendous development boom. Private development corporations have developed and planned a variety of small and large development projects. The state government of Pennsylvania has proposed a new superhighway to be built through the communities, and new residents, in pursuit of the jobs being created there by investors in light industry and tourism and of the housing created in new urban subdivisions by developers, have moved in at a rate of 300 a month. The Amish and Mennonite populations now find themselves outnumbered by the new Lancaster residents. In the late 1980s Alan Mussellman, a Lancaster Planning Commission specialist, stated that environmental reviews may prevent the highway from knifing through the heart of the Amish community, but unless something "dramatic" is done to protect the area from accelerated development, "we'd almost be securing the fact that over the long term, the Amish community is going to be under too much pressure to stay."[45]

Another example of this displacement by urban developers can be seen in the dislocation of long-time residents of New England towns and farms, as this part of New England comes under increasing development pressures from expanding metropolitan areas. Thus Rory O'Shaughnessy, a deputy sheriff in the town of Litchfield, Connecticut, recently wrote to journalist Edie Clark of *Yankee* that the developers are "pimping off the town!...County farms are folding like a house of cards....Natives of Litchfield are being exiled for an inherent lack of buying power that is now necessary to remain in Litchfield."[46] Despite the fact that Litchfield has had a zoning code since 1939, the metropolitan developers' presence there is creating big-city problems, including rapidly escalating land prices. One group of developers paid $550,000 for some property in the town's historic district, in which they then proposed to erect a condominium project. But before the developers were able to break ground, Litchfield's Planning and Zoning Commission, concerned about rapid growth, implemented a construction moratorium. After 9 months the outside developers decided to move on, selling the land for $400,000 more than they paid for it; their eyes were now set on another town in the same county with less stringent planning regulations. With the town's local newspaper (and its real estate section) being sold to very affluent New Yorkers in Manhattan, it is now all but impossible for local citizens to afford land or housing in their hometown. In less than two decades, houses that sold for $20,000 now fetch $600,000. As O'Shaughnessy sums up the situation, "Litchfield is dying as a community so that some New Yorkers can go back to New York City on Monday and say that they had a nice weekend. They are taking away my birthright to stay in the town I was born in, the town that I love."[47]

From these examples and others like them, we can see that the preferences and choices of individuals develop in a social context that is fundamentally shaped by markets ruled by capitalists and top managers in industrial and development corporations. This context involves not only the production of goods and services but also an intricate web of relations of unequal power and wealth. In U.S. society the production of goods and services precedes consumption, but the two processes go hand in hand. The physical structure of production builds barriers and sets limits to individual choices. Moreover, citizen preferences are frequently created or manipulated by powerful investors and their associates working through advertising, public relations, and the mass media.[48]

To a large extent, it is the unequal distribution of resources, of income and wealth, that limits cousumer choices. The choices of moderate- and middle-income Americans are far more restricted than those of the rich and super-affluent. And it is not just average workers and consumers who are affected by this unequal distribution of resources. Small businesses are destroyed as real estate investors and developers shove them aside and build office towers. Much of the suburbanization literature argues that middle-income Americans express their free choice for more housing space by moving to suburbia. This line of reasoning leads to the conclusion that the *poor* choose and prefer central-city locations. But this is not necessarily true. The urban poor and the urban rich alike can live in large central cities, but only the latter have the incomes that make it easy to *choose* where to live.[49]

GOVERNMENT AND URBAN DEVELOPMENT

Pluralist and Market Politics Analyses In addition to economic structures and decision makers, we must give substantial attention to political structures and decision makers in understanding city building. Most social scientists have either neglected the role of government in city development or have assumed a pluralist or "market politics" perspective. The pluralist outlook has dominated much political science analysis of U.S. cities: Political decision makers, on the whole, promote the general welfare because their decisions result from responding to and coordinating pressures from a multiplicity of contending pressure groups. Advocates of urban pluralism see a competitive market in the urban political sphere that is analogous to the economic market; there is a political market in which individual voters and an array of diverse interest groups, in ever changing coalitions, compete for influence on local governments within a general value consensus.[50] Yet traditional pluralists have tended to neglect private economic decision making.

More recently, some political scientists have argued for a market model of urban politics. Political scientist Paul E. Peterson, in his book *City Limits*, has argued that local government officials should (and usually do) seek to enhance the general welfare of their particular cities and pursue economic growth in partnership with business elites. Government policies making a city attractive for investors benefit all urban residents. In Peterson's perspective, the general public "interests of cities" are roughly identical with the "interests of their export industries." Thus city officials expand local export industries by working with business elites and seeking outside firms by various means, including the provision of a business-oriented service infrastructure; by pursuing a "good business climate" and economic development from mobile (outside) capital they bring benefits to the "community as a whole." Peterson recognizes that many city officials also implement redistributive policies favoring the needy; but he accents the superiority of local business-oriented developmental policies in fostering the "common welfare" of urbanites. As with other "market" analysts of cities, such as Berry and Kasarda, political scientists such as Peterson do not provide a critical analysis of oligopoly capitalism, investors, and investment capital; they generally view the fostering of "free markets" as maximizing the general welfare. These markets should not be restructured by governmental action; at the most their rough edges should be smoothed.[51]

Critical Perspectives on Government In contrast to this market-knows-best perspective on urban economics and politics, critical urban analysts note the overwhelming evidence that certain groups have *far* more power than others to shape both economic and political decisions. Just as markets generally favor powerful capitalist investors over ordinary consumers, the urban political process favors the interests of powerful business and other groups over ordinary voters. Neither U.S. markets nor U.S. political arrangements are neutral. And both economic and political arrangements are dominated by the few. Some critical social scientists emphasize the economic and political decision makers, while others accent economic and governmental structures. But all critical analysts reject the pluralist and market-knows-best perspectives. Certain critical researchers such as Ralph Miliband and G. William Domhoff have accented the importance of specific business decision makers, particularly the capitalists, in state decisions. They view powerful economic decision makers as generally dominant over governmental decision makers and their decisions. Miliband and Domhoff have emphasized the specific ties between the capitalist class and various governments, including the movement of business leaders into and out of key political positions. In the United States, at the federal and local government levels, there is the everyday reality of interpersonal connections between business leaders and governmental officials. Domhoff has demonstrated that in the United States individual capitalists and their close subordinates do in fact rule by serving in critical governmental positions at both the national and the local levels. These governmental actors generally work hard to maintain favorable conditions for capitalists' enterprises and profits.[52]

Some social scientists, such as Nicos Poulantzas, have been critical of Miliband and Domhoff for assessing government action too much in terms of specific decision makers, rather than in terms of the government's structurally determined position in a capitalistic society. These scholars accent the *structures and institutions* of a capitalist society and how these limit the actions of all political decision makers. From Poulantzas' perspective, government officials, whether they are former business leaders or career civil servants, are structurally constrained by the dominance of the capitalistic economy in Western countries, including the United States; thus those who are not from business backgrounds generally serve the economic needs of capitalism and the capitalist class.[53] However, Domhoff has also recognized the importance of both the institutional structures surrounding the political decision makers and the individual decision makers themselves. As Domhoff visualizes it, economic classes and political institutions are abstract conceptual units, while "individuals are the basic elements for building networks that make up classes and that locate the institutions in sociological space."[54]

Other critical political analysts, while recognizing the constraining effects of capitalism, have given greater emphasis to the relative independence of government officials in shaping societies than do Miliband, Domhoff, or Poulantzas. For example, sociologist Fred Block has suggested that for the most part capitalists do not directly manage local or national governments, but leave that to civil servants and politicians. Block recognizes that some capitalists are recruited into government, but argues that those who do serve as "state managers" are not typical of their class, because they must look at the world from their governmental vantagepoints. Moreover, even corporate executives serving at the top of local or national government bureaucracies may sometimes represent particular interests within the government, rather than the interests of their corporations. Some seek to enlarge their own bureaucracy's power or work to coordinate business leaders who would otherwise be in conflict. However, like Poulantzas, Block recognizes that government officials are generally limited by their capitalistic economic context; they must maintain "business confidence" in government.[55]

Levels of Government   For our purposes it is important to distinguish the dimensions of government in the United States. Three levels can be distinguished: (1) the federal government, (2) regional governments (the "State of New York"), and (3) local governments (a city or county government). Many scholars have noted that local governments have limited independence in the United States; they are dependent in numerous ways on the federal government, particularly for funding.

Some analysis of the city government level has emphasized the importance of local political officials and "political entrepreneurs" in pursuing their own state-centered or bureaucratic goals. For example, political scientists Ted Robert Gurr and Desmond King are critical of the business dominance perspective of analysts like Domhoff. Gurr and King argue that city government officials often pursue specific governmental goals—maintaining public order, raising taxes, and pursuing programs *they* have independently conceived to promote their cities.[56] Similarly, in *The Contested City* John Mollenkopf has examined urban development, particularly for Boston and San Francisco, and has argued that the success of downtown redevelopment and progrowth efforts has depended on the leadership of a political entrepreneur, "one who gathers and risks political capital or support in order to reshape politics and create new sources of power by establishing new programs."[57] However, in Mollenkopf's own data on Boston and San Francisco, as well as data we will examine in later chapters, there is substantial evidence of business elites initiating and guiding urban development projects, shaping public taxation policies, and actually serving in top government positions. Political actors and entrepreneurs are important in many U.S. cities, and should not be neglected as a source of new development ideas or as a coordinating force in city politics, but they are not generally *the* dominant force in urban policy making in regard to growth and development.

Growth Coalitions: Private-Public Teamwork We have underscored the importance of local growth coalitions in shaping how cities grow and decline. In many cities, particularly in the Sunbelt, business leaders in growth coalitions have also been leading political officials. For instance, a Dallas mayor was quoted in the *Wall Street Journal* as saying: "The system probably works better when a poor man is not in [political] office." A major real estate developer, this Sunbelt mayor probably had in mind the operation of the growth coalition and of the urban development system. When he was Dallas mayor, he was also a president, vice-president, partner, manager, and board member of many businesses. Many American cities have been directly governed by individuals with real estate or banking ties that are fostered by the decisions they make as government officials.[58]

City political leaders vary in the degree to which they are concerned with developer and citizen needs. Todd Swanstrom has distinguished between two types of efforts by local government officials to enhance the economic attractiveness of cities for investors: *conservative* growth politics, where there is little attention to the social welfare needs of local citizens and the planning for economic growth is left substantially to the private sector; and *liberal* growth politics, where local politicians provide social service programs and also guide economic development planning and furnish incentives for corporations interested in locating in their city. One should add to Swanstrom's categories a third—cities where growth politics involves government officials in planning for economic development, but does not involve much action by government to improve social services for the citizenry. Sunbelt cities, such as Dallas and Houston, often have a type of conservative growth politics, with few local politicians independent of business linkages, while northern cities, such as Minneapolis, are more likely to have the liberal type of growth politics.[59]

Specific Government Decision Makers Urban real estate development is not only organized around a network of private entrepreneurs and corporations but is also linked to a complex array of governmental agencies and decision makers. Table 1.2 lists some of the many important development-related decisions made by officials at the local and national government levels.

TABLE 1.2   Urban development: Decision categories
and selected government decision makers

1. Actions on utility services, building codes, zoning, tax
    abatements; boosterism and progrowth actions
        Mayors and city council members
        County government officials
        Officials on local zoning and planning commissions
        Officials in special local authorities

2. Housing, redevelopment, and tax decisions
        Members of Congress
        Department of Housing and Urban Development officials
        Local and state government officials

Subsidies and the Business Philosophy   In the United States industrial and
real estate investors have not been able to supply all the conditions for
profitable location and development. The decisions and actions listed in
Table 1.2 have been taken to address the continuing problems of individual
and corporate capitalists involved in industrial location and real estate
development, including their recurring need for subsidies and services.
Local and federal governments provide a developmental aid system to
assist profit making in urban areas. Local governments subsidize, by
means of taxation, many public services, such as roads, sewers, and
utilities linked to business development. Urban land is valuable because
it is usually not raw but "serviced." Government-subsidized labor has
been expended on it. Services for business development are often provided by local governments, at least in part out of working people's taxes.
Thus much urban land has taxpayer-subsidized features, which add to its
value as a marketed commodity. As Michael Peter Smith has underscored
in his recent book *City, State, and Market,* U.S. business and political elites
have frequently tried to convince the public that uneven economic development in the United States is the result of welfare-maximizing market
forces. But, in reality, uneven economic development across cities and
regions is best understood as the outcome of decisions made by economic
and political actors at both the local and national levels.[60]

One important feature of our society is the institutionalized value
system held not only by business leaders but also by many political
officials and rank-and-file Americans. Most business people have adhered
to a free-enterprise philosophy that is hostile to governmental interference
in business profit making. They subscribe to the idea that markets operating freely lead to rational and efficient outcomes. This value system asserts
a laissez-faire view of government, one preferring government not to
interfere in the market economy as a *general principle.* Yet this general
principle is not adhered to in much of the everyday behavior and many of
the decisions of capitalists, including real estate capitalists. They often

ignore this value system when it comes to particular types of governmental subsidies. As Karl Polanyi demonstrated in his classic book *The Great Transformation*, a freewheeling market system and unrestrained capitalist competition become economically and socially irrational, even from the point of view of capitalists.[61] For example, early capitalist cities had a freer land and buildings market and less government intervention than modern capitalist cities, but they also had extreme water, sanitation, garbage, utility, and other service problems that not only harmed urban workers but brought diseases to the families of capitalists.

Savvy real estate developers have long used local and national government aid to promote their own business interests. Historian Marc Weiss has documented, for the decades 1910–1950, how the larger housing developers gradually became dominant in cities by using local and federal government regulations to displace smaller homebuilders. First, in the 1910s and 1920s the larger homebuilders, most of whom were real estate brokers, worked with local government and other professional planners to secure public land-use planning and regulation. Prior to the 1940s most leading residential developers were organized through the Home Builders and Subdividers Division or the City Planning Committee of the National Association of Real Estate Boards (NAREB), a powerful real estate organization. From the 1910s to the 1940s, these organizations represented large developers building expensive residential subdivisions and sought not only government infrastructure services but also zoning and other regulations forcing all housing developers to build high-quality subdivisions. Private real estate organizations helped to secure governmental zoning laws and subdivision regulations. Many smaller subdividers and builders were indifferent to these regulations, or were openly hostile.[62]

By the 1930s the larger developers associated with the NAREB (now the National Association of Realtors) and other industry organizations had found that land-use laws were not being administered locally in ways that provided the desired market control and developmental stability. So the NAREB, together with other real estate interests and finance capitalists, worked for the passage of the 1934 National Housing Act, which created the Federal Housing Administration (FHA). With a staff recruited from the private development sector, the FHA wrote regulations that not only shored up the ailing U.S. lending industry by insuring banks from defaults on individual mortgages, but also standardized subdivision development nationwide with minimum requirements for the design and engineering of streets and other subdivision services (see Chapter 8). FHA regulation thus gave greater market control to the larger developers who could afford to comply; and it provided leverage to get local officials to provide the comprehensive zoning. Weiss' data show large homebuilders organizing to increase their control over the housing market by working with local government officials to enforce zoning and subdivision regulations. When this strategy was not fully adequate, they lobbied the federal government to provide an FHA with the power to guarantee the land-use rationalization desired by larger developers.

In spite of this use of government for business purposes, most business leaders still adhere to the laissez-faire philosophy in general, perhaps because that gives them the opportunity to oppose governmental intervention on behalf of social programs for the general citizenry. The laissez-faire ideology allows them to accept government aid for one project and yet reject "any *quid pro quo* for the government support they receive." Thus acceptance of utility subsidies or tax breaks does not mean they must support governmental programs for the unemployed or housing programs for the elderly.[63]

PROTESTING AND HUMANIZING DEVELOPMENT: URBAN CITIZEN MOVEMENTS

Challenges to Developers   The development of the urban landscape by industrialists and developers, bankers, and allied politicians, has its countervailing forces—people's movements that periodically force developers and governments to make concessions and to alter their plans. A number of critical urban analysts, such as Manuel Castells, Pierre Clavel, and Robert Fisher, have emphasized the importance of group conflict and community struggles in city development. Thus in his important book *The City and the Grassroots,* Castells has called for refocusing urban analysis on city conflict. Citizens' movements emerge in order to protect neighborhood and community spaces; many city residents find themselves in conflict with the goals of the industrial and development capitalists. Like Castells, Fisher and Clavel argue that many urbanites struggle for a city organized around human, family, and neighborhood concerns that go beyond capital accumulation and profitability.[64]

One important concern in much critical analysis is the way households struggle to survive and force a restructuring of the priorities of business and political elites. In contrast to analysts like Peterson and Kasarda, these critical urban scholars do not see cities as having a common interest in maximizing growth and development, but rather accent the disagreement and conflict in cities over decisions about economic and physical development.[65] Well-organized groups of workers and consumers can sometimes make a difference in patterns of urban development. This chapter opened with the example of well-organized workers and renters in Santa Monica, California, who threw out a developer-oriented city council and replaced it with a council seeking to restrict growth initiatives to projects which met at least some community needs. These initiatives were still having a positive impact for Santa Monicans in the late 1980s. To take another example, progressive activists in San Francisco have pressured city officials to establish restrictions on office tower architecture and related wind patterns and sunlight blockage. They have also been successful in passing measures modifying development south of Market Street, reducing traffic congestion, putting a 900,000-square-foot annual cap on downtown office development, and exacting contributions from developers for such community needs as child care and housing.[66]

East and West, North and South, citizen movements have pressed for changes in urban development projects. Major expressway projects in cities such as Boston, New York, Philadelphia, and Washington have generated grassroots resistance movements. And there have been numerous attempts, and a few successes, by citizens' groups seeking to stop large mall developments. One attempt was in Burlington, Vermont, where the citizens fought on environmental grounds against a nearby mall planned by a major corporation. Citizens protested against the traffic congestion and likely decline of the downtown area that the new mall would bring. Moreover, in Hadley, Massachusetts, another citizens' group took on a national mall development corporation. At issue were the questionable need for another mall in this small town and the air, water, soil, and traffic problems that a mall would create.

Lake Tahoe Struggles   Environmental damage was also the critical issue raised by the 50,000 urban and rural residents of the Lake Tahoe Basin in Nevada when they took steps to manage growth there. While the Basin can handle the permanent population of 50,000 with little adverse impact, the community is inundated by the annual 12 million tourists and part-time residents drawn by "high-rise casinos, strings of cheap motels and businesses sporting garish signs."[67] In the case of Lake Tahoe, citizen pressure forced a temporary growth moratorium implemented by local officials, after which an agreement was reached to limit growth in the basin and provide for the repair of the lake's ecosystem. In addition to these environmentally oriented resistance movements, in recent years renters' movements have grown up, protesting condominium conversions by developers, the lack of development of moderate-rent housing, and the ever-rising rents that the now short supply of affordable housing generate. Rapid growth in tenants' organizations can be seen in states like New Jersey, where they began in earnest in the 1960s. By the 1970s and 1980s the New Jersey Tenants' Organization had organized many large-scale rent strikes. Many of the strikes have been effective in reducing rent levels and improving conditions in apartment buildings and complexes. Much current resistance aimed at developers and development projects has received stimulation or leadership from veterans of civil-rights and antiwar movements in the 1960s and 1970s. Ronald Shiffman explains that "people in the anti-war and civil-rights movements started working in urban areas because they could achieve their goals there, and by now they're very sophisticated and using their political skills to great advantage."[68]

The movements to control or halt urban development altogether are neither localized in California nor confined to a small group of activists. A Washington-based environmental group, Population Environment Balance, Inc., recently surveyed 1,650 communities across the country. They found that one in five had instituted various growth management controls, and that many others planned to bring in growth-restriction strategies soon. By the late 1980s it had become clear that growth-control efforts attract a wide range of supporters, including conservatives and liberals, urban reformers, and environmentalists. As a leader of "Not Yet New York," a Los Angeles antigrowth coalition, expresses it, "it's a new ball game politically."[69] An illustration of this emerging political reality can be seen in California's politically conservative Orange County. There, a liberal former mayor and a conservative former head of the county Republican organization have joined forces on a comprehensive growth-management campaign. We will explore citizens' movements at length in Chapter 10.

CONCLUSION: THE NEED FOR PUBLIC BALANCE SHEETS

In this chapter we have examined the traditional social science and governmental perspectives on urban growth and development and have seen them to be substantially grounded in neoclassical economics. These traditional perspectives put heavy emphasis on a "free" land and property market, on allegedly equal individuals competing freely, on private property, on efficient land use, and on the benefits that markets in land are supposed to bring to all urbanites. But the realities are not what these perspectives suggest. As we have seen from examples, there are no free competitive markets in cities, because corporate location, urban land purchase, and urban development are disproportionately controlled, often monopolized, by powerful capitalistic decision makers. The newer critical perspective, also described in this chapter, focuses on these power and inequality realities of city growth and decline.

For the most part, the actions of urban industrialists, developers, bankers, and their political allies are visible and quantifiable. Using the language of the accountant and the economist and calculating profit and loss on their private balance sheets, they are prepared to spell out what they see as the need for and benefits of constant urban growth. Down to the last square foot, they can tell us how much new office space is needed and how much has been created. They inform us of the number of jobs produced by their construction projects, and, once completed, they speculate with great precision about the number of additional employees the employers in their urban monuments will require. They calculate, and often exaggerate, the expected amount of additional tax revenues their large projects will generate, and, using the concept of the multiplier effect, speculate upon the economic benefits of their actions for the city as a whole.

On the other hand, the negative fallout from urban development is noticeably absent from the industrialists' and developers' lexicon. Just as critical, and usually just as obvious, the *social costs* generated by urban growth are less studied and are sometimes more difficult to specify and quantify. For example, why do we not attempt to measure the long-term physical and psychological impact of increasing pedestrian and auto congestion on consumers and workers? How can we eliminate unsafe pollution levels and prevent health damage? How should we measure the psychological impact on urbanites of routinely being deprived of sunlight as high-rise skyscrapers obstruct the sun? And what is the total community cost of the growing numbers of the homeless and those displaced by the processes of condominium conversion and gentrification in our cities? Finally, how can we calculate the fading sense of community that is produced in many neighborhoods as constant development and redevelopment converge to constitute the modern city?

In the last few years a start on studying social costs has been made. The idea that what is efficient and rational for developers is not necessarily so for workers, consumers, and society as a whole has even been documented in a study of Phoenix, Arizona, by the Center for Business Research at Arizona State University. According to this study the benefits of Phoenix's growth to businesses included more customers, improved market potential, greater availability of labor, and higher profits; the study's research manager stated that "most businesses enjoy a substantial net benefit from urban growth." His evaluation of the net effect of urban growth for ordinary citizens was less favorable. The benefits of expanded job opportunities, a greater selection of goods, and higher incomes for some workers are offset by higher taxes, an increased cost of living, urban sprawl and traffic congestion, water and air pollution, destruction of the natural environment and depletion of resources, waste disposal, a higher crime rate, greater demand for social services, and problems such as homelessness.[70]

Industrial and real estate capitalism does indeed shape the major development projects in cities—the factories, shopping centers, suburbs, business parks, office towers, and apartment complexes. Once the decisions of the powerful are made, smaller scale builders must work around the larger-scale projects, and average workers and their families have to choose within the limits provided. Workers and consumers, especially those with inadequate economic resources, endure the brunt of many social costs of our capitalistic development system. And these costs, as we will document in later chapters, have been enormous. However, we must not forget that group struggle is at the heart of capitalist cities. Citizens' movements are pressing for the community costs of urban development and decline to be addressed and eliminated.

NOTES

1. Richard J. Margolis, "Is the Next Step Penn Station?," *The New Leader* 69 (February 10, 1986): 11.
2. Michael H. Zisser, "Bright Lights, Big City...Limited Vision?," *Planning* 53 (March 1987): 9.
3. Dave Lindorff, "About-Face in Santa Monica," *Village Voice*, December 2–8, 1981, 20.
4. "Who's Gone This Year," *Forbes* 140 (October 26, 1987): 308. See also Howard Banks, "Real Men Don't Need Tax Breaks," *Forbes* 135 (June 3, 1985): 78, 80.
5. Herbert Gans, *The Levittowners* (New York: Random House, 1967), p. 6.
6. Ibid., pp. 5–13.
7. "The Master Builder," *Newsweek*, August 31, 1981, 45; Joe R. Feagin, "Sunbelt Metropolis and Development Capital," in *Sunbelt/Snowbelt: Urban Development and Regional Restructuring*, edited by Larry Sawers and William K. Tabb (New York: Oxford University Press, 1984), pp. 110–111.
8. Robert E. Park and Ernest W. Burgess, *Introduction to the Science of Society* (Chicago: University of Chicago Press, 1924), p. 507.
9. W. Parker Frisbie and John D. Kasarda, "Spatial Processes," in *The Handbook of Sociology*, edited by N. Smelser (Newbury Park, California: Sage, 1988), pp. 629–666.
10. Brian J. L. Berry and John Kasarda, *Contemporary Urban Ecology* (New York: Macmillan, 1977); Michael Micklin and Harvey M. Choldin, eds., *Sociological Human Ecology* (Boulder: Westview, 1984); Harvey M. Choldin, *Cities and Suburbs: An Introduction to Urban Sociology* (New York: McGraw- Hill, 1985). This paragraph draws on Joe R. Feagin, *Free Enterprise City: Houston in Political-Economic Perspective* (New Brunswick: Rutgers, 1988), pp. 15–21.
11. Stephen E. Harris, *The Death of Capital* (New York: Pantheon, 1977), p. 64.
12. Ibid., p. 65.
13. John Kasarda, "The Implications of Contemporary Redistribution Trends for National Urban Policy," *Social Science Quarterly* 61 (December 1980): 373–400.
14. Katherine Bradbury, Anthony Downs, and Kenneth Small, *Urban Decline and the Future of American Cities* (Washington, D.C.: The Brookings Institution, 1982), p. 296.

15. Lewis Mumford, *The City in History* (New York: Harcourt, Brace and World, 1961), p. 452.
16. Francis X. Sutton et al., *The American Business Creed* (Cambridge, Mass.: Harvard University Press, 1956), pp. 361–362.
17. Edward A. Filene, *Successful Living in the Machine Age* (New York: Simon and Schuster, 1932), p. 98.
18. William Alonso, *Location and Land Use* (Cambridge, Mass.: Harvard University Press, 1964); Richard Muth, *Cities and Housing* (Chicago: University of Chicago Press, 1969).
19. David L. Birch, "Wide Open Spaces," *Inc.* 9 (August 1987): 28.
20. Paul E. Peterson, "Introduction: Technology, Race, and Urban Policy," in *The New Urban Reality* (Washington, D.C.: Brookings Institution, 1985), pp. 2–12.
21. Amos Hawley, *Urban Society*, 2nd ed. (New York: Wiley, 1981).
22. Micklin and Choldin, eds., *Sociological Human Ecology*.
23. Berry and Kasarda, *Contemporary Urban Ecology*, pp. 353, 402.
24. Hawley, *Urban Society*, pp. 228–229, 262–263; see also Frisbie and Kasarda, "Spatial Processes."
25. President's Commission for a National Agenda for the Eighties, Panel on Policies and Prospects, *Urban America in the Eighties: Perspectives and Prospects* (Washington, D.C.: U.S. Government Printing Office, 1980).
26. Ibid., pp. 12, 104.
27. Manuel Castells, "Is There an Urban Sociology?" in *Urban Sociology*, edited by C. G. Pickvance (London: Tavistock, 1976), pp. 33–57; Manuel Castells, *The Urban Question* (London: Edward Arnold, 1977); David Harvey, *The Urbanization of Capital* (Baltimore: Johns Hopkins University Press, 1985); Henri Lefebvre, *La Revolution Urbaine* (Paris: Gallimard, 1970).
28. Michael Peter Smith, *The City and Social Theory* (New York: St. Martin's, 1979); Susan Fainstein, Norman Fainstein, Michael Peter Smith, Dennis Judd, and Richard Child Hill, *Restructuring the City* (New York: Longman, 1983); Richard Child Hill, "Urban Political Economy," in *Cities in Transformation*, edited by Michael P. Smith (Beverly Hills: Sage, 1984), pp. 123–138; J. Allen Whitt, *Urban Elites and Mass Transportation* (Princeton, N.J.: Princeton University Press, 1982); Mark Gottdiener, *The Social Production of Urban Space* (Austin: University of Texas Press, 1985); Gordon L. Clark and Michael Dear, *State Apparatus: Structures and Language of Legitimacy* (Boston: Allen and Unwin, 1984), pp. 131–145; John R. Logan and Harvey M. Molotch, *Urban Fortunes: The Political Economy of Place* (Berkeley: University of California Press, 1987).
29. As we will document in later chapters, other pressures for land-use controls have stemmed from local merchants concerned with protecting their business places for profitable marketing uses. In such cases

the commitment by local merchants to land is primarily to its use value as a place to make a profit. Thus we actually have three basic interests in land: (1) in the exchange value of the land itself; (2) in the use value of the land for living, family, and neighborhood; (3) in the use value of the land for local commercial or industrial profit making.

30. See Mark Gottdiener and Joe R. Feagin, "The Paradigm Shift in Urban Sociology," *Urban Affairs Quarterly* 24 (December 1988): vol. 24, pp. 163–187.

31. Sam Bass Warner, *The Urban Wilderness* (New York: Harper and Row, 1972), pp. 16–17. See also pp. 8–15.

32. Ibid., p. 18.

33. Henri Lefebvre, *Everyday Life in the Modern World* (New York: Harper and Row, 1971), p. 66; Harvey, *The Urbanization of Capital*; David Harvey, *Consciousness and the Urban Experience* (Baltimore: Johns Hopkins University Press, 1985).

34. Mark Gottdiener, "Crisis Theory and Socio-Spatial Restructuring," in *Crisis Theory and Capitalist Development*, edited by M. Gottdiener and N. Komninos (New York: St. Martin's, 1989), pp. 365–375.

35. David Vail, "Uneven Development Downeast," *Dollars and Sense* 127 (June 1987): 9.

36. Ibid.

37. Berry and Kasarda, *Contemporary Urban Ecology*; Micklin and Choldin, eds., *Sociological Human Ecology*; Choldin, *Cities and Suburbs: An Introduction to Urban Sociology*.

38. D. Claire McAdams and Joe R. Feagin, "A Power Conflict Approach to Urban Land Use," Austin, Texas, University of Texas, unpublished monograph, 1980; and D. Claire McAdams, "Powerful Actors in Public Land Use Decision Making Processes," unpublished Ph.D. dissertation, University of Texas, 1979, chaps. 1–3.

39. John Walton, "A Systematic Survey of Community Power Research," in *The Structure of Community Power*, edited by Michael Aiken and Paul Mott (New York: Random House, 1970), pp. 443–464.

40. Harvey Molotch, "Strategies and Constraints of Growth Elites," in *Business Elites and Urban Development*, edited by Scott Cummings (Albany: State University of New York Press, 1988), p. 25.

41. Elizabeth Ashton, "Houston's Doctor of Urban Decay," *Texas Business Review*, March 1982, 53.

42. Ibid., p. 52.

43. Century Development Corporation, Greenway Plaza brochures and fact sheets, in author's files; interview with senior research official, Rice Center, Houston, Texas, May, 1981.

44. James Lorimer, *The Developers* (Toronto: James Lorimer, 1978), p. 220.

45. William K. Stevens, "For Amish, Progress Can Be Threat," *New York Times*, December 2, 1987, 12.

46. Edie Clark, "Litchfield: Connecticut's Worst Kept Secret," *Yankee Magazine*, March 1988, 77.

47. Ibid., p. 78.

48. Eric S. Sheppard, "The Ideology of Spatial Choice," in *Papers of the Regional Science Association*, edited by Morgan D. Thomas, vol. 45 (1980), p. 206.

49. Ibid., pp. 206–297.

50. See Robert Dahl, *Who Governs?* (New Haven: Yale University Press, 1961); Thomas M. Guterbock, "The Political Economy of Urban Revitalization," *Urban Affairs Quarterly* 15 (March 1980): 429–438.

51. Paul E. Peterson, *City Limits* (Chicago: University of Chicago Press, 1981); for a good critical analysis of this view see Ted Robert Gurr and Desmond S. King, *The State and the City* (Chicago: University of Chicago Press, 1987), p. 7ff.

52. Ralph Miliband, "State Power and Class Interests," *New Left Review* 138 (1983): 57–68; Ralph Miliband, *The State in Capitalist Society* (London: Weidenfeld and Nicolson, 1969); G. William Domhoff, *Who Rules America?* (Englewood Cliffs, N.J.: Prentice-Hall, 1967); this and the next few paragraphs draw on Feagin, *Free Enterprise City: Houston in Political-Economic Perspective*, pp. 34–40.

53. Nicos Poulantzas, "The Problem of the Capitalist State," *New Left Review* 58 (1969): 67–78.

54. G. William Domhoff, "I Am Not an Instrumentalist," *Kapitalstate* 4 (1976): 223.

55. Fred Block, "The Ruling Class Does Not Rule," *Socialist Revolution* 7 (1977): 13; Fred Block, *Revising State Theory* (Philadelphia: Temple University Press, 1987), pp. 9–10.

56. Gurr and King, *The State and the City*, pp. 8–9.

57. John Mollenkopf, *The Contested City* (Princeton: Princeton University Press, 1983), pp. 6, 9.

58. John Fullinwider, "Dallas: The City with No Limits," *In These Times*, December 17–23, 1980, 13.

59. Todd Swanstrom, *The Crisis of Growth Politics: Cleveland, Kucinich, and the Challenge of Urban Populism* (Philadelphia: Temple University Press, 1985).

60. Michael Peter Smith, *City, State, and Market: The Political Economy of Urban Society* (Oxford: Basil Blackwell, 1988), pp. 6–15.

61. Karl Polanyi, *The Great Transformation* (Boston: Beacon, 1944).

62. Marc A. Weiss, The Rise of the Community Builders: The American Real Estate Industry and Urban Land Planning (New York: Columbia University Press, 1987).

63. Fred Block, *Revising State Theory* (Philadelphia: Temple University Press, 1984), p. 11. See also pp. 10–12.

64. Manuel Castells, *The City and the Grassroots* (Berkeley: University of California Press, 1983); Robert Fisher, *Let the People Decide* (Boston: Twayne, 1984), Pierre Clavel, *The Progressive City* (New Brunswick: Rutgers, 1986).
65. See, for example, Clarence N. Stone, "The Study of the Politics of Urban Development," in *The Politics of Urban Development*, edited by Clarence N. Stone and Heywood T. Sanders (Lawrence: University Press of Kansas, 1987), pp. 8–10.
66. Andrew Reinbach, "Cities Clamp Tough Rules on Downtown Builders," *Barrons*, December 2, 1985, 81.
67. Jay Stuller, "Battle-Weary Lake Tahoe Combatants Try Compromise," *Audobon* 89 (May 1987): 46.
68. Cited in Reinbach, "Cities Clamp," ibid.
69. Frederick Rose, "Curbing Growth: California Towns Vote to Restrict Expansion as Services Lag Behind," *Wall Street Journal*, November 27, 1987, 4.
70. Tom R. Rex, "Businesses Enjoy Benefits; Individuals, Society Pay Costs," *Arizona Business* 34 (August 1987): 3.

2

CORPORATE LOCATION
DECISIONS

A typical maquiladora operates with two American-owned manufacturing facilities figuratively facing each other across the international border. Components of a product are warehoused on the U.S. side and assembled by cheap labor on the Mexican side. The goods to be assembled flow into Mexico duty-free. Under two "sweetheart" U.S. tariff regulations, the finished product frequently returns to the United States with no import taxes to be paid. Twenty one years ago, Mexico had 12 maquiladoras, employing 3,000 people. At the start of this year [1987], there were 844, providing work for 242,000 people.[1]

...the plant-closings language [in the 1988 trade bill debated by Congress and the White House] is nothing more than a modest effort to make sure that the few companies inclined to do so don't hide plans to close a plant until the last minute, leaving workers and communities in the lurch. It is squarely in the tradition of such social reforms as the child labor and minimum wage laws. These act to soften the social consequences of free market decisions and thus permit the market continued public acceptance without the sort of deep government involvement often practiced abroad.[2]

INTRODUCTION

All U.S. regions and cities have been affected by a company closing down a plant, warehouse, store, or office facility. Many areas have experienced major shutdowns and losses of jobs. This is part of the uneven development process being aggressively carried out by U.S. and foreign capitalists. Some areas are actually losing plants, called "runaway" plants, to other areas. In many cases plants, offices, and stores are closed in one area and the investment capital is moved elsewhere—to the Sunbelt or to Third World countries. Capital flight from one city to another or from the United States to overseas can be part of a broad corporate plan to escape taxes, to build on less expensive land, or to find cheaper and less militant workers. The withdrawal of capital from an area has often been the work of large firms, including the multinational corporations. In one New England study, Barry Bluestone, Bennett Harrison, and Lawrence Baker found that large companies were responsible for half of the jobs lost in that area by plant closings. Such a disinvestment has disrupted communities, cost workers their homes, increased health problems, and remade the face of the industrial heartland of America.[3]

SCALE AND CHARACTER OF THE JOB LOSSES

Examples of Disinvestment   This job loss scenario frequently occurs in the United States: In the fall of 1979, U.S. Steel closed down operations in Youngstown, Ohio—with 3,500 jobs lost. In the spring of 1980, Ford closed its Pico Rivera plant in Los Angeles—with 2,000 jobs lost. In the winter of 1982, General Electric laid off hundreds of workers at its Ontario, California, electric iron plant. That corporation's capital is reportedly being invested in plants in Singapore, Brazil, and Mexico—areas with much lower wages. The Ontario plant was profitable, but in the corporate view not profitable enough. In the spring of 1982, it was announced that the famous Seth Thomas clock factory, resident in Thomaston, Connecticut, for more than 160 years, would be moving its operations to Atlanta, Georgia. The president of General Time, Inc., the parent company that owns the factory, was quoted to the effect that relocation to Georgia would mean lower operating costs. As a result, most of the plant's 175 workers lost their jobs.[4]

Many plant closures have involved short periods of notice for workers. For example, on a Tuesday in February 1983, Maria Carson was midway through her morning's work at Atari's Santa Clara, California, plant when her manager asked the workers in her department to gather around. He said that they and several hundred other Atari workers at neighboring plants were being laid off immediately because the company was moving its video game and home computer operations overseas to Hong Kong and Taiwan. "He said we could pick up our final checks Friday at Sunnyvale High School and then we were made to leave by the back door....I didn't even get a chance to clean out my desk."[5] Carson's experience was neither isolated, nor one that was limited to the recession years of the early 1980s. For example, the Department of Labor reported that 5.1 million workers who had been at their jobs at east 3 years were displaced because of plant closings or employment cutbacks between January 1981 and January 1986. Among these, 45 percent received no notification from their employer prior to displacement.[6]

Indeed a series of recent surveys of displaced workers demonstrates that mass layoffs and plant closings have generated much hardship during the heralded "economic recovery" of the 1980s. In the latest of these reports, the Labor Department's Employment and Training Administration uncovered these research findings[7]:

Despite the longest peacetime economic expansion in the nation's history, nearly 10 million Americans lost their jobs to plant closings and layoffs from 1983 to 1988.

Nearly 4.7 of the 9.7 million people laid off were "tenured" workers—defined as holding their previous job three years or longer.

Thirty percent of these longtime workers still did not have new jobs as of January 1988.

Among those who did find new jobs, 30 percent reported an income loss of at least 20 percent from their old jobs, while 28 percent reported that their earnings had increased by 20 percent or more in their new jobs.

During the 1980s plant closings and other layoffs created severe life problems for many U.S. workers, with older, minority, female, and workers in the north central states paying the greatest price. Indeed, plant closings have become so important that even the once reluctant U.S. Bureau of Labor Statistics has begun keeping a record. Late in 1987 the U.S. Labor Department transmitted its first report covering the year 1986. The data collected covered *only* 11 states that provided data for the full year. In 1986 these 11 states reported a total of 1,335 layoffs in 926 establishments; nearly 275,000 workers were displaced as a result of these mass layoffs and plant closings.[8]

Human Cost   A major example of the mechanics of corporate relocation can be seen in the closing of a large Campbell, Ohio, steel plant owned by the Youngstown Sheet and Tube Company. In 1969 this profitable plant was sold to the Lykes Corporation, a large conglomerate with no experience in steel production. Before the sale to Lykes, the major steel plant had received millions of dollars for annual maintenance and development, but Lykes reduced that investment substantially, allowing the quality of the steel facilities to deteriorate. Reportedly, Lykes used the profits from the Ohio plant to pay off other debts and to buy nonsteel companies. After 8 years, most of the Campbell steel-making facility was closed as unprofitable. In recent decades many conglomerates have bought up profitable companies and slowly "milked" them of their profits, which have been used for other nonrelated investments. Local workers and communities have paid a heavy price for this type of milking and disinvestment. In the Campbell case the local community lost millions of dollars in tax revenues and had to borrow money to run its public schools. In addition, 4,900 jobs were lost. The total social cost of the death of this plant has been estimated at $72 million over the first few years in terms of increased welfare and food stamp costs, related governmental expenditures, and lost taxes to government. Ripple effects, including the loss of thousands of jobs in other local businesses, could be seen across the Youngstown area.[9]

Corporate flight is more than a matter of money. It involves serious family and community costs, including broken lives for working people, who lose jobs and livelihoods as well as their homes and their consumer goods. One problem is the loss of health insurance. A study of displaced workers from 1979 through 1984 concluded that such workers "did, in fact, face a high risk of losing health insurance coverage for an extended period of time following displacement, even after new employment was secured."[10] Moreover, whole cities become economically depressed when companies leave. There are no longer enough firms and people to pay the taxes that finance good schools and city services. People who are permanently laid off, particularly older workers, can have great difficulty in finding new jobs. Corporate flight and plant closings have ripple effects across the faces of cities. Municipal revenues decrease because companies leave, and companies and unemployed workers pay fewer taxes. The tax base erodes. Urban services are reduced; school teachers, police officers, and fire fighters are laid off. Local small businesses, grocery stores, taverns, and gas stations go bankrupt. Downtown shopping areas become ghost towns, with many stores boarded up.[11]

Plant-Closing Laws   The traditional U.S. business and social science perspectives on plant or capital relocation from one area of a city to another or from northern cities to southern cities suggest that unrestrained corporate mobility is necessary for the health of the U.S. economy. We discussed this argument in Chapter 1. Capital must be free to move. Corporate executives do not wish governments to intervene, except to facilitate capital mobility with tax incentives and other business-oriented subsidies. Some suggest that working people should follow footloose corporations wherever they or their capital go.

The United States is the only advanced industrial nation that allows this freewheeling mobility for corporate enterprises. Western European nations, Canada, and Japan limit the ability of corporations to move plants and offices; governmental permission is usually required. Advance warning of a plant closure to workers is mandated. In Canada employers are required to provide 1 to 16 weeks of advance notice to their workers depending on the situation; in Germany the advance notice period is 30 days after the firm has officially notified the government; in Britain up to 90 days of notice are required; and in Japan "sufficient" advance warning is required.[12] But in the United States, proposals for similar requirements have met with limited success. Business opponents have argued such policies represent government intrusion on private enterprises and restrict the ability of U.S. firms to compete internationally. However, the weakness of this argument is suggested by the fact that the United States regularly runs a balance-of-trade deficit favoring European and Asian countries with plant-closing and advance notice policies.

In 1988 the U.S. Congress passed an advance notice bill, which was initially vetoed by President Ronald Reagan. Yet the vetoed proposal was modest. Mossberg has described the bill: "It wouldn't bar a single closing or layoff. It wouldn't require companies to get worker or government approval to close plants or conduct layoffs. It wouldn't affect companies with under 100 workers....It merely requires stable companies that know well beforehand of plans to close plants or order mass layoffs to share this information 60 days in advance with the affected workers and local governments."[13] However, the Worker Adjustment and Restraining Act (WARN) became law in the summer of 1988 when President Reagan decided not to veto the legislation a second time so that the trade bill to which it was attached could be enacted.

The WARN law, which took effect in early 1989, only applies to most corporations with at least 100 full-time employees that plan to lay off more than 50 of those employees. The relatively weak notification law stipulates that an affected business must notify (1) any labor union or other group representing workers, or if no employee representatives exist, the affected employees directly, (2) the State Dislocated Worker Unit, and (3) the chief elected official of the local government in the area where the closing or layoff is to occur. A corporation violating WARN's provisions is subject to fines (up to $500 a day for local officials) and penalties including up to 60 days of back pay and benefits to employees. WARN's supporters hope it will assist U.S. workers in finding new employment on a timely basis while offering some protection for local governments from being faced suddenly with major service increases and tax decreases.

THE LOGIC OF CORPORATE LOCATION DECISIONS

Traditional Explanations   There is an extensive business and social science literature on how companies make location decisions. This literature is highly technical, but its major assumptions are simple. Corporate location decisions hinge on profitability. August Lösch, one of the founding fathers of industrial "location theory," suggested that industries should locate at the point of maximum profits, where the total income exceeds total costs by the greatest amount. Cutting costs is thought to be a critical aspect of location decisions.[14] Melvin Greenhut has examined the business view of location and has listed factors he perceives as influencing decisions:

1. Cost factors at the location: transportation costs, extent of unionization, wage costs, taxation
2. Demand factors at the location: extent of competition by other firms
3. Cost-reducing factors: cities that specialize in one type of industry

4. Revenue-increasing factors: areas that especially need the product made
5. Personal interaction factors: advantages from interaction with other companies and executives[15]

A study examining changes in manufacturing employment between 1970 and 1980 put the traditional industrial location theory to empirical test and found a number of the traditional factors to be of little value in explaining shifts in corporate investment. Using data on the 48 contiguous states, researcher Jaffe found explanations related to the strength of organized labor, the level of taxation, and the extent of social welfare provisions to be more useful in explaining recent changes in manufacturing employment than most other cost-demand and retail-market factors. In particular, he found that the general level of labor organization within a state was "the strongest and most consistent predictor of the expansion and movement of manufacturing jobs between 1970 and 1980." His findings indicate that many manufacturing employers have in recent decades increasingly preferred the nonunion states, as well as those with lower rates of business taxation and weaker welfare programs.[16]

Large-Scale Capitalism and Location   Many conventional location analysts envision a huge "free" market of modest-sized, autonomous companies competing with one another for plant and other business locations in various regions and cities. Their simplified model is one of numerous companies, no one of which has unduly coercive or dominant market power. But this is a critical error. The cost and profit factors conventional scholars identify do play a major role in location decisions, but their theories tend to neglect the dominant role of large national and international companies. The European scholar Ernest Mandel, among others, has argued that the large corporation is the central organizational form of capital in late capitalism. The history of capitalism since the late nineteenth century has been of *capital centralization*, the fusion of different capitals under a single command, and *capital concentration*, the growth of very large corporations resulting from the elimination of weaker companies.[17] Before 1900 most capitalist companies in the United States were small, but by the early 1900s company mergers were creating giant corporations, first in the oil, steel, and grain industries, and later in the auto industry. By 1901 U.S. Steel, a company formed from mergers, controlled $1.4 billion worth of industrial plants. And industrial concentration was the trend, one that continues unabated today. Every week newspapers detail mergers, acquisitions, and takeovers of corporations, which serve to generate greater concentration and centralization of wealth in many industries. Today just 100 companies, with Exxon and General Motors at the top, control 61 percent of all the manufacturing plants and other industrial assets, a substantial increase since 1961. Such asset control directly translates into national economic and political dominance for the larger companies.[18]

To a large degree, locational decision making is shaped by the size of a corporation and its access to capital. Many large companies have the internal profit-generated funds to expand and relocate without borrowing much; other giant corporations can use their credit worthiness to secure capital from lenders for new urban development projects. Substantial size gives corporations the ability to build long-term projects and enables them to separate major operations spatially with ease because they have the resources to reintegrate operations using transportation and communication networks, even across the world. For example, Exxon, the world's largest corporation by some measures, has widely dispersed its major subsidiary and affiliate offices, including the Exxon Corporation (the international headquarters in New York), the Exxon Chemical Company (Darien, Connecticut), the Exxon Company International (Florham Park, New Jersey), the Exxon Pipeline Company (Houston), Exxon Coal, U.S.A. (Houston), and the Exxon Company, U.S.A. (Houston). There are also four organizations coordinating operating affiliates across the globe: Latin America (controlled from Coral Gables, Florida), Europe and Africa (from London), the Middle East (from New York), and the Far East and Australia (from Houston). Operating facilities such as offshore oil wells and petrochemical plants are located in dozens of countries.[19] Many large corporations have placed their principal administrative operations in office towers in downtown areas of cities such as New York, Chicago, San Francisco, Los Angeles, and Houston; they have placed field management, operations, and research facilities in suburbia or regional cities; and they have located manufacturing operations in widely dispersed areas, including both the rural areas and cities in Africa, Latin America, and Asia.

Large-scale building projects in U.S. cities frequently reflect a specialized dispersion of corporate functions. Industrial parks house the manufacturing facilities of large corporations and related smaller companies. Office towers contain managerial and information processing (for instance, computerized accounting), thus becoming the administrative centers for corporations. Shopping centers are filled with retail corporations, which sell the products of the manufacturing firms. Suburban developments are often built by development and construction corporations to house those who work for large corporations and the smaller businesses dependent on them. Sometimes downtown development is explained in terms of the need of business people to have much face-to-face contact. But this business need existed well before downtown skyscrapers began to increase dramatically in numbers. It was not until 1910–1925 that many national corporations needed to separate administrative and production facilities. Downtown office tower development exploded only when corporations became large enough to separate their various administrative and production operations. Today's cities reveal the different functional components of large corporations in their physical faces, in their geographical contours.[20]

Abandoning Central-City Locations   In the last few decades many companies have decided to locate their manufacturing and other production operations in the "better business climates" of southern cities, outlying suburbs, rural areas beyond the suburbs, or cities outside the United States. Corporate executives cite high wages, strong unions, and expensive city services as problems with doing business profitably in many older central cities. For example, a 1988 survey of manufacturers in the San Francisco Bay area found broad dissatisfaction with local conditions there. Approximately 40 percent of the 210 manufacturers polled said their next expansion would be outside the Bay area, because of the high cost of Bay area business space, high payroll costs, and what they saw as a hostile public attitude toward business needs.[21] Mainstream social scientists, including urban ecologists, have seen this movement of industries out of the older central cities as normal and good:

> *Directed by the sixth sense of profit, entrepreneurs of blue-collar industries have sought alternative, more cost-effective sites in the suburbs, exurbs, and nonmetropolitan areas which are far better suited to today's advanced transportation and production technologies and which avoid what have become serious negative externalities of inner-city locations.*[22]

The quote reveals the business-oriented assumptions that underlie much urban analysis. Profit is here described as a unique human attribute, a "sixth sense," which drives entrepreneurs to avoid the inner-city locations.

A survey by the Fantus Company, a firm providing major location assistance to industrial corporations, found that *only* 112 of 700 companies surveyed would consider building a plant in or near poverty areas in cities. These firms would build in such locations only under the following conditions:

1. A large docile labor pool
2. Lack of well-organized opposition from unions and community groups
3. Ample land and adequate utilities and roads
4. Lower taxes
5. Absence of massive housing deterioration
6. Government-subsidized training programs and services

The Fantus report summed up much of the current corporate logic on location decisions this way: "These companies are interested in good

publicity and profits. None of them indicated any interest in philan-
thropy."[23]

Seeking the "Good Business Climate": Ranking States   A number of accounting and consulting firms assist corporations in locating "good business
climates." One widely followed listing of business climates is the "Annual
Surveys of General Manufacturing Climates" compiled by Grant Thornton, a Chicago-based accounting firm. Grant Thornton allows state manufacturing associations and chambers of commerce to establish the criteria
it uses. Consequently, business costs such as wages, changes in wage rates,
levels of workers' compensation, and productivity figure prominently in
the 21 factors that make up each state's business climate ranking. Table 2.1
shows the best and worst "business climate" states according to Grant
Thornton's 1988 surveys.[24]

Table 2.1   Grant Thornton's ranking of business climates

Best states
1. North Dakota
2. Nebraska
3. South Dakota
4. Virginia
5. Colorado

Worst states
43. West Virginia
44. Wyoming
45. Louisiana
46. Montana
47. Ohio
48. Michigan

The best states include those with relatively low wages and weak
unions. However, there are some odd qualities to rankings such as these.
Such evaluations do not jibe with actual manufacturing output by state.
For example, Grant Thornton ranks North Dakota as the state with the best
climate for manufacturing in the United States despite the fact that it ranks
near the very bottom among all 50 states in factory output. Moreover,
Grant Thornton places Ohio and Michigan at the very bottom of its list of
good business climates despite the fact that both remain major locations
of manufacturing activity. One analysis has concluded that "businesses
don't really use business climate indices to guide their decisions about
where to locate. Instead, they use them to pressure state and local governments to adopt more pro-business policies."[25]

Moreover, if one evaluates a state's quality of employment and
environment from a worker's point of view, a different picture emerges.
In a report titled "The Climate for Workers in the United States," Kenneth

Johnson and Marilyn Scurlock compiled 33 factors for each state to produce a composite index of the quality of work. In contrast to the aforementioned corporate rankings, Johnson and Scurlock used such criteria as job creation, income level and distribution, job rights, health and safety, equal employment opportunity, and job loss benefits to rank the states. Table 2.2 identifies the five states with the best and worst work climates.[26]

TABLE 2.2   Best and worst work climates

Best states
1. Massachusetts
2. Connecticut
3. Minnesota
4. California
5. New York

Worst states
46. Kentucky
47. Tennessee
48. Arkansas
49. South Carolina
50. Alabama

The Johnson and Scurlock worker's index is quite different from the Grant Thornton type of business index. For example, the Johnson and Scurlock index found that the 10 worst states for working people were in the Southeast. The best states are large states in the north and west. And many of the states that the business climate indices rank as poor for new manufacturing plant location rank much higher on the Johnson and Scurlock index. This latter index highlights the extent to which traditional business climate indices neglect worker and family welfare considerations in evaluating potential and actual company locations.

Location Decisions and Government Regulations   Government regulations, including environmental standards, are generally not major considerations in most company decisions about plant and office locations inside and outside cities. Even though corporate officials complain about governmental regulations, they generally do *not* cite these as significant factors affecting their siting of new plants and offices. Not surprisingly, many government regulations reflect a compromise between business and citizen pressures. Unless citizens organize to protest, the routine behavior of most government officials is to enforce local regulations to the degree that business leaders will accept. Variations from zoning laws protecting residential areas from commercial development are granted; environmental reports are filed and ignored; development permits are granted without the studies required by law. Unless local citizens protest, property development interests in cities get much of what they want. For example, in the late 1970s Dow Chemical Company dropped its plan to build a half-billion-dollar petrochemical plant on the metropolitan fringe of San Francisco because a coalition of community groups, a labor union, and environmental groups threatened lawsuits and forced officials to enforce local environmental laws, which Dow decided would be too costly to obey. Still, this corporate retreat may be the exception that proves the rule because there are few community protest examples in other cities.[27]

CYCLES OF UNEVEN DEVELOPMENT: SOME URBAN HISTORY

Waves of Urban Growth For two centuries U.S. cities have grown and declined in response to oscillating capital investments. Urban centers are often old creations, but their character and existence have reflected the investment choices of the powerful, as well as struggles between powerful decision makers and ordinary citizens. Over the last century among the most important decision makers have been industrialists and other top corporate executives. Large corporations have commonly sought out the most favorable places for their operations—often the metropolitan areas. By the 1920s large cities dominated most states, even though a majority of the population lived outside of them. Virtually all industrial production was located in factories in the top 25 metropolitan areas. New York City, Chicago, Philadelphia, Cincinnati, Pittsburgh, and Milwaukee were dominant manufacturing areas. Many cities became specialized centers. Albany made shirts; Troy, shirt collars; New Bedford and Fall River, textiles. In addition, Waltham made watches; Bridgeport, furniture; Dayton, cash registers, and Detroit, automobiles. In turn, these centers of corporate investment attracted many skilled and unskilled workers to their factories and other workplaces.[28]

Typically, a few key industries are at the heart of each successive epoch of urban industrial growth. Usually the location decision of any one company does not give a city its characteristic industrial structure—rather, the set of decisions made by several, dozens, or hundreds of companies are involved. Moreover, in each distinctive period of urban economic growth, older industries such as steel or automobile production have not necessarily died out. They may have just become less dominant in an urban area. There are often distinctive cycles of investment in the "primary circuit" of manufacturing production, to use the term of Harvey's discussed in Chapter 1. Ann Markusen has developed a suggestive model of the profit cycles of large industries and the cycles' impact on regional and city development. Many large industries go through cycles of initiation of product manufacturing, maturation, and decline. And the internal corporate problems of profit and market control can have a major impact on the cities and regions where they are located. Markusen has argued that the global patterns of investment and disinvestment of manufacturing capital are substantially shaped by the oligopolistic character (that is, the concentration of capital control in a few firms) of a particular industry, as well as by the character of its labor struggle, its competition, and its profits at a particular stage of industrial development. Particularly important for city development and decline are the periods of initial growth and late maturation in manufacturing industries. In the later stages of an industry, a decline in investment return has regularly resulted in a greater velocity of capital movement into and out of particular urban places, thereby increasing the problems of community adjustment we cited earlier.[29]

For example, the U.S. iron and steel industries have been highly localized; during the period 1920–1960 most steel was made in the midwestern areas around Pittsburgh, Cleveland, Detroit, Youngstown, and Chicago. In these areas the steel industry grew up, consolidated and became oligopolistic, and declined. Over the twentieth century there was a slow shift westward in steel making, reflecting in part western demand for steel and in part the new sources of ore and coal, but this shift was gradual. In addition, each wave of capital investments by newly created and emerging corporations, such as in the case of the electronics industry today in the Silicon Valley of California, is commonly reflected in distinctive urban development in some region inside or outside the United States. New industries frequently locate in newer cities. Older cities may continue as before or they may stagnate and decline, as in the case of Detroit. Sometimes older cities capture part of the newer high-tech industries, as is the case for Boston and its electronics industry; yet others may actually lose older industries and secure no replacements, as is the case for some New England towns that lost their textile factories to southern cities. In general, older cities often give way to the industrial dominance of newer cities, which themselves eventually suffer through capital disinvestment at a later point in time.

Designing Cities for Worker Control   The critical urban scholar David Gordon has suggested the controversial argument that U.S. cities have been shaped by the changing character of the class struggle between capitalists and workers in three distinctive periods: commercial capitalism (1750–1850), industrial-competitive capitalism (1850–1900), and monopoly capitalism (1900–present). The cities that grew most dramatically and conspicuously in each of these periods tended to have different characteristics. In the early commercial period, commercial merchants' activities generated and influenced the character of the cities; ports became major cities as national and international trade expanded. It was during this period that New York City became the dominant commercial metropolis.

Central cities of the large metropolises were diversified in terms of income, and in this period poorer workers often lived *outside* the central areas, as was the case in early Boston. Some capitalist investors engaged in land speculation; interestingly, the lot-and-block grid system found in most cities was first created by these early land speculators in order to maximize land profits.[30]

Later, from 1850 to 1900 industrial capitalism and the factory system were the social forces that shaped city structure in fundamental ways. According to Gordon's analysis, the many new factories located in the central cities required very large numbers of wage laborers; large numbers of immigrant workers were recruited from Europe to the central cities, which became centers of industrial capitalism. Large-scale investments often lead and shape the movements of workers and their families. These capital transfers are what Michael P. Smith calls "mobility-inducing investments." For example, the movement of industry to central cities had a significant effect on workers and small businesses.[31] Traditional discussions of capitalist location decisions have emphasized that transportation and communication efficiency and access to other companies were among the most important factors in business choices of centralized city locations. However, these early industrial cities grew well beyond the point where transportation and access were efficient. Indeed, many cities became inefficient in transport and greatly congested.

Gordon suggests that a primary concern of these manufacturing employers was *labor control*, that is, maintaining the availability of low-wage workers in large numbers. In the beginning, the impersonality and anonymity created by cities as large as New York and Chicago made it difficult for workers to organize successfully. During this period factories were located in downtown areas; segregated working-class residential areas—the familiar tenements—sprang up nearby. More fortunate middle-income and upper-income urbanites tended to leave the downtown centers, moving to suburban locations as streetcar and railroad lines expanded. Gordon argues that these industrial cities became clogged not because of technological necessity, but because the dominant capitalists there required a concentrated mass of relatively impoverished workers to make their enterprises profitable.

The twentieth-century city, in contrast, has grown up under monopoly (or, more accurately, oligopoly) capitalism, an economic system dominated by a few hundred large national and multinational corporations. One key characteristic of monopoly capitalism is its significant decentralization of production—the movement out of many older central-city areas. Modern technology is usually offered by conventional social science analysis as the reason for this change: Trucks and telephones made manufacturing in outlying areas possible. Autos speeded the movement of workers. But Gordon notes that this decentralization had already begun in 1900, well before the truck and auto were important. To a substantial degree, Gordon argues, this early manufacturing decentralization was a reaction to the emergence in the central cities of organized workers seeking better wages and working conditions and thus a growing number of struggles with employers. Many companies able to finance plants outside the central cities moved there to find cheaper labor and to reduce the ability of workers to organize. Large-scale union organizations and rebellion in major central cities took place during the period 1870–1915, and this contributed significantly to the decentralization of much industry to outlying city areas.32 While Gordon has been criticized for providing only a partial analysis—there were other major factors involved in the decentralization of corporate facilities—his suggestions about the "flight" reaction of corporations to organized workers has the ring of truth even today, as we saw in the data in the previously noted Jaffee study. In the last few decades many of the states with weak union organization, such as those in the Southwest and West, have seen an influx of corporate facilities.

Recent Urban History: Manufacturing Shifts to the Sunbelt   The 1980 census revealed significant population losses for major northern cities. For example, St. Louis, Cleveland, Detroit, and Pittsburgh witnessed losses of more than one-fifth of their populations over the 1960s and 1970s. Chicago, Boston, Newark, and New York also lost a sizable proportion of their populations. During the decade before 1980, in contrast, many Sunbelt cities flourished. The investment and population shift to selected areas in the Sunbelt was continuing in the 1980s. Donnelley Marketing Information Services has reported that 8 of the 10 fastest-growing counties are located in the South. For the period 1980–1985, Gwinnett County northeast of Atlanta topped the list. The Houston metropolitan area county of Fort Bend, Texas, was close behind. At the other end of the spectrum, Wayne County, which includes Detroit, Michigan, headed the list of counties in decline, with an 8 percent population decline between 1980 and 1985.[33]

Substantial manufacturing and other employment opportunities have shifted from the northern states to the South in the last two decades. This Sunbelt shift began in the 1960s, considerably before the fiscal crises of northern cities such as New York. Many urban fiscal crises are substantially the result of that shift, not its cause. Consider, for example, that between the 1960s and the 1980s "capital stock" (new plant and equipment) grew at twice the pace in the South as in the North. In roughly the same period the North lost a total of 800,000 manufacturing jobs, even though the nation gained 2.3 million jobs. Moreover, the shift of jobs from the North has been faster than the population shift.[34]

Why the tilt to the Sunbelt? Several explanations have been offered. Some traditional analysts have argued that capital movements to the South have followed workers seeking more attractive life-styles. We have previously discussed the problems with this explanation, including the data that show that jobs generally move faster than the workers needed to fill them. Business and allied political leaders commonly talk about "fiscal responsibility," "balanced budgets," and "a good business climate" in describing "good" and "bad" cities. What does the phrase "a good business climate" in the Sunbelt cities mean? As we suggested earlier, and as also has been discussed in an Urban Land Institute (a developers' think tank) handbook, the "good business climate" is a code phrase for lower wages, moderate operating costs, low unionization rates, minimal taxes, and pro-business local governments.[35] There are yet other reasons for this urban growth in the Sunbelt states. From the beginning many Sunbelt cities have had fewer physical barriers to new industrial development. Many were initially less built up, with an abundance of open space; they did not have the established and extensive physical infrastructures of Frostbelt cities.

The Mechanics behind the Sunbelt Shift   Capital has been moved to the Sunbelt in a variety of ways. Some giant multilocation corporations may disinvest by delaying maintenance or ignoring machinery replacement needs in a northern plant, store, or office facility; then they invest the savings in new and similar operations in Sunbelt cities. Or sometimes facilities may be moved from plants being phased out to expanding plants already in the Sunbelt. Or the profits from northern manufacturing plants may be rechanneled to entirely *new* types of plants, warehouses, or office buildings in the Sunbelt. Only an estimated 2 to 5 percent of manufacturing changes result from the actual physical relocation of the *same* plants. Rees' study of location decisions by manufacturing firms in the Sunbelt cities of Dallas, Fort Worth, and Houston followed nearly 6,000 plant location decisions; 4 in 10 were plant expansions, and just over one-third were new plants. Only one-seventh of these decisions involved actual plant relocations from outside to the area studied; the rest involved acquisitions of other companies' facilities. The majority of plant-siting decisions did not involve the movement of existing plants from one region to another. The dominant causes of Sunbelt economic growth are the expansion of existing companies and the creation of new companies. An important component of this process is the shifting of operations by a large multilocational company from one region to another, expanding employment in one region—the Sunbelt—and contracting employment in another—the Frostbelt.[36]

The Role of Government   In the Sunbelt case much manufacturing and other business growth stems from capital shifts into certain distinctive areas of investment. The "six pillars" of this Sunbelt development, according to

Kirkpatrick Sale, are defense, oil, advanced technology, real estate and construction, tourism, and agriculture—some of these are relatively new and have seen a dramatic infusion of capital since World War II. The boom in the Sunbelt thus reflected a new round of corporate investment in selected Sunbelt cities.[37] It is important to note that many Sunbelt cities have good business climates in part because the federal government for a time channeled financial aid to them and away from northern cities. This federal aid accelerated with major *military* expenditures during World War II. In the last few decades substantial federal expenditures have gone to support military-industrial complexes (for example, Los Angeles, Dallas–Fort Worth), as well as to subsidize highway, water, electric, and other services, providing the infrastructure necessary for expanded corporate investments in the West and South.

According to a study by Havemann and Stanfield in the 1970s, the declining industrial areas of the Frostbelt were sending far more tax dollars to Washington, D.C., than they were receiving back in federal expenditures. In 1975 the Sunbelt was accumulating a surplus of $51.6 billion of federal expenditures over tax dollars paid, while the Frostbelt endured a deficit of nearly $31 billion. This massive imbalance was accelerating the economic development of the Sunbelt while hastening the decline of numerous areas in the Frostbelt.[38] And subsequent research on the 1980s has shown that the western United States still receives the highest per capita allocation of federal funds, but that the disparity between regions has narrowed in recent years. These expenditures make the linkage between the rise of the Sunbelt cities, the decline of Frostbelt cities, and the role of the national government in those contrasting processes clear. Some have spoken of this regional conflict over federal subsidies as the "second war between the states." Exacerbating this war has been the reduction in expenditures the federal government distributes to local and state governments, especially since the 1980s. The likely redistribution of power and money that will follow the completion of the 1990 census will also have an impact. Two research groups central to the conflict are the Sunbelt Institute and the Northeast-Midwest Institute. Both research groups represent their respective regions armed with competing studies of federal expenditures and how they affect each. For example, the Sunbelt Institute released a report asserting that New York received $1 for each 75 cents it sends to the nation's capital, while Southern states, on the average, pay $1.56 for every $1 returned. The Northeast-Midwest Institute, meanwhile, published a study contending that its members pay $33 billion more in federal taxes than they receive in benefits, while the South gains $27 billion and the West $29 billion. In addition, regional rivalries are punctuated by the political difficulties of governments and politicians in various regions. For example, when Speaker of the House Jim Wright was accused of political corruption in the late 1980s, many northern newspaper editors revelled in the difficulties of this leading Sunbelt politician. And when in 1989 the federal government moved to bail out ailing savings and loan institutions, many of them in the Sunbelt states, numerous northern politicians and business leaders objected to aid for the formerly prosperous Sunbelt states.[39]

In Chapter 1 we discussed the *Urban America* report of the President's Special Commission for a National Agenda for the Eighties; this important report called on government to stay away from the declining cities of the North such as New York and Cleveland; government officials should keep their "hands off," or at most help workers migrate to the Sunbelt where corporations have been generating new jobs.[40] However, the report does not feature the billions of dollars in federal government money that had subsidized the economic boom in the South and West. This *Urban America* report viewed the Sunbelt as an area of "economic viability, benefitting large numbers of poor southerners." But that business climate in the South has not been as good for poorer working people as for the affluent in the South. Firestine has analyzed demographic data that show that "despite the dramatic income expansion in the Sunbelt in recent years, this economic growth has apparently done little to alleviate the relative extremes in income distribution which have marked the South."[41] Census data indicate that very large proportions of inner-city residents in southern cities remain poor in spite of the region's heralded prosperity. Incomes are almost as unequally distributed in the South today as in the past. And the southern state governments are much less generous than the northern governments in their educational, health, welfare, and other social service expenditures. Part of the price low- and middle-income workers have paid for the business prosperity in the South is less desirable working conditions and a lower quality of services.

Changes in the Sunbelt Yet even the booming Sunbelt cities have not been immune to the cycles of investment and disinvestment. Business investment in the Sunbelt cities is not permanent. Surprisingly, the South has lost certain types of manufacturing jobs. One study found that in the South for every 100 new manufacturing jobs created, 80 manufacturing jobs were lost. (In the North for every 100 jobs created, 110 were lost, so the net gain in employment still favored the South.) If this balance has been favorable for the South in recent decades, the question arises as to why there are many plant closings there. Even the *Urban America* report is candid on this point: "Industrial activity that was attracted to the South since the 1950s by lower wages, greater labor control, and lower energy costs is often found relocating outside the United States to achieve even lower production costs."[42]

The uneven oscillation of investment in the Sunbelt shows the lack of a permanent commitment that modern corporations exhibit toward the communities in which they settle. They do not exclusively prefer rural or urban areas, or the Sunbelt or Frostbelt, as places to make profits. Nor for that matter do they exhibit a pronounced preference for remaining in the United States. In some cases, there has been movement out of certain Sunbelt cities into other Sunbelt areas. For example, in the early 1980s there was advertising in the Houston metropolitan area that proclaimed the advantages of good schools, more jobs, less pollution, and fewer traffic jams *outside* the metropolitan area. The ads were intended to attract firms to outlying cities within a 100-mile radius. Even some southern business leaders and publications such as the *Houston Business Journal* had come to recognize the costs of the earlier free enterprise boom: that "a city, like a macrocosm of businesses that create it, can reach a point of diminishing returns."[43] In the economic boom years of the 1970s and early 1980s, Houston's sewage crisis, traffic, air pollution, and poverty-related crime—all related to Sunbelt capitalism—had escalated business and workers' costs. Even before the oil-related recession of the mid-1980s, companies such as Brown Oil Tools, Inc., an old Houston firm, had moved out from the city to small towns nearby.

Even more strikingly, other corporations have relocated outside the Sunbelt. Seeking cheap labor, such as workers paid a dollar or two an hour, many manufacturing operations have been moved to other countries. We have previously noted the flight of Atari from California to Hong Kong and Taiwan. Other firms have moved just across the U.S. border. For example, in the late 1980s there were 850 maquiladoras (factories) operating just inside the Mexican border. These plants use cheap Mexican labor and represent investments by U.S. firms in the primary circuit of manufacturing, but this time outside the Sunbelt.[44]

Revival and Stability in the North   Some parts of the northern industrial heartland have revived as a desirable place for profitable investment, as we will see in more detail in Chapter 5. By the early 1980s some real estate investors were saying that big money was to be made in northern cities and their suburbs. One investment consultant noted that moderate growth areas outside the Sunbelt did not have the increasing Sunbelt problem of the supply (too many office buildings, too many new housing subdivisions) exceeding demand. Developers in the Sunbelt were, in the investment consultant's view, too optimistic; they were overbuilding and outracing demand.[45] This investor recommended urban areas where developers were not building so aggressively, specifically suggesting investments in Boston and Columbus. This consultant's predictions were on target, for in the late 1980s the Boston economy was in better shape than that in the former boomtowns of Houston, Dallas, and Oklahoma City.

Indeed, the contrast between the Frostbelt and the Sunbelt has been overdrawn in much of the social science and popular literatures. There were, and still are, many investments being made in the prosperous cities in the North. A survey by the magazine *Sales and Marketing Management* has revealed that much personal wealth remains in the North—in such Frostbelt areas as Nassau County, New York, Stamford, Connecticut, Lake County, Illinois, and Newark, New Jersey. These communities house large numbers of very affluent homeowners, those who can buy expensive housing in new suburban subdivisions.[46] In addition, even in the Sunbelt boom from the early 1970s and to the early 1980s corporate investment was more substantial in certain Frostbelt cities, for example, Minneapolis, than in certain major Sunbelt cities such as New Orleans and Birmingham. Indeed, Minneapolis has been rated by the Urban Institute as the best American city in its general quality of life. The city has a major corporate headquarters center and has an orchestra, prominent art museums, much park land, little pollution, a low crime rate, and an excellent array of health and welfare programs, libraries, and public schools. A manual for newcomers published by local business interests admits that "Minnesota taxes tend to be higher than those in some parts of the country, because Minnesota offers a wide range of services to all of its citizens, with a special emphasis on meeting the needs of the disadvantaged."[47] The excellent middle-income services have long attracted companies with large white-collar workforces to this premier Frostbelt city.

GOVERNMENT SUBSIDIES FOR CORPORATE LOCATIONS

Growth Coalitions and Governments Compete   Corporations move freely from one place to another, encouraging competition between local communities, whose growth coalitions and local governments often bid for these footloose corporations with tax incentives and other pro-business subsidies. Thousands of local growth coalitions and government officials compete for corporations seeking to move their investments. The result is a broad array of tax and other subsidies that are usually unnecessary, again forcing the average taxpayer to shoulder business costs. For example, a vice-president of a major industrial location firm emphasized his company's success in winning $30 million of subsidies in Canada for one of his client corporations, including "a free, fully serviced site with heavy utilities in place, reduced local property tax levies, a federal grant of over $10 million, [and] a provincial training grant."[48]

In the mid-1980s ConAgra, an Omaha-based food-processing conglomerate, began looking for a site for a new research facility and headquarters. ConAgra's chief executive informed Nebraska governmental officials that his company would consider staying in the state if they would modify the tax laws. He told the governor and the state legislature that these specific changes would be necessary for ConAgra to remain: a reduction in the personal income tax for the high-income bracket, a shrinkage of the taxable base of corporate earnings to reflect only in-state sales (a major tax break), a package of investment and payroll tax credits, and property and equipment tax exemptions (including some for ConAgra's jet airplanes). Despite resistance from the head of the state legislature's Special Committee on Economic Development, who called the plan "corporate blackmail," ConAgra executives got what they asked for. Originally, it was estimated that the tax breaks would deprive the state treasury of $24 million in the first few years, but a closer examination revealed a loss of at least $160 million. According to the Center for Rural Affairs, it would probably take 50 years for increased economic activity to make up for the tax concessions. Meanwhile, ordinary Nebraskans have had to pay the bill. For example, the income tax shifts will add 50 percent to the tax burden of a two-wage-earner family with a $15,000-a-year income.[49] Similar package deals have been worked out for companies threatening to migrate in many areas of the United States.

Bowing to corporate pressure, some state governments, especially in the Sunbelt, have restricted unionization with right-to-work laws. Texas, Virginia, and Oklahoma have advertised that "labor-management relations are excellent" and that "wage rates are considerably below those found in major manufacturing areas." Northern states such as New Hampshire have also advertised this lack of unionization. North Carolina has proclaimed in a promotion brochure that its right-to-work law "*guarantees* employee freedom" and "*preserves* right to manage."[50] An advertisement for plant location in Florida ran as follows: "*Got Labor Pains? Central Florida Delivers!* Florida's 'right-to-work' laws contribute to a low incidence of labor unrest and work stoppages. We are ranked 43rd among the fifty states, with less than 13 percent of non-agricultural labor unionized."[51] This ad was placed by a county development group working in cooperation with the Florida State Department of Commerce.

State and City Advertising   State governments spend at least $100 million a year on economic development advertising. One of the biggest spenders has been Michigan, which paid $3.3 million in 1986 to advertise its good business climate and quality of life. New Jersey spent nearly $3 million for the same purpose. New York, Arkansas, and Maryland have also been generous spenders in the effort to secure companies seeking new locations for their cities. Some cities have expended as much or more than states on economic development advertising. For example, in recent years Houston's private-public economic development council has been spending about $2 million a year on city promotion. Mobile, Alabama, has paid more than $4 million on advertising. Some of this advertising has begun to accent quality-of-life issues. San Antonio, for example, ran an ad campaign promoting "the good life for business," while picturing its scenic downtown "Riverwalk." Near the nation's capital, Loudoun County, Virginia, already beset by traffic congestion from its suburban real estate boom, advertises "an idyllic lifestyle, with lush countryside, peaceful villages, and a community spirit." However, most development advertising is reserved for long-standing recruitment angles: low wages, weak or absent unions, and corporate tax breaks. Nevada promotes its "favorable corporate tax structure." Kentucky uses brochures outlining favorable policies in the state tax code. Georgia solicits businesses by promising wage rates "among the nation's lowest."[52]

Special Government Advertising and Subsidies: Do They Make a Major Difference? In recent years a number of research studies have indicated that special governmental subsidies for industrial corporations rank down the list for most corporate executives making location decisions. In spite of the many millions of dollars spent by local governments on advertising and special concessions to recruit industrial and commercial corporations, most corporate executives make their decisions on the basis of other important locational factors, as we noted earlier in the chapter. Various aspects of the general tax situation certainly influence corporate locations in many cases. But even more important for most industrial firms locating plants and warehouses seems to be the labor situation, such as type of workers available, the extent of unions, and wage rates. In addition, the subsidies do not offset marketing considerations. For example, firms desiring a presence on the Pacific Rim locate in the west coast cities whether or not the best governmental subsidies are provided there. And, perhaps most significant is the fact that many industrial and commercial corporations can now get some type of location subsidy in many cities in all regions.

Free-Enterprise Zones: The Return of the Company Town? As suggested above, government subsidies for business location and relocation have been substantial. They have included major programs for urban renewal in central cities and similar governmental investments that cleared land for business development, a topic given fuller consideration in Chapter 9. Here we will note one major 1980s proposal to transform central cities as places attractive for manufacturing corporations. The Reagan administration presented, as its serious program for dealing with urban problems, an "urban enterprise zones" proposal for poverty-stricken central-city areas. The underlying principle was to entice industrial companies to move their factories back into cities by providing an array of subsidies. Companies setting up plants in central-city areas were promised a sharp reduction in taxes, including investment tax credits, payroll tax reductions, and income tax and capital gains tax reductions. Also promised was a significant reduction in social and environmental regulations in central-city areas where companies would relocate. Eligible areas would, in theory at least, be chosen on the basis of high poverty and unemployment levels. Local governments would be able to apply to the federal Department of Housing and Urban Development for designation as urban enterprise zones.[53]

The Reagan Administration's 1982 Enterprise Zone Tax Act was presented to Congress in a form less extreme than the original proposal. Despite this humanizing of the enterprise zone legislation, it failed to pass in Congress. Nevertheless, cities and states across the nation have implemented this free-enterprise zone concept. By the late 1980s, 26 states had created more than 1,300 free-enterprise zones in 615 communities. Three Sunbelt states accounted for more than half of all the zones: Louisiana, with 623; Arkansas, with 181; and Florida, with 136. Like the proposed national legislation these local zones offer corporations many incentives to invest in designated urban areas, including property tax incentives, low-interest loans, and regulatory relief. However, most of the state-generated programs have not been directed at boosting employment in poverty areas. Only nine of the zones have requirements for state subsidies that include a minimum number of residents living in poverty.[54]

Given the historical record for similar programs, it seems likely that the corporate commitments to these U.S. enterprise zones will be temporary. Consider the case of the Volkswagen plant in New Stanton, Pennsylvania. In 1976 state and local governments provided the company with $88 million in low-interest loans, tax abatements, and road and rail improvements in its effort to induce the company to manufacture automobiles in the city. Given the state's generosity, Volkswagen agreed, but a little more than a decade later, the company announced it was halting production, permanently idling 2,500 production jobs.[55]

In general, the enterprise zone concept is in line with providing corporations with a "good business climate" wherever possible and is clearly consistent with the business climate surveys presented earlier. The various ingredients of the zones encompass many of the governmental subsidies that corporate executives seek. An official of a public employees' union called the urban enterprise zone proposal simply "an excuse for the creation of company towns." Employment for urban workers is in fact created, but at the cost of letting large multinational corporations control the terms. In this sense, urban enterprise zones are "company towns" built and fortified with federal government assistance.

CONCLUSION

Corporate location decisions are among the most fundamental in shaping the spatial environments of our cities, as well as in creating their basic economic climates and propensities to prosper or decline. U.S. cities are changing, as industrial and commercial corporations make decisions to abandon one area and move to another. This constant threat of job loss has made many U.S. workers fearful. The sense is that their community, their city, may be next. Bluestone and Harrison have articulated the dynamics succinctly:

> *Working people's feelings about this are not without foundation. Deindustrialization is occurring—on a surprisingly massive scale. It can be seen from North to South and East to West. It is happening as the largest most powerful corporations in the nation shut down older plants in the industrial heartland (and in the Old South) to move to new industrial zones in the New South and overseas...in an effort to maximize their profits and increase their span of control over the global economic system.*[56]

We can now turn to a discussion of the urban land and property developers who provide many of the industrial parks, office parks, and other projects suitable for corporate production, marketing, and administrative use.

NOTES

1. Seth Kantor, "Caucus Opens Twin-Plant Debate," *Austin American Statesman*, March 12, 1987, c11.
2. Walter S. Mossberg, "Plant-Closings Quarrel Distorts a Modest Idea," *Wall Street Journal*, April 25, 1988, 1.
3. Barry Bluestone, Bennett Harrison, and Lawrence Baker, *Corporate Flight* (Washington, D.C.: Progressive Alliance, 1981), pp. 12–13; "Capital Moves: Who's Left Behind," *Dollars and Sense*, April 1981, 7–8; Barry Bluestone and Bennett Harrison, *The Deindustrialization of America* (New York: Basic Books, 1982), pp. 9–30.
4. "Capital Moves," p. 7; "Seth Thomas," *Austin American Statesman*, April 1982, A7.
5. Tamar Lewin, "Atari Layoff Case Highlights Question of Workers' Rights," *Austin American Statesman*, July 25, 1984, G6.
6. Francis W. Horvath, "The Pulse of Economic Change: Displaced Workers of 1981–85," *Monthly Labor Review* 110 (June 1987): 3–12.
7. "Despite a 5-Year Upturn, 9.7 Million Jobs are Lost," *New York Times*, December 13, 1988, 14.
8. Lewis B. Siegel, "BLS Surveys Mass Layoffs and Plant Closings in 1986," *Monthly Labor Review* 110 (October 1987): 39.
9. "Capital Moves," p. 8; David Smith, *The Public Balance Sheet: A New Tool for Evaluating Economic Choices* (Washington, D.C.: Conference on Alternative State and Local Policies, 1979), pp. 3–4.
10. Michael Podgursky and Paul Swaim, "Health Insurance Loss: The Case of the Displaced Worker," *Monthly Labor Review* 110 (April 1987): 32.

11. Bluestone, Harrison, and Baker, *Corporate Flight*, pp. 24–35.
12. Mossberg, "Plant-Closings Quarrel Distorts a Modest Idea," 1.
13. Ibid.
14. August Lösch, *The Economics of Location* (New Haven: Yale University Press, 1954), pp. 28–30.
15. Melvin Greenhut, *Plant Location in Theory and Practice* (Chapel Hill, N.C.: University of North Carolina Press, 1956), pp. 175–285. I am drawing on the summary in David M. Smith, *Industrial Location*, 1st ed. (New York: Wiley, 1971), pp. 144–146.
16. David Jaffee, "The Political Economy of Job Loss in the United States, 1970–1980," *Social Problems* 33 (April 1986): 310.
17. Ernest Mandel, *Late Capitalism* (London: Verso, 1978), pp. 310–316.
18. Nancy Folbre, *A Field Guide to the U.S. Economy* (New York: Pantheon, 1987), p. 18.
19. Exxon Corporation, *This Is Exxon* (New York: Exxon Corporation, 1985), pp. 7–20.
20. M. Storper, R. Walker, and E. Widess, "Performance Regulation and Industrial Location: A Case Study," *Environment and Planning* 13 (1981): 321–338; David M. Gordon, "Capitalism and the Roots of Urban Crisis," in *The Fiscal Crisis of American Cities* (New York: Vintage, 1977), pp. 104–105.
21. Eugene Carlson, "Some Manufacturers Sour on San Francisco," *Wall Street Journal*, May 4, 1988, 19.
22. John D. Kasarda, "The Implications of Contemporary Redistribution Trends for National Urban Policy," *Social Science Quarterly* 61 (December 1980): 385.
23. The report is quoted in Richard A. Walker, "A Theory of Suburbanization: Capitalism and Construction of Urban Space in the United States," in *Urbanization and Urban Planning in Capitalist Society*, edited by Michael Dear and Allen J. Scott (London: Methuen, 1981), p. 401.
24. Cited in Eugene Carlson, "Rating Business Climates Becomes a Confusing—and Nasty—Game," *Wall Street Journal*, May 3, 1988, 25. Grant Thornton does not rate Alaska and Hawaii.
25. "How's the Labor Climate Where You Live," *Dollars and Sense* 125, (April 1987): 16.
26. Ibid., p. 15. The source is the Southern Labor Institute.
27. Storper, Walker, and Widess, "Performance Regulation and Industrial Location," pp. 325–327.
28. Diana Klebanow, Franklin L. Jonas, and Ira M. Leonard, *Urban Legacy* (New York: Mentor, 1977), pp. 157–158.
29. Ann Markusen, *Profit Cycles, Oligopoly, and Regional Development* (Cambridge, Mass.: MIT Press, 1985); see also Alfred J. Watkins, *The Practice of Urban Economics* (Beverly Hills: Sage, 1980), pp. 130, 154; Smith, *Industrial Location*, pp. 350–360.

30. Gordon, "Capitalism and the Roots of Urban Crisis," pp. 93–94.
31. Michael P. Smith, *The City and Social Theory* (New York: St. Martin's, 1979), p. 240.
32. Ibid., pp. 94–102.
33. Sharon Thomason, "Suburban Sprawl: How Counties Cope," *American City and County* 101 (July 1986): 64.
34. President's Commission for a National Agenda for the Eighties, Panel on Policies and Prospects, *Urban America in the Eighties: Perspectives and Prospects* (Washington, D.C.: U.S. Government Printing Office, 1980), pp. 18, 27, 42.
35. Urban Land Institute, *Industrial Development Handbook* (Washington, D.C.: Urban Land Institute, 1975), p. 229.
36. John Rees, "Regional Shifts in the U.S. and the Internal Generation of Manufacturing Growth in the Southwest," paper presented at Conference on the Committee on Urban Public Economics, Baltimore, Johns Hopkins University, May 1978, pp. 11–13; John Rees, "Manufacturing Change, Internal Control and Government Spending in the Growth Region of the United States," paper presented at 24th North American Meetings of the Regional Science Association, Philadelphia, November 1977, pp. 1–7.
37. President's Commission, *Urban America in the Eighties*, pp. 41–42; Kirkpatrick Sale, *Power Shift* (New York: Random House, 1975).
38. Joel Havemann and Rochelle L. Stanfield, "Federal Spending: The North's Loss Is the Sunbelt's Gain," *National Journal* 26 (June 26, 1976): 878–891.
39. David Lowery, Stanley D. Brunn, and Gerald Webster, "From Stable Disparity to Dynamic Equity: The Spatial Distribution of Federal Expenditures, 1971–83," *Social Science Quarterly* 67 (March 1986): 98–106; Kenneth R. Weiss, "States Circle Their Wagons for the Money Wars," *New York Times*, April 25, 1989, p. 12.
40. President's Commission, *Urban America in the Eighties*, pp. 18–42; see also "Burning up in the Snowbelt," *Time*, January 12, 1981, 19.
41. Robert E. Firestine, "Economic Growth and Inequality, Demographic Change and the Public Sector Response," in *The Rise of the Sunbelt Cities* (Beverly Hills: Sage, 1977), p. 199; cf. also Peter A. Lupsha and William J. Siembieda, "The Poverty of Public Services: An Analysis and Interpretation," in *The Rise of the Sunbelt Cities*, p. 174.
42. President's Commission, *Urban America in the Eighties*, p. 42.
43. "Corporate Flight to the Suburbs," *Houston Business Journal*, January 12, 1981, 1.
44. Kantor, "Caucus Opens Twin-Plant Debate," c11.
45. Steven Lewis, "Institutions Will Dominate Development in 1981, Predicts White: Money Market to Remain Volatile," *National Real Estate Investor* 23 (February 1981): 60.

46. "Housing May (or May Not) Follow Population Trends," *Builder* 7 (January 1984): 97.
47. Tomi J. Martella et al., *The Minneapolis New Resident Guide* (San Diego: MARCOA, 1987), p. 42.
48. Robert M. Ady, "Shifting Factors in Plant Location," *Industrial Development*, November–December 1981, 16–17.
49. Neal Peirce, "Corporate Tax Breaks Can Be Too Expensive," *St. Louis Post-Dispatch,* January 1, 1988.
50. Quoted in Goodman, *The Last Entrepreneurs,* p. 37.
51. Advertisement in Conway Publications, *Site Selection Handbook/78* 23 (February 1978): 70.
52. Robert Guskind, "Bringing Madison Avenue to Main Street," *Planning* 53 (February 1987): 7–8.
53. John Herbers, "New Urban Program," *New York Times,* March 28, 1982.
54. Edward Hayes, "From Rags to Riches," *American City and County* 101 (November 1986): 64–72.
55. Peirce, "Corporate Tax Breaks Can Be Too Expensive."
56. Bluestone and Harrison, *The Deindustrialization of America,* p. 47.

3

DEVELOPERS, BANKERS, AND SPECULATORS
Shapers of American Cities

In Canada, wealth has several classifications: Rich, superrich and Reichmann. If not the world's wealthiest family, it comes awfully close, with a net worth approaching $10 billion, double that in assets. And the clan is extending its global reach. Yet though the three Reichmann brothers are the earth's biggest real-estate developers and have erected such U.S. landmarks as Wall Street's World Financial Center, few Americans know their name.[1]

...a new breed of entrepreneur has reshaped the developer's image. Trump is only one of a group of well-publicized builders that includes Mortimer Zuckerman of Boston, New York and Washington, D.C., California's Donald Bren and Gerald Hines of Houston. These moguls have emerged from behind their buildings to cultivate high-rolling lifestyles, move in powerful circles—and put up distinctive buildings that have made them celebrities in their own right.[2]

INTRODUCTION

A Pioneering Developer The age of the large-scale property developer began in earnest after World War II, not only in the United States but also in Canada and in many European countries. Developers have commonly cast themselves as the conceptualizers, organizers, and supervisors of real estate development projects. They are centrally concerned with the exchange value of urban land and urban construction. One leading pioneer in conceptualizing, building, financing, and marketing large-scale development projects was Bill Zeckendorf, who from the 1940s to the 1960s became involved in office, hotel, shopping center, and apartment projects in the United States and Canada. "Real estate is one of the few businesses," Zeckendorf once commented, "in which you can get into the big-time without money." Borrowing extensively, Zeckendorf followed his prescription and built a multinational real estate empire from a small beginning. By the 1950s his development corporation, Webb and Knapp, had half a billion dollars in construction and was the most important real estate developer in urban renewal areas in U.S. cities.

According to Zeckendorf's autobiography, his company packaged and built the first giant suburban shopping center in New York, started a Denver construction boom with an office complex and a hotel, built a famous office and shopping center in Montreal (the Place Ville-Marie), and fathered large-scale reconstruction projects in Washington, D.C., Philadelphia, Pittsburgh, and numerous other cities across the nation. Zeckendorf packaged land for the Chase Manhattan Bank Plaza, and in his heyday he owned numerous New York office towers. He was a real estate capitalist who hobnobbed with then-president Dwight Eisenhower and the Queen of England, as well as prominent bankers who helped get Zeckendorf projects developed. He was a wizard at leveraging—buying and developing property with other people's cash.[3]

However, in the late 1950s Zeckendorf's company ran into major financial trouble, in part because of construction problems and extensive borrowing. Zeckendorf began to sell land and buildings. British bankers bought some of his projects, and millions of dollars were consequently lost by the British. Ever resilient, Zeckendorf survived this fiasco to become involved in real estate operations again. Today, the Zeckendorf family continues to mold the urban landscape of New York. In 1986 the Zeckendorf Company submitted a winning bid to New York City to codevelop the South Ferry Plaza site, a $400 million 60-story office tower located at the confluence of the Hudson and East Rivers. More recently, the Zeckendorfs, in a joint venture with others, broke ground on a condominium project called Central Park Place. The development is attracting considerable attention as it will offer a sweeping view of Central Park to the residents of its 310 luxury apartments.[4]

William Zeckendorf, Jr., has gained a reputation for being more cautious than his father. In most instances he reportedly has put up a small percentage of the money for a project and has taken responsibility for managing it, in exchange for a share of the ownership. Though the younger Zeckendorf's fortunes are but a fraction of his father's, they are more secure. Unlike his father, he refuses to start new office projects until a major tenant commits to lease space; for example, he did not start construction on a 2-million-square-foot project at the old Madison Square Garden until the Ogilvy advertising agency agreed to lease 600,000 square feet of the space. In this case, a pioneering development corporation has persisted across two generations.[5]

Today the real estate development industry is one of the largest in the United States. Real estate development, construction, and services account for about 16 percent of the U.S. gross national product. And in recent years employment in the construction industry alone has approached 5 million workers.[6] A variety of urban development projects account for much of that construction employment. Developers such as the Zeckendorfs, together with major construction companies and banks, build a variety of large projects from office towers to residential subdivisions. They are major shapers of our cities. It is not sufficient to discuss, as the mainstream social scientists often do, the character of cities, their growth, or their demise primarily in terms of small businesses or rank-and-file workers and consumers, for their choices are limited in many ways not only by the large industrial corporations but also by the major real estate developers.

THE ROLES AND TYPES OF DEVELOPERS

Developers as Catalysts In Chapter 1 we discussed the primary and secondary circuits of capital investment. The reader will remember that Lefebvre and Harvey, among other critical scholars, have developed the concept of the secondary circuit of capital, an investment circuit distinct from primary production (for example, manufacturing) investments and one that includes real investment. During crises or surpluses in the primary circuit, capital often flows in the direction of the secondary circuit of real estate investments. These real estate investments often take the form of large-scale urban development projects. Land and property developers conceptualize, package, and organize the funding and construction of urban development projects. Developers act as catalysts, notes Lorimer, as they

> look for sites to erect a profitable apartment building or shopping center or suburb, they assemble the site, draw up some kind of plan for the project, get the necessary approvals from governments and public bodies, line up tenants if this is appropriate, line up mortgage lenders to lend them the bulk of the cost of the project once it's built, get the architectural plans for the scheme drawn up, hire the contractors to do the construction, and arrange to rent or sell the building once it's finished.[7]

Enhancing the exchange value of the land and buildings is a principal concern.

A report on Sunbelt development has noted that "the location, timing, and form of future urban development is determined in the project planning stage of the development process." It is the private developers and their associates, the report notes, who make the land tract and purchase decisions, taking into account highway patterns, regional growth patterns, the availability of utilities, and the general "feasibility" (that is, profitability) of the development project. Typically, the developers also decide on the financing, such as Federal Housing Administration (FHA) guaranteed loans or conventional loans for a suburban subdivision. The developers procure the necessary utilities, securing governmental assistance in subsidizing them. Developers secure the construction and long-term financing, bringing banks and other financial institutions into the picture. They may divest what they develop, as in the case of suburban developers who sell off serviced lots to smaller builders, or they may retain ownership and lease out space to tenants, as in the case of many office building developers. The developers who fashion large urban projects can do so partly because of a legal system which protects their property ownership, their right to dispose of property, a point made in Chapter 1. The legal protection of individualized property ownership gives landowners and developers much control over urban space. Within broad limits land can be developed, and buildings constructed, as they wish.[8]

Reorienting Cities: Early Entrepreneurs   Real estate entrepreneurs and developers can have profound effects on the physical face of cities. Take, for example, the powerful nineteenth-century capitalists Marshall Field and Potter Palmer, whose real estate operations remade the face of Chicago. At the end of the Civil War, the Lake Street area was the central retail district of Chicago. A single powerful capitalist, Potter Palmer, rechanneled major business growth to another section of Chicago. The location he chose, around State Street, was then run down. Palmer bought up much of the property, pushed for a wide street heading into the area, and then developed a plush hotel to entice businesses there. He thereby succeeded in relocating the center of Chicago's business activity. Moreover, after the great Chicago fire, Marshall Field, another famous Chicago entrepreneur, made investment decisions that again relocated substantial business activity in the city. Like Palmer, Field avoided former business centers and chose another dilapidated area inhabited by the poor. Field rebuilt his large retail store in a poor Irish area, displacing the local residents in the process. Numerous businesses followed his lead, another indication of the early importance of leading capitalists in shaping urban patterns. Eventually, Field's real estate investments and land speculation became more profitable than his retail business. Yet, compared with modern developers, Palmer and Field were not as centrally involved in real estate development in itself.[9]

Types of Modern Developers   Some land and property developers are diversified, building and managing a variety of urban projects, including office towers, shopping centers, warehouses, industrial plants, hotels, and motels. In the 1980s the giant diversified U.S. developers included Trammell Crow (Dallas), Urban Investment and Development (Chicago), Gerald D. Hines Interests (Houston), Vantage (Dallas), Daon Corporation (Newport Beach), Century Development Corporation (Houston), and Maguire Partners (Los Angeles). While many of these development corporations are based in the Sunbelt, their projects can be found in many cities. Other developers are specialists. They focus their attention on particular areas of activity such as shopping centers or multifamily housing. For example, in the mid-1980s major shopping center developers included the Edward J. DeBartolo Corporation, General Growth Companies, and Ernest W. Hahn, Inc. Such companies own and manage millions of square feet in shopping centers.

Some large developers dominate particular types of urban construction. For example, in 1982 Trammell Crow, one of the largest U.S.-based developers, dominated the commercial warehousing market as owner and manager of a $2 billion empire. These warehouses have typically been located in industrial parks near major traffic arteries. But Trammell Crow has also developed office buildings, hotels, and residential subdivisions. In 1985 alone, Trammell Crow started $2.2 billion worth of new buildings. Trammell Crow has established itself as the preeminent American homebuilder; in 1987 Trammell Crow's 12,037 housing starts led the nation (see Chapter 8). Trammell Crow has also been involved in the development of hotels (see Chapter 4). By 1986 the journal *Institutional Investor* had Crow pegged as the nation's largest developer, controlling properties valued at $7.5 billion. And in 1988 the *Wall Street Journal* reported Trammell Crow to be the nation's biggest landlord, owning and managing 287.5 million square feet of office, industrial, and retail space valued at $14 billion.[10] The Crow example shows that many of the giant developers started in one specific type of construction such as warehouses or shopping centers, then diversified into other projects such as office towers, apartment buildings, houses for resale, and land development to maximize profits. These developers, as capitalists, transform today's profits from development projects into banked funds, and then into tomorrow's development projects. The secondary circuit of investment has many branches.

Developers and Shady Deals? Developers can be inventive in pursuing their goals. Most operate aboveboard, but others press against ethical limits. One developer who pushed against the limits of legal conduct was J. R. McConnell. After being convicted of securities fraud in Florida, McConnell headed to Houston in 1978 where few people in this free-enterprise city asked about his past. The magazine *Texas Business* featured McConnell in a section called "Houstonians to Watch," describing him as a "publicity-shy investor...he's sketchy about details of his past, and his business associates are fascinated by his mystery."[11] As it happened, Houstonians should have scrutinized McConnell more closely. Upon his arrival in Texas, McConnell became a vice-president of Texas Guaranty Investments (TGI). In return for their money, investors in the company believed they were receiving first liens on TGI-owned property. Investors were driven through the posh River Oaks neighborhood in Houston and told they were looking at their property. Only later did they discover their "property" referred to a few square feet here and there, a tree, fire plug, or a room within a house. Yet, investors continued to sink their individual retirement accounts and sometimes their entire life savings into TGI, until the firm eventually amassed more than $35 million. McConnell then took the money and used it to buy real estate in Houston and Galveston.

Late in 1986 McConnell and his enterprises were forced into Chapter 11 protection of the bankruptcy court in Houston, with debts totaling $427.8 million and hundreds of properties that had been acquired through dubious means. According to civil lawsuits in U.S. district court in Houston and bankruptcy court records, the empire was reportedly amassed in part through questionable title and financing arrangements and bogus records created in a "sophisticated document-alteration room."[12] Upon hearing of the investigation, McConnell left Texas for a life on the lam in several countries. In a statement sent to the *Galveston Daily News*, McConnell blamed the bankruptcy filing of his companies on the "collapse of the Texas economy and the problems of the Texas financial institutions."[13] McConnell was indicted in October 1987 for defrauding banks, thrifts, and real estate insurers of at least $160 million. After months in hiding, McConnell surrendered to federal agents. In July 1988 the 41-year-old mastermind behind the largest title fraud case in U.S. history electrocuted himself in jail.[14]

While most developers do not cross the line into fraud and other crimes, many press ahead rather vigorously in pursuing their goals. For example, during the 1980s in New York City wealthy developer Donald Trump wanted the tenants evicted from a building next to Central Park which he hoped to raze. In an attempt to drive the tenants out of his rent-controlled building, Trump offered to shelter some of the city's homeless in its vacant apartments. The current tenants, claiming Trump was trying to drive them out in order to erect a new high-rise project, fought back and eventually won a favorable settlement. Meanwhile, the city refused Trump's offer to house some of the homeless there.[15] Other developers and land speculators have used "parking-lot blockbusting" to force homeowners to sell to them. To displace a whole neighborhood of homeowners, developers have been known to buy a few houses scattered throughout the area and then let them deteriorate. An alternative strategy has been to bulldoze selected houses in a neighborhood and replace them with noisy and unsightly parking lots. Eventually other residents must leave because of adjacent deterioration.

THE ORGANIZATION, BUREAUCRATIZATION, AND OPERATION OF DEVELOPERS

The real estate development industry is complex; as already suggested, there are many sizes of development companies, and their internal organizational structures vary significantly. Many developers in the decade after

World War II started as relatively small entrepreneurs and used early profits to move into one land enterprise after another. Even today, the real estate entrepreneur has frequently been seen as the crucial risk taker, the one who seeks to invest and reinvest in new business enterprises. However, in recent decades, as is true with many other sectors of the U.S. economy, even the most visible entrepreneurs have developed large-scale development companies; the bureaucratized corporation has come to dominate much real estate development.

A Major U.S. Developer: Entrepreneur Donald Trump Many large development corporations have grown up around one or a few powerful individuals; most of these are white and male. Sometimes, as is true of the Canadian Reichmann brothers and Denver's Philip F. Anschutz, the developers keep a low public profile. Anschutz, for example, has been described as "shy, secretive, and filthy rich—a Denver billionaire with vast holdings in mining, energy, real estate, and railroads. Few people in his home town have ever seen him on the party circuit, much less on the local news."[16] In other cases, the developers are well known to the public. Many of the latter are colorful figures who wheel through deals and social life with a flair for publicity. A major example of the latter is New York developer and New Jersey casino operator Donald J. Trump. Compared with the Reichmanns (see below), Trump's accomplishments do not place him at the very top. But Trump has catapulted himself into the national limelight. He learned about real estate from his father, Fred Trump, a successful developer who built and managed low- and middle-income housing in Queens and Brooklyn. Educated at the Wharton School of Finance, Trump reportedly found his real estate courses to be less than challenging because they stressed small projects.[17]

Not long after graduation he had a chance to work on major projects. In the mid-1970s his first major project involved transforming the distressed Commodore Hotel into the Grand Hyatt Hotel. Like the Reichmanns, Trump chose to invest in a property that few would have chosen. The Commodore, owned by the Penn Central Corporation, owed $6 million in back taxes and was losing $4.6 million annually. For $250,000, Trump signed an agreement to purchase an option on the property, but Trump did not have the money. When the city's Board of Estimate asked to see Trump's option agreement with Penn Central, he sent along a copy with only his signature on it (since he had no financing), but no one seems to have noticed. Trump persuaded lenders to loan $70 million for the project, convinced the Hyatt organization to manage the facility, and prevailed on city government to grant tax concessions. New York City officials, fighting off a city bankruptcy at that time, agreed to give Trump its first-ever tax abatement for commercial property. The value of the pivotal tax break has been estimated at $120 million. When the converted hotel opened, the Grand Hyatt was a multiple-purpose palace with 1,400 rooms, a presidential suite renting at $2,000 a night, a ballroom, a shopping arcade, and five restaurants.[18].

During the Grand Hyatt project Trump built a major development corporation, the Trump Organization. He also had learned how to involve government officials. He hired key government people after they left public service, thereby securing their intimate knowledge of the city bureaucracy and their access to important politicians and regulators. Following the 1974 election of Hugh L. Carey, to whose gubernatorial campaign the Trump Organization had contributed, Trump hired Louise M. Sunshine, the former head of Carey's finance committee, as a key official. With her help Trump was able to persuade officials of the financially strapped city (in concert with state authorities) to build the New York Convention Center on the site of the Penn Central railroad yards; this earned him a $500,000 commission fee.[19] According to one former government official, when other developers made relatively small campaign contributions to politicians, "Trump was giving $50,000—and bragging about it."[20]

Since the Hyatt development, Trump's development firm has been involved in numerous large-scale projects. Buying land cheaply and securing tax abatements, he erected Trump Tower, a retail-office-apartment complex next to Tiffany's on Fifth Avenue in New York City. In the mid-1980s he began construction on Trump Parc, a 42-story condominium project in Manhattan's Central Park South. Now completed, Trump receives between $2.5 million and $4 million for three-bedroom apartments that face Central Park. According to the magazine *Building Design and Construction*, in 1987 Trump ranked twenty-seventh among major developers in the United States.[21] Trump's latest forays in real estate and development have been in the field of casinos. As of the late 1980s he owned three, two in New Jersey and one in the Bahamas; and he had also acquired controlling interest in Resorts International, Inc., owner of the largest casino in Atlantic City. Although the exact figures cannot be ascertained because the Trump Organization's holdings are private, the major real estate holdings of Trump's North American empire are estimated to be worth about $3.8 billion.[22]

The Trump story illustrates the complexity of the contemporary real estate investment process. Here the movement of capital into selected branches of the secondary circuit of capital investment was fostered by a real estate entrepreneur who made extensive use of governmental connections and subsidies for his development projects. Government facilitation of capital flow was essential, and this complex web of developmental actions and decisions so integrates economic and political organizations and decision makers that it is difficult to disentangle the component parts.

A Canadian Developer in the United States: Robert Campeau   Over the last two decades many of the largest developers operating in the United States have been Canadian. These have included Olympia and York, Cadillac Fairview, and the Campeau Corporation. About half the assets of these giant developers are located in the United States. Only a few U.S. developers such as Texas-based Trammell Crow and Gerald Hines Interests have been large enough to compete in the same league with these billion-dollar Canadian companies. Robert Campeau, the head of one major development company, has entertained Canada's leading citizens and prime ministers in his mansion in Ottawa. Unlike Donald Trump, whose father had established a successful development business, Campeau's ascension has been arduous. Growing up in an Ontario mining town, he quit school at the age of 14 and went to work in a factory to help support his family. At the age of 25, he got his start in real estate by selling a house intended for his family for a $3,000 profit. Sensing the opportunity, he built 40 more houses that same year.[23] Over the next decade and a half he created the Campeau Corporation, a large integrated development firm. The corporation has built hundreds of Canadian apartment and office buildings, as well as 20,000 houses. And three-quarters of its development projects have been located in the United States, including office buildings and shopping centers. Campeau is aggressive; an associate has been quoted as saying that "he knows what he wants and goes for it, and if he doesn't get it, he fights back."[24]

In the 1980s the Campeau Corporation began to move beyond real estate development and to diversify with investments in retail stores. Thus in 1986 Campeau completed the largest-ever Canadian investment in a U.S. company when he paid $4.9 billion to merge his company with the New-York-based Allied Stores Corporation. The acquisition seemed dubious to many corporate analysts, given that Allied's 1985 revenues were 27 times greater than Campeau's. But Campeau was able to succeed because he had the backing of powerful investment bankers.[25] In early 1987 the combined debt of Allied and Campeau Corporation was $4.5 billion, compared to annual revenue of $4.3 billion. Stock market analysts were predicting dire consequences for his merger. But within a year, Campeau had sold off 16 divisions of Allied that were not performing well, while retaining possession of Allied's more lucrative stores. He also initiated widespread firings, cut expenses, and made changes in management. Nonetheless, Campeau Corporation was still losing money; in May 1988 the company announced that for the previous 13 months it had lost nearly $255 million.[26]

Despite these losses, in the late 1980s Campeau completed the largest-ever acquisition in the retail field by capturing Federated Department Stores—a $6.6 billion transaction, complete with the issuance of junk bonds. At the time Campeau-Allied Corporation had 290 stores with 32,000 employees, while Federated had 650 stores and 133,000 employees. Campeau had long-term debt of roughly $4.5 billion, compared with

Federated's $1 billion. Once again, Campeau had put himself under the gun to divest many of Federated's underperforming units, while maintaining the more profitable and prestigious divisions.[27] The Campeau Corporation history not only demonstrates the growth of a complex and diversified corporation, but also the ways in which capital can move first into the secondary circuit, into urban real estate investments such as houses and office buildings, and then back into the primary circuit, in the form of investments in manufacturing or retail firms.

Complex Companies   Most large development corporations today are complex organizations. They are bureaucratized companies with multiple levels of managers and other white-collar employees, associated professional experts like architects and lawyers, numerous divisions, and complicated rules and regulations. The land and development industry was once dominated by relatively small entrepreneurs and corporations. As we discussed in Chapter 1, Weiss has examined one type of developer-builder, those involved in residential developments. From the beginning of subdividing in the 1890s to the 1940s, Weiss explains how the larger homebuilders, later called community developers, became dominant by using the local and federal government regulations to displace smaller builders, a process that continues today.[28] A similar concentration and centralization process has taken place for developers of other large-scale projects such as office buildings and shopping centers. In the last decade or two, large corporations have dominated much urban real estate development and financing. Since the 1960s numerous smaller firms have merged to form larger ones, large firms have bought up smaller ones, smaller builders have expanded into larger-scale commercial development, and the super-developers like Campeau have sometimes become conglomerates by acquiring non-real estate enterprises.

There are various building and development specialties: constructing itself, manufacturing prefab houses or parts of houses and other buildings, packaging and subdividing land, financing, and managing ongoing income properties such as office towers and shopping malls. Some development companies incorporate several functions. Yet many of the largest development corporations that have been active in North American real estate have been unknown to the general public—for example, Cadillac Fairview Corporation, once one of the largest and most diversified development companies operating in North America. Typical of the large developers, Cadillac Fairview operated in more than one country and at one point engaged in many different types of projects, including (1) corporate rental projects, (2) the development and operation of office buildings, shopping centers, apartment buildings, and industrial plants, (3) the development and construction of single-family homes, and (4) land development. By the early 1980s the company controlled 33 office towers andmultiple-useprojectsin North America, encompassing over 20 million square feet of space. An additional 8.5 million square feet was scheduled for completion by 1987. By the mid-1980s the firm also operated or was constructing more than 40 shopping centers and was planning to add to its stock of 94 industrial buildings by adding more than a dozen in the United States and Canada by the early 1990s. The firm also controlled more than 50 residential subdivisions in such cities as New York, Philadelphia, Atlanta, Houston, Los Angeles, Seattle, and Toronto.[29]

The complexity of a modern corporation is indicated by the eight divisions Cadillac Fairview was operating in the early 1980s:

1. Corporate Financial Group: Financial services, planning
2. Land and Housing Group: Condominiums, single-family homes, planned communities
3. Shopping Centers Group: Shopping center management, construction
4. Construction Services Division: Construction services
5. Urban Development Group: Office towers, MXDs
6. Industrial Division: Industrial parks, buildings
7. U.S. Southern Region: All types of development
8. U.S. Western Region: All types of development

As can be seen, Cadillac Fairview has been involved in virtually every type of urban development project. Yet the fortunes of even the largest of the international development companies ebb and flow. Until recently, Cadillac Fairview was controlled by two of the most powerful families in Canada—the Bronfmans (who control Seagrams, the largest distillery in the world), who had a 50 percent stake in the firm, and the Reichmanns (see below), who had a 23 percent share. In the mid-1980s the owners of this development corporation tried to sell off all or part of its holdings to reduce its debt. In 1987, in a deal that ranked as one of the largest development sales ever made, the Bronfmans and Reichmanns sold Cadillac Fairview's Canadian commercial interests and its U.S. shopping centers to JMB Realty, a Chicago-based real estate syndicator, who paid $2 billion. In the same year developer Michael Prentiss and New England Mutual bought Cadillac Fairview's U.S. office and industrial park interests for $435 million. The secondary circuit of real estate is a very volatile and ever-changing arena of investments, and it is the large corporations that are the most powerful players.[30]

The World's Biggest Developer: Olympia and York, Ltd. Ironically, the world's largest urban developer got a boost from Bill Zeckendorf's financial crisis, which we discussed in the opening to this chapter. By the late 1980s Olympia and York Developments, Ltd., a multinational Canadian corporation headed by Paul, Albert, and Ralph Reichmann and still unknown to most Americans, owned 50 million square feet of space in North America alone; the little-known Canadian company was Manhattan's *largest* commercial landlord. Altogether, in the late 1980s the Reichmann brothers held total assets approaching $18 billion. Estimates of their direct real estate holdings range from $11 billion to $15 billion. This family originated in Hungary, but migrated to Vienna. Fleeing Nazi terror there, they eventually moved to Morocco. In 1956 the family moved to Toronto and established a tile importing business, which led them into real estate development. By the early 1960s Zeckendorf was overextended in terms of debt and on the brink of fiscal disaster. In 1964 the Reichmann brothers bought nearly 600 acres of land near Toronto from him for $25 million, land that became the center of a major industrial and residential district. The Reichmanns soon became involved in warehouse construction.[31]

Taking advantage of "distressed" properties has been a trademark of the Reichmann approach. For example, in 1977, amid the fiscal crisis that depressed property values in New York City, the Reichmanns purchased eight Manhattan skyscrapers for $320 million. Today the buildings are valued in excess of $3 billion. Since that time, their firm, Olympia and York, has built many major development projects across the United States and overseas. These include a $750 million redevelopment project in downtown San Francisco (the Yerba Buena Garden, a mixed-use project), as well as major projects in Boston, Miami, Hartford, and Dallas. Their most impressive U.S. project to date is the World Financial Center in lower Manhattan (the Battery Park City project) that was finished in the late 1980s at a cost of $1.5 billion. Residing in the new complex are such powerful financial companies as Merrill Lynch, American Express, and Dow Jones. The biggest development in New York City since Rockefeller Center was built some five decades earlier, this project is larger than four Empire State buildings. Its construction raised the amount of office space controlled by the Reichmanns to nearly 25 million square feet out of a total of 300 million in New York City. By 1987 the Reichmann brothers had become New York's largest commercial landlord.[32]

A multinational enterprise, Olympia and York has been active in the secondary circuit of real estate capital investment worldwide. In their largest metropolitan project to date, the Canadian brothers have worked with the British (Conservative Party) government to develop the Canary Wharf in the Docklands area of East London. Consisting of 24 buildings encompassing 12.5 million square feet of floor space, the $6 billion project is part of a major restructuring of the city's East End, which is destroying blue-collar communities and replacing them with white-collar developments. Beginning in the early 1980s, the Reichmanns set out to diversify into a variety of businesses, including related companies specializing in financial services and real estate development. They also symbolize the growing concentration of real estate development capital under one roof. In the late 1980s

Olympia and York had a large share of the stock (altogether worth $5 billion) in these major companies: Gulf Canada Resources (70 percent of the company's stock); Abitibi-Price (77 percent); G.W. Utilities (88 percent); Trilon (13 percent); Campeau (22 percent); Santa Fe/Southern Pacific (20 percent); Trizec (37 percent); and Landmark Land Company (25 percent).[33]

Concentration and Centralization in Development This list illustrates not only that the largest real estate development firms are multinationals, but also just how centralized and concentrated the real estate industry has become. Olympia and York is the world's largest real estate development firm—and also owns a significant share in other major development corporations such as Campeau, Trizec, and Landmark. Today there are fewer and larger development companies than a decade ago. Traditionally, a few key rationalizations have been used to defend the domination of fewer and fewer corporations; one such rationalization is that large corporations provide better planned developments than smaller companies. Real estate analyst Lewis Goodkin justifies larger companies by noting that the smaller "entrepreneurial builder, short on bankroll and long on leverage, has to follow a hedgehopping pattern of suburban development, so large-scale development can mean less hedgehopping and less sprawl."[34] Those large firms with more cash can be, in their view, more efficient in real estate projects. As one developer put it, "the last few years have eliminated a number of players. Cash has been king."[35] Over the last several decades the development and land industry trend has generally been toward control by fewer companies. Inflation creates tighter margins, forcing many smaller developers and builders out of business. This has been true in many areas of development, from shopping malls to residential subdivisions. For example, by the early 1980s three dozen publicly owned homebuilding firms delivered a fifth of all single-family homes sold in the United States, an increase in share over the prior decade. By one estimate, 200 major developers will be in control of most suburban housing projects by the end of the century.[36]

In addition, from time to time a number of the largest homebuilding and other development companies have become, or been started as, subsidiaries of large non-real estate corporations, including corporations as diverse as Exxon, Aetna, Penn Central, and Phillip Morris. By the 1970s many large multinational corporations were moving into some aspect of the real estate development industry. Three hundred of the top one thousand corporations, including those in the oil, food, chemical, paper, and machinery industries, had real estate departments and subsidiaries. Thus 250 major corporations replying to a 1971 survey had moved $25 billion of investment capital into the secondary circuit of real estate. Chrysler Corporation, which was beset by financial problems in the late 1970s and early 1980s, had set up a real estate department in 1967. Three years later its holdings exceeded $300 million and included a wide range of real estate projects around the country, from urban townhouses to a Montana ski resort. Aerospace companies, major utility companies, timber corporations, and oil companies, too, have gotten into urban development projects. Large companies have also become involved in huge "new towns," massive suburban projects such as Reston, Virginia (Gulf Oil), and Rancho, California (Kaiser Aluminum).[37]

Oil company profits and borrowed funds have, on occasion, been invested in urban development. We have noted Gulf Oil's Reston, Virginia, satellite city project. Exxon's real estate subsidiary has heavily invested in Houston metropolitan area real estate. Another oil firm project, one of the largest satellite cities in the world, is The Woodlands, situated on 23,000 acres north of downtown Houston. This development is the brainchild of an oil capitalist, George Mitchell, who has moved some of his oil-generated capital (plus other financial resources) into a new investment: the building of a multibillion-dollar satellite city of his own design. Built by Woodlands Development Corporation, a subsidiary of Mitchell's Texas oil company, this planned development housed 13,000 residents and 200 businesses by the early 1980s. According to its 36-year master plan, it will eventually accommodate 160,000 residents and encompass 25 million square feet of office space. Everything from schools, shopping malls, apartments, single-family homes, churches, and transportation lines have been provided. The Woodlands represents Mitchell's vision of how urban problems are to be solved. The Woodlands, Mitchell further notes, is "not Utopia, but it's a step better than anything done in the past."[38]

Richard Walker and Michael Heiman noted that behind this dramatic expansion of non-real estate corporations into the development industry has been the "search for profitable outlets for surplus capital, product diversification, tax benefits, and the use of surplus land. Large-scale development, in particular, absorbed large blocks of capital, allowed internalization of profitable neighborhood effects, and promised monopoly control over local housing markets."[39] Here is a clear example of surplus capital flowing from the primary circuit of oil investment to the secondary circuit of real estate investment. Of course, there have been major setbacks, which have slowed the penetration of non-real estate multinational corporations into real estate development. Major economic recessions have reduced investments in land and in urban development projects. On occasion, the large non-real estate companies have even abandoned the secondary circuit.

A Note on Profitability   Investments in secondary-circuit development projects provide the opportunity for capitalists to make substantial profits. Inflation in land and building prices, especially with financing at fixed-interest loans prior to the late 1970s, brought large profits to hundreds of developers in the decades after World War II, enabling many to make further ventures and to expand. One analysis of profits found that selected North American development companies were making from a low of 9 percent to a high of 430 percent returns on shareholders' investments. In addition, because many developers in boom areas own land and other speculative property that is appreciating, they may eventually make high profits from the sale of that property, income not figured into annual profits until projects are sold. Except in regional or national recessions, profitability has been high for many development subsidiaries and companies.[40]

BANKERS, INSURANCE COMPANIES, AND OTHER LENDERS

Fueling the Secondary Circuit of Investment An understanding of complex financial arrangements is necessary to comprehend how developers and their lenders make substantial profits. We have noted previously that surpluses of capital in the primary circuit can shift capital in the direction of the secondary circuit, into land and building investments. In addition, contrary to the arguments of David Harvey, capital need not originate in the primary circuit of production; capital regularly flows from one part of the international secondary circuit, such as a profit from a huge apartment project in London, to another, such as a new office tower project in Los Angeles. Harvey has underscored the critical mediating role of state-subsidized banks and other finance capitalists in facilitating the flow of capital into the secondary real estate circuit. Individual capitalists may have difficulty in switching capital from one circuit to another without the protection of government-backed banks and other governmental protection. Thus a functioning capital market, a wide range of banking institutions, and governments willing to back up that capital market are essential to the flow of capital between different circuits.

Cash and borrowed funds make urban real estate development possible. A developer's capital may come from shares sold to stockholder-investors, profits retained from previous projects, loans from U.S. lenders, or loans from overseas banks. Equity investors and debt lenders are critical actors in most large urban projects. A developer's own funds or those of friends and relatives may provide the basic start-up capital. But this is only a small part of the money needed. The necessary debt capital is usually provided by institutions such as commercial banks, insurance companies, pension funds, real estate syndicates, and foreign investors. Commercial banks, savings and loan institutions, and insurance companies are leading members of the group sometimes called *finance capitalists,* the complex network of organizations that make profits by trading in various types of financial instruments, including bonds, and by servicing clients with loans and mortgages. Developers are dependent on finance capitalists, because one of the major functions of developers is to secure financing for their secondary-circuit projects. Moreover, finance capitalists are a direct factor in development as well; finance capital "is partly responsible for stimulating demand for property in the first place, by its own needs for office space, by lending money to developers, and by pouring money into property as a hedge against inflation."[41]

Banking Arrangements   Real estate developers and other operators usually need less of their own money to get started than do most other entrepreneurs. They can borrow more of the total purchasing price of their projects from banking institutions than their peers can for industrial equipment. This process, called *leveraging*, gives developers a lot of clout beyond their own resources. Leverage is the mechanism that allows the pyramiding of operations, such as those of Bill Zeckendorf, by borrowing millions after a small personal investment. Over the last few decades loans have come from commercial banks, savings and loan institutions, insurance companies, real estate investment trusts, wealthy individual investors, and pension funds. Commercial banks often provide the short-term construction financing for development projects. Construction loans are usually paid back by another loan, such as a longer-term mortgage provided by an insurance company after construction is completed.

Mortgages provide one type of borrowing developers use; they pay interest and principal payments over several years to the lender. A mortgage loan is a written legal agreement in which the borrower pledges the physical property as security to the creditor to receive the loan. The lender has a lien against the property, which allows the lender to take title or sell the property if payments are not made. Ordinarily mortgage loans provide the majority of the longer-term money for development projects. Active developers constantly search for new loans. When a loan comes due, money must be found to cover it. "Prepayments on huge [property] loans create a constant demand for cash so that the only ways in which profits can be made are by raising additional mortgages and selling off buildings and land."[42] Mortgage insurance and other protection provided by the *federal government* since the 1930s have made it possible, and more profitable, for lending corporations to channel capital into the secondary circuit of real estate. Moreover, because lenders loan so much money to real estate actors, many lending executives maintain close ties to the development companies. Local banking officials, as one Long Island study has documented, even got into land speculation partnerships themselves; and some bank officials served on zoning and planning boards, to which their developer friends have applied for permits.[43]

The traditional role of the commercial banks has been to make short-term construction and development loans and to place long-term commercial financing with other finance capital institutions. However, in recent years many commercial banks have used their own capital sources to make longer-term loans. In addition, new real estate lenders such as national and international investment bankers have been added, and older lenders now face vigorous competition in the secondary circuit of investments. By the late 1980s major real estate lenders, and arrangers of financing for other clients, included such large investment bankers as J.P. Morgan and Salomon Brothers. These Wall Street investment bankers have become involved in real estate markets by establishing their own mortgage trading departments, which package and securitize loans. This sometimes has even meant a bypassing of the intermediate role of the local commercial mortgage bankers and the mortgage brokers, the firms with an understanding of local real estate markets. The nationalization and internationalization of the real estate financing can be clearly seen in the movement of the investment bankers into major local real estate projects.[44]

Complex lending arrangements can fall apart. For example, in the mid-1970s several New York banks put together a $62 million short-term loan for the developer of an office building and later had to take ownership of the building when the developer was unable to get long-term financing. Borrowing has created problems on the opposite coast, as the default of a Los Angeles developer revealed. The developer had borrowed a large amount from a Beverly Hills bank and when he defaulted, the bank's worried customers began withdrawing money. The U.S. Comptroller of the Currency intervened, and the bank had to be sold to another large banking corporation.[45]

Moreover, banks and other lenders commonly set limits on real estate development by requiring that certain conditions be met before they will loan; financial institutions are in a position to dictate such conditions as size and scope of projects, type of financial statements, interest rates, bank access to records, legal fees, and even access to mass transit. In the case of smaller developers, finance capitalists can dictate virtually all important conditions. In making loans, lenders have considerable power to shape how, and whether, urban communities grow. When they have decided to finance corporations building office towers in central cities, they have contributed to the growth of administrative centers there. When they have decided to deny loans to black homeowners in black communities (a practice known as *redlining*), they have hastened the decline of housing in many low-to-moderate-income areas. In addition, lenders tend to prefer the larger developers and industrial corporations as borrowers, because they figure a big company is less likely to go bankrupt than a small one. In this way they contribute to concentration and centralization in the real estate development sector of the U.S. economy.

Insurance Companies Many mortgage loans, especially for substantial development projects, have been provided by insurance companies. As early as the 1920s the country's largest insurance companies, Metropolitan Life and Prudential, were putting $50 million into home and apartment loans, funneling the funds through local banks. By the early 1980s, according to the *Life Insurance Fact Book,* insurance companies were third among all institutional investors in the amount of such loans made. Loans held by life insurance companies totaled $138 billion, a significant proportion of their assets. In the late 1950s fully 70 percent of mortgages held by insurance companies were for single-family and multifamily housing; but by the 1980s just 26 percent of insurance-financed mortgages were for residential loans. The nonresidential (nonfarm) mortgages made up nearly two thirds of their mortgages. Life insurance companies had more than $86 billion in such mortgages. These corporations have placed the money they hold from their own clients, and from pension funds they manage, into shopping centers, office towers, industrial factories, medical centers, apartment complexes, and industrial parks. Although many insurance companies have reduced investments in new mortgages during the periodic recessions of last two decades, they continue to make a significant proportion of commercial mortgage loans.[46]

In addition, insurance companies have become direct owners of much real estate—altogether $18 billion in 1981, up substantially over the previous decade. About 80 percent of this was then real estate investment property—the aforementioned skyscrapers, shopping centers, and other major development projects. Moreover, insurance firms have increasingly become involved in loan origination by setting up their own subsidiaries for brokering real estate loans. For example, in the late 1980s a subsidiary of New England Mutual Life Insurance Company invested $28 million in several industrial parks built by a Phoenix developer. Insurance companies not only have purchased real estate, but also have developed commercial projects. Thus Urbco, Inc., the real estate development arm of Connecticut Mutual Life Insurance Company, developed one million square feet of office, shopping center, and residential space during 5 years in the mid-1980s. Some have become involved in joint ventures. In the late 1980s New York's Guardian Life Insurance Company became a 50-50 partner with a local developer in a large office building in Los Angeles.[47]

Pension Funds The 1980s have sometimes been described as the "era of pension fund investment in real estate."[48] By the 1980s the money in many pension funds had grown to the point that their managers were investing heavily in "trophy," or high-quality, real estate investments, such as office buildings, regional shopping malls, and industrial buildings in prime locations such as New York, Boston, and Washington, D.C. For example, in 1988 the Teachers Insurance and Annuity Association (TIAA) owned $2 billion worth of trophy real estate including the Seagram's Building in New York City and major office buildings in Chicago, Cincinnati, and Minneapolis. Total pension fund money was well over a half-trillion dollars by 1980 and was expected to be one trillion dollars by 1990. Banks, insurance companies, and financial management companies typically control the investment decisions for most pension funds. The Equitable company alone managed $11 billion of real estate investments for U.S. pension funds in the late 1980s. Also in the late 1980s the Metropolitan Life Insurance Company purchased five shopping malls for its own portfolio and for pension fund clients.[49]

Even the union pension funds are managed by finance capitalists. Half the 192 union funds in one AFL-CIO survey were invested by only four bank and insurance companies: Morgan Guaranty Trust, Bankers Trust, Equitable, and Prudential. For the most part, these companies have invested as they see fit, including investing union pension funds in non-union construction projects. According to one report, Prudential loaned union pension funds to finance a building for the National Right to Work Committee, an organization vigorously opposed to unions. A number of building trade unions, in states from California to Florida, have organized to take back control of their pension fund money, and put more control into the hands of the workers themselves. Some struggles have been successful, and there will likely be more struggles over who will manage workers' pension funds in regard to real estate ventures.[50]

Developers Become Bankers   The quest for real estate capital has taken some interesting turns. One result of banking deregulation during the Reagan administration of the 1980s was less regulation of bank ownership and bank operations. The U.S. comptroller of the currency even permitted developers themselves to open their own banks. For example, in the Houston area at least 15 banks have been opened by real estate developers, most of whom went into banking in order to facilitate development activities; and at least 3 of these went bankrupt during the oil-related decline in the Southwest during the 1980s. These Southwest banks' loan portfolios were heavily tied into real estate projects. "Most often, developers opened banks as lead tenants in their office buildings in order to secure long-term financing for their property."[51] Thus one 10-story office building, called Petro Center I, was built in Houston in 1982; its developer also founded Petrobank, which served as the building's lead tenant until the bank failed in 1986. As a result, the first floor once occupied by the bank was soon vacant, and the building itself was taken over by outside corporations headquartered in Pennsylvania and Delaware. These new bankers have been creative in their loan policies. While the law prohibits more than 15 percent of a bank's capital being loaned to any one person, the law does not prevent loans from being made to several different individuals active in the *same* development project. This practice lessens a bank's loan diversification and has contributed to the failure of some banks across the Sunbelt, including the new developer banks.[52]

Pooled Investments: Syndicates and REITs   Real estate syndicates are another device used by real estate operators to obtain money for development. These syndicates typically involve the issuing of securities and have helped generate money for major projects such as skyscrapers. Until the 1986 tax reform legislation, the "tax shelter" (depreciation) advantages of real estate attracted wealthy investors such as doctors and lawyers into real estate tax shelters, including syndications involving part ownership in real estate projects. Real estate syndicates became increasingly common-place, and in the early 1970s syndicates accounted for one-tenth of new security offerings by the large Wall Street firms. However, some went bankrupt, and the luster for the wealthy began to wear off. By the late 1980s the rates of return on investments in these syndications had gone "from being spectacular to simply attractive."[53] The 1986 tax reform law length-ened the depreciation period, required the use of straight-line deprecia-tion, and limited the ability of investors to shelter ordinary income such as salaries and fees with losses from passive real estate investments. Most real estate arrangements no longer provide such lucrative tax shelters; most are now being sold for their income-producing advantages.

A related real estate financing device is the Real Estate Investment Trust (REIT). This arrangement permits "smaller" investors to get together and invest in land and buildings. The trust funds are like mutual funds. By the early 1970s stocks in REITs were "hot properties" on Wall Street, with a volume of about $20 billion. In those years, the REITs accounted for one-fifth of the money loaned out for development and construction. Major banks, including Chase Manhattan and the Bank of America, launched trusts of their own; even insurance companies such as Massa-chusetts Mutual were involved. But between 1973 and 1975 several large developers went bankrupt; and shares in many REITs dropped sharply, to one-fifth of their former value.[54] However, by the late 1980s the tarnished REITs had regained their popularity under the new tax reform laws, which had liberalized REIT rules. A qualified REIT can now avoid federal taxa-tion by returning its taxable income to shareholders; so-called "smaller" investors can pool their investments (for example, $100,000 each) in a diversified REIT which owns several real estate properties. Pension funds can also invest in the REITs and receive income tax-free. The 1980s tax reform legislation also created new real estate mortgage investment con-duits (REMICs) to encourage investment in real estate mortgages. These REMICs are nontaxable pools of real estate mortgages, which are used as backing for revenue-producing securities issued to well-off investors.[55]

Changes in the Secondary Circuit: Two-Tiered Investments   During the 1980s many U.S. metropolitan areas became overbuilt. Nonetheless, there has still been much financing activity, some of it in the cities that are still underbuilt, but much of it involving the resale and refinancing of existing properties in many cities. One real estate analyst at Cushman and Wake-field has noted the growth of a two-tiered property investment market, with a lot of surplus capital chasing the higher-quality buildings in pre-ferred locations in the top tier and much less capital available for buildings and projects in the lower tier. Not surprisingly, there have been major changes in the commercial loan industry in the last decade or so. Because of the oscillations in the U.S. economy, most lenders are no longer willing to make long-term, fixed-interest, fully amortizing loans. Instead, a variety of short-term and flexible devices have been used to facilitate real estate loans. These include floating interest rates, joint ventures and equity participation, securitization, sales/leaseback arrangements, and even a proposed real estate financial futures market.

Because of oscillating interest rates in the last decade many firms have arranged floating-interest-rate loans. For example, the investment banker Salomon Brothers has arranged a number of short-term floating-interest-rate loans for several regional shopping centers; the ultimate source of the capital was in this case the foreign banking community, which offered less expensive loans than U.S. sources. This type of financ-ing signals the *international* nature of much contemporary financing (see below). The global character of this financing can also be seen in the use of the London Interbank Offered Rate (LIBOR) as the basis for calculating interest rates worldwide.[56]

Direct participation by lenders in the loans has become common-place. One major developer, Portman Washington, noted that during the 1970s "a developer borrowed 110 percent of his costs, bought a Porsche, and didn't fret about equity partners."[57] By the mid-1980s, however, many lenders had become more selective and sought out equity participation in projects. As we have already seen in the case of the insurance corporations, many mortgage lenders now require a large share of a project's equity ownership, as well as high interest rates, before they will make a loan. Thus they have more protection than if they just make the loan; and they secure some future cash flow. For example, in the late 1980s New York's Chemical Bank arranged a $26 million mortgage for a Trammell Crow project in Tennessee; the bank held a participating interest in the mortgage. Part of such a loan may also be syndicated to other financial institutions.[58] A complicated financing mechanism that has become more popular is the sales/leaseback arrangement. A Westinghouse real estate subsidiary, for example, has arranged financing for developers who buy land with un-completed projects on them. The developers buy the land and buildings from the current occupying firms, then lease them back to the *same* firms. Then the developers use the rest of the land for new developments. Another device used to facilitate financing of large developments is "securitization," which involves the repackaging and reselling of existing real estate loans by one financial institution to other investors, thereby creating a new source of capital for further development. For example, in the late 1980s the Equitable company packaged $500 million of its commercial mortgages and sold them as mortgage pass-through securities. Pension funds sometimes purchase these packages of existing mortgages. By 1987 an estimated 4 percent of commercial mortgages had been securitized.[59] In addition, some real estate companies have issued their own publicly traded securities. Los Angeles' Westfield International, Inc., a mall development company, recently sold $308 million in preferred stock, with First Boston Corporation as the underwriter.[60]

In addition, the wave of corporate mergers since the early 1980s has had an effect on the ownership, sale, and financing of real estate property. Companies with large real estate holdings have become targets for takeovers. The property held by the target firm is later sold or mortgaged to help finance the takeover. For example, Campeau's aforementioned takeover of Allied stores involved the use of substantial mortgage debt to help finance the move of this development corporation into the ownership of department stores. In a complex finance capital arrangement, the real estate property of Allied is to be used to help pay off the "junk" (high-interest) loans used to finance the initial takeover.[61]

Tax Shelters and Tax Laws   Much real estate development in the United States since World War II has been facilitated, if not directly stimulated, by favorable tax laws. For example, between 1981 and 1987 there was an unusually large spurt of real estate investment and much overbuilding in cities across the nation. In 1981 the federal government established a 15-year accelerated depreciation schedule for buildings. Coupled with relatively high interest rates, this formed a climate where deep-shelter tax loss vehicles could be marketed vigorously to wealthy investors. As one knowledgeable expert put it, "This spurred investors to throw money at 'see-through' buildings."[62] With so much money available, some developers ignored questions of the economic viability of projects; there was much overbuilding of office buildings, hotels, and multifamily apartment housing for the affluent.

Until 1987 the federal tax laws provided "a safety net" for wealthy lenders and real estate owners and speculators. Not surprisingly, the change in the tax laws that occurred in 1987 had major effects on overbuilding, and on the related buying and selling of real estate. A number of tax reforms, including the reduction in general tax rates, the elimination of special treatment for capital gains, the limitation on deducting excess losses, and the increase in the depreciable lives of real property, significantly reduced the desirability of real estate projects as tax shelters for wealthy investors. As a result, those concerned with packaging real estate deals are no longer presenting them as tax shelters, but rather as direct income producers and as a hedge against inflation. In the short term, real estate property values were predicted to decline as a result of the tax law's less favorable protection of investors; there would be less money invested by those seeking the tax shelters, activity that inflated real estate prices. However, so far this prediction has been true mostly for lesser-quality real estate property. In the past, poor-quality real estate could be marketed to a wealthy investor seeking a tax shelter, because of the favorable tax laws, but since 1987 only economically viable properties such as shopping centers and apartment buildings for the affluent have been widely and actively bought and sold.[63]

THE INCREASING IMPORTANCE OF FOREIGN INVESTMENT

Global Capital Markets Since 1980 global investments in the secondary circuit of real estate have expanded greatly; capital for development now flows with ease across national boundaries. For instance, during the 1970s the Prudential and Metropolitan Life insurance companies were among the top 10 lenders in Canadian real estate. A significant portion of Canada's urban real estate development has been financed by U.S., German, Italian, British, and other foreign interests. Moreover, by the late 1980s, U.S. assets held by foreigners exceeded $1.2 trillion; corporate stocks and bonds made up one third of this amount, with another quarter in governmental securities. The rest, nearly $500 billion, was in miscellaneous assets, much of that being real estate.[64]

An important reason for the growing presence of foreign capital is the huge capital surplus held by pension funds, banks, and other corporations in certain foreign countries. Thus the success of numerous European and Asian corporations, and countries, in foreign trade and the falling value of the U.S. dollar in the 1980s radically changed the structure of international banking and the flow of capital in the secondary circuit in the United States. Foreign banks have expanded with the foreign trade. By the late 1980s the formerly dominant U.S. banks were no longer the world's largest; European banks held nearly $4 trillion in assets, while non-U.S. Pacific Rim banks held $3.7 trillion. North American banks were in third place with a more modest $1.75 trillion. In addition, the deregulation of banks and other financial institutions in European and Asian countries has contributed to the international flow of capital.[65]

The Europeans and Canadians Because of the periodic shortage of reasonably priced capital for development projects, many U.S. developers, and their brokers or bankers, have sought overseas capital. Foreign banks, investors, and pension funds have responded. Since the early 1980s the declining value of the dollar in relation to European and Japanese currencies has made investment in U.S. real estate attractive. For example, Dutch investors have invested in development projects and buildings in East Coast cities from New York and Boston to Raleigh and Atlanta. By the late 1980s the employees' pension fund for the Dutch airline KLM had $150 million of its money invested in U.S. real estate, including 100 acres in the Raleigh-Durham, North Carolina, area.[66]

Canadian development firms have also increased their investments in the United States since the 1970s. Canada's direct investment in the United States grew from $11.4 billion to $16.7 billion between 1983 and 1985 alone. While all of this money was not put into real estate projects, the billions of dollars do highlight the attractiveness of the United States to Canadian investors. In the 1980s Canada ranked fourth among all foreign investors in the United States, behind only Great Britain, the Netherlands, and Japan. In some cases, existing buildings are bought and held as investment property; in other cases the Canadian investments have taken the form of construction of major new development projects. We have documented the heavy involvement of Olympia and York Developments, Ltd., in a number of U.S. cities. Other major Canadian firms that have invested heavily in U.S. real estate include Bramalea, Ltd., the Trizec Corporation, Costain, Ltd., and B.C.E. Development. Costain, Ltd., is a residential developer with more than half its capital assets in the United States. A B.C.E. Development subsidiary bought $1 billion worth in real estate in five U.S. cities in 1986 alone, including much office space in Minneapolis. Bramalea, Ltd., has been investing here since 1979, with 60 percent of its total assets now in office buildings, residential housing, shopping centers, and industrial parks in cities from Los Angeles to Dallas.[67]

Trizec, Canada's largest publicly traded development corporation, has more than half its $4 billion assets invested in 98 U.S. properties, running the gamut from office towers and mixed-use centers to nursing home facilities. Trizec owns Hahn Company, a developer of 44 U.S. shopping centers, and controls one quarter of Rouse Company, a developer of 59 U.S. shopping centers. However, Trizec does not stand alone; it is closely linked to Canada's other large real estate firms. As we explained previously, Trizec is owned in part by Olympia and York. It is also partially owned by another Canadian firm, Cadillac Fairview. Interestingly, Trizec in turn holds a 43 percent ownership stake in Bramalea. These interlocks among major Canadian development firms have increased in the last decade and signal the increasing concentration and centralization of capital in the complex international development industry.[68]

Japanese Investors In addition to the Canadian and Dutch firms, other overseas banking and development companies have invested in U.S. real estate. These have included West Germany's Deutsche Bank, the U.K.'s

Heron Corporation, Australia's Hooker Corporation, and numerous Japanese companies. The success of Japanese capitalists in world trade has built up large surpluses of capital. The first Japanese investments in U.S. real estate markets were made in Hawaii; by 1988 Japanese investors owned $2.6 billion in property there. In one year in the late 1980s Japanese investors and institutions poured nearly $6 billion into U.S. real estate, with New York and Los Angeles being the principal destinations. Moreover, in 1987 the Los Angeles firm Hokubei sponsored 30 real estate tours for Japanese investors, showing them properties in New York, Chicago, Dallas, San Francisco, and Los Angeles. Tours have been sponsored by large banks, such as Mitsui Bank and Nomura Securities, which hope to be the lenders for sales.[69]

Unlike the Canadians, most Japanese investors have so far invested in existing properties. Japanese banks and other investors prefer to purchase trophy office buildings—and, less often, hotels, malls, and expensive condominiums—in major metropolitan areas. Sumitomo Realty and Development Company recently paid $500 million for a 41-story building in New York City. Mitsui Fudosan expended more than $610 million for New York's Exxon Building. The real estate subsidiary of Nippon Life Insurance paid more than $300 million for office buildings in New York City, Houston, and Los Angeles. And the hotel subsidiary of Japan Air Lines purchased New York's historic Essex House Hotel for $175 million. Boston's World Trade Center, a redevelopment project on the harbor, was offered to U.S. and Japanese insurance firms, but a Japanese company ended up with the 10-year $95 million in financing for the project.[70] A banker at J.P. Morgan noted in the late 1980s that "if you're a big player in arranging real estate financing you must do one half of your business with the Japanese or you're not keeping up with the times."[71] U.S. insurance firms and other banking firms have helped arrange Japanese financing for major real estate projects. In 1987 Equitable, for example, arranged financing for the Park City Mall in Lancaster, Pennsylvania. Equitable Real Estate held a $64 million first mortgage with a 10-year term; this was divided into two parts, a senior interest ($52 million) and a subordinated interest ($12 million). Japan's Sumitomo Bank took over the senior interest, with Equitable holding the rest. This was the first time a major Japanese bank had become involved in U.S. retail property.[72]

Only a handful of Japanese firms have become involved in real estate development. Kumagai Gumi stands out. Nearly a third of its $6 billion in total construction and property development activity is outside Japan. For more than half a century the firm has been active in neighboring countries, but since 1980 it has focused on the United States. By the late 1980s one-tenth of the firm's overseas activity was in the United States. In the mid-1980s Kumagai Gumi undertook 11 projects in New York worth $1.2 billion, 6 office building projects in Los Angeles and San Francisco, and a

hotel in Indianapolis worth $70 million. One of Kumagai Gumi's promi-
nent projects is One Union Square East, the Zeckendorf Towers, a joint-
venture project with William Zeckendorf, Jr. This is a 1.32-million-square
feet multiple-use project with four 20-story towers placed atop a seven-
tiered structure that will have nearly 700 condominiums and 312,000
square feet of office-retail space.[73] In addition, Japanese homebuilders
have scrutinized the U.S. housing markets. They have paid attention to
residential housing because a majority of Japan's houses are built in
factories with computerized assembly processes and high-technology
materials. Daiwa House, Japan's fourth-largest prefabricated housing
manufacturer, has constructed traditional homes in California and Texas,
thereby learning U.S. homebuilding and marketing techniques.[74] The
movement of surplus capital from Japan has become obvious from coast
to coast.

CONSTRUCTION FIRMS AND REALTORS

Often coordinated with industrial firms, developers, and lenders, a variety
of other land-interested actors play key supportive roles in the drama of
urban growth, development, and decline. Among these are thousands of
small builders, independent construction companies, real estate agencies,
architectural firms, engineering companies, management firms, and leasing companies. Small local builders can be found in many of the
developers' subdivisions actually supervising the construction of individual houses. Construction companies, small and large, are critical to urban
development projects. Those that are not subsidiaries of development
corporations are often closely held private companies that make little
information available about themselves. The public view of construction
tends to be one of a lot of little companies feverishly competing with one
another. Yet large construction companies do most of the major commercial and residential construction in the United States. In an examination of
New York City, Kleinfield has noted that "only a smattering of general
contractors regularly build tall office towers in New York City....They are
the hired hands, the ones that for a flat fee take the dream of skyscraper
and wrench it into reality."[75]

Real estate brokers and agents are another category of land-interested actors whose decisions, often in coordination with developers and
bankers, have had an impact on the urban landscape. Some specialize in
selling commercial real estate space; others, in sales of houses. Traditionally, brokering was highly fragmented and localized, but in the last two
decades local real estate brokers have faced increasingly intense competition from giant national brokers such as Coldwell Banker and Cushman
and Wakefield, the emergence of which reveals concentration and centralization of capital in yet another sector of contemporary real estate capital-

ism. Associations of real estate sales agents were organized in larger cities prior to 1900, but it was not until the 1910s that the forerunner of the National Association of Real Estate Boards (NAREB) was created. As we will discuss in Chapter 8, the NAREB (later renamed the National Association of Realtors) initially included homebuilders and community developers; it has long been one of the most powerful and effective governmental lobbies for real estate interests in Washington, D.C. Together with the National Association of Home Builders, the NAREB has fought for certain types of government housing and banking assistance programs, and lobbied against others. In Chapters 8 and 9 we will discuss the role that these real estate organizations have played in securing government assistance for home mortgages and land use regulation programs supportive of the real estate industry.

LAND DEVELOPMENT AND LAND SPECULATION

The consequences of urban land development placed under the direction of the powerful land-oriented decision makers of modern capitalism can be seen in U.S. patterns of landownership. One noteworthy phenomenon is *landbanking*. Developers, particularly large developers, their financial associates, and large landowners own or control an increasingly large percentage of urban land. Development corporations can buy up land and hold it in land "banks," waiting for the land's value to rise in response to adjacent city development, including the building of government-financed highways. Development firms often undertake joint ventures with other owners and financiers of land. Billions of dollars in land assets are held in this fashion by land development and allied companies. This land can serve several purposes. It can be held for future development by the company holding it, or it may be a speculative investment held for future sale. Developers, as well as land-oriented subsidiaries of non-real estate companies, not only shift capital from one real estate sector to another—as from profits off land developed in downtown areas to investments into suburban land, and back—but they also bank capital drawn from manufacturing operations in the primary circuit into land holdings in the secondary circuit of real estate. This banked profit and wealth can be returned to real estate development or to industrial manufacturing activities when future profitability dictates. Yet investment in land is distinctive; unlike investment in manufacturing it is not productive, that is, it does not increase goods or services.

Large amounts of money can be realized in urban land holding, buying, and selling. The creation of money value, often on paper, occurs as land ages and changes hands, often many times, in its life span. Land developers and other real estate investors acting as speculators are at the heart of this recurrent processing. A real estate speculator is a distinctive type of investor. A speculator is primarily interested in the unearned profits from property values and thus less interested in developing the land for productive uses or in managing buildings. Some speculators are not interested in holding property for a long time. Of course, in everyday practice it is difficult to tell where ordinary land investment ends and speculation begins—the two are closely interconnected.[76]

Speculation in the Nineteenth Century   Rural and urban land speculation by individuals and corporations has been characteristic of capitalism since the early days of this nation. In the first centuries of North American development, real estate speculators and developers, often merchants, large farmers, and railroaders with wealth and means, launched or shaped city development from Washington to Omaha and San Francisco, setting the pattern for future city growth. Legally and illegally, they bought land, pressured legislators, and bribed officials in a quest for profits. In the nineteenth century huge railroad corporations were among the first to become heavily involved in real estate speculation and development, rural and urban. Actions taken by railroad executives had a significant effect on land development, especially in the West. Many railroad lines were extended into unoccupied territory primarily for land speculation. Railroad capitalists expanding lines westward often received large federal government subsidies, including large gifts of land along the rails. These grants of government land rose in value with the growth of railroads and the towns that accompanied them, often leading to large land profits for railroad corporations, to the present day. By 1900 about 183 million acres had been given to the railroads, far more than the 80 million acres sold or granted to the much more publicized 600,000 American farmers. Interestingly, land sales and development were often a greater source of profit for railroad corporations than the actual building of railroads.[77] The growth of some midwestern and western cities was significantly accelerated or depressed by the actions of railroad capitalists. On some occasions, railroad corporations actually developed the towns. But even when they were not directly involved in building towns they had a profound effect on urban development. Because the placement of railroads heavily shaped land values, some railroad companies sought bribes from local officials in return for putting the towns on a new railroad line. Railroad capitalists and their subordinates sometimes negotiated with town developers or promoters to obtain the best right-of-way land and to secure monetary contributions. Towns and cities usually had to pay the "fee" or confront serious economic troubles, possibly even death, if the railroads bypassed them.[78]

Urban promoters were important in town and city development as the frontier of the United States moved westward. These town and city promoters, argues Richard Wade, were the real pioneers who opened up the West. They chose many town sites, and most were heavily involved in local landownership, speculation, and development. Many were local business people, such as merchants, looking to expand their clientele or invest surplus profits. Town and city "boosterism" (see Chapter 9) dates from this early period. Local officials and promoters with real estate investments lobbied railroad corporations to come their way. For example, cities such as El Paso and Kansas City became major urban centers because of railroad company decisions to deal with local promoters. And, at least in part, Los Angeles owes its current prominence to the fact that local land promoters gave a major railroad $600,000 and other subsidies to secure a rail route to the area.[79]

Impact of Speculation Today Today land speculation continues to be a critical part of profit making in cities, particularly on the urban fringe. A variety of powerful actors are currently involved, including developers, land speculators, bankers, and industrial corporations. Many developers of shopping centers, suburbs, and industrial parks are actively involved in land speculation. They seek profits not only from building and leasing but also from buying land near their developments and around the city fringe. Speculators ordinarily are interested in the sale of undeveloped land, which they may subdivide for others to build upon. For example, Patten Corporation, founded in Stamford, Vermont, and owned by Harry Patten, is reportedly the largest marketer of undeveloped land in the Northeast. By buying large tracts of rural land, then subdividing and selling the unimproved properties, Patten has often doubled or tripled his money in a few weeks. In just one year (1987) the corporation's 15-state operation sold 49,784 acres nationwide in 3,242 separate transactions. In 5 years its sales rose from $3 million to nearly $82 million.[80]

   The executives heading the Patten firm are aggressive land speculators. One of their strategies is to buy land in or near small towns in Vermont, Maine, Connecticut, and New York, areas that are increasingly sought out by affluent urbanites desiring a place away from big-city life. According to a late 1980s' count by Maine's attorney general, Patten had at least 34 subdivisions underway in that state, with some as large as 4,500 acres. A part of the firm's strategy is to purchase land, break it up into saleable parcels, and leave the social costs of the consequent growth, including increased congestion and environmental problems, and the probable higher taxes to be borne by the local residents. Tim Kerwin, a Boston developer, has said that he experienced a sense of fraternal shame as he watched Patten come to his "home away from home" in Hartford, Maine:

> I was appalled at the way Patten was conducting this. They were going into meetings and screaming at people and threatening them. It was clearly intimidation. I'm not against development, but Patten is in the develop and run business, and I'm concerned that the [Canton] lake be developed carefully.[81]

Yet the Patten executives are not unique. Their firm is just one of at least half a dozen land speculation firms at work in New England today. Next to Patten, the largest of the land speculators is Properties of America, Inc. (POA), of Williamstown, Massachusetts. This firm was founded in the mid-1970s by Philip Grande after his partnership with Harry Patten dissolved. Many land corporations have bought large tracts of raw land, subdivided them into lots large enough to bypass local government environmental reviews, and then marketed lots aggressively to affluent city residents by advertising in newspapers in large metropolitan areas.[82]

While some speculators are content to wait passively for their land values to rise, others work actively to increase those values in other ways. By aggressively seeking governmental subsidies in the form of utilities for their lands, for example, speculators can adopt an active stance in promoting their land values. Rather than the designated zoning and planning commissions in communities, developers and speculators can become the real planners of a given urban area. Some operate by looking a decade ahead, trying to predict the next round of urban or suburban sprawl. Other developer-speculators become involved when development seems imminent, making a profit by getting the necessary rezoning and other political decisions for a parcel of land. In addition, there are frequently intimate relationships between real estate capitalists and industrial capitalists. Sometimes industrial capitalists lead the development process by virtue of their own site location decisions. At other times, property capitalists make strategic land purchase decisions that shape development by attracting industrial corporations. A study by Gottdiener has documented the role of land investors and speculators in channeling urban growth in distinctive directions on Long Island. Central-city land speculation can drive prices up substantially and thus encourage outward expansion of a city. Transitional areas ("slums") near existing central-city development are sometimes speculation targets. These areas may be bulldozed and banked as parking lots, until the time is ripe for further development.[83]

Land banking and speculating have numerous negative consequences. Bruce Lindeman has suggested that speculation alters the *nature* of urban space, of the land commodity itself, by restricting the supply of land and forcing prices *above* what they would have been without speculative activity. Market prices can rise to extraordinary levels. These higher-than-necessary prices result in part from the expensive financial arrangements into which speculators frequently enter, as well as from the speculative pricing itself. Financing costs are passed along in the form of higher prices for the eventual users of the property. Exchange value takes precedence over use value. Restrictions on land supply also arise because of the complex legal and financial arrangements that a series of speculators, one after another, can bring to a given parcel of land. Complex legal entanglements sometimes hamper the sale of land later to developers and builders. Encumbered by mortgages, land changes its character as a commodity. One result of this speculation is an acceleration of urban sprawl as developers try to leapfrog land tied up by legal or financial complications or by speculators holding out for higher prices. In this way, much suburban sprawl might be characterized as the recurring flight of speculators and developers to cheaper land farther out.[84]

One of the penetrating discussions of land speculation in the United States appears in *Progress and Poverty*, a neglected book by nineteenth-century reformer Henry George. George argues that it is mostly the work and effort of an *entire* community that really brings a steady advance in land values there and nearby, *not* the efforts of land speculators. He notes that "this steady increase naturally leads to speculation in which future increase is anticipated." Interested only in the exchange value of the land, the speculator thus secures, unjustly and with little or no productive effort on the land, the increased value generated by the whole community's efforts. By control of land, the speculator ultimately secures hard-earned dollars from working people who must use the land for home and family space.[85]

CONCLUSION: THE DOWNSIDE OF DEVELOPMENT

In this chapter we have closely examined developers, land speculators, and their development allies, including the large financial institutions of the United States and certain foreign countries; we have underscored the important and continuing impact of these powerful decision makers on U.S. cities. We touched on the social and community costs that stem from our undemocratic system of real estate development. Substantial control over urban space, over the urban physical environment, comes with control over real estate projects. For example, a development corporation may build a large office park with several office towers, while smaller real estate operators develop the areas surrounding that project, such as by providing residential condominiums for the affluent. Normally, this action does not involve input from those city residents displaced in the process, those seeking affordable housing, or those affected by changes in traffic, wind, or shadow patterns. In this process a large area of a city changes, and environmental problems may be created; viable older communities and smaller businesses may be destroyed. The actions of developers and speculators can also contribute to inflation for consumers. New development projects on speculative land can mean higher housing and apartment costs. Higher leasing costs in the large shopping centers also put upward pressure on consumer prices charged by the companies that rent and use these facilities. New office tower projects may make a central city look more modern, but frequently the residential housing problems in the central city remain unresolved.[86]

Even supporters of the existing system of real estate investment have raised questions about the decisions of many developers. Is the capital used by development companies put to productive use? Lorimer suggests that the answer depends on the project:

> *If it is all used to build new factories, schools, or hospitals one can see that it has been a productive investment, provided of course the new buildings are quickly put to use. If it is used to tear down an old, but perfectly usable, office block and replace it with another, or to produce a large building that stands empty for years, society may doubt the wisdom of the system.*[87]

A theme of this book is that cities are zones of conflict between competing claims for land, such as exchange-value and use-value concerns, and that those with less wealth and power usually lose in this urban competition. Development projects, large and small, benefit some town and city residents while exacting costs from others. The conflict over land use and development in central cities and outlying areas is frequently a barely hidden class conflict—between those who build and profit from office towers, shopping centers, and the like, and those workers and consumers who seek "home" spaces in the form of affordable housing and livable cities. Property developers go where the profits are, not necessarily where the human or societal needs are. Societal resources used to meet luxury needs, such as for expensive suburban shopping malls or downtown condominium apartments, cannot be used simultaneously to increase the supply of affordable low- or middle-income housing, one of many persisting human needs that remain unmet in U.S. society.

NOTES

1. Jack Egan and Eva Pomice, "The New Rothschilds," *U.S. News and World Report*, March 14, 1988, 37.
2. John Schwartz, "The Stars of Brick and Mortar," *Newsweek*, September 28, 1987, 62.
3. Leonard Downie, *Mortgage on America* (New York: Praeger, 1974), p. 69; William Zeckendorf, *Zeckendorf* (New York: Holt, Rinehart and Winston, 1970), pp. 5–10.
4. Oliver Marriott, *The Property Boom* (London: Hamish Hamihou, 1967), pp. 199–202; Albert Scardino, "They'll Take Manhattan," *The New York Times Magazine*, sect. 6, Part 2, December 7, 1986, 35; Andree Brooks, "Central Park Vista from New Tower," *New York Times*, January 1, 1988, 42.
5. Scardino, "They'll Take Manhattan," 112; Alex Taylor, III, "Smart Moves for Hard Times," *Fortune* 114 (December 8, 1986): 32.
6. Taylor, III, "Smart Moves for Hard Times," p. 29.

7. James Lorimer, *The Developers* (Toronto: James Lorimer, 1978), pp. 61–62; cf. Marriot, *The Property Boom*, p. 24.

8. Rice Center Research and Development Corporation, *Houston Initiatives: Phase One Report* (Houston: Rice Center, 1981), pp. 1–15.

9. Dana L. Thomas, *Lords of the Land* (New York: G.P. Putnam's Sons, 1977), pp. 137–175.

10. "How Building Better Makes Crow Tops in Warehouses," *Building Design and Construction* 20 (August 1980): 68–72; Taylor, III, "Smart Moves for Hard Times," p. 31; Joe Kolman, "A Tighter Ship at Trammell Crow," *Institutional Investor* 20 (May 1986): 129; "Two More Partners Quit Trammell Crow to Form Own Firm," *Wall Street Journal*, May 23, 1988, 19.

11. "Houstonians to Watch: J. R. McConnell," *Texas Business*, August 1986, (reprint).

12. Todd Vogel, "J. R. McConnell: The Ballad of a Texas Tornado," *Business Week*, November 9, 1987, 80; Caleb Solomon, "Indictments Awaited in Real-Estate Case Related to McConnell's Collapsed Empire," *Wall Street Journal*, October 10, 1987, 14.

13. Solomon, "Indictments Awaited on Real-Estate Case Related to McConnell's Collapse," p. 14.

14. Jim McTague, "Fugitive Turns Himself in as Fraud Hearing Begins," *American Banker* 152 (November 19, 1987): 3; Peter Applebome, "Texas Real Estate Tycoon Takes His Own Life in Jail," *New York Times*, July 6, 1988, 18.

15. See "Trump, Donald J.," *Current Biography Yearbook 1984*, vol. 45, p. 402; Bill Powell and Peter McKillop, "Citizen Trump," *Newsweek*, September 28, 1987, 55.

16. Mark Ivey and Marc Frons, "Denver's Quiet Billionaire Comes out Fighting," *Business Week*, July 27, 1987, 70.

17. Louis Menand, "The Triumph of Trumpery," *The New Republic* 198 (February 1, 1988): 29; "Trump, Donald J.," *Current Biography Yearbook 1984*, p. 400.

18. Rick Hampson, "A Trump Who Holds All the Cards," *St. Louis Post-Dispatch*, October 25, 1987, 1F; Bill Powell and Peter McKillop, "Citizen Trump," *Newsweek*, September 28, 1987, 55.

19. "Trump, Donald J.," *Current Biography Yearbook 1984*, p. 401.

20. Powell and McKillop, "Citizen Trump," p. 55.

21. Cited in Gary Belis, "Donald Trump Explained," *Fortune* 117 (January 4, 1988): 92.

22. James R. Norman, "Donald Trump: What's Behind the Hype?" *Business Week*, July 20, 1987, 94; Powell and McKillop, "Citizen Trump," p. 52; Richard Koenig and Pauline Yoshihashi, "Trump, Griffin Reach Impasse in Resorts Talks," *Wall Street Journal*, May 12, 1988, 4.

23. Kate Ballen, "A Canadian with a Chip on His Shoulder," *Fortune* 115 (January 5, 1987): 102.
24. Susan Goldberg, "Campeau Not Afraid to Speak His Mind," *Dallas Morning News*, September 29, 1981, microfiche 109, F9–10.
25. Ann Shortell, "Victory on a Wide Field," *Maclean's*, November 17, 1986, 58.
26. Sidney Rutberg and Pete Born, "Campeau: Retailing's New Dynamo," *Daily News Record* 18 (January 28, 1988): 1; Jacquie McNish, "Campeau Posts 13-Month Loss of $254 Million," *Wall Street Journal*, May 16, 1988, 4.
27. Carol Hymowitz and Jacquie McNish, "Campeau-Federated Is off to Rocky Start," *Wall Street Journal*, May 13, 1988, 6; Carol Hymowitz, Jacquie McNish, and Bryan Burrough, "Campeau Seeks Federated Chain for $4.2 Billion," *Wall Street Journal*, January 26, 1988, 2; Rutberg and Born, "Campeau," p. 5; Carol Hymowitz and Jacquie McNish, "Campeau Seeks Retailing Chief Amid Disarray," *Wall Street Journal*, May 9, 1988, 2.
28. Marc A. Weiss, *The Rise of the Community Builders: The American Real Estate Industry and Urban Land Planning* (New York: Columbia University Press, 1987).
29. Linda Monroe, "In-Depth Report: Cadillac Fairview," *Buildings* 80 (February 1986): 62; *Cadillac Fairview, Annual Report*, 1981; Michael V. Prentiss, "Canadians Setting the Pace in the U.S.," Speech to the National Association of Real Estate Investment Trusts, New York, October 1981.
30. Bruce Wallace and Ann Shortell, "Selling off a Family Jewel," *Maclean's* 99 (August 18, 1986): 32; "The Top 200 Deals," *Business Week*, April 15, 1988, 51, 58.
31. Egan and Pomice, "The New Rothschilds," pp. 37–39; D'archy Jenish, Rose Laver, Larry Black, and Ann Shortell, "Capital Developments," *Maclean's*, August 24, 1987, 28; Harvey D. Shapiro, "Olympia & York's American Empire," *Institutional Investor* 20 (February 1986): 154.
32. Janice Castro, "The Canadians Come Calling," *Time*, November 17, 1986, 68; Terri Thompson and Edith Terry, "What the Reichmanns Plan Next for Their Real Estate Billions," *Business Week*, October 28, 1985, 97; Egan and Pomice, "The New Rothschilds," p. 37.
33. Egan and Pomice, "The New Rothschilds," p. 39.
34. Lewis M. Goodkin, *When Real Estate and Homebuilding Become Big Business: Mergers, Acquisitions, and Joint Ventures* (Boston: Cahners Books, 1974), pp. 20–22.
35. Stephen P. Jarchow, "An Interview with an Average Super-Builder," *Real Estate Review*, Summer 1985, 74.
36. "The Public Builders in 1980–1981: Hanging Tough against Mounting Odds," *Housing* 59 (June 1981): 10–15.

37. Goodkin, *When Real Estate and Homebuilding Become Big Business: Mergers, Acquisitions, and Joint Ventures*, pp. 20–22.
38. Interview with George Mitchell, published by Ginger H. Jester in *Houston North Magazine*, November 1980, and published as a brochure for The Woodlands, p. 5; we have also used Woodlands Development Corporation fact sheets here.
39. Richard A. Walker and Michael K. Heiman, "Quiet Revolution for Whom?" *Annals of the Association of American Geographers* 71 (March 1981): 71.
40. Lorimer, *The Developers*, pp. 70–71; "Still an Inflation Haven, with the Right Deal," *Business Week*, December 29, 1980, 140–142.
41. Peter Ambrose and Bob Colenutt, *The Property Machine* (London: Penguin, 1975), p. 127. Also see pp. 41–45.
42. Ambrose and Colenutt, *The Property Machine*, p. 58; see also Goodkin, *When Real Estate and Homebuilding Become Big Business*, p. 6.
43. Mark Gottdiener, *Planned Sprawl* (Beverly Hills: Sage, 1977), p. 110.
44. Lauralee E. Martin, "Commercial Property Loan Changes of Past Decade Could Impact Mortgage Banker/Broker's Future," *National Real Estate Investor* 30 (October 1988): 96.
45. Martin Mayer, *The Bankers* (New York: Ballantine, 1974), pp. 265–266, 407.
46. Pearl Janet Davies, *Real Estate in American History* (Washington, D.C.: Public Affairs Press, 1958), p. 141; American Council of Life Insurance, *1982 Life Insurance Fact Book* (Washington, D.C.: American Council of Life Insurance, 1982), pp. 80–84.
47. Phyllis Feinberg, "Too Much Money Chasing Too Little Product," *National Real Estate Investor* 30 (September 1988): 62–64.
48. Feinberg, "Too Much Money Chasing Too Little Product," p. 55.
49. Ibid., p. 58.
50. Marc Erlich, "Building Trades Aim for Union Control over Pension Fund Investments," *Labor Notes* 30 (July 28, 1981): 11.
51. Doug Miller, "Bank Troubles Linked to Developers," *Houston Business Journal*, May 2, 1988, 14–15.
52. Ibid., p. 1.
53. Richard H. Thielen, "Real Estate Syndications after Tax Reform," p. 68; see also Downie, *Mortgage on America*, pp. 76–78.
54. Anthony Sampson, *The Money Lenders* (New York: Viking, 1981), pp. 135–136; Thomas, *Lords of the Land*, pp. 285–290.
55. DeLeo et al., "A Return to the Fundamentals," p. 42.
56. Phyllis Feinberg, "Real Estate Lenders Search for Good Deals," *National Real Estate Investor* 30 (October 1988): 71–76.
57. Jarchow, "An Interview with an Average Super-Builder," p. 74.
58. Feinberg, "Real Estate Lenders Search for Good Deals," pp. 84–88.
59. Ibid., p. 84.

60. Ibid., p. 88.
61. Ibid., p. 72.
62. Alfred DeLeo, Marc Jacobowitz, and Michael Bernstein, "A Return to the Fundamentals: Marketing Real Estate after Tax Reform," *Real Estate Finance* 3 (Winter 1987): 43; see also Charles Wetterer, "Developing an Investment Strategy for the Late 1980s," *Real Estate Finance* 3 (Spring 1986): 18.
63. Steve Brown, "Lenders, Investors Seek New Strategies for Deals," *National Real Estate Investor* 30 (July 1988): 72; Richard H. Thielen, "Real Estate Syndications after Tax Reform," *Real Estate Finance* 3 (Winter 1987): 68.
64. "Benefits Abound for Users of Foreign Capital," *National Real Estate Investor* 30 (April 1988): 104.
65. Ibid.
66. Feinberg, "Too Much Money Chasing Too Little Product," pp. 55, 68.
67. David Lake, "Building across Borders," *American Banker* 150 (July 29, 1985): 43; Andrew Marton, "The World's New Property Barons," *Institutional Investor* 21 (August 1987): 102.
68. Aubin, *City for Sale*, p. 319; Castro, "The Canadians Come Calling," p. 68.
69. Marton, "The World's New Property Barons," p. 99.
70. Kenneth R. Sheets, Andrea Gabor, and Cindy Skrzycki, "Landlords from the Far East," *U.S. News and World Report*, April 7, 1986, 53.
71. Feinberg, "Real Estate Lenders Search for Good Deals," p. 89.
72. Ibid., p. 80.
73. Marton, "The World's New Property Barons," p. 100.
74. Sheets et al., "Landlords from the Far East," p. 54.
75. N. R. Kleinfield, "Boom Times for the Builders of New York," *New York Times*, July 26, 1981, sect. 3, 1.
76. Gottdiener, *Planned Sprawl*, pp. 104–108.
77. Aaron M. Sakolski, *Land Tenure and Land Taxation in America* (New York: Robert Schalkenbach Foundation, 1957), pp. 53–55; Aaron M. Sakolski, *The Great American Land Bubble* (New York: Harper and Brothers, 1932); Edward P. Eichler and Marshall Kaplan, *The Community Builders* (Berkeley: University of California Press, 1967), p. 15.
78. Thomas, *Lords of the Land*, pp. 70–87; Sakolski, *Land Tenure and Land Taxation in America*, pp. 163–174; Dee Brown, *Hear That Lonesome Whistle Blow* (New York: Bantam, 1977), pp. 244–268.
79. Richard C. Wade, *The Urban Frontier, 1790–1830* (Cambridge, Mass.: Harvard University Press, 1959), pp. 27–40; Charles N. Glaab and A. Theodore Brown, *A History of Urban America* (New York: Macmillan, 1967), pp. 119–120; Sam Bass Warner, *The Urban Wilderness* (New York: Harper and Row, 1972), pp. 19–22.
80. Cited in Edie Clark, "Dreams for Sale," *Yankee Magazine*, April 1988, 72.

81. Ibid., p. 75.
82. Ibid., pp. 66–67.
83. Cf. Gottdiener, *Planned Sprawl*.
84. Bruce Lindeman, "Anatomy of Land Speculation," *Journal of the American Institute of Planners* 42 (April 1976): 149–151.
85. Henry George, *Progress and Poverty*, reprinted ed. (New York: Robert Schalkenbach Foundation, 1962), pp. 264, 268.
86. Lorimer, *The Developers*, p. 233.
87. Ibid., p. 36. See also p. 127.

4

SKYSCRAPERS
AND MULTIPLE-USE PROJECTS

New Yorkers are finally awakening to the realization that the city of their future is a city they do not want. It is a city of 30- and 50-story towers in the middle of residential neighborhoods, a city in which light and air are declining in direct proportion to the rise in congestion on the streets and sidewalks, a city in which disjointed new projects interrupt the continuous walls of storefronts that, for 150 years, have successfully provided the framework for New York's retail commerce.[1]

California is weary of the growth that has made the state the most populous in the country. Large and small cities throughout the state are experimenting with ways to stop the sprawl...San Francisco voters recently put a stop to the "Manhattanization" of their city by prohibiting more skyscrapers. In Los Angeles, the pro-growth chairman of the city council was defeated after 17 years in office by a relatively unknown antigrowth activist. Even state courts have gotten into the act.[2]

INTRODUCTION

"Manhattanization"—this and harsher terms have been used by Americans to describe the widespread development of high-rise office towers in their cities. In earlier decades the public quietly accepted high-rise architecture as a vertical sign of progress, but since the 1970s a growing number of citizens' groups have questioned the process of "burying our city under a skyline of tombstones."[3]

With its increasingly obscured scenic views of bays and hills, San Francisco has become a national symbol of discontent over the Manhattanization of cities. By the mid-1970s a substantial majority of citizens there were in favor of high-rise building controls. A local initiative petition to have every high-rise building approved by the general public was supported by 40 percent of the voters. The battle in San Francisco started in the 1960s with the construction of curved high-rise apartment buildings, the Fontana Towers, which were built on the shoreline and blocked the view of the bay from major sections of San Francisco. Other giant buildings constructed over the next decade became targets of public hostility. Increasingly, environmentalists were joined by a contingent of middle-income neighborhood residents. One advertisement by a citizens' group opposed to developers building more skyscrapers put the public view forcefully: "San Francisco was once light, hilly, pastel, open. Inviting. In only twelve years it has taken on the forbidden look of every other American city. Forty more skyscrapers are due in the next five years. They are as great a disaster economically as they are aesthetically."[4] Finally, in 1986 San Franciscans passed a proposition restricting annual office construction to the small amount of 475,000 square feet, or one medium-sized office building!

An increasing number of citizens in other cities have begun to question the dominating skyscraper architecture. From Boston, where one major tower has produced cracked windows and pieces of falling facade, to New York, where skyscrapers have created sunless canyons for the urbanites below, these structures are dramatic symbols of the dominance of cities by the leading industrial, retail, service, utility, and development corporations. Working with industrial corporations or working on their own, developers and associated construction firms plan and build most high-rise developments; they build office towers and office parks as well as hotels and industrial buildings. They erect hospitals and buildings for government agencies. They put up shopping malls and housing facilities for those who work in the towers, parks, and hotels. And they construct apartment buildings and subdivisions on city fringes.

Today certain projects, such as office towers, tend to be located in central-city areas, where they reflect a concentration of business activities. Other major development projects, such as industrial parks and suburban subdivisions, tend to be located outside the central cities and represent a decentralizing tendency in urban development, a shift outward from central areas. These contrasting trends are part of the broader process of uneven and oscillating urban spatial development, a process generated by the channeling of capital into secondary-circuit real estate investments by private-sector decision makers, the powerful city shapers who are often assisted by government officials.

CHANGING SKYLINES: SKYSCRAPERS AND OTHER OFFICE BUILDINGS

Shifting City Faces   The dominance of skyscrapers is rather new in American cities. Most sizable office buildings have been built since World War II. Many house large corporations. In building industry handbooks office buildings are sometimes described simply as structures where services are provided or where information is processed. But they signal much more than that. The giant office buildings in the larger cities, in particular, reflect the shift in the U.S. economy from an older (competitive) capitalism of smaller firms to a modern (monopoly or oligopoly) capitalism dominated by larger firms.

There is a relationship between the character of capitalism in a particular historical period and the type of urban physical structure and spatial organization. City landscapes of giant office towers, hotels, and apartment buildings are a new invention, for until the 1940s and 1950s most cities had only modest-sized buildings either downtown or in outlying areas. In the mid-nineteenth century, cities were mostly composed of commercial buildings with fewer than five stories and organized around the needs of merchants and early manufacturers. For example, in 1850 Boston was a walking city of small buildings stretching two miles out from the city hall. Hills had been cut down and marshes filled in, and builders were constructing three- and four-story homes for the small, prosperous middle-income sector. They also built wharves and concentrated warehouses and manufacturing buildings in low-rise structures near the coast. Residences and manufacturing facilities were adjacent. However, within a few decades development in such cities created more segregation, with areas for factories, railroad yards, suburban housing, and office buildings, with more substantial projects than before.

Interestingly, the development of the technology necessary for constructing skyscrapers—for instance, steel-skeleton construction and electric elevators—preceded the great expansion of high-rise construction by several decades. A few steel-skeleton skyscrapers, rising higher than the 12-story limit of the older stone-wall construction, were built in New York and Chicago in the 1880s. Yet skyscraper building did not begin in earnest until the period 1905–1930. Then such construction increased, particularly in New York and Chicago, which became major nerve centers for the new supercorporations. In New York residents saw the Singer Building (1908, 47 stories), the Metropolitan Life Insurance Building (1909, 50 stories), and the Woolworth Building (1913, 55 stories) spring up in less than a decade. As the headquarters city for many large firms, New York became famous for its major buildings, such as the Empire State Building, the steel-framed 102-story office tower completed in 1931 and the largest such building for the next several decades.

Mergers and Mammoth Corporations In addition to the emergence or expansion of substantial independent firms, mammoth companies were created in the hundreds of mergers during the period 1897–1904, just prior to the upsurge in office construction. This first major wave of mergers in U.S. history involved the uniting of 15 percent of the nation's business assets; and this merging wave created more than 70 huge firms, many of them in manufacturing, including U.S. Steel, General Electric, United Fruit, Standard Oil, and American Can. A second great wave of mergers encompassed a tenth of business assets and about 12,000 companies during the period 1925–1930. These latter mergers included banks and utility firms, as well as manufacturers. Most involved investment banking firms as creators and coordinators of the mergers. The increase in skyscrapers in the first three decades of the twentieth century paralleled the growth of the large independent and merged corporations in this period, one that some have called the "rise of oligopoly capitalism." Earlier competitive capitalism, with its smaller businesses, had little need for such towering and centralized office facilities. But the large firms sought larger buildings, for their functional utility and for their symbolism of power; and the giant new firms also had the capital to move into the large-scale secondary-circuit projects. For several decades now, high-rise office buildings have been seen as necessary to house the considerable groups of managerial and clerical employees who coordinate and administer the copious paperwork and extensive information processing of the large industrial and banking corporations and their supportive array of law, accounting, and other service firms.[5]

The proliferation of skyscrapers has differed by region. The cities of the East and Midwest were the nation's dominant headquarters cities and office tower complexes until the 1970s. As late as 1972 most major skyscrapers were east of the Mississippi. Los Angeles, for example, had only five high-rise buildings at that time. By the mid-1980s, however, the Los Angeles scene had changed dramatically: In the 30 square blocks of the central business district there were more than 45 buildings, with 23 million square feet of office space. As *Forbes* noted in 1986, "thanks in part to the slow-growth attitudes of the northern Californians, downtown L.A. has as much office space as downtown San Francisco."[6] The increase in both cities, moreover, was substantially related to the emergence of multinational corporations whose control over widespread operations in the Pacific Rim countries increasingly required centralized administrative centers on the West Coast. Similarly, Houston, a global trade city often called the "oil capital of the world," has seen the development of most of its 160 million square feet of office space since the international oil boom of the 1970s. However, even today, as can be seen in Table 4.1, New York and Chicago have the six tallest U.S. buildings, with Houston a relatively new contender.[7] This continuing dominance of New York and Chicago in massive skyscraper competition is a signal of their continuing centrality as two leading corporate headquarters cities in the United States.

TABLE 4.1 Tallest Skyscrapers

City	Building	Stories	Height (in feet)
Chicago	Sears Tower	110	1,454
New York	World Trade Center	110	1,377
New York	Empire State Building	102	1,250
Chicago	Amoco Building	80	1,136
Chicago	John Hancock Center	100	1,127
New York	Chrysler Building	77	1,046
Houston	Texas Commerce	75	1,002
Houston	Allied Bank	71	985

Skyscraper Builders Rising in prominence alongside the high-rise buildings have been the major development corporations reviewed in the last chapter. Major U.S. and Canadian developers have often been involved in the construction of many larger buildings. For example, we have already discussed the dramatic reception developer Gerald Hines gave at the foundation-laying ceremony for a huge bank-and-office tower in Houston. Since the 1950s Hines' company has built hundreds of major urban development projects—altogether about tens of millions of square feet of office and shopping space in cities from coast to coast. Among his famous projects are the Galleria shopping mall and the Texas Commerce Tower in Houston (see Table 4.1) Hines has become internationally famous for hiring prominent architects to provide unique designs for some of his new buildings. A *Fortune* story notes that he "did so because he thought well-designed buildings would make more money for him and his partners."[8] Monumental buildings by architects such as Philip Johnson and I. M. Pei were generally shunned by developers until Hines decided these projects could be undertaken at reasonable cost. Hines also brought high-powered marketing techniques into the development picture. Prospective business tenants have reportedly received a grand tour, called the "processional" in the firm, during which they have been presented with huge models of the building under construction, a slide-show presentation on multiple screens, and the implied message that such original architecture is on the cutting edge of Western civilization.[9]

Generally speaking, office buildings are measured not by their contribution to the community but by their height, architectural distinctiveness, and profitability. In the development of office buildings U.S. and Canadian developers typically work with a variety of landowners, bankers and other lenders, and construction company executives. The operations and negotiations may be secretive and may on occasion involve dummy corporations to conceal corporate interests from competitors and the public. A first step is gaining control of the land where the building is to be constructed. Another important step often involves securing prior leasing commitments from companies to occupy space in the proposed building, for lenders often require these. Other steps include acquiring the financing and the necessary planning and zoning approval from government officials.

BOOM AND BUST:
CYCLES IN OFFICE CONSTRUCTION

Supply of Office Space   By 1990 the U.S. office market consisted of more than 11 *billion* square feet of occupied space. This space was occupied by a diversity of corporate offices, including the management and headquarters offices of financial, insurance, real estate, business and professional service, manufacturing, transportation, public utilities, agricultural, oil, and construction companies. Some space was also occupied by small firms and government agencies. From the 1960s to the early 1980s, U.S. businesses kept the demand for office space at a high level in many cities. Indeed, a third great wave of corporate mergers, which peaked in the late 1960s, contributed to the boom. During that period 25,000 firms were involved in mergers. Unlike the 1897–1904 wave, which involved horizontal expansion within industries, and the 1925–1930 wave, which accented vertical mergers within a particular industry, the 1960s mergers involved the bringing together of companies into sizable conglomerates of unrelated businesses. Many of the new firms sought new office space. However, because many such mergers were not driven by horizontal or vertical integration, but by stock market considerations, some conglomerates eventually sold off unprofitable acquisitions, helping fuel yet another round of acquisitions and mergers in the late 1970s and 1980s.[10]

During the 1970s and early 1980s, hundreds of major office towers and other corporate buildings sprang up in key northern and southern cities. In the decade 1975–1985 developers constructed 36 percent of *all* the office space ever built in U.S. cities.[11] For a while the construction could not keep up with the demand for offices. During this period major Sunbelt cities, including San Francisco, Los Angeles, Phoenix, Dallas, Houston, Denver, Atlanta, and Miami—as well as Washington, Chicago, and New York—experienced shortages of downtown space. The average vacancy rate in buildings in the United States and Canada declined over the 1970s.

By 1982, however, the construction boom was replaced by a bust in numerous cities. Owners of many new buildings had difficulty finding tenants. Even major developers and land speculators were caught in the general recession. They had often invested with the idea that continuing inflation would guarantee profits in the leasing and sale of their buildings. The recession of the mid-1980s, as well as corporate defenses taken against the hostile takeovers characteristic of the merger wave in the 1980s, forced many corporations to cancel plans to expand, to move into new offices, or to move to new urban areas. Those that could relocate often considered office space outside expensive downtown areas. These decisions meant less demand for, and less capital for, the formerly soaring office construction and leasing business. Caught in the glut were major Canadian corporations, such as Cadillac Fairview and Olympia and York, Ltd., that had rushed into U.S. real estate. During the period 1979–1982, Canadian companies controlled one-quarter of all new office construction, but began selling off a significant share of their investment when the business downturn became a lasting reality.[12]

Cycles of Office Building   Office-building development, like other types of construction, has moved up and down with movements in the general economy. But the movements have not been as synchronous with broader economic changes as one might expect. The office glut of the early 1980s should have provided sufficient incentive for developers and corporate development managers to slow construction significantly. Despite high vacancy rates in numerous downtown and suburban locations, some developers kept on building. The accelerated depreciation rates of the Reagan administration's 1981 tax legislation were a spur to investment and development in many, but not all, cities. The pace of U.S. office construction continued upward from 1977, with 138 million square feet constructed in that year, through 1985, with 330 million square feet constructed. In addition, more than 1 billion square feet were completed between 1984 and 1987. According to Birch, much of this has been overbuilding in the extreme: "In general, one in five office buildings built between 1975 and 1985 was not needed. In the Mountain West it was almost one in two; in the Oil Patch, more than one in three; in the Pacific West, about one in three."[13] As Mason observed, "With an average office vacancy rate of 17 percent and handfuls of former boomtowns disastrously overbuilt, the result should have caused major cutbacks in construction and falling prices. Instead, U.S. and foreign institutional investors picked up the slack."[14] Here is a clear example of the distinctive dynamics of the secondary circuit of real estate investments. Surplus capital worldwide often moves into the U.S. secondary circuit seeking a better rate of return than can be found in the primary or secondary circuits here or in other countries. And in this case, the world's real estate investors were gambling that the overbuilt condition in the United States would soon be corrected.

Even after the 1986 tax reform act reduced the depreciation and tax shelter advantages of real estate investments, many developers continued to alter selected U.S. cityscapes by placing additional office space on the market. For example, in the late 1980s the development subsidiary of Prudential Insurance Company was seeking joint-venture partners for at least four major projects. Just one, a $1.2 billion office tower in New York's

Times Square was expected to add 4.1 million square feet, or nearly 2 percent, to Manhattan's top-grade office stock in 1989.[15] Because of the relatively high vacancy rates found in some major metropolitan centers, developers and finance capitalists have increasingly sought outlets in smaller or less-developed cities. They have often followed industrial and commercial firms to these areas. For example, in the late 1980s Trammell Crow opened offices in Tucson, Columbus, and Baton Rouge. Other regional cities such as Nashville and Albuquerque experienced a tripling of available office space in the mid-1980s. Moreover, there has been considerable regional variation in vacancy rates. For example, in 1987 Hartford, Connecticut, had the lowest city rate at 4.6 percent. The likelihood that Hartford would retain that position was doubtful, because the city then had enough construction underway to expand its supply by a third. At the other end of the spectrum, the highest urban vacancy rate was recorded in Austin, Texas, with nearly 37 percent of downtown space vacant.[16]

By the late 1980s even the high-growth cities of the Northeast, with their relatively strong real estate markets, had growing office vacancy rates. Two cases in point were Boston and New York. In early 1989 construction was underway on the largest office project in Boston in four years. The project, known as 125 High Street and scheduled for completion in 1991, includes towers of 30 and 21 stories that will add 1.8 million square feet of space to the city's office market. The development, designed to attract large tenants, is proceeding despite the addition of 4 million square feet in 1988 and a jump in the vacancy rate for prime office space from 5 to 12 percent. Moreover, several notable office projects were part of New York's growing inventory of empty structures, including the million square feet of vacant property owned by Olympia and York and a glittering new tower built by Melvin Kaufman. Despite these increases, however, the vacancy rates in the Northeast seem unlikely to increase to the level of those in the Southwest in the near future. Stricter zoning regulations and a general lack of land in key central cities figure prominently in keeping eastern vacancy rates relatively low.[17]

Benefitting from Overbuilding Office gluts benefit some businesses at the expense of others. As vacancy rates climb, the perquisites offered to potential tenants usually grow. The obvious benefit emerging from the rash of overbuilding was a reduction in the cost of office space per square foot. A late 1980s report rated Denver as the least expensive of 27 major cities in the United States and Canada. In contrast, corporations leasing space in the growth cities of the Northeast were paying relatively high prices; in Boston and New York the average price was $46 to $49 per square foot. In Sunbelt cities there were other major benefits. In Houston, Denver, and Los Angeles reports of 2 years of free rent for a 5-year lease were commonplace. For one offer in Dallas the tenant's only 5-year obligation for thousands of square feet of offices was to keep lights on until 11 P.M. and to post a security guard.[18] Other deals included substantial space renovations at no cost and options on adjacent property. As Ross noted, "landlords are offering brokers unprecedented incentives to sign up renters."[19] Indeed, one San Francisco owner gave brokers who showed his building to a prospective tenant a bottle of California wine; if the tenant signed up, the broker got the commission immediately, rather than half the commission on signing and half later.

Efficiency and Profitability Except in times of recession, office building has been among the most successful and profitable real estate projects over several decades. A common explanation for extensive downtown construction is couched in terms of improved business efficiency; that is, this clustering of corporate offices increases access for businesses, their executives, and workers. However, massive traffic jams downtown highlight major inefficiencies in centralizing office towers. In reality, several factors lie behind this concentration: the desire of leading firms for *spatial* dominance, the differentiation of administration from production in many corporations, the social interaction of capitalist and managerial elites from large companies, and a desire for a prestigious image—the last factor being conspicuous consumption by corporate executives seeking to be linked to distinctive buildings. Office-building centralization did not involve a vote of the people working in central cities—these profoundly life-shaping decisions were made by top corporate executives, albeit usually with the aid of governmental officials.[20]

Office buildings are sometimes favored by developers over other projects such as apartment complexes, because business tenants can more easily pass rental costs onto their consumers and are unlikely to press for rent control. Except during recessions and crises, once the office structures are in successful operation rising office rents cover mortgage and operating expenses and provide developer-owners with a good rate of return on investments. Office buildings are frequently marketed by the managing firms the same way as other commodities. One office-building advertisement, for example, emphasized the following: (1) its "prestige" address, (2) its flexible floor plans, (3) its central atrium and panoramic views, and (4) its special climate-control system. Expensive color brochures and advertising techniques are used to build interest in a new office building among executives in possible tenant corporations.[21]

HIGH-RISE HOTELS: ANOTHER TYPE OF SECONDARY-CIRCUIT DEVELOPMENT

In the board game *Monopoly* people buy and mortgage little plastic houses and hotels as they develop their properties from Marvin Gardens to

Boardwalk. Rents charged to passersby determine a player's success. In the real world of Atlantic City, New Jersey, from which *Monopoly's* street names are actually drawn, the huge new casino hotels are owned by a few major corporations. High room rents charged to visitors enhance the profits of hotel chains, most of which earn gambling profits as well. Meanwhile, many of the city's residents have been displaced by hotel development and are relegated to substandard housing. But Atlantic City is not alone. Interspersed among office skyscrapers, new high-rise hotels dot many central-city skylines. International corporations often own or control these hotels. For example, in the early 1980s the Hilton company owned or leased 17 hotels, managed 31 more, and collected franchise fees from 165 additional hotels that use its name. More than 200 hotels, mostly sizable ones, rose up under the Hilton name, which covered real estate assets estimated at nearly $2 billion. Today's complicated ownership and financing for many hotels can be seen in the way the Hilton company operates. In the mid-1970s the company sold half interest in six of its hotels to the Prudential Insurance Company for $83 million, with Hilton collecting the management fees for running the hotels.[22] Hotels have been important places for surplus capital infusion, and finance capital firms such as Prudential have played an important role in channeling capital into hotels.

Development Specialists   A small number of development firms specialize in hotels. According to the trade journal *Restaurant and Hotel Design*, the following were the eight notable developers operating in the late 1980s: Charles H. Shaw (building 8 hotels, for such firms as Embassy Suites and Hilton); Galbreath-Ruffin Corporation (5 hotels, for Hyatt, Sofitel, Four Seasons, and Westin); Hemmeter (5 hotels, for Hyatt and Westin); MAT Associates, Inc. (11 hotels, for Americana, Hyatt, Hilton, Loews, Marriott, Radisson, Sheraton, Sofitel, Swissotel, and Trusthouse Forte); Trammell Crow Hotel Company (25 hotels, for Wyndham); Tishman Realty and Construction (5 hotels, for Hilton and Nikko); VMS Realty Partners (6 hotels, for Arvida Management, Four Seasons, Holiday Inn, Omni, Sanesta, and Westin); and Webb Companies (9 hotels, for Comfort Inns, Hampton Inns, Hilton, Hyatt, Quality Inns, Radisson, and Days Inn).[23] Altogether these developers were involved in 74 hotel projects for more than a dozen major hotel companies. Trammell Crow, a major U.S. developer of warehouses, office buildings, and other corporate projects, has become directly involved in building and managing large hotels. In 1979 he built his first, the Anatole in Dallas, with others following soon thereafter in Atlanta and Chicago. In 1982 he built the Market Center Hotel in Dallas, while setting up Wyndham Hotels to manage it and others he was planning. By 1986 Wyndham was managing 15 Crow hotels. Crow's reported plan is to erect several dozen Wyndham hotels by the early 1990s, in order to compete with Hyatt and Marriott, at an average cost of $60,000 to $120,000 per room.[24]

Office development projects frequently set the pattern within which much other small- and large-scale development takes place. Hotels and apartment buildings are commonly constructed near office towers and office parks. Hotel construction and ownership have often been very profitable. Hotel chains can increase profits and keep up with inflation by raising room prices, a practice that generally seems to have little effect on occupancy rates, at least in the corporate headquarters cities. As Barron Hilton, head of the Hilton company, once said "...pricing flexibility has been one of the most favorable aspects of our business. We can change rates overnight."[25]

FINANCING HIGH-RISE DEVELOPMENT

Financial Institutions The financing of large projects such as office buildings can be a complex process. Developers of office projects compete with other users of credit for available money; alternative investment opportunities for lenders, in the branches of the primary or secondary circuits across the globe, affect interest in office projects. This oscillation shapes the boom-bust office construction cycles in many cities. As we discussed in Chapter 3, longer-term financing for major office projects now comes from a variety of U.S. and foreign sources, replacing a commercial bank's construction loan. Prior to the mid-1980s, permanent financing often involved 25- to 30-year amortization and a modest real interest rate. Since then, variable-rate loans have been written so that lenders can raise (or lower) interest rates as the market changes. Instability in the U.S. and world capitalist economy, especially in finance capitalism, signaled by oscillating interest rates, has made such loans necessary.[26] It has become common for a developer to work together with a bank, insurance company, or foreign investor as a major financial or equity partner on a joint-venture project. Once silent financial partners, lenders frequently wish today to own a piece of the buildings they finance. Since the late 1970s a new trend can be seen in the close organizational ties developing between lending organizations and developers. We noted earlier that Prudential and New York's Guardian Life Insurance Company have been joint-venture partners in major New York City office projects.

Swelling U.S. pension funds and surplus capital from Europe, the Middle East, and Japan have been loaned to fund much office construction. In some Sunbelt cities a fifth or more of all new investment money for office constellations, both new construction and resales, has come from foreign sources. In Chapter 3 we discussed the capital investments of Nippon Life

Insurance and Kumagai Gumi in office buildings in New York City, San Francisco, Houston, and Los Angeles, as well as numerous ventures by Canadian firms such as Olympia and York, Trizec, and B.C.E. Development, with the latter owning much office space in Minneapolis. According to *Forbes,* in the late 1980s nearly one-third of buildings in downtown Los Angeles were owned by foreign investors, with Japanese, British, and Dutch investors playing the dominant role.[27] Since the early 1980s a major market has opened up in used office towers; many of the hundreds of office buildings built in the 1970s and 1980s have been sold at least once since their construction. The buyers have often been domestic and foreign pension funds and other foreign investors. For example, late in 1988 the financially troubled Sears corporation put the world's tallest skyscraper up for sale. Originally built in 1974 for $200 million, the 110-story Sears Tower had by the late 1980s become a liability for the firm, whose executives probably hoped that a pension fund or foreign investor would pay the $1 billion-plus record asking price for this unique "trophy" investment.[28]

Government Assistance for Office Development   As with suburban developments (see Chapter 8), government officials commonly play a supportive role in downtown office development. They provide money for governmental services such as new roads and sewers, give away public land by closing streets as part of redevelopment projects, and construct business-oriented projects such as convention centers and downtown parking garages. Office-building and other developments in central business districts often receive tax reductions (tax abatements) and utility benefits. Local public services and utilities for the corporations to be housed in the skyscrapers may be partially subsidized by smaller commercial and residential customers in the central-city areas, because the latter may pay proportionately higher tax and utility rates.[29]

Most residents of New York City are aware of the two 110-story World Trade Center towers in lower Manhattan, high-rise columns costing a billion dollars and housing thousands of employees and visitors on a typical weekday. Eight hundred tenants, when the buildings are fully occupied, sprawl across 9 million square feet of office space, linked by 95 elevators. Tenants have included international import and export companies, bankers, government trade agencies, and business trade organizations. The idea for the World Trade Center came from the Downtown–Lower Manhattan Association, a business group organized and led by David Rockefeller, then head of the Chase Manhattan Bank. Its goal was to raze older structures in the area and create a new center of business prosperity in Manhattan, with a public agency (the New York Port Authority) paying for construction. In this case, governmental capital was specifically used to build a business office project. In the case of a more recent New York project, Philip K. Howard, director of the Municipal Art Society, has described how city planning officials worked closely with developers on the Columbus Circle project. City planning officials apparently followed three guidelines in negotiations with developers: sell public land, approve the largest possible building, and sell it to the highest bidder. Howard, who helped lead the fight against the construction of office towers near Central Park, has accented the point that the construction of massive towers does not represent some "natural law" of the "free market," but rather an intentional collaboration between developers and government officials to speed downtown real estate development and maximize revenue.[30]

PROBLEMS IN HIGH-RISE DEVELOPMENT

Community Effects   High-rise building development can have serious negative effects such as demolition of single-family homes, destruction of neighborhoods, increased fire hazards, and altered local weather patterns. Older but much-needed residential housing is sometimes destroyed by downtown development of new office buildings, apartment towers, and hotels. One study in Calgary, Canada, found that 65 percent of the buildings demolished in downtown areas were single-family houses. Moreover, examining the New York case, Philip Howard, the Municipal Art Society director just mentioned, has described the negative effects of high-rise development on New York neighborhoods: Residential areas like Murray Hill and Carnegie Hill have been "invaded by blockbuster projects with fancy names that resemble nothing so closely as inflated versions of 1930s public housing projects"; neighborhoods on the Upper East Side have been besieged by towers that are "separated from the sidewalk and the rest of the community by cold useless plazas"; and the area south of Lincoln Center has become a maze of "unconnected apartment towers that exceed 50 stories and do not even offer the pretext of fitting into the fabric of the surrounding areas."[31]

Smaller retail corporations and other small businesses may be displaced from downtown areas by large-scale development ventures. Owners of older buildings may have to sell because of the competition with new office towers. In other cases, a new office building replaces an old office building that would be serviceable for many more decades but is not used because greater profit can be made from new construction. New buildings mean more space to rent and, depending on the city and the timing, more profit. In addition, some urban analysts have asked whether the newer, and often cheaply built, office buildings will have a relatively short life expectancy; the average such building, according to the Federal Bureau of Standards, can be expected to last no more than 40 years. Many office structures seem designed for replacement in another round of real estate investments and construction in the not-too-distant future.

A New Climate?   Office towers can create their own weather patterns. Warner has observed that the "skyscrapers shut off light and air from the passing pedestrian...[and] the lofty height of the towers creates a special microclimate of high winds in winter and sizzling streets and oven-hot masonry walls in summer."[32] Evidence demonstrating the weather impact has been provided by Peter Bosselmann, director of the University of California's Environmental Simulation Laboratory, who was commissioned by the New York City Parks Council to assess the impact of new high-rise development on Central Park, including the effect of Trump's Television City complex with its 1,946 foot tower. Bosselmann's research showed that a playground in Central Park would be shadowed and colder after 4 P.M. in early spring and summer, that the running track in Riverside Park would have no noontime sunlight for much of the fall and winter, and that the northwest wind would be 160 percent stronger in the proposed park in Television City. Bosselmann has been quoted as saying, "I've never measured wind ratios of this kind."[33] Interestingly, the old expression "twenty-three skiddoo" came from the wind-generating feature of New York's Flatiron Building, an early skyscraper built on Twenty-third Street; the winds there played havoc with men's hats and women's skirts.

From the 1950s to the 1980s the "international" style of office-building architecture—boxy, concrete, glass, steel, and aluminum structures—flourished in North American and European cities. Before 1950 most high-rise buildings had modest windows with exteriors of concrete, brick, and metal, but between the 1950s and the 1970s there was a dramatic shift to high-rise "glass-box" buildings often looking something akin to a person with opaque wrap-around sunglasses. However, during the late 1970s and 1980s, in many cities, architects and developers reacted to criticisms of the international style of glass boxes by developing significant modifications to the glass-box concept. The "boxyness" of the larger buildings was softened or changed dramatically. During the last decade we have seen more eclectic architectural styles, with glassy construction modified significantly with neo-baroque ornamentation and unusual shapes, as can be seen in recent construction in cities such as San Francisco and Los Angeles. Some of the skyscraper structures began to zig and zag, with slanted tops, pyramidal bases, and other architectural variations from the basic glassy box shape. Some were built with tops looking like cathedrals or Chippendale furniture. Such buildings are sometimes termed "signature" buildings because of their uniqueness. A growing number of the new office buildings, Kay suggests, look like "wacky sculpture."[34]

In the 1950s British glass companies invented the thick float glass that made the massive glass buildings possible. A few companies make most of the glass used in this distinctive type of office tower construction. Moreover, the shift to glass-box architecture reflected elitist, not democratic, decision making. One city analyst has commented that

> *we have no figures to tell us how the urbanite reacts to the adamant geometry of the glass box, or how the bleakness of our main streets, studded with parking lots, hits small town and rural folk. Who can doubt, though, that our architecture of the slick, boring highrise, the empty plaza, the desolate shopping mall in the suburbs—all those structures that forbid human congress—contribute to the poverty of...public life.*[35]

We do have a few opinion surveys on how urbanites react to the geometry of high-rise buildings, whether glass boxes or otherwise. In a survey 300 University of Maryland students were asked what they liked and disliked about tall buildings. A majority said they liked the views from the buildings; a significant percentage felt they made efficient use of space. However, the majority mentioned more features that they disliked: (1) waiting for elevators, (2) absence of greenery, (3) threat of fire, and (4) impersonality. Many disliked the monotonous architecture and feared getting stuck in skyscraper elevators. Among those who lived near a tall building, one-third said it was annoying. When asked, "What do you think would improve tall buildings?" the major answers were greater fire safety, more greenery, and a maximum height of 12 stories. On the West Coast a survey of Bank of America employees found that a substantial proportion felt oppressed by the large buildings around them. What seemed to bother them were the scale, the closed-in feeling, and the lack of breathing space. Yet most Americans are not consulted in the decision-making process lying behind investments in, and the construction of, their workplaces.[36]

Energy Problems Do the new office buildings, hotels, and apartment buildings squander energy unnecessarily? Environmental and other citizen groups have begun to raise this question. Because the windows usually do not open, many open air shafts are needed for expensive, energy-consuming air-conditioning systems. And because glass as a rule does not insulate as well as masonry, there is greater energy consumption in the new buildings. Even some savvy developers and their corporate tenants have become aware of the savings of structures built to conserve energy. For example, the relatively low-rise, 28-story West Monroe office building in Chicago saves at least 30 percent in energy costs, compared with a higher-rise 50-story building with the same amount of space in square feet, because it has less exterior wall area exposed to the elements and less glass as part of those walls. Nonetheless, most buildings with energy-wasting plazas and central atriums are still seen by business analysts as beautiful signature buildings.[37]

Problems of the Vertical Office Culture   Office towers create a distinctive office climate, one different from that created in low-rise, horizontal facilities. Many corporations have concentrated thousands of their employees in skyscrapers without seriously considering the organizational implications. Take the aforementioned Sears Tower in Chicago, for example. When built in 1974, the tower was envisioned as a unique monument to Sears' dominance as the world's largest retail firm. Thousands of Sears managerial and clerical employees were moved to the skyscraper. Over the next decade Sears executives saw their firm's "hometown" image change to that of a large impersonal corporation, with the giant tower contributing to that change. By the late 1980s Sears' dominance of U.S. retail sales was being seriously challenged; the firm's sales were declining to the level of the improving sales of such challenging firms as K Mart. In addition, there is the operational and organizational problem of a vertical corporate environment. To quote Edward Brennan, the chairperson of Sears, "when your world is vertical and all your movement is by elevator, your contacts are inhibited, you don't see people as frequently as you do in other environments and decision making is difficult."[38] This hyper-vertical corporate environment led to the development of a "slow-to-react" corporate culture, which some cite as a major reason for Sears' competitive problems. As a result, Sears' top executives prepared a plan for a critical organizational and physical restructuring that included not only selling the skyscraper but also moving thousands of employees to decentralized urban settings in an attempt to regain Sears' hometown image. Yet Sears is not unique. The impersonality and slow-to-react character of the corporate cultures of many firms are substantially reinforced by spatial considerations that corporate executives and urban scholars alike have neglected.

Threat of Skyscraper Fires   Based on the novels *The Tower* and *The Glass Inferno*, the movie *Towering Inferno* was a famous disaster film about hundreds of people trapped at the top of a fire-consumed, 130-story skyscraper in San Francisco. In this 1974 movie people were trapped in a tower that had been built with shady business practices, shortcuts leaving the structure without adequate fire protection. Unfortunately, a real-life reenactment of the movie occurred in November 1980 when a fire engulfed the MGM Grand Hotel in Las Vegas; this towering inferno killed 84 people. The National Fire Protection Association has noted that the most lethal high-rise fires have been in hotels and apartment buildings. In May 1988 the scenario was repeated in the 62-story First Interstate Bancorp Tower in Los Angeles. *Wall Street Journal* reporters wrote that the scene was "reminiscent of the movie *Towering Inferno*" as flames moved from the twelfth to the sixteenth floors injuring 40 and killing 1.[39] The fire not only posed an immediate hazard to the occupants of the tower but also threatened passersby as it rained down glass and other debris. This fire also underscores the continuing threat of high-rise fires because of inadequate measures taken by owners. In the wake of the First Interstate fire, Fire Chief Donald Manning said that three quarters of the 800 major office buildings in Los Angeles lacked sprinkler systems. According to the president of the American Fire-Sprinkler Association, while "there aren't any comprehensive figures on how many buildings in the U.S. lack sprinkler systems,...the majority of them lack sprinklers. If the office building was built more than 10 years ago, the chances are it isn't sprinklered."[40]

Before the early 1950s most high-rise buildings were constructed in ways that stalled or reduced the hazards of fire. Concrete floors, steam heat, no air conditioning ducts, windows that opened, hard plaster walls, dropped ceilings—these features produced buildings with few open air shafts and much solid, heat-absorbing material throughout. Modern buildings, however, have panel walls hung from floor slabs, insulating materials that reflect rather than absorb heat, windows that will not open, and multiple air shafts for heating and air conditioning. These features can facilitate the spread of fires. And the new plastic materials often increase toxic fumes. Extreme heights make it difficult for fire fighters to combat fires in upper stories, and the concentration of high-rise buildings in one area can make it difficult for fire engines to approach because of traffic congestion.

The development industry has been concerned about films such as *Towering Inferno* and has tried to push forward an image of skyscraper safety. Developers, owners, and leasing companies vigorously argue that high-rise buildings are safe because of the absence of fire trouble spots such as cooking facilities and because of the presence of alert security personnel. Developer pressure for favorable treatment means that exceptions to fire codes flourish. Many have fought the implementation of expensive new safety systems for office towers. Developers and owners have usually been able to derail efforts to require new safety technologies. The building permit for the First Interstate Building was issued in 1972, when sprinkler systems were not required for Los Angeles buildings. The code was changed in 1974 so that buildings more than 74 feet tall must have sprinkler systems, but the First Interstate Building was not required to install sprinkler systems, so long as it met other upgrading standards, including stairwell and elevator system improvements.[41]

The construction of large office and hotel buildings has raised questions other than the question of fire hazards. In *Risk, Ruin and Riches* Jim Powell has detailed the July 1981 Hyatt Regency hotel disaster in Kansas City. Two 71,000 pound concrete skywalks fell several stories down the atrium on a dance crowd estimated at 2,500 below. Rescuers found 113 dead and 239 injured. Powell concludes that a number of people involved in the hotel construction were responsible for the design changes in the skywalks that led to the disaster: the owner, an engineering firm that produced drawings with deadly mistakes, the licensed structural engineers at the construction site, and the city building inspectors. In this case, the development of a state-of-the-art atrium building was not accompanied by procedures adequate to protect the public from design flaws. There are built-in dangers in relying on high-rise construction for urban development. For this reason, among others, many developers now emphasize medium-scale office and hotel buildings.[42]

MULTIPLE-USE DEVELOPMENTS

Integrated Complexes of Business   Visionaries have portrayed the city of the future as one giant integrated physical structure housing all the people in a city from cradle to grave. If this really is the city of the future, a scaled-down version already exists today in some of the urban multiple-use developments, called MXDs in the trade. These MXD developments are so huge that they can shove aside other urban uses. In Houston, for example, Greenway Plaza encompasses more than 100 acres of central-city land. In its first two phases nearly 4 million square feet of office space were constructed. Greenway Plaza includes the 32-story Conoco Tower, an 11-story Union Carbide building, the multistory Dow Center Complex, a 22-story Kellogg building, the Richmond and Buffalo towers, a chemical company building, a luxury hotel, high-rise apartment buildings, a parking garage, a heliport, and a sports arena. Construction of Greenway Plaza began in the late 1960s; and it was still being built into the 1980s, at a total cost of more than $1 billion. Preparation for this mammoth undertaking involved the acquisition and destruction or removal of several hundred single-family houses.

An example of a MXD in progress is the project undertaken in North Brunswick, New Jersey, by K. Hovnanian Companies, one of New Jersey's leading developers. Choosing 189 acres of vacant land off Route 1 in the central part of the state, the firm announced in 1987 that its 10-year MXD project would include 1 million square feet of offices, 50,000 square feet of retail space, a hotel, and 1,000 condominiums at a cost of $225 million. Another example can be seen in San Antonio. In 1987 the San Antonio development company Wender/Wright Interests began construction of a $10 billion 7,500-acre complex which would eventually house a computer microchip factory, a Sea World theme park, and a Union Carbide plant. Moreover, in 1987 Honolulu developer James Campbell was planning a $2 billion 6,000-acre MXD project with 6 million square feet of commercial space, about 15,000 housing units, a park, a civic center, and amphitheater.[43]

Defining MXDs   There are many MXD developments in North America. According to the developers' think tank, the Urban Land Institute (ULI), these developments are reshaping metropolitan life.[44] Developers and allied real estate operators see the MXDs not just as profit-making enterprises but as major examples of societal restructuring. MXD's are "projects that incorporate three or more revenue-producing uses in a physically integrated and planned development. Mixed-use developments often include such components as office, retail, hotel, residential, and entertainment space."[45] A mid-1970s study found 88 existing or planned multiple-purpose centers, 50 of which were in central business districts, 31 in central cities, and 7 in suburbs. Most were in cities with populations over 1 million. By the late 1980s there were already more than 130 MXDs.[46] Even in the mid- to late-1980s the continued planning and construction of MXDs demonstrated continued viability of this type of large-scale project. One important reason for MXD viability is the assistance frequently provided by local government officials. A ULI survey of 131 MXDs revealed significant governmental involvement, with nearly 50 percent of them requiring some local code or ordinance change, 36 percent receiving indirect economic incentives or infrastructure improvements, 34 percent including governmental investment in supporting projects, and 16 percent involving direct governmental ownership or shared risk.[47]

The Scale Multiple-use projects are huge sets of buildings extending over a city block or more. These are different from other projects because they involve integrated building patterns and substantial organizational and financial power over a longer period of time, requirements that can only be met under the conditions of modern oligopoly capitalism, that is, where giant development and lending corporations can put them together. In such cases, the powerful developmental actors include the developers who package and develop the MXDs, the financial institutions, and the large retail and service corporations that acquire space from, or go into a joint venture with, a developer. Among the major U.S. corporations operating as MXD developers or financiers have been the following: Alcoa Properties; Metropolitan Life Insurance Company; Hallmark Cards, Inc.; David Rockefeller Associates; Aetna Life and Casualty Company; Texas Eastern Transmission Corporation; Equitable Life Insurance Company; John Hancock Mutual Life Insurance Company; and Ford Motor Company. Even this abbreviated list includes principal U.S. nonconstruction corporations.[48]

The enormous scale and cost of MXDs can be seen in three famous projects:

Place	Name	Size (in million square feet)	Estimated cost in millions (1975)
Washington, D.C.	Watergate	1.8	$ 45
San Francisco	Embarcadero	3.9	$175
Houston	Galleria	4.6	$ 70

The Watergate Complex is a well-known MXD that became part of the history of burglary and political corruption during the Nixon administration. These three older MXD projects are located in the nation's chief cities, have involved major U.S. or foreign corporations, and have cost at least $45 million in investment capital each. The scale is monumental.[49]

At one point, Houston's Texas Eastern Transmission Corporation was building what was billed as the largest MXD ever undertaken. About 1970 this oil and gas company bought 33 city blocks on the east side of downtown Houston. Once an expensive residential area, this had become a diverse area of commercial buildings, small hotels, apartment houses, and older homes. Called Houston Center, this MXD project was seen as a new model for city life. According to its own advertising, the center would mean "the creation of an entirely new city offering fresh approaches to work, recreation and residence. It may well be the prototype of the city of the future."[50] Local government was cooperative. The Houston Center developer, Texas Eastern, received permission from the city government to close major city streets and gave several blocks to the local government, which built a convention center complex using local tax revenues. However, Texas Eastern ran into a problem with its Houston Center development schedule and sold half its interest to the Canadian-based Cadillac Fairview corporation, which later ran into major financial problems of its own. Although several high-rise buildings were completed in the project area, the downturn in the fortunes of the supervising corporations, as well as the major recession in Houston's oil-centered economy in the 1980s, had the consequence that this MXD has not become the largest development project in urban history.[51]

An Early Multipurpose Project   Rockefeller Center, constructed in Manhattan by the Rockefeller family, is the earliest and perhaps the most-famous major multiple-use project. Described by one admiring writer as "a cathedral of the mid-twentieth century," this multibuilding complex dwarfs St. Patrick's Cathedral across from it.[52] Thus it symbolizes the rise to prominence of oil, banking, and communications corporations and the decline of religious edifices as the high points of Western cities. This business and entertainment center was begun during the first years of the Great Depression and is still one of the largest multipurpose projects. It was made possible by the fortune built by John D. Rockefeller, Jr. (1874–1960). Rockefeller himself controlled the development of the center by choosing the members of the board of Rockefeller Center, Inc., and of the companies tied to it. By the late 1970s it consisted of 21 skyscrapers; it had 2 miles of underground passageways and planned services for its 200-plus tenants. Although Rockefeller Center is not an MXD by the strictest definition, because it has only two of the major land uses, it is similar in overall conception: office buildings, landscaped plazas, theaters, skating pond, and many restaurants.[53]

Mammoth projects such as Rockefeller Center have inspired strange reactions from some commentators. One author, apparently unaware of the irony in her statement, notes that the "influence of Rockefeller Center extends even to Walt Disney World, also designed under single-minded control. Like the Center, it has underground facilities, plants, an almost obsessive interest in cleanliness, and an up-to-date if not avant-garde standard of modern architecture."[54] The comment is ironic because critics of projects such as Rockefeller Center have argued that they embody the negative characteristics sometimes associated with a Disney World: a plastic, contrived, and artificial character. Rockefeller Center became the model for many other multipurpose developments. Indeed, Rockefeller Center, Inc., has itself participated in designing, developing, financing, and running similar massive projects across the United States, including the Wells Fargo Building in Los Angeles, the Continental Center in New York City, the Irving Trust Operations Center in New York City, and the ill-fated Renaissance Center in Detroit.

Building the New Capitalist City Multiple-use projects are seen by some developers, architects, and architectural critics as the wave of the urban future. They have been called the most viable form of new metropolitan development. An MXD, planner Alan M. Vorhees argues, provides for "a variety of life styles....It tends to reduce energy requirements, particularly if it replaces vehicle trips with walk trips....It tends to break up the monotony of the urban environment."[55] From this perspective the MXDs and other huge shopping malls are portrayed as moving city life from the streets into air-conditioned complexes where people can live, work, and even die inside one privately owned urban project—a business version of cradle-to-grave existence. Developers argue that multiple-use malls with entertainment, housing, and other nonretail facilities are easier to sell to communities. One producer noted that making an issue of the multiple-use features of his planned business-and-shopping-center project helped to defeat a local ballot proposal to prevent its being built. Thus MXDs are seen as a way to keep "central cities alive."[56]

To take one prominent example, Houston's Galleria MXD, with its many shops, hotel, office building, and theaters, is often claimed to be "the place" to be seen in Houston. And it has been cited as a reorganizer of Houston's metropolitan growth, providing a major "focal point" for western development outside the downtown area. Many MXDs are touted as reversing blight, wherever they may in fact be located. Multiple-use developments such as the famous Watergate complex in Washington, D.C., have been viewed as bringing new recreational and residential life to areas that would otherwise be dead at night. However, much housing and many smaller businesses were destroyed to make the developments possible. Although they are sometimes erroneously called "urban villages," most giant multiple-use developments tend to operate like new central business districts. Some MXDs, such as the fortresslike Renaissance Center in Detroit, are similar to the castles of the Middle Ages and reflect some of the same concerns about crime and protection of the affluent. Their builders sometimes see them as exclusive oases in downtown deserts. Their luxury component is emphasized, and their class character is freely admitted. Upper- and upper-middle-income people are preferred clients.

MXDs can be money-making machines; typically they, like any of the independent shopping malls, permit above-average rents to be charged to their business tenants. They are viewed as commodities by their producers; exchange value is a central consideration for the developers and their occupants. One ULI handbook portrays the MXD image as a new means of product differentiation, as being different enough shopping space to attract people away from other marketing areas. Many developers, and their clients, also view the MXDs as good advertising for their companies, as prestigious locations that bring them public attention.[57] One study, *The Costs of Sprawl*, prepared for the federal government, defends these high-density developments. They are seen as less costly in terms of land consumption, air pollution, and energy consumption than lower-density developments. Advertising the advantages of such higher-density land use is done to generate government and public support for the profitable MXDs. However, the same arguments for high density are rejected when it comes to suburban development. In suburbia many developers and their government defenders see low-density sprawl as best.[58]

Problems of Aging Many modern office tower and MXD projects have a certain transitory character; they are not built to last. For instance, there is the Place Ville-Marie, one of the first curtain-wall MXDs in North America, once a jewel in the crown of developer Bill Zeckendorf, who built this cross-shaped complex in Montreal, Canada, in the early 1960s (see Chapter 3). With a large shopping area, a 41-story tower, other buildings, and transportation linkage to nearby buildings, Place Ville-Marie became the model for many subsequent MXD projects in Canada and the United States. It was later sold to the Trizec Corporation. Once Canada's premier office address, housing companies like the Royal Bank of Canada, Air Canada, numerous oil companies, and top law firms, Place Ville-Marie was described in the 1980s by a real estate broker as a "twenty-five-year-old Chevy" that was already technologically obsolete. What the broker had in mind was the aging of Place Ville-Marie—its energy-inefficient architecture of single-glazed, floor-to-ceiling glass windows, its absence of sprinkler systems, and its lack of current fashionability for many corporate clients seeking Montreal locations. The turnover of capital in the secondary circuit of real estate investment appears to be increasing; the MXDs like Place Ville-Marie are distinguished by built-in obsolescence.[59]

CONCLUSION: CITIZENS QUESTIONING LARGE-SCALE DEVELOPMENT

The distinctive spatial features of the modern Western city include large-scale development projects such as the omnipresent towering skyscrapers and MXDs. These represent the concentration and centralization of capital in the larger industrial, commercial, retail, and development corporations that characterize modern capitalism. And these huge projects also signal the extraordinary flows of capital into the secondary circuit of real estate investment since the early twentieth century. Large amounts of capital have been transferred to U.S. real estate from the manufacturing circuit, as well as from secondary-circuit real estate profits in other countries. The secondary circuit of real estate investment has become a global circuit.

The dominance of these major development projects in cities has not meant that they represent the sentiments of a majority of city residents. Indeed, the dehumanizing and environmental impact of large-scale office and MXD developments has led to an increasing number of citizens' protests concerned with neighborhood and family use-value considerations. Thus in San Francisco voters put a stop to the "Manhattanization" of their central city by prohibiting major skyscrapers. The California Supreme Court blocked an $88 million development opposed by citizens in the Westwood area of Los Angeles. And in Boston a group called Citizens for a Better New England tried to stop the New England Life Insurance Company and Gerald D. Hines Interests from developing a 25-story office tower in that city's Back Bay area. The members of the group argued that the high-rise building would change the low-rise character of their neighborhood, create greater traffic problems, and worsen a parking problem. Others opposed the project on aesthetic grounds. Boston City Councilor David Scondras called the building "stupid," "pompous," and a replica of the architect's (Philip Johnson's) buildings elsewhere. The neighborhood group fought the project at every level from city government to the state's highest court and finally succeeded in getting the project downsized.[60]

Another indicator of citizen resistance to the continued construction of skyscrapers is the increasing number of "view-protection" zoning laws springing up around the country. Rodney L. Cobb, editor of the *Land Use Law and Zoning Digest*, has noted that "a couple of decades ago, you rarely saw zoning used to protect aesthetic values...now zoning is becoming more sophisticated in terms of protecting views."[61] Such a zoning law is on the books in Seattle; since the mid-1980s the city government has ensured that views of the Seattle bay area and of nearby mountains will not be obstructed by high-rise construction. Moreover, in Austin a new Texas law protects views of the old state Capitol building by barring high-rise development in certain view corridors around it. And Cincinnati law now protects vistas of the rolling hills near downtown by controlling the height of office buildings. While many view-protection ordinances have been challenged by developers around the country, citizens' groups have won unexpected victories. The future is likely to be one of continued conflict over the vertical culture and impact of high-rise building. The home and neighborhood use value of urban space for its residents is featured in this conflict.

NOTES

1. Philip K. Howard, "New York Is Becoming a City We Don't Want," *New York Times*, November 28, 1987, 23.
2. Tim Schreiner, "Putting on the Brakes," *American Demographics* 10 (January 1988): 54–55.
3. Donald Appleyard and Lois Fishman, "High-Rise Buildings versus San Francisco: Measuring Visual and Symbolic Impacts," in *Human Response to Tall Buildings*, edited by Donald J. Conway (Stroudsburg, Pennsylvania: Dowden, Hutchinson, and Ross, 1977), p. 82.
4. Cited in ibid., p. 83.
5. John Brooks, *The Takeover Game* (New York: E.P. Dutton, 1987), pp. 171–172; Larry Sawyers, "Urban Form and the Mode of Production," *The Review of Radical Political Economics* 7 (Spring 1975): 65–66; Institute of Real Estate Management, *Managing the Office Building* (Chicago: National Association of Realtors, 1981), pp. 7–8.
6. Ellen Paris, "Are You Listening, Woody Allen?" *Forbes* 137 (July 28, 1986): 106.
7. David Landis, "Towering Dream: Harry Grant Boosting Tallest Building," *USA Today*, September 1, 1988, 2B; Julie Stacey, "How Buildings Stack up," *USA Today*, June 3, 1988, 1; Otto Johnson, "Notable U.S. Skyscrapers," in *The 1988 Information Please Almanac* (Boston: Houghton Mifflin Company, 1988), p. 586.
8. Alexander Stuart, "Texan Gerald Hines Is Tall in the Skyline," *Fortune* 101 (January 28, 1980): 101; and Gerald D. Hines Interests news release, in author's files.
9. Stuart, "Texan Gerald Hines Is Tall in the Skyline," pp. 102–104.
10. "America's Office Needs, 1985–95," *Buildings* 81 (January 1987): 46–47; Brooks, *The Takeover Game*, pp. 173–174.
11. David L. Birch, "Wide Open Spaces," *Inc.* 9 (August 1987): 28–29.
12. "End of the Office Boom," *Business Week*, October 4, 1982, 94–98; "Office Space Review, 1981," *Buildings* 75 (January 1981): 52–65;

"News," *Buildings* 75 (March 1981): 16–17; Stanford Hory, "San Francisco Bounces Back," *Building* 73 (July 1979): 92; Peter Meyer, "Land Rush," *Harper's* 258 (January 1979): 45–60; "Office Space Goes Begging," *Newsweek*, October 11, 1982, 96.

13. Birch, "Wide Open Spaces," p. 28.

14. Todd Mason, "Real Estate: Less Frisky, but Still Kicking," *Business Week*, January 11, 1988, 131; see also David R. Mosena and Mary Ludgin, "Look for Less Office Space, More Frills," *Planning* (January 1987): 7.

15. Gary Weiss, "The Office Glut: That Empty Feeling Spreads," *Business Week*, October 20, 1986, 112.

16. William Celis, III, "Mid-Sized Cities Feel Effects of Increased Building Activity," *Wall Street Journal*, July 15, 1987, 21; Mosena and Ludgin, "Look for Less Office Space, More Frills," p. 7.

17. Susan Diesenhouse, "Towers Add to Boston's Office Glut," *New York Times*, April 19, 1989, p. 30; William Celis, III, "Office-Space Vacancies Growing in Northeast," *Wall Street Journal*, April 29, 1988, 17; Roger Lowenstein, "Manhattan's 10-Year Real Estate Boom Is Weakened by the Stock Market Crash," *Wall Street Journal*, January 15, 1988, 20.

18. "Denver Rated Best for Offices," *Springfield (Mo.) News-Leader*, April 23, 1988, E1; Irwin Ross, "Bargains Galore in Office Space," *Fortune*, February 17, 1986, 58; Birch, "Wide Open Spaces," p. 29.

19. Irwin Ross, "It's a Glorious Glut for Brokers," *Fortune*, February 17, 1986, p. 62.

20. Richard A. Walker and David B. Large, "The Economics of Energy Extravagance," *Ecology Law Quarterly* 4 (1975): 963–985; James Lorimer, *The Developers* (Toronto: James Lorimer, 1978), pp. 170–171.

21. Institute of Real Estate Management, *Managing the Office Building*, p. 97.

22. "Leaving Nothing to Chance," *Financial World* 150 (February 1, 1981): 24. See also p. 25.

23. Stephen Rushmore, "14 Notable Hotel Development Firms," *Restaurant and Hotel Design*, December 1987, 23–38.

24. "As the Crow Flies," *Forbes* 137 (March 10, 1986): 10.

25. "Leaving Nothing to Chance," *Financial World* 150 (February 1, 1981): 24.

26. Institute of Real Estate Management, *Managing the Office Building*, pp. 287–288, 293–295.

27. Paris, "Are You Listening, Woody Allen?," p. 108.

28. William McWhirter, "Moving Back to Main Street," *Time*, November 14, 1988, 52.

29. Sam Bass Warner, *The Urban Wilderness* (New York: Harper and Row, 1972), pp. 34–35.

30. Philip K. Howard, "New York Is Becoming a City We Don't Want," p. 23.
31. Ibid.
32. Warner, *The Urban Wilderness*, p. 34; Henry Aubin, *City for Sale* (Toronto: James Lorimer, 1977), p. 116.
33. Sam Roberts, "As Towers Rise, a Slow Fade-Out of Sun and Sky," *New York Times*, December 7, 1987, 18.
34. Jane Holtz Kay, "Rubik's Cube in Steel," *Christian Science Monitor*, January 8, 1982, 15; "The Sky's the Limit," *Newsweek*, November 8, 1982, 67.
35. Quoted in Aubin, *City for Sale*, p. 95. See also pp. 116–118.
36. Gilda Moss Haber, "The Impact of Tall Buildings on Users and Neighbors," in *Human Responses to Tall Buildings*, pp. 51–57; Appleyard and Fishman, "High-Rise Buildings versus San Francisco," p. 81.
37. Institute of Real Estate Management, *Managing the Office Building*, pp. 14–15.
38. McWhirter, "Moving Back to Main Street," p. 52.
39. Earl C. Gottschalk, Jr., and Daniel Akst, "Los Angeles High-Rise Fire Prompts Louder Calls for Sprinkler Systems," *Wall Street Journal*, May 6, 1988, 20.
40. Gottschalk and Akst, "Los Angeles High-Rise Fire Prompts Louder Calls for Sprinkler Systems," p. 20.
41. Neal D. Hougton, "The Myth of the Towering Inferno," *Buildings* 75 (May 1981): 48–50; Gottschalk and Akst, "Los Angeles High-Rise Fire Prompts Louder Calls for Sprinkler Systems," p. 20.
42 Jim Powell, *Risk, Ruin and Riches* (New York: Macmillan, 1986), pp. 299–336.
43. Century Development Corporation, Greenway Plaza brochures and fact sheets in author's files; some data are drawn from an interview with a research official at the Rice Center research facility in Greenway Plaza, Houston, Texas, May, 1981; Rachelle Garbarine, "Hovnanian Planning a Mixed-Use Project," *New York Times*, November 22, 1987, R12.
44. Robert E. Witherspoon, Jon P. Abbett, and Robert M. Gladstone, *Mixed-Use Developments: New Ways of Land Use* (Washington, D.C.: Urban Land Institute, 1976), p. 3.
45. Matt Kane, "Mixed-Use Commercial Developments Staying Strong," *Nation's Cities Weekly* 10 (June 1, 1987): 1.
46. Witherspoon, Abbett, and Gladstone, *Mixed-Use Developments*, pp. 6, 11, 17, 40–44.
47. Kane, "Mixed-Use Commercial Developments Staying Strong," p. 1.
48. Witherspoon, Abbett, and Gladstone, *Mixed-Use Developments*, pp. 52–53, 84.
49. Ibid., pp. 91–153.

50. Quoted in Bernard H. Siegan, *Land Use without Zoning* (Lexington, Mass.: Lexington Books, 1972), p. 70.
51. Ibid., pp. 74–76.
52. Carol Herselle Krinsky, *Rockefeller Center* (New York: Oxford University Press, 1978), p. 31.
53. Ibid., p. 15; Lillie A. Mikesell, "Rockefeller Center, Inc.," *Buildings* 75 (April 1981): 44–50.
54. Krinsky, *Rockefeller Center*, p. 7.
55. Quoted in ibid., pp. 3, 5.
56. Ibid., pp. 4–5.
57. Witherspoon, Abbett, and Gladstone, *Mixed-Use Developments*, p. 64, 74–76.
58. Council on Environmental Quality, Department of Housing and Urban Development, *The Costs of Sprawl: Environmental and Economic Costs of Alternative Residential Patterns* (Washington, D.C.: U.S. Government Printing Office, 1974).
59. Alan Freemen, "Top Montreal Office Complex Encounters Trouble as It Ages," *Wall Street Journal*, November 10, 1982, sect. 2, p. 1.
60. Schreiner, "Putting on the Brakes," pp. 54–55; Neil McGhee, "New England Life's Home Office Tower Raises Local Controversy," *National Underwriter*, August 30, 1986, 3, 14.
61. William Celis, III, "More Cities Pass Zoning Laws to Keep Local Sights in View," *Wall Street Journal*, July 22, 1987, 23.

5

GENTRIFICATION
AND REDEVELOPMENT
IN CENTRAL CITIES

Lowertown, a neighborhood near downtown St. Paul, Minnesota, has become "quite trendy" in the last five years....Formerly a depressed warehouse district, Lowertown is now burgeoning with new restaurants, apartment buildings, and single-family houses. Gentrification has a dark side, when residents of a formerly depressed center city cannot afford to live in their new, upscale surroundings....Between 1976 and 1985, 514 single-room residences in downtown St. Paul were displaced by redevelopment. In February 1985, the city estimated that the number of downtown rental units affordable to those with low incomes had declined from 410 in 1980 to 185 in 1984, while the number of higher-priced units had increased.[1]

Walter Reinhaus, a white graduate student, is renovating a Charles Adamsesque mansion in the middle of an all-black Chicago neighborhood. "With gentrification," he says, "it's easy to go too far. There are people and places here I deeply love. There's some of the best barbecue I've ever had. Stores are cheap, unpretentious." Thanks to him, perhaps, not for long.[2]

INTRODUCTION

Ernestine Turner, mother of eight, was evicted from her somewhat dilapidated row house in a changing area of Washington, D.C. Given 45 days' notice, she was unable to find a new place that she could afford on her low monthly welfare check. According to a *Washington Post* story, she collapsed with a nervous breakdown and was taken to the hospital. Ms. Turner reportedly said, "I've been to the mayor's office, the Department of Human Resources, and the public housing office. Everybody says there's nothing available for a family of my size." Her landlord owned many houses in the area and was selling them to developers and other affluent individuals interested in developing centrally located properties in the nation's booming political capital. Long ago abandoned by whites, many central-city areas have in the last two decades received renewed attention from white land speculators and developers.³

Central cities have long been discussed in terms of decay, poverty, and fiscal crises. Numerous social scientists and journalists have written that the central cities are "doomed," "physically obsolete," and deserving of "abandonment." In recent decades, however, new images have been articulated, envisioning central cities with new investment, rejuvenation of central-city neighborhoods, and the back-to-the-city movement of affluent whites called *gentrification*. This vision can easily be discerned in popular publications. In an article in *Harper's* T. D. Allman argued that central-city revitalization was well underway by the mid-1970s and that central cities were attracting new investment to projects such as office towers and rebuilt residential areas. Writing about the same time in the *Saturday Review,* Horace Sutton spoke eloquently on revitalization: "It is dusk, many have strayed far, but mother [the city] beckons and the wayfarers [middle-income people] are on the way back."⁴ Moreover, in a late 1980s cover story *Time* declared: "So the tide has turned. Today it is almost obligatory for a city to have a fine old theater or train station or office building that has been saved, spiffed up, and put back to good, if not necessarily its original use...buying paperbacks and chocolate-chip cookies in what used to be a warehouse and watching stand-up comedians in what used to be a stable and living in what used to be a factory are now, happily, coast-to-coast cliches, not novelties."⁵

UNEVEN URBAN DEVELOPMENT

Urban Centers of Modern Capitalism   The central cities of larger metropolitan areas have long been control centers for U.S. capitalism. The major central cities have been the hub for economic, political, and cultural dominance by corporate elites. Thus decline in downtown areas is often viewed negatively by local and national business groups. Economic contraction there may be tolerated for an interim period, but new pressures frequently arise for urban revitalization. As a result, over the last several decades we have seen an urban renaissance in many central cities. The new office towers, hotels, MXDs, and exclusive neighborhoods of historic homes, marinas, and specialty shops signal the channeling of much new capital into the secondary circuit of real estate investments in central cities. They also signal the return of well-off residents to the housing areas of central cities. But the widely praised downtown resurgence is yet another chapter in the long-term process of uneven investments across cities, a process with winners and with losers.

Do All Benefit from Redevelopment? Stanford University professor Richard Muth has asserted the widespread myth of central-city development:

> To make money and to survive, the private developer must convert less highly valued to more highly valued real estate, making everybody richer as a result. To paraphrase Adam Smith, the private developer in seeking his own interest promotes society's even though this was not part of his intention....In the process, the city's housing stock will have been upgraded and the city's tax base increased. All of us consumers will benefit.[6]

In contrast to the idyllic picture painted by Muth, there is the everyday reality of people being hurt by redevelopment. Many central-city residents concerned with the use value of their apartments and homes, particularly those who are black, Hispanic, poor, or elderly, do not benefit from the exchange-value decisions of the powerful city rebuilders.

In many cities residential areas once populated by white city dwellers were abandoned between the 1930s and the 1970s as whites left for the suburbs. Later, many of the same areas were reclaimed by whites of a different generation. This seesawing can be seen in the Bunker Hill area near downtown Los Angeles. Once an area of mansions owned by doctors, lawyers, and merchants, by the 1920s and 1930s it had become populated by poorer whites and Mexican-Americans. Well-off whites moved to the suburbs. This abandonment was followed in the 1950s and 1960s by a new round of investment in the secondary circuit of central-city real estate—and the resulting human and community costs for the residents then in the area. In 1954 the city council voted to seek $33 million to redevelop Bunker Hill. City officials had earlier rejected a plan for moderate-income public housing in the area as "socialistic." Yet the preferred redevelopment plan included *large* federal subsidies and local tax benefits (some critics say corporate "welfare") for business-oriented redevelopment. In the 1960s the houses were leveled, their low-income inhabitants were displaced, and huge buildings—a bank complex, oil company offices, a music center complex, and luxury apartment towers—were erected. Altogether, 6,000 people were pushed out of their neighborhoods. The city's Community Redevelopment Agency worked closely with the business interests.[7]

San Francisco's Tenderloin area—home for 20,000 low-income and elderly citizens—was invaded by the hotel industry. Three large hotels were constructed there, bringing a "touristification" that threatens this important residential area. Moreover, in Atlantic City, New Jersey, casino hotels and specialty shops have displaced many moderate-income and elderly residents. Real estate speculation has driven taxes so high that homeowners must sell out. Reportedly, landlords have forced black and Hispanic tenants out by reducing maintenance, then selling off to developers of resort projects. The hotel and casino building boom has resulted in severe displacement, particularly displacing minorities, the poor, and the elderly.[8] Across the nation central-city redevelopment has had its low-income, minority, and elderly victims. For example, in the decade 1970–1980 various urban investment-disinvestment processes resulted in an average loss of 125,000 low-rent housing units a year in the United States. Approximately half the 2 million units in single-room occupancy hotels, hotels where many low-income urbanites reside, were razed, abandoned, or gentrified. And since 1980 the trend toward abandonment and conversion has continued: Another million low-rent housing units were lost between 1980 and 1988.[9]

CENTRAL-CITY DEVELOPMENT: WHO DECIDES?

We have previously examined numerous examples of downtown redevelopment projects, including Rockefeller Center, the World Financial Center, and Trump Tower in New York, the Watergate complex in Washington, D.C., the Bunker Hill project in Los Angeles, and the Renaissance Center complex in Detroit. In some cities such as Houston and Austin developers have worked with government officials to build downtown convention centers. And in cities such as Baltimore, older retail and industrial buildings in the central area have been converted to chic shops and expensive restaurants serving conventioneers, tourists, and white-collar workers. Yet even in redeveloped central cities, development tends to be spotty and uneven. Beauregard notes that "a new, vigorous and highly capitalized central core is surrounded by gentrified and affluent neighborhoods, declining industrial districts, and both stabilizing and deteriorating neighborhoods."[10]

A Good Business Climate? In examining possible downtown and other central-city projects, executives of industrial and development corporations are again concerned about the "business climate." They are most likely to participate in downtown revitalization if they are given special tax abatements, if labor unions are restrained, if business leaders are pivotal in the public planning groups, and if government officials cooperate with private economic activity. The profit-minded transformers of our cities put these conditions into their own language, saying they are interested in situations where "the municipal administration treats labor and management evenly."[11] These basic concerns are essentially the same as those we identified for corporate location decisions in Chapter 2. The Urban Land Institute (ULI) has been active in promoting downtown areas as good places for business development—accenting the existing transportation networks, the unemployed central-city work force, and the pro-business attitude of central-city governments as attractive.[12]

Behind the Scenes: The Local Power Structure How does a typical central business district (CBD) project develop? A ULI handbook describes the process as follows:

> *Individual businessmen, developers, or investors may be the first to recognize and pursue the opportunity for development of a project in the CBD. This fairly random operation of private market forces may be assisted by public or quasi-public groups seeking to stimulate downtown revitalization, perhaps to stabilize the economy.*[13]

Note the ULI emphasis on the privately controlled character of CBD development. In Chapter 1 we discussed the emphasis that urban analysts such as Mollenkopf, Gurr, and King have placed on the origination of redevelopment projects by local government officials. While this political entrepreneurship does indeed take place, the ULI quote suggests a more common process of project origination. Most often, the CBD redevelopment process is coordinated and managed by a growth coalition centered around developers, landowners, and executives of industrial and banking corporations, who are assisted by other private groups and by local and state government officials.

Formally, every city is guided by government officials—the mayor, city council, zoning commission, and planning commission. Behind the scenes, however, we commonly find a less visible "government" by business leaders and organizations that influence actual governmental decisions. In Los Angeles, for example, a powerful be-hind-the-scenes organization of business leaders for many years shaped much private and governmental decision making. At the heart of this group were powerful local corporations such as the *Los Angeles Times*. Its owner, Otis Chandler, once said, "I think the *Times* is the only thing in Los Angeles that brings cohesion to the entire area. Even more than the mayor, the City Council, the Board of Supervisors. It is the only thing that tells you what is happening every day and what might happen. It's a tremendous force."[14] The *Times* executives and organization were indeed powerful in Los Angeles, but they have shared power with other corporate leaders; their united efforts reshaped that city's physical form. In the 1970s a downtown development group was formed, the Committee for Central City Planning (CCCP), Inc., made up of top executives from major downtown businesses. They persuaded the city council to help pay for a study of downtown development. Approved by city officials in the mid-1970s, the new plan proposed business-oriented redevelopment that would be subsidized substantially by county taxes. The *Los Angeles Times* supported the plan, playing up its advantages in editorials.[15]

Newspaper executives are frequently part of the local power structure. Many newspapers are controlled by local wealthy families or, increasingly now, by large corporate chains. Their editorial boards are drawn from a variety of sources, including industrial executives, journalists, and former government officials sympathetic to growth. For instance, in the late 1980s Herbert Sturz, a seven-year veteran of the New York City Planning Commission, became a member of the editorial board of the *New York Times*, a paper one knowledgeable planner has called "conspicuously kind to the planning commission despite increasing public criticism."[16] Newspapers in general are heavily dependent on local business advertising, and for this reason tend to be aggressive defenders of local growth and downtown development. Since World War II, leading business people in many other cities have organized themselves to prepare central-area redevelopment plans: the Dallas Citizens Council, the Central Area Committee of Chicago, Civic Progress in St. Louis, the Allegheny Conference in Pittsburgh, the Civic Conference in Boston, and the Greater Philadelphia Movement. Business leaders are the heart of most local growth coalitions; they meet privately to set out economic development and downtown redevelopment agendas for their cities and commonly coordinate their activities with the press and sympathetic politicians.

Government Subsidies   In the situations where central-city development projects are not too risky and profits are likely to be substantial, developers and other investors may proceed with modest government involvement. Where risks are greater, however, even the most conservative executives in major corporations will often seek out some type of government assistance. In many cities these executives are not willing to put up most of the front-end money for central-city development; they prefer for local governments to pay for some or most of the utilities, land clearance, market surveys, and building analyses, as well as, in some cases, to provide low-interest development loans.[17] In recent years a range of private-public partnerships have been created to develop central-city projects. We will examine these in detail in Chapter 9.

    In unemployment-troubled Detroit, to take one important example, General Motors (GM) executives expressed their desire to build a new Cadillac plant rather than rehabilitate an older one, so city officials worked with GM to clear and provide land east of downtown, cleared at taxpayer expense—a project with serious human costs. A *New York Times* story described the scene:

> *Ann and Andrew Giannini have, they say, everything they want: a home they enjoy, neighbors who watch over one another, stores within walking distance....But the Gianninis live in the path of a major project designed to preserve jobs for Detroit and to help revitalize the American auto-mobile industry....Under present plans the site would be sold or leased to G.M. at prices comparable to those of open land in suburban or rural areas.[18]*

One Detroit City Council member commented on the dilemma of city administrators: "I think we are so desperate for jobs we will do anything. The multi-national corporations are doing the economic planning for the world."[19] At stake was the destruction of Poletown, a large multiethnic neighborhood, cleared at public expense to provide land for private use. The newly cleared land was the result of bulldozing a stable, racially integrated, residential neighborhood with 3,500 people in 1,500 homes. General Motors was unresponsive when a local citizens' group proposed alternative sites for this much-needed job-creating auto plant.

Federal Aid for Development One important federal subsidy for private development has been provided by the 1977 Housing and Urban Development Act, which authorized Urban Development Action Grants (UDAGs) to local governments for development in areas with specified poverty, housing, and unemployment problems. Between 1977 and 1987, the federal government spent nearly $4.5 billion on nearly 3,000 UDAG projects in 1,180 cities. Local governments are supposed to use the grants to encourage private investment in depressed areas. Instead, UDAGs have frequently been used for the streets, utilities, and other services needed for various types of private residential, commercial, and industrial projects benefitting businesses and affluent urbanites. For example, in 1987 Cleveland officials received six UDAGs. One went toward a supermarket; another was a $7.7 million grant for an office building. Yet another was awarded to assist in the development of a neighborhood shopping center.[20] The *Wall Street Journal* has noted abuses connected with UDAG spending; "ski resorts in Stowe, Vt., posh hotels in Newport, R.I., and the headquarters of the Kellogg Co. in Battle Creek, Mich." were all built with UDAG money; the program was described as "a lush picnic basket for private developers."[21]

During the redevelopment of central business districts, city governments have frequently been pressured to provide a variety of subsidies and support—parking facilities, tax abatements, public services, zoning permissions, and administrative assistance in finding federal grants and loans. Support has included debatable zoning changes. A typical situation involves a developer requesting a variance from planning officials to construct a building in excess of existing height requirements. In many cities controversy surrounds the politics of these zoning variances. Edward L. Sadowsky, a former New York City Council member, has said that the zoning variance process "always opens you up to charges of cronyism and corruption. And you sometimes allow both aesthetic and environmental values to be sacrificed for some cash."[22] Tax abatements, which reduce a development's taxes (often for long periods), are a major subsidy sought by central-city developers. For example, the city of St. Louis has relied heavily on the use of tax abatements for most downtown projects for the past two decades and for many residential and commercial improvements throughout the city. In Cleveland major tax abatements have been provided for bank and hotel projects. Missouri's abatement law permits local governments to waive all or part of the property taxes spent on improvements for a maximum of 25 years and allows developers to use the governmental power of eminent domain within city-approved redevelopment areas to force property owners to sell their land for a "fair market price." Even though school district officials and others have complained about the drain on local property tax revenues, many local government administrators persist in granting long-term tax abatements. Indeed, in numerous cities downtown redevelopment has in effect been subsidized by school children, whose inferior school facilities deteriorate because necessary tax revenues have been reduced.[23]

Other Taxpayer Subsidies   Tax credits for preserving historic structures are, in effect, another subsidy for developers. Many commentators see historic preservation as providing "a new alternative vision of the future downtown," making downtown areas more "fun" for middle- and upper-income residents. Since the early 1980s the historic tax credits program has allowed developers to recover a fifth of their renovation costs in tax credits, provided the renovated buildings are put to commercial use. The impact of these credits has stimulated much investment in historic rehabilitation projects. As one trade publication has noted, "Couple that [the tax credit] with the availability of Urban Development Action Grants (UDAGs)…and you have a strong basis for why developers, including those specializing in retail properties, have gotten into the rehab business in a big way."[24] In numerous cities developers, usually assisted by local governments, have built developments centered around rehabilitated historic structures in order to attract (white) suburbanites downtown on evenings and weekends. One such redevelopment project has been called the "festival marketplace," which involves the rehabilitation of old buildings into a complex of chic shops and restaurants such as the Faneuil Hall Marketplace (Boston), Ghirardelli Square (San Francisco), Harborplace (Baltimore), and South Street Seaport (New York). These have generally become profitable retail centers and have persuaded some uncritical planners that they are creating new civic "gathering places" and "dramatically changing the image of American cities."[25]

Local government officials have gone to extraordinary lengths to subsidize private enterprise. Business interests in Greenville, South Carolina, offered to build a hotel, office building, and retail facilities for the Greenville Commons project only if the city administrators would build support facilities—including a convention center, a parking garage, and a landscaped atrium. The city officials put out $7.5 million, while business interests risked only $4 million for the hotel and office buildings. Similarly, in the Fountain Square project in Cincinnati, Ohio, the city government spent $18 million of the $84 million for that large project, including the costs of land clearance and packaging and a parking garage.[26]

In these various ways, taxpayers have subsidized business redevelopment projects whose profits are privately appropriated by businesses. An important issue here is whether the private developers would have invested without government incentives. A strong argument can be made that many corporate recipients do not in fact require the government assistance. For example, the Des Moines city government applied for a $4 million UDAG to help a private developer with an 840,000-square-foot shopping mall. The mall developer readily acknowledged that the mall would have been built without the grant. Yet he noted that the federal money would enable him to build a "much nicer project."[27]

In addition, in Missouri and elsewhere state legislatures have passed laws easing downtown redevelopment by giving developers quicker access to the power of "eminent domain," the traditional governmental power to take private property for an ostensibly public purpose. Removing "blight" has been the usual rationalization for using this major governmental power to force residents to move. In recent years some state governments have expanded the definition of blight to make governmental clearance of land for *private* projects easier. Eminent domain has been used not just for public projects such as highways but also for private development projects. For example, a Michigan law, the Downtown Development Authority Act, permits government authorities to demolish buildings and acquire property for private economic development. A city government can use its powers to condemn property and transfer it to a public development authority, which can in turn prepare it for private development. Other states, including Ohio, have passed similar legislation. A basic objective of these arrangements is to pass along the right of eminent domain from elected officials to public agencies run by nonelected officials largely for the benefit of private developers or directly to developers themselves. These nonelected agencies are easier to shield from citizens' democratic input than are elected officials.[28]

Growth Cities and Decreasing Developer Subsidies: The New Linkage Policies
Since the late 1970s, in certain cities with expanding private economies, the number and extent of developer subsidies have been significantly curtailed, or developers have been required to pay "exactions" or "linkage development fees" in order to receive building authorization from local government officials. We have noted already in Chapter 1 the community welfare concessions made by developers in Santa Monica. In Chapters 9 and 10 we will discuss concessions made by developers in other cities such as Boston and San Francisco. We should note, however, that many of the most substantial linked development contracts seem to have come in

prosperous California cities, in part as a result of the declining tax base resulting from property tax limitation laws such as Proposition 13. City governments without a substantial tax base find it much more difficult to provide the usual array of subsidies for private development. In addition, the major linkage concessions from development interests have for the most part come in high-growth metropolitan areas. Linkage policy does not seem to work as well in cities without expanding private economies.

GENTRIFICATION: A CLOSER LOOK

Locations for Residential Renovation   Gentrification is a process of residential development that often accompanies industrial and commercial development projects in central-city areas. It involves housing renovation and an increased movement of middle- and upper-income people into central-city areas, pushing out poorer residents. By the late 1970s a Department of Housing and Urban Development survey estimated that renovation projects were taking place in a quarter of western cities, 43 percent of north-central cities, half of northeastern cities, and the majority of southern cities.[29] The most likely areas for gentrification and housing revitalization are in larger cities, in the Northeast and South, in neighborhoods near central business districts and on mass transit lines, in areas with housing built originally to the standards of affluent families, and in neighborhoods with good governmental services such as libraries and hospitals. Phillip Clay's study of 195 neighborhoods in 30 cities found many cases of gentrification. The majority were neighborhoods with one- and two-family houses; newly rehabilitated housing was priced well above the central-city average. These areas were near commercial, business, or governmental projects.[30]

Residential gentrification has been commonplace in corporate headquarters cities, including New York, Chicago, San Francisco, and Houston. Known for their skyscrapers, luxury apartments, and thousands of white-collar workers, these cities have experienced much housing revitalization. Corporate headquarters cities tend to be growth areas for professional and managerial jobs. The office and residential area requirements of these cities are different than those of industrial-factory cities such as Jersey City and Youngstown. Not surprisingly, housing redevelopment varies greatly by region and city character. Predominantly manufacturing cities in the Midwest and Northeast have seen less gentrification.[31]

The Gentrification Pattern   Drawing on a study of gentrifying areas in Washington, D.C., Dennis Gale has suggested that housing change and neighborhood resettlement go through three stages.[32] We can elaborate on Gale's typology a bit:

Stage 1: A few pioneering households migrate to a deteriorating area. Among them are many young professionals. These initial "resettlers" often supply their own funds, because banking institutions are reluctant to extend credit in risky areas. Because the number of newcomers is small, the displacement of indigenous residents is minimized.

Stage 2: After a year or two, some realtors, developers, and local media "discover" the area. Now, larger numbers of people become attracted to its accessibility and investment potential. They buy houses and renovate them. Financing is still difficult to obtain. Newcomers are disproportionately young couples, and those in professional, technical, and managerial occupations are overrepresented. As their numbers grow, tensions with lower-income residents increase. Rents are raised and tenants are evicted to provide renovated housing for higher income households. Some commercial shops such as boutiques move into the area. Local government begins to pay attention to the quality of services. Developers and speculators begin to buy up property for resale.

Stage 3: Developers and speculators are operating widely. Resettlement increases at a rapid rate. Indigenous residents are squeezed out of the neighborhood completely. Renovation is now a large-scale process. Older couples with children join the ranks; they are more likely to have moved from the suburbs. Local government may adopt a more active role in helping to advertise the area; more improvements are made in local services. Banking institutions become more interested; financing is easier to secure for renovation.

According to one analysis, those who arrive in the last stage lack the diversity and inspiration of earlier gentrifiers; the original settlers "attract mobs of merely stylish followers who diminish the diversity and sweep away every last speck of grit. The old-line residents and the anchors of their communities—the hardware stores, the cobblers, the taverns—are driven out by suddenly high rents. Gentrification is not fun for everyone."[33] This portrayal exaggerates the virtues of early-stage gentrifiers, but it does accurately depict the last stage. We can flesh out this portrait with some specific examples. The Capitol Hill area in Washington, D.C., began gentrification in the 1960s, and several other neighborhoods subsequently started the process. New homebuyers were mostly white couples and individuals without children; most were college graduates; there were no black couples. The Capitol Hill neighborhood is a typical seesaw investment area. The Victorian houses, once occupied by affluent whites, were abandoned to poorer blacks in the 1950s and 1960s. In the late 1960s the area began to change. White professional families, preferring city life and excitement, moved in; builders and developers bought up and renovated the housing. This white immigration forced black families out as landlords sold houses to speculators and developers. More recently, this process of gentrifying investment has spread throughout the city. Washington, D.C., has numerous neighborhoods that have undergone gentrification, with thousands of affluent white families moving in and thousands of poorer, disproportionately nonwhite, families moving out. In 1984 the Census Bureau reported that the population of Washington, D.C., had actually stopped declining for the first year in 16 years.[34]

An ironic example of gentrification can be glimpsed in San Francisco's Haight-Ashbury, a once vibrant counterculture ("hippie") community, which had declined into a drug-scarred ghetto by the early 1970s. Once again, most of the gentrifiers who came during the 1970s and 1980s were young professionals. They brought a new life-style to the area; head shops and crash pads were replaced with professional offices, boutiques, and restored townhouses. Older counterculture residents, as well as poor and black families, were forced to move to other areas of the city. Yet those displaced were the very people who had worked hard to improve the public services and who added the diversity to the area that attracted the gentrifying newcomers.[35]

Speculators and Developers   Speculators and developers commonly play a critical role in the gentrification process. A Washington, D.C., study found speculators combing "neighborhoods on foot and by telephone just ahead of the restoration movement, making attractive cash offers to owners."[36] If owners do not wish to sell, government building inspectors may be called in by the potential buyers; the inspectors may order expensive repairs, thereby forcing the sale. For example, in one 2-year period one-fifth of all recorded property sales in Washington, D.C., involved two or more sales of the same property, a sign of speculation. A National Urban Coalition report found significant speculative activity in the 44 cities it surveyed.[37]

Developers play an important part in gentrification, sometimes early, sometimes later. Central-city gentrification can occur when local developers purchase buildings at a bargain price, obtain loans to rehabilitate them, and then market the renovated housing to higher-income households at a profit. One survey of 30 cities found developers playing an integral role at a relatively early point in 40 percent of the gentrifying districts. Developers also become active later in the gentrifying maneuvers; many have access to the capital needed to spur changes in a community with little or no participation by local residents in the decision-making process. In some cases the executives of development firms play the role of speculators, buying properties in a deteriorating area and waiting for land appreciation. They may or may not begin renovation of housing later. In addition to speculators and developers, there are other important actors in the gentrification drama. Much gentrification occurs when banks become willing to make loans to older neighborhoods they formerly had abandoned ("redlined"). Decisions by finance capitalists can determine whether or not gentrification will occur on a large scale. Moreover, government officials have commonly played their part in spurring development of gentrifying areas by providing improvements in services and advertising the neighborhoods.[38]

URBAN DISPLACEMENT

Displacement transpires when people are forced to move by local housing or neighborhood conditions beyond their control, conditions that make housing hazardous or prohibitively expensive. Urban displacement, which is common in central cities, has been caused by a variety of factors, including gentrification, airport and highway construction, public urban renewal, and school construction. A congressional *Displacement Report*, assessing the impact of gentrification and other housing-related causes of urban displacement, estimated that at least 370,000 households were displaced in metropolitan areas each year. The private sector accounted for most of the displacement.[39] We can distinguish between three different types of private displacement: displacement by condominium construction and conversion, gentrification displacement, and abandoned area displacement.

Condominiums and Displacement Much central-city growth has involved the conversion by developers of apartments for rent to condominiums, as well as construction of new condominiums. By the late 1970s potential homebuyers, many of them young first-time purchasers, began to seek other housing alternatives as prices for single-family homes rapidly escalated. One increasingly common option has been for young people to stay at, or return to, their parents' homes. Thus the proportion of young people aged 18–34 living in their parents' home increased from just over one-fifth in 1960 to just under one-third in 1983. In 1984 fully 37 percent of children aged 18–29 lived in their parents' home.[40] The other alternatives for the young have been to compete for the limited pool of affordable apartments or to buy apartment condominiums. Some new condominium buildings have been constructed, and many older apartment buildings have been converted by developers from rental units into condominiums for sale. There were few condominium units before 1970. The number of apartments built as condominiums increased to 1.3 million by 1975 and to more than 4 million by the mid-1980s. Condominium construction has exceeded detached housing construction in many areas. Moreover, just under half a million existing apartment units were converted to condominiums between 1970 and 1980; more than a millon more were converted by the mid-1980s. Condominium and co-op sales exceeded 360,000 in 1987 and were selling at an annual rate of 408,000 in the first quarter of 1988.[41]

An example from Philadelphia sheds light on the impact of the condominium conversion process on low- and moderate-income households. In that city an apartment building worth $25 million was sold to a condominium development corporation for $50 million. That firm converted the rental apartments, with little renovation, into condominiums for sale. Reportedly, a typical rental charge was about $560 per month before conversion, but afterward the total payment (for mortgage and interest, taxes, and fees) was $1,200 per month. Most existing renters have to leave such a building because they cannot afford the higher cost. Profits from condo conversion can be substantial. For example, profits from one owner's conversions in Chicago have been estimated at 44 percent for one complex and nearly 100 percent for another. Because of this high level of profitability, banks were eager to finance conversions at high interest rates.[42]

Tenants bear the brunt of the human costs when apartment buildings are converted to condominiums. Peter Dreier and John Atlas report that 50 to 75 percent of existing tenants cannot afford condo-converted apartments, because, as the example above suggests, monthly costs often double after conversion. Even when condo converters provide discounts to existing tenants, the cost for households skyrockets. In most cases low- and middle-income families will never again be able to afford housing in such apartment buildings. They are displaced and are forced to look elsewhere, often finding only inadequate accommodations available. Sometimes the end result is an additional increment in the nation's homeless count. As *Time* noted in 1986, "The new homeless are the economically dispossessed...they include blue-collar families who have been forced out of apartments when their low-income housing is converted to condominiums."[43]

Most condo conversions have been in large cities. One study puts the amount of rental stock converted in the 37 largest metropolitan areas at a rate seven times higher than that for the rest of the United States. Federal housing authorities have estimated that half of all families may live in condominiums by the year 2000. The concentration of condo activity in major cities has sometimes led to an oversupply similar to the glut of office space discussed in Chapter 4; in some cities landlord-developers are offering waivers of monthly maintenance payments, modest down payments, and low-interest rates to lure condo customers. In New York City, the Zeckendorf Company, Manhattan's largest developer of condominiums, cut its usual 10 percent down payment in half for condominium purchases in a building on Broadway.[44]

One factor likely to spur further conversion of rental apartments to condominiums is the expiration of the federal law that for a time created developer incentives to build low- and moderate-income housing. In the late 1960s the federal government began to offer developers subsidies—

tax breaks, federal mortgage insurance, and subsidized low-interest loans—if they would charge below-market rents to tenants seeking afford able housing. But as part of the deal with developers, the agreements covering this valuable housing are now expiring. With expiration comes the developers' option to convert the units into rental housing or condo miniums for upper-income families. Although it is not clear how many low- and moderate-income tenants will be displaced by conversions, the signs are not encouraging. For instance, in Chicago, owners of a building in the Lakeview section of the city hiked rents 230 percent in 1987 after they paid off their 20-year low-interest loan. Elderly residents, confronted with a jump in rent from $300 to $750, were forced to moved out. Moreover, the industry publication *Mortgage Banking* has estimated that the loss of federally assisted low- and moderate-income housing sites to condo con versions, cooperatives, and upper-income housing could range anywhere from 154,000 to 1 million units. By the year 2005 the owners of up to 1.7 million units will be eligible to end contractual arrangements and convert their properties.[45]

On occasion, the condo conversion process has been met by grass roots resistance. The practice of mailing "buy or move" letters has spurred tenants to form protest organizations across the nation. Pressure by tenants' groups on legislatures and city councils has resulted in modest laws to protect renters from "condomania" in many cities and states. One outgrowth of the controversy surrounding the social impact of conver sions was the preparation of a special federal report, entitled *The Conver sion of Rental Housing to Condominiums and Cooperatives.* Yet this report played down the impact of conversions on displaced renters. Federal housing authorities acknowledged the extent of displacement, but gave their stamp of approval to the condominium trend, thus reflecting the owners', not the tenants', perspective.[46]

Gentrification Displacement Condo construction and condo apartment conversions are one source of displacement. A related source is gentrifica tion, which as we have seen often involves central-city housing renovation and rehabilitated home sales to middle- and upper-income people moving into central-city areas, thereby pushing out the former, and usually poorer, residents. Estimates of gentrification-related displacement are imprecise. Grier and Grier have concluded that displacement by the private renewal processes affects a small number of families. Yet an estimate by Cushing Dolbeare, a national housing consultant, has put the number displaced by gentrification at approximately 100,000 per year.[47]

Some social scientists such as sociologist John Kasarda see "displace ment" as a "loaded term." Kasarda argues that "from the standpoint of the city, the movement represents neighborhood upgrading and urban rein vestment." He criticizes those analysts who worry so much about poor renters that they do not envision the advantages of gentrification and argues that from the standpoint of the city as a whole gentrification represents a positive revitalization.[48] However, this argument does not bear up under close scrutiny. Urbanites are not a homogeneous group and do not benefit uniformly from these development processes. Among those who benefit most from gentrification are profit-oriented speculators and developers and the new affluent families moving in. Gentrification brings some higher-income people into the core areas of central cities, but it also engenders problems of social justice. Low- and moderate-income families that are pushed aside during urban "revitalization" suffer. Thus the National Urban Coalition found displacement of low- and moderate-income families in two-thirds of the gentrified neighborhoods it examined. A Portland, Oregon, study of displacement found that about 3,000 families were forced to move involuntarily each year, with 40 percent displaced by central-city rehabilitation. Most of the displaced were young renters between the ages of 25 and 35; 40 percent had incomes below $7,500. Those doing the displacing tended to have higher incomes.[49]

Gentrification creates "little gilded islands" and forces low- and moderate-income families into competition for housing in a decreasing number of central-city areas. Displaced tenants (less often homeowners) tend to move to nearby poverty areas, to move several times, and to pay higher rents in their new housing. Some of those displaced by private redevelopment are the same families displaced in previous decades by public urban renewal projects. Under the private system of real estate capitalism, the private housing market does not have to provide moderate-rent accommodations elsewhere for the displaced. Moreover, a move has been found to be high on the list of causes of major stress for people of any age or income level, but especially for the aged and the poor.[50] Few urban observers in the late 1980s were optimistic about reversing gentrification-related displacement. Referring to the continuing gentrification of central-city apartments, William Apgar of the Harvard/MIT Joint Center, noted that "America is increasingly becoming a nation of housing haves and have-nots." And James Roark, Mayor of Charleston, West Virginia, and a National League of Cities housing specialist, suggested that "over the next few years, hundreds of thousands of families will be displaced."[51]

Abandonment Displacement Many U.S. cities have central-city areas that look like the bombed-out cities of Europe after World War II; many houses are boarded up or stand with their windows broken out. Fires break out periodically. Families struggle to get by, living under substandard conditions in dilapidated and deteriorating houses owned by absentee landlords. When they must leave, their houses frequently become additions to the pool of abandoned housing. The famous South Bronx area in New York

City, with its extensive abandoned housing, is similar to areas in Brooklyn, Seattle, Cleveland, St. Louis, and Los Angeles.[52]

This large-scale abandonment of central-city housing is stereotypically viewed as being the fault of the tenants, who allegedly destroy the buildings. But large-scale abandonment is part of the disinvestment process central to urban real estate capitalism. Some abandonment is the result of homeowners or small landlords getting in over their heads, but most results from ownership of buildings by a series of landlords who, one after another, let the property run down. Typically, this is a conscious activity by absentee landlords looking for profits. Buildings are often bought with a small down payment and a big mortgage; tenants are charged rents, but little or no maintenance is provided. Often utility bills are not paid by the investor-landlord, who until recently has received major depreciation deductions that reduced taxes on these housing investments. He or she soon sells the property to another profit-seeking investor, and so on, until the last landlord abandons the dilapidated property. These "disinvestment" profit makers commonly walk away from their deteriorated investments, leaving urban taxpayers with the community costs. A *Washington Post* story gave an example of a 52-unit apartment complex abandoned by a landlord who owed the city $140,000 in unpaid utility bills and back taxes. Another obvious example of some real estate investors taking deliberate steps to destroy central-city housing can be seen in the hiring of arsonists to destroy residential buildings for insurance money, a process that not only has destroyed buildings but taken tenants' lives in many cities.[53]

URBAN REDEVELOPMENT AS INSTITUTIONALIZED RACISM

Government Urban Renewal   Central-city disinvestment and reinvestment are part of the dynamics of urban racial relations. Whether it is brought by urban renewal, gentrification, or other means, the negative impact of central-city redevelopment has frequently fallen on black, Hispanic, and Asian-American communities. We saw this in the case of the Turner family in the opening paragraph of this chapter. Ironically, the 1949 Housing Act, which legitimated massive urban renewal, originally envisioned the use of federal money for "slum" clearance and the provision of *decent low-rent replacement housing* by private enterprise. Instead, during the 1950s and 1960s the new law created a federally subsidized program, called "urban renewal," that bulldozed large central-city areas, usually for resale to developers uninterested in providing such residential housing (see Chapter 9). A heavy price was paid by central-city residents. Some of those displaced were moderate-income whites, especially those in recent immigrant groups. Thus in the late 1950s, the Boston Redevelopment Agency uprooted 7,000 residents from the city's West End, most of whom were Italian-Americans. About 2,700 low-rent housing units were demolished to make way for 2,300 luxury apartments. However, more than three-quarters of those displaced by redevelopment programs have been black or Hispanic. For example, in the late 1960s, 2,500 mainly black and Hispanic residents were forced to leave 20 acres of land in Brooklyn set aside for urban renewal. Although 2,400 affordable units were planned to replace the lost housing stock there, only 800 units were actually constructed—and those were in high-rise buildings not completed until a decade later.[54]

Since the end of the governmental program officially called urban renewal in the 1970s, other governmental and private redevelopment programs, as well as the activities of real estate speculators, have continued to force black, Hispanic, and other minority families out of one residential area after another so that white businesses and affluent families could convert the land for their use. For example, for that most famous of black urban areas—Harlem in New York City—estimates of the number of blacks displaced by whites between 1970 and the mid-1980s have ranged up to 30,000. Philadelphia's black areas have experienced similar displacement. In the late nineteenth century the famous sociologist W. E. B. Du Bois conducted a major study, published as *The Philadelphia Negro*, of the all-black area of Philadelphia called the Seventh Ward. Today he might not believe its changed appearance; that Seventh Ward is now Society Hill, a virtually all-white redeveloped community with homes starting at about $150,000.[55]

Uneven Racial Development   Since World War II, a basic dynamic creating racial polarization in U.S. cities has been the movement of white middle-income families to the suburbs, leaving behind a substantially poorer, often minority, population in the central cities. As we have documented throughout this book, this suburban migration of whites has been stimulated by the primary- and secondary-circuit investment decisions of industrial corporations, banks, and developers and has been assisted by federal government subsidies for home mortgages and road building. In this uneven development process, capital has flowed to housing in the suburbs and away from housing development in the central cities. Yet a recent phase of the cycle, capital has been flowing back into certain central-city areas, into the construction of new commercial and housing projects. Housing is renovated to accommodate white professional and managerial families returning to central-city areas.

Norman Nager highlights the contrast here: "Serious attempts are being made to make the city attractive to these people. When whites moved out of the cities, deterioration was allowed to occur by the public as well as the private sectors."[56] Streets, schools, and parks were allowed to deteriorate. Now the whites moving back demand a change. They desire neighborhoods and housing comparable in quality to what they, or their parents, had in the suburbs. Meanwhile, the land occupied by minority Americans becomes a prime target for real estate speculation and development. In this way the disinvestment-investment process has a racially discriminatory impact. This central-city seesawing may be rational from the points of view of profit-seeking white developers and the retail corporations and affluent homeowners they serve, but it is clearly irrational for the minority urbanites whose lives are uprooted. Here again the dominant exchange-value concerns of the development interests come into direct conflict with the use-value concerns of the poorer central-city families and neighborhoods.

Speculation and Displacement New York's Harlem, originally constructed for middle-income whites, but inhabited almost entirely by blacks between the 1920s and the 1980s, is one locality where real estate speculators have become conspicuous in the last decade. In one 5-year period the number of building sales doubled annually from 503 in 1980 to 1,131 in 1985. During the same period the average price per building rose from $130,000 to $230,000. During the late 1980s there were more daily property transfers in Harlem than elsewhere in Manhattan. Speculators in Harlem vary widely, from white physicians living in other parts of Manhattan, to long-term residents of the area, to foreign investors. One of Harlem's active traders in land and buildings has been John F. Arcella. In 1980 Arcella bought a building on West 116th Street for $6,000; 2 years later, he sold it to other Harlem speculators for $190,750, making a huge profit. Eventually, after changing hands five times, the building sold for more than $600,000. Between 1980 and 1983, Arcella bought 15 properties, most for less than $10,000. According to Arcella, he never makes money operating the buildings he buys; rather, his profits come from "flipping." As he relates it, "believe me, I've flipped a lot of buildings." Exchange value is the dominant concern. What Arcella and the other speculators in Harlem real estate ignore is the use value of the land and buildings for the poor black residents. There are major human costs to flipping. Exchange-value-motivated speculation and safe, affordable housing for existing residents seldom go together in Harlem or any area. Not unexpectedly, the aforementioned building that was flipped so many times accumulated 142 uncorrected building-code violations during the process, including exposed wiring, rodents, water leaks, and missing windows. Existing residents were less important than the future use, and probable destruction, of the building. Tenants even paid their rent to a corporation that had neither offices nor a telephone; this absentee arrangement translated into maintenance problems that went unresolved for long periods.[57]

Ironically, speculative activity in Harlem has, in recent years, been fueled by the release of city-controlled (for example, formerly abandoned) housing. The New York City government owns much of Harlem's housing stock and, after curtailing its program of selling the tax-delinquent properties for several years in the 1980s, has resumed public auctions of Harlem real estate in the late 1980s. Harlem's city-aided speculative and redevelopment processes displace its long-term, usually black, residents, who are as a rule replaced by whites. As Samuel Freedman notes, "the implicit question in renewing Harlem is whether it will be done for the ultimate gain of whites."[58]

CONCLUSION

U.S. cities, and their constituent communities, grow and decline as part of a process of uneven investment in various parts of the secondary circuit of real estate, with some areas of cities getting much needed capital and other areas being neglected by investors—a process that reflects the exchange-value goals of local and national industrial, development, and banking capitalists and the use- and exchange-value goals of the affluent managers and professionals moving back to central cities. The spatial seesawing of capital investments in real estate developments, from one region to another, from central cities to suburbs, from one suburb to another, and then from the suburbs back to central cities, is a central and defining feature of our capitalistic system. Earlier we cited a *Time* article heralding the redevelopment tide washing across many central cites. Yet even that report noted that "many cities have not revived. Detroit is comatose, Gary, Ind., is not much healthier and development in Oakland is lagging."[59] In the uneven investment process some central cities have benefited much more than others.

In this chapter we have focused on the processes of uneven investment and development within central cities. In Chapters 9 and 10 we will describe citizen efforts to force changes in these patterns by forging linked development. In the next three chapters we will turn to the development of the U.S. highway and freeway systems, and then to the decentralization and suburbanization of cities that such governmental transport investments facilitated.

NOTES

1. Brad Edmondson, "The Midwest: St. Paul's American Beauty," *American Demographics* 8 (May 1986): 44.
2. Kurt Anderson, "Spiffing up the Urban Heritage," *Time,* November 23, 1987, 82.
3. Joseph D. Whitaker, "Convalescence of an Area Causes Pain for the Poor," *Washington Post,* May 29, 1977, A8.

4. T. D. Allman, "The Urban Crisis Leaves Town," *Harper's* 257 (December 1978): 41–56; Horace Sutton, "America Falls in Love with Its Cities—Again," *Saturday Review*, August 1978, 16–21.

5. Kurt Anderson, Daniel S. Levy, and Edwin Reingold, "Bringing the City Back to Life," *Time*, November 23, 1987, 74.

6. Richard Muth, in *San Francisco Chronicle*, January 30, 1978, as quoted in Chester W. Hartman, Dennis Keating, and Richard LeGates, *Displacement: How to Fight It* (Berkeley: National Housing Law Project, 1982), p. 27.

7. Robert Gottlieb and Irene Wolt, *Thinking Big: The Story of the Los Angeles Times* (New York: G.E. Putnam's Sons, 1977), pp. 260–268, 365, 530–531.

8. Hartman, Keating, and LeGates, *Displacement*, p. 6.

9. David Whitman and Michael Bosc, "The Coming of the Couch People," *U.S. News and World Report*, August 3, 1987, 19; Elizabeth Ehrlich, "Homelessness: The Policy Failure Haunting America," *Business Week*, April 25, 1988, 134.

10. Robert A. Beauregard, "The Redevelopment of the Advanced Capitalist City." Paper presented at the conference on New Perspectives on Urban Political Economy, Washington, D.C., American University, May 1981, p. 17.

11. Urban Land Institute, *Downtown Development Handbook* (Washington, D.C.: Urban Land Institute, 1980), p. 15.

12. Urban Land Institute, *Industrial Development Handbook* (Washington, D.C.: Urban Land Institute, 1975), p. 227.

13. Urban Land Institute, *Downtown Development Handbook*, p. 39. See also pp. 59, 93–98.

14. Gottlieb and Wolt, *Thinking Big*, pp. 524–526.

15. Ibid., pp. 532–534.

16. Howard Zisser, "Bright Lights, Big City...Limited Vision?" *Planning* 53 (March 1987): 10.

17. Urban Land Institute, *Downtown Development Handbook*, p. 50.

18. The *New York Times* story (September 15, 1980) is quoted in Hartman, Keating, and LeGates, *Displacement*, p. 100.

19. Ibid.

20. Robert M. Byrne, Douglas R. Porter, and Elizabeth D. Baker, "Urban Development Action Grants," *Urban Land*, June 1980, 3–10; James Kilpatrick, "Housing Bill Exceeds U.S. Responsibility," *St. Louis Post-Dispatch*, November 23, 1987, 3B.

21. *Wall Street Journal* (editorial), "Urban Slush Fund," *Wall Street Journal*, May 18, 1988, 30.

22. David W. Dunlap, "New York City to Reassess Zoning Trade-offs," *New York Times*, January 11, 1988, 1.

23. Tim O'Neil, "Agency Weighing Fine-Tuning of City Tax Abatement," *St. Louis Post-Dispatch*, December 1, 1987, 6A; Charlene Prost, "Comeback City," *Planning* 51 (October 1985): 8.

24. Eric C. Peterson, "Rehabbing: Good Deals!" *Stores* 69 (May 1987): 77.

25. John Fondersmith, "Making Cities Fun: Downtown 2040," *The Futurist*, March/April 1988, 9–17; Anderson, Levy, and Reingold, "Bringing the City Back to Life," p. 79.

26. Urban Land Institute, *Downtown Development Handbook*, pp. 53–63.

27. *Wall Street Journal*, "Urban Slush Fund," p. 30.

28. Urban Land Institute, *Downtown Development Handbook*, pp. 16, 170–172.

29. J. Thomas Black, "Private-Market Housing Renovation in Central Cities: An Urban Land Institute Survey," in *Back to the City*, pp. 3–13; the HUD study is cited in "Back to City Moves Displace the Poor," *New York Times*, October 14, 1979, 51.

30. Philip L. Clay, *Neighborhood Renewal* (Lexington, Mass.: Lexington Books, 1979), pp. 18–25; see also Biliana Cicin-Sain, "The Costs and Benefits of Neighborhood Revitalization," in *Urban Revitalization, Urban Affairs Annual Review*, edited by D. B. Rosenthal (Beverly Hills: Sage, 1980), vol. 18, pp. 52–53.

31. David Perry and Alfred Watkins, "The Urban Renaissance for Business," *Nation*, March 1, 1980, 236–238; Franz Shurmann and Sandy Close, "The Emergence of Global City USA: New Affluence and a New Kind of Misery," *Progressive*, January 1979, 27–29; S. Gregory Lipton, "Evidence of Central-City Renewal," *Journal of the American Institute of Planners* 42 (April 1977): 138.

32. Dennis E. Gale, "Neighborhood Resettlement: Washington, D.C.," in *Back to the City*, edited by Shirley B. Laska and Daphne Spain (New York: Pergamon, 1980), pp. 106–109.

33. Anderson, Levy, and Reingold, "Bringing the City Back to Life," p. 82.

34. Ibid., pp. 96–97; Dennis E. Gale, *The Back-to-the City Movement Revisited: A Survey of Recent Homebuyers in the Capitol Hill Neighborhood of Washington, D.C.* (Washington, D.C.: Department of Urban and Regional Planning, George Washington University, 1977), pp. 2, 13–14; Frank White, III, "The Yuppies Are Coming: Young, Affluent Whites Are Taking over Urban Ghettos," *Ebony* 40 (April 1985): 155.

35. Marilyn Chase, "The Haight-Ashbury Turns into a Bastion of the Middle Class," *Wall Street Journal*, July 24, 1978, 1.

36. Carol Richards and Jonathan Rowe, "Restoring a City: Who Pays the Price?" *Working Papers for a New Society* 4 (Winter 1977): 196–197.

37. National Urban Coalition, *Displacement: City Neighborhoods in Transition* (Washington, D.C., 1978).

38. Clay, *Neighborhood Renewal*, pp. 30–37; Robert M. Byrne, Douglas R. Porter, and Elizabeth D. Baker, "Urban Development Action Grants," *Urban Land*, June 1980, 3–10.

39. Office of Policy Development and Research, Department of Housing and Urban Development, *Displacement Report* (Washington, D.C.: U.S. Government Printing Office, 1979), p. 23.
40. Cited in Al Carlson, "More Adults Making Home with Parents," *Springfield (Mo.) News-Leader,* March 24, 1988, 1D.
41. David Landis, "Condo Sales Hit Record Level in First Quarter," *USA Today,* May 27, 1988, 1B.
42. CBS *News,* "60 Minutes," March 29, 1981; Dreier and Atlas, "Condo Mania," p. 20; Robert Sheridan, "Condo Conversions," *Buildings* 75 (September 1979): 67.
43. Richard Stengel, "Down and Out and Dispossessed," *Time,* November 24, 1986, 27.
44. U.S. Department of Housing and Urban Development, *The Conversion of Rental Housing to Condominiums and Cooperatives: A National Study of Scope, Causes and Impacts* (Washington, D.C.: U.S. Government Printing Office, 1980); "Condominium Conversion Controls," *Society,* March/April 1984, 59; Peter Dreier and John Atlas, "Condo Mania," *Progressive,* March 1981, 19–21; Mark McCain, "Battling the Doldrums in Condo Sales," *New York Times,* December 13, 1987, R1.
45. Susan Dentzer, "A New Squeeze on Housing," *Newsweek,* August 10, 1987, 48; Mortgage Banking, "Federally-Assisted Housing: Now You See It, Soon You Won't?" *Mortgage Banking* 47 (July 1987): 26; Whitman and Bosc, "The Coming of the Couch People," p. 20.
46. U.S. Department of Housing and Urban Development, *The Conversion of Rental Housing to Condominiums and Cooperatives.*
47. George Grier and Eunice Grier, *Urban Displacement: A Reconnaissance* (Washington, D.C.: U.S. Department of Housing and Urban Development, March, 1978), p. iii; Cushing Dolbeare is quoted in "Fixing up Big-City Neighborhoods; Who Loses Out," *U.S. News and World Report,* February 19, 1979, 73.
48. John D. Kasarda, "The Implications of Contemporary Redistribution Trends for National Urban Policy," *Social Science Quarterly* 61 (December 1980): 394.
49. National Urban Coalition, *Displacement,* pp. 3–7.
50. Clay, *Neighborhood Renewal,* p. 31; Cicin-Sain, "The Costs and Benefits of Neighborhood Revitalization," pp. 69–72.
51. Cited in Whitman and Bosc, "The Coming of the Couch People," p. 19.
52. Brian D. Boyer, *Cities Destroyed for Cash* (Chicago: Follett, 1973), p. 3.
53. Hartman, Keating, and LeGates, *Displacement,* p. 62.
54. Boston Urban Study Group, "The City Vs. the Vault," *Dollars and Sense* 102 (December 1984): 7; Jennifer Stern, "A Project Grows in Brooklyn," *Planning* 53 (March 1987): 29.
55. White, "The Yuppies Are Coming," pp. 155–156.

56. Norman Nager, "Continuities of Urban Policy on the Poor," in *Back to the City*, edited by Shirley B. Laska and Daphne Spain (New York: Pergamon, 1980), p. 240.
57. Samuel G. Freedman, "Harlem and the Speculators: Big Profits but Little Renewal," *New York Times*, December 19, 1986, 1, 19; Martin Mittelstaedt, "The Gentrification of Harlem," *World Press Review*, April 1987, 44 (excerpted from the *Toronto Globe and Mail*, February 23, 1987).
58. Freedman, "Harlem and the Speculators: Big Profits but Little Renewal," p. 19.
59. Kurt Anderson, "Spiffing up the Urban Heritage," *Time*, November 23, 1987, 82.

6

AUTOS, HIGHWAYS, AND CITY DECENTRALIZATION

In all, the nation wasted an estimated 1.25 billion vehicle-hours and 1.38 billion gallons of gas in traffic congestion on limited access highways in 1984. By 2005, waste could soar to 6.91 billion hours and 7.32 billion gallons.[1]

"The name 'expressway' in Boston is clearly a misnomer, because it's a distressway" (Commuter).[2]

INTRODUCTION

Jamaica Plain is a blue-collar neighborhood southeast of downtown Boston. In 1970 its Lamartine Street had a diverse population of blacks, Puerto Ricans, and white Catholics. A colorful neighborhood, it was a residential area typical of older U.S. cities. Yet the business and political powers that be, those who decide on massive highway systems and where they go, picked Lamartine Street as the right-of-way for a section of Boston's Interstate 95 highway.

To find out what Lamartine Street was like, you have to look on the odd-numbered side of the street, because that's not part of the rite-of-way. It ranges from well kept two- and three-story houses to somewhat shabby three-deckers....Some houses on the even-numbered side also remain. Number 260, for example, is a yellow house with brown trim and a neat garden. Its occupants are an elderly couple. Their home is not needed for the highway. But they have seen and heard the bulldozers and the earth movers rip up their neighbors' homes and leave a flat dirt wasteland all the way to Number 226, a vacant space two blocks long and a block from the street to the railroad tracks.[3]

In U.S. cities people are regularly displaced by highway projects. People, particularly the poor, blacks and other minorities, and the elderly, make sacrifices. New roads often connect central cities to suburbs, or older suburbs to newer suburbs, thereby facilitating the movement of workers and real estate investments from one part of the city to another.

In earlier chapters we examined major real estate development projects in central cities. In the next few chapters we will look at the development projects farther out—the business parks, shopping centers, and omnipresent suburbs. As we noted in Chapter 1, most U.S. cities have become *multinucleated*, with major commercial, industrial, and residential areas no longer closely linked to or dependent upon the downtown center. Decentralization has become characteristic of our cities from coast to coast. Essential to decentralization has been the development and regular extension of an automobile-dominated transportation system serving businesses and the general citizenry, but mostly paid for by rank-and-file taxpayers. With and without citizen consent, corporate capitalists, industrialists and developers, and allied political officials have made key decisions fundamentally shaping the type of transportation system upon which all Americans now depend.

THE RISE AND FALL OF MASS RAIL TRANSIT

The Auto-Oil-Rubber Industrial Complex The auto-oil-rubber industrial complex has long been central to both the general economy and the urban transportation system in the United States. Automobile and auto-related industries provide a large proportion, sometimes estimated at one-sixth, of all jobs, although this proportion may be decreasing with the decline and stagnation in the auto industry over the last two decades. An estimated one-quarter to one-half of the land in central cities is used for the movement, storage, selling, and parking of automobiles, trucks, and buses. The expanding production of automobiles and trucks has been coordinated with the expansion of highways and freeways and has facilitated the bulging suburbanization around today's cities.

Because of the dominance of autos and trucks in the U.S. transportation system, the traditional social scientists examined in Chapter 1 have typically viewed that transportation system as preordained by the American "love" for the automobile. For example, in a recent book on Los Angeles, historian Scott Bottles argues that "America's present urban transportation system largely reflects choices made by the public itself"; the public freely chose the automobile as a "liberating and democratic technology."[4] Conventional explanations for auto-centered patterns focus on the response of a market system to these consumers. Auto-linked technologies are discussed as though they force human decisions: Thus "the city dweller, especially in recent times, has been a victim of the technological changes that have been wrought in transportation systems."[5] As we discussed in Chapter 1, traditional ecologists and other social scientists view the complexity and shape of cities as largely determined by technological developments in transportation—a reasonable view—but these technologies are not carefully examined in terms of their economic contexts, histories, and possible technological alternatives. For example, unlike the United States, numerous capitalist countries in Europe, including prosperous West Germany, have a mixed rail transit/automobile transport system. There interurban and intraurban rail transit remains very important. For this reason, the U.S. system cannot be assumed to be simply the result of "free" consumer choices in a market context. The capitalistic history and decision-making contexts that resulted in the positioning of automobiles at the heart of the U.S. transportation system must be examined.

Early Mass Rail Transit Rural and urban Americans have not always been so dependent on automobiles for interurban and intraurban transport. In the years between the 1880s and the 1940s many cities had significant mass transit systems. By 1890 electric trolleys were in general use. Indeed, electric trolley routes, elevated railroads, and subways facilitated the first urban expansion and decentralization. Some investor-owned rail transit companies extended their trolley lines beyond existing urbanized areas out into the countryside in an attempt to profit from the land speculation along the rail lines. Glenn Yago has documented how transit owners and real estate speculators worked together to ensure the spatial and economic development of cities by private enterprise. Transit companies were a significant force in urban sprawl. The suburban spread of Los Angeles, for example, got its initial push from the expansion of trolley rail lines. Not initially laid out as an automobile city, this sprawling metropolis developed along streetcar tracks; only later was the streetcar network displaced by automobiles.[6]

The reorganization and disruption of mass rail transit that took place in the early 1900s did not result just from the challenge of improved automobile technology. Rather, capitalist entrepreneurs and private corporations seeking profits reorganized and consolidated existing rail transit systems. Electrification of horse-drawn streetcars increased investment costs and stimulated concentration of ownership in larger "transit trusts" of landowning, finance, and utility entrepreneurs. Mergers of old transit firms and the assembly of new companies were commonplace, and there was much speculation in transit company stock. Yago has provided evidence on the corrupt accounting practices, overextension of lines for real estate speculation, and overcapitalization which led to the bankruptcy of more than one-third of the private urban transit companies during the period 1916–1923.[7] Sometimes the capitalists involved in the transit companies were too eager for profits. "These actions in turn," Charles Cheape notes, "drained funds, discouraged additional investment, and contributed significantly to the collapse and reorganization of many transit systems shortly after World War I and again in the 1930s."[8]

Ironically, one consequence of the so-called "progressive" political reform movement in cities in the first decades of the twentieth century was that supervision of rail transit systems was often placed in the hands of business-dominated regulatory commissions, many of whose members were committed to the interests of corporate America (for example, transit stock manipulation for profit), rather than to the welfare of the general public. In numerous cases the extraordinary profits made by rail transit entrepreneurs, together with their ties to corrupt politicians, created a negative public image—which in turn made the public less enthusiastic about new tax-supported subsidies and fare hikes for the troubled rail transit systems. Moreover, as the profits of many of the private transit firms declined, public authorities in some cities, including Boston and New York, were forced to take over the transit lines from the poorly managed private companies in response to citizen pressure for mass transportation. This fact suggests that there has long been popular *demand* for publicly owned rail transit that is reliable, convenient, and inexpensive. Indeed, during the period 1910–1930 a *majority* of Americans either could not afford, because of modest incomes, or could not use, because of age or handicap, an automobile.[9]

A Corporate Plan to Kill Mass Transit? By the late 1910s and 1920s the ascension of the U.S. auto-oil-rubber industrial complex brought new corporate strategies to expand automobile markets and secure government subsidies for road infrastructure. Mass rail transit hindered the profit-oriented interests of this car-centered industrial complex, whose executives became involved not only in pressuring governments to subsidize roads but also in the buying up of mass transit lines. For example, in the early 1920s, Los Angeles had the largest and most effective trolley car system in the United States. Utilizing more than a thousand miles of track, the system transported millions of people yearly. During World War II, the streetcars ran 2,800 scheduled runs a day.[10] But by the end of that war, the trolleys were disappearing. And their demise had little to do with consumer choice. As news analyst Harry Reasoner has observed, it "was largely a result of a criminal conspiracy":

> The way it worked was that General Motors, Firestone Tire and Standard Oil of California and some other companies, depending on the location of the target, would arrange financing for an outfit called National City Lines, which cozied up to city councils and county commissioners and bought up transit systems like L.A.'s. Then they would junk or sell the electric cars and pry up the rails for scrap and beautiful, modern buses would be substituted, buses made by General Motors and running on Firestone Tires and burning Standard's gas.[11]

Within a month after the trolley system in Los Angeles was purchased, 237 new buses arrived. It is important to realize that, for all the financial and management problems created by the private owners of the rail transit firms, the old transit systems were still popular. In the year prior to the takeover, the Los Angeles electric lines made $1.5 million in profits and carried more than 200 million passengers. The logic behind the corporate takeover plan was clear. The auto-related firms acted because a trolley car can carry the passengers of several dozen automobiles.

During the 1930s GM created a holding company through which it and other auto-related companies channeled money to buy up electric transit systems in 45 cities from New York to Los Angeles. As researcher Bradford Snell has outlined it, the process had three stages. First, General Motors (GM) helped the Greyhound corporation displace long-distance passenger transportation from railroads to buses. Then GM and other auto-related companies bought up and dismantled numerous local electric transit systems, replacing them with the GM-built buses. Moreover, in the late 1940s, GM was convicted in a Chicago federal court of having conspired to destroy electric transit and to convert trolley systems to diesel buses, whose production GM monopolized. William Dixon, the man who put together the criminal conspiracy case for the federal government, argued that individual corporate executives should be sent to jail. Instead, each received a trivial $1 fine. The corporations were assessed a modest $5,000 penalty, the maximum under the law.[12] In spite of this conviction, GM continued to play a role in converting electric transit systems to diesel buses. And these diesel buses provided more expensive mass transit: "The diesel bus, as engineered by GM, has a shorter life expectancy, higher operating costs, and lower overall productivity than electric buses. GM has thus made the bus economically noncompetitive with the car also."[13] One source of public discontent with mass transit was this inferiority of the new diesel buses compared to the rail transit cars that had been displaced without any consultation with consumers. Not surprisingly, between 1936 and 1955 the number of operating trolley cars in the United States dropped from about 40,000 to 5,000.

In a lengthy report GM officials have argued that electric transit systems were already in trouble when GM began intervening. As noted above, some poorly managed transit systems were declining already, and some had begun to convert partially to buses before GM's vigorous action. So from GM's viewpoint, the corporation's direct intervention only accelerated the process. This point has been accented by Bottles, who shows that GM did not single-handedly destroy the streetcar systems in Los Angeles.[14] These privately controlled systems were providing a lesser quality of service before GM became involved. The profit milking and corruption of the private streetcar firms in Los Angeles were not idiosyncratic but were common for privately owned mass transport in numerous cities.

Also important in destroying mass transit was the new and aggressive multimillion-dollar marketing of automobiles and trucks by General Motors and other automobile companies across the United States. And the automobile companies and their advertisers were not the only powerful actors involved in killing off numerous mass transit systems. Bankers and public officials also played a role. Yago notes that "after World War II, banks sold bankrupt and obsolete transit systems throughout the country at prices that bore no relation to the systems' real values."[15] Often favoring the auto interests, local banks and other financial institutions tried to limit government bond issues that could be used to finance new equipment and refurbish the remaining rail transit systems.

Because of successful lobbying by executives from the auto-oil-rubber complex, and their own acceptance of a motorization perspective, most government officials increasingly backed street and highway construction. They cooperated with the auto industry in eliminating many mass transit systems. Increased governmental support for auto and truck transportation systems has meant systematic disinvestment in mass transit systems. Over the several decades since World War II, governmental mass transit subsidies have been small compared with highway subsidies. This decline has hurt low- and moderate-income people the most. Less public transit since World War II has meant increased commuting time in large cities where people are dependent on the automobile, which is especially troublesome for moderate-income workers who may not be able to afford a reliable car; less mass transit has also meant increased consumer expenditures for automobiles and gasoline. Auto expansion has frustrated the development of much mass transit because growing street congestion slows down buses and trolleys, further reducing their ridership. As a result, governmental funding for public rail transit has been cut, again chasing away riders who dislike poorly maintained equipment. And fares have been increased. Riders who can use automobiles do so. And the downward spiral has continued to the point of extinction of most public rail transit systems.[16]

Mass transit was allowed to decline by the business-oriented government officials in most cities. Consumer desires were only partly responsible for this. Consumers did discover the freedom of movement of autos, and even in cities with excellent rail transit systems many prefer the auto for at least some types of travel. But consumers make their choices *from the alternatives available.* With no real rail transportation alternative to the automobile in most urban areas, consumers turned to it as a necessity. Ironically, as the auto and truck congestion of the cities has mounted between the 1950s and the 1980s, more and more citizens, and not a few business leaders, have called for new mass transit systems for their cities, a phenomenon we will assess below.[17]

Mass Transit in Other Capitalistic Countries Comparative research on U.S. and German transportation systems by Yago has demonstrated the importance of looking at corporate power and economic structure. Mass rail transport developed in Germany before 1900. In the 1870s and 1880s the German national and local governments became interested in mass transit; at that time the coal, steel, iron, chemical, and electrical manufacturing companies were dominant in German capitalism. Interestingly, corporate executives in these industries supported the development of rail transportation; by 1900 the national and local governments had subsidized and institutionalized intraurban and interurban rail transport systems, which served the transport needs not only of the citizenry but also of the dominant coal, steel, chemical, and electrical industries. These industries also supplied equipment and supplies for the rail networks. In contrast, in the United States early transport companies were involved in manipulation and land speculation; transit service was rarely the central goal of the early rail transit firms. In contrast to Germany, dominance of U.S. industry by a major economic concentration did not come to the United States until after 1900, and when it did come, the auto-oil-rubber industrial complex was dominant. There was no other integrated industrial complex to contest this dominance of the auto-related firms, and governmental intervention was directed at support of motorization and the automobile. In Germany governmental intervention for mass rail transit had preceded this dominance of the motorization lobby. This suggests that the *timing* of the implementation of technological innovations in relation to corporate development is critical to their dominance, or lack of dominance, in cities and societies.[18]

Interestingly, it was the Nazi interest in motorization and militarization in the 1930s that sharply increased the role of auto and truck transport in Germany. Adolf Hitler worked hard to motorize the military and the society. After World War II, the German auto lobby increased in power, and an auto transport system was placed alongside the rail transport system. However, the West German government and people have maintained a strong commitment to both systems; and the OPEC-generated oil crises of the 1970s brought an unparalleled revival of mass transit in Germany, whereas in the United States there was a more modest revival. The reason for the dramatic contrast between the two countries was that Germany had retained a rail passenger transport system, one that is still viable and energy conserving to the present day.

CENTRALIZATION AND COSTS OF THE AUTOMOBILE

Centralization in the Auto Industry In the first decade of the twentieth century, the owners of automobiles were primarily capitalists, small and large, and self-employed professionals such as physicians. By 1915 two auto markets had developed: the elite market, with its expensive automobiles; and a market of Model-T-type cars for average workers with decent-paying, full-time jobs. In the United States the number of autos increased from 10.5 million in 1921 to 26.5 million in 1929. Automobile manufacturing increasingly accounted for a huge proportion of the basic resources such as oil and iron ore consumed in the United States. Gradually the automobile industry became oligopolistic. Great centralization and concentration of capital came to this industry in the 1920s. During the period 1900–1924 there were 500 auto firms, but this number had declined to 44 firms by the late 1920s; by the 1970s there were just 3 major companies. For two decades General Motors, Ford, and Chrysler have made most of the cars produced by U.S. manufacturers for U.S. consumers. Historically, the U.S. auto industry has kept out new competitors by its high-cost styling, exclusive dealerships, and administered prices. Until the 1970s, except for periodic recessions, the automobile companies have been profitable enterprises. In recent decades the Big Three auto manufacturers have faced stiff competition from foreign companies, in part because of past management decisions not to invest in making what top executives regarded as less profitable smaller cars. Indeed, from the 1970s to the 1990s top auto executives have sought government subsidies (for example, the government bailout of the Chrysler corporation) and union concessions to improve their profitability.[19]

Marketing   As we have noted previously, mainstream social science analysis of cities has often assumed that the dominance of the automobile was more or less natural and inevitable. Coupled with this view is an emphasis on consumer preferences: Consumers have always demanded automobiles. An example of this consumer-as-dominant bias can be seen in Ralph Gakenheimer's statement that "in the postwar years, the pent-up demand for automobile travel was resulting in the very rapid increase of car ownership."[20] This perspective neglects the critical role of auto companies, such as General Motors, in killing off mass transit. Neglected too is the aggressive advertising and mass marketing that shaped consumer tastes for automobiles characterized by annual model changes and, often, questionable quality. Forceful advertising has played a significant part in wedding Americans to the automobile. In the mid-1920s General Motors had pioneered in developing new marketing techniques, including installment buying, annual model changes, and widespread advertising.

　　Product designers and advertisers have worked together to market a broad array of options they have decided to put into cars. For example, a 1940 Chevrolet ad emphasizes a powerful engine and size: "It measures a thrilling fifteen feet plus—181 inches from front of grille to rear of body—and it's 'every inch the king' of lowest-priced cars."[21] A 1965 Pontiac GTO ad shows a car covered with a tiger rug. The caption reads:

"Purrs if you're nice. Snarls when you prod it. Trophy V-8, standard in Pontiac GTO. 389 cubic inches. 335 horsepower. 431 lb-ft of torque...then prowl in a Wide-Track a while. You'll know who's a tiger."[22] A 1968 Dodge 440 Magnum ad shows a blond woman posed provocatively next to the car on a beach, with the caption: "Mother warned me...that there would be men like you driving cars like that. Do you really think you can get to me with that long, low, tough machine you just rolled up in?"[23] Billions of dollars have been spent on advertising that emphasizes style and snobbery, sex, and speed. Annual model changes, however trivial, are sold as necessary for the new car buyer. Product designers incorporate unnecessary features that can enhance profitability. And there is a definite suggestion in much advertising that one cannot be intelligent, comfortable, or a "real man" without a new automobile.

CONSTRUCTION OF ROADS AND HIGHWAYS

The Interstate Highway System Government subsidies have been critical to the process by which automobile transportation substantially replaced railroad and mass transit (passenger) transportation. For many decades now, the federal government has emphasized highways in its subsidies for ground transportation. During the 1950s a major escalation of the governmental commitment was made. Military defense requirements constituted the rationale President Dwight Eisenhower used in defending his mid-1950s proposal for a $50 billion intercontinental highway network. He appointed a member of the military elite, former General Lucius D. Clay, to head an official committee to report on the nation's transportation needs. The committee included a top construction company president, the head of a major bank, the head of an auto-related corporation, and the head of a truck drivers' union—not exactly an objective review panel. Most people who testified before the panel were from organized groups of auto-related companies, oil companies, and other large corporations, or were government highway officials. Not surprisingly, the report recommended a greatly expanded highway system to meet military and civil defense needs, as well as the needs of an expanding economy.[24]

Soon Congress had before it a number of bills designed to expand government subsidies for highway building. Testifying before Congress on the highway bills in the mid-1950s, Robert Moses, a prominent New York official and defender of new road systems, said, "I still have not found anybody who can tell me how you are going to keep on turning out all these cars without decent, first-class modern highways for them to run on, in particular on the routes that connect the big cities and their suburbs, and run through the cities, because that is what we have today."[25] Moses, who was responsible for proposing and supervising extensive highway systems himself, is candid. Not only does he explicitly link the expanding production of autos to expanded highway systems, but he also emphasizes the role of these road systems in linking suburban land development to workplaces in big cities. Business leaders and government officials developed a major public relations campaign to generate public support for the expensive, tax-funded national system of highways; most local growth coalitions across the country supported the proposals. In 1956 a law was passed setting up a Highway Trust Fund collected from gasoline taxes to build an interstate highway system. In effect, the federal government provides a huge subsidy for the auto-related industries in the form of gasoline taxes collected for this trust fund; other types of surface passenger transportation have received relatively small government subsidies.

The Highway Industry   The highway industry exerts its dominance through coalitions of corporate capitalists and state and federal highway officials. The highway construction and auto lobbies have dominated the Federal Highway Administration as well as state highway departments. Government officials, elected and unelected, usually see eye to eye with the lobbies.

> *Their implicit (and sometimes explicit) national goals are usually two cars in every garage, a gasoline station on every corner, and cities devoted overwhelmingly to streets, parking lots, and maintenance facilities for the auto. Progress is measured in terms of car ownership and highway and street mileage. If the cities seem choked and under strain the solution is to improve and expand car-carrying capabilities.*[26]

Thus during the 1960s the *Asphalt Institute Quarterly* strongly supported a statement by the U.S. Secretary of Commerce, who said that traffic problems would be solved by providing better roads for cars, not by restricting the number or caliber of cars. "We shout a 'Hear, hear!' and let's construct those better roads out of asphalt so they will cost less to build and thus be easy on taxes—at the same time providing more roads for more cars to travel more miles and use more petroleum products."[27]

One major lobbying force for expanded highway programs has been the American Road Builders Association. Representing highway construction corporations, materials suppliers, engineering companies, and investment corporations, the association labored vigorously for expanding highway construction and against citizens' groups protesting highway construction projects. One association official wrote that local business leaders should actively create public opinion:

> *The truth is, however, that the local people are not entirely aware of their best interests. They do not know for sure what the new highway will mean to them. That is why those who oppose a proposal usually appear in large numbers and talk longer and louder than do those who favor the project. And that is precisely why a softening-up or pre-selling public relations campaign must be waged in those communities before the public hearing is held.*[28]

The highway construction organizations have regularly organized large-scale public relations campaigns on behalf of expanded highway construction. Highways are defended as critical to industrial and residential growth. Freeways open up new areas for developers, make suburbanization possible, and increase land values. Other auto-related organizations, such as the National Asphalt Pavement Association, the Truck Trailer Manufacturing Association, the American Petroleum Institute, the National Automobile Dealers Association, and the Rubber Manufacturers Association, have been important in lobbying for an extensive highway system. Key members of Congress have been lobbied directly by auto-related interests. Campaign contributions help shape government officials' responsiveness. Corporate officials sometimes move into the executive branch or Congress, and vice versa. These lobbying efforts have been extraordinarily successful. As a result, by the late 1980s the 43,000-mile interstate system was nearly complete.[29]

The U.S. highway system represents a continuing governmental subsidy not only for auto and truck corporations but also for other corporations that rely heavily on highway networks. These corporations, especially the large ones, often do not pay a fair share of the total cost, and much of what they do pay is passed on to consumers in the prices of their products. The average worker and consumer through his or her taxes heavily supports this expensive and inefficient transportation system.

Extending Federally Subsidized Highways Interestingly, the extension of the Interstate Highway System into freeway belts and highways *within* metropolitan areas was not the original goal. Rather, cities were to be linked with other cities by the interstate system. Yet by the 1960s federally funded expressways around, within, and through metropolitan areas had become an important part of the growing system. With the federal government providing most of the money, local business and government leaders sought new highways. Yet the interstate highways in and around cities are primarily used by commuters and for other local transportation, not for the interstate and military travel that was the system's original purpose. Not surprisingly, these "interstate" highways have played a very significant facilitating role in the decentralization of residential and industrial development. Transportation networks do not just reflect technological developments such as the emergence of automobiles. They also signal the actions, or inaction, of governmental agencies, in this case agencies heavily lobbied by business interests representing the auto, oil, rubber, and highway construction industries.

Highway Superbuilder: New York City's Robert Moses Just one strangely curved mile of the Cross-Bronx Expressway was at issue. Local neighborhood groups, mostly low- and middle-income Jewish residents in the

Bronx area of New York City were protesting that the proposed express-way route would destroy more than 1,530 apartments; they knew that far more than the official figure of 5,000 people would be displaced by that one mile of new expressway. What puzzled neighborhood leaders and their advisory engineers was that an alternative route along an existing city avenue would have made a straighter expressway and would have consumed fewer buildings. Instead, city officials proposed to destroy the homes of thousands. Neighborhood groups aggressively protested the threatened loss of homes, neighborhoods, shopping, parks, and schools. They were angered by the bureaucratic form letters giving them just 90 days to move. The neighborhood residents went to official meetings where they were abused, ignored, and stonewalled. While they did slow the political process down, they lost the battle. Together with business leaders and politicians, the powerful New York official Robert Moses, the same activist who had lobbied for federally funded highways, had imposed his own will on the people. The expressway was built with its strange curve. According to Robert Caro, no one is sure why the expressway was con-structed that way—perhaps, some speculate, to show neighborhood resi-dents that they have so little power to shape transportation systems.[30]

Until 1945 most superhighways had been built around or between cities, not within them. But by the mid-1940s Moses, head of a powerful public agency in New York, was planning to build 100 miles of express-ways in the city, more superhighway mileage for this one city than existed *in the world* in that year. Moses eventually built 700 miles of expressways and roads in and around New York City. Thousands of houses, apartment buildings, and businesses were destroyed. Caro sums up the impact.

> *Even for the "easiest" of these monster roads, those traversing relatively "open" areas of the city, there were always private homes, small apartment houses—and whole factories—which had to be picked up and moved bodily to new locations. For most of these roads, Moses had to hack paths through jungles of tenements and apartment houses, to slash aqueducts in two and push sewers aside, to lift railroads in the air or shove them underground.[31]*

By the time he was through Robert Moses had built $2 billion worth of highways and roads in New York City. He built most of the city's major expressways and many major bridges. More than 250,000 people had been displaced in the process. Neighborhoods, schools, and parks had been destroyed to provide room for more automobiles, with little demo-cratic input from neighborhood residents into the critical decisions. Again we see the critical determinative decisions of specific actors, in this case a government decision maker, in creating existing U.S. transporta-tion arrangements. Moses shaped, and was shaped by, his structural (bureaucratic) context.

CONGESTION AND OTHER SOCIAL COSTS

The Vicious Cycle of Congestion There is a vicious auto-freeway-congestion cycle in many urban areas. Freeways are constructed. But soon they become filled with cars. This overflow is in turn used to justify even more freeways. As Cervero puts it, "the most serious flaw in all supply-side responses to traffic congestion is that they all too often exacerbate the very problem they attempt to solve. The literature is replete with examples of expanded roadways generating new traffic, which in turn necessitates further expansion, which induces more traffic, and so on and so on."[32] Part of the reasoning behind the tremendous increase in highway expenditures after World War II was the idea that traffic congestion and the absence of parking were causing central-city decline. Yet the vigorous road construction created even more problems. In many cities the expensive highway system does not work at the very hours—rush hours—when it is supposed to work. Indeed, the concept of "rush hour" has become meaningless in many central-city areas; traffic on many urban freeways is the same, congested, at noontime as in the morning and evening. And in many cases the average speed on major traffic arteries was greater in the horse-and-buggy days of the past.[33]

There are several factors contributing to the traffic congestion problem. One is the increase in number of commuters. In 1950 there were 59 million commuters in the nation, but by the late 1980s that figure had swollen to 110 million. Moreover, three-quarters of commuting autos have no passengers other than the driver. Then there is the increase in the number of motor vehicles. Between 1950 and 1986, when the U.S. population grew by approximately 60 percent, the number of motor vehicles grew by nearly 260 percent.[34] Table 6.1 reveals the urban areas where traffic congestion was the most extreme in the mid-1980s, together with the U.S. Department of Transportation's forecast of the worst areas shortly after the turn of the century.[35]

Table 6.1 Urban areas with the worst traffic congestion

1984
1. Houston
2. New Orleans
3. New York
4. Detroit
5. San Francisco
6. Seattle
7. Los Angeles
8. Boston
9. Charlotte
10. Atlanta

Table 6.1 Urban areas with the worst traffic congestion (*cont'd.*)

2005
1. Charlotte
2. Houston
3. Detroit
4. San Antonio
5. Dallas
6. Miami
7. New Orleans
8. Seattle
9. Boston
10. San Francisco

While the southern cities of Houston, New Orleans, and Charlotte, cities famous for relatively low local taxes and "good business climates," lead both lists, they are not the only metropolitan areas with serious traffic congestion problems. Note that seven major cities, on three coasts, are on both lists.

Other Problems of Auto Dependence Congestion means time wasted. According to the U.S. Department of Transportation, a worker who stays on the job for 45 years and is tied up in traffic 20 minutes each day will spend nearly 2 working years sitting in congested traffic. In addition to time, automobiles require a large share of consumer income. The average motorist pays out five to seven times the initial cost of an automobile if she or he retains it for 10 years or so, for gasoline, insurance, and other expenses. Traffic engineers estimate that commuters spend $150 billion a year just to travel to work and back. There are, in addition, human and community costs to consider, including the impact on the environment and the health of Americans. Tens of thousands of people are killed each year by cars and trucks. Pollution damages the lungs of millions. Executives at Northrop Aviation in Los Angeles have calculated that its company's propane-powered van fleet, which is used by 900 employees, prevented 800 tons of pollutants from entering the atmosphere over a 4-year span.[36]

Cracks in the Road: The Infrastructure Crisis At the cost of billions of dollars an interstate highway system has been constructed, one of the largest public works projects in history. Today this expensive system is deteriorating in many rural and urban areas. Officially, at least one-tenth of it is in poor condition, with numerous potholes and deteriorating bridges. Many other highways are in similar deteriorating condition; many roads are being used well beyond their expected lifetimes. A major reason for highway deterioration is that auto traffic and truck usage has been much greater than expected. Particularly harmful is the truck traffic, because one overweight truck can do damage comparable to that of thousands of automobiles. A number of analysts have noted that many trucks are operated at illegally high weights to increase profitability; it is often cheaper to pay fines than to run with less weight. This problem of over-weight trucks has increased with the deregulation, and enhanced competition for trucking contracts, in the 1980s. Yet the U.S. highway system has not been built to withstand such punishment. Maintenance and replacement costs to keep it in shape have been estimated at billions of dollars a year, but only a few hundred million dollars a year have been made available for this purpose. The growing maintenance costs for these highways mean that new taxes will be required. The Highway Trust Fund no longer provides enough revenue.

In 1983 the Mianus River Bridge on the Connecticut Turnpike collapsed and killed three motorists. This tragic event contributed to a growing national concern about the public infrastructure. In 1986 a congressionally mandated report, titled *The Nation's Public Works*, reported that the nation's infrastructure of roads and bridges was in serious trouble and that since the early 1970s governmental spending on public works had grown very slowly.[37] Some estimates of the cost of repairs and reconstruction on U.S. roads go as high as $600 billion. Moreover, at least 200,000 bridges—40 percent of all bridges—need to be replaced or repaired at a cost of tens of billions of dollars. During the Reagan "revolution" of the 1980s, a major share of the traditional federal financing of infrastructural improvements was shifted to state and local governments. Thus in November 1988 New York voters gave their state government the authority to issue $3 billion in new bonds to pay for the repair of deteriorating bridges and roads. This came on top of $1.25 billion authorized in 1983. The spending was required because 4,000 miles of New York's highways were in poor condition; and 7,405 bridges were in serious disrepair. Most of the bond money was directed to road and bridge repairs.[38]

Spending billions on the auto-centered transport system is especially difficult in times of government fiscal crisis, such as the 1980s. Not surprisingly, there have been major government reductions in highway expenditures. During the 1960s the state of California spent more than $1 billion a year on highways, but in contrast spent just $400,000 on new freeway projects in 1985. Between 1980 and 1987 California built the equivalent of only 50 miles of eight-lane freeways. Moreover, inflation-adjusted figures show that general governmental outlays for highway construction and maintenance declined sharply from $3.82 per mile traveled by motor vehicles in 1960 to $1.98 in 1986.[39]

This infrastructure crisis signals that the dependence of Americans on an automobile-truck transport system has had extraordinary *long-term* costs that were not seriously considered in the beginning. These costs are already more extensive than troubled local and state governments can bear; and at some point they will doubtless require substantial tax increases.

THE IMPACT OF CITY DECENTRALIZATION

Suburban Traffic Congestion In many cities, suburban sprawl and traffic congestion go hand in hand. There is a tendency for those who can afford it to shift their use of automobiles, and the location of their residences, as new freeways and other highways are developed. At first, home-to-work trips take less time than before, even over greater distances, because of the new highways. But then more developers of residential subdivisions are attracted to locations along the new highways, congestion increases, and travel time frequently increases again. Moreover, changing to the automobile because of the early advantages of a freeway can affect the remaining urban rail mass transit lines, which may become unprofitable and die out, even though motorists later experience severe freeway congestion and then cry out for mass transit. At that later point, however, building mass transit to service low-density sprawl becomes a very expensive undertaking.

Because it is spread out, much of suburbia is not easily serviced by mass transit. Commuters need cars to get to mass transit stations. For the most part, developers of residential subdivisions since World War II have oriented their subdivisions to automobiles. Builders of office buildings often construct huge garages for employees to park their cars in; some office towers have many floors of parking. Shopping centers, particularly larger regional centers, reserve most of their acreage for cars, which are often the only means of access. Decentralized development along freeways is increasingly creating congestion problems outside major cities. For example, planners now anticipate that the increasingly built-up 20-mile corridor along U.S. Route 1 from Trenton to Brunswick, New Jersey, will take at least 5 hours to traverse by the year 2005. The corridor, heavily populated with office parks and shopping centers, was largely made up of farms just a few years ago.[40]

Suburban Employment Corporate plant, warehouse, and office location decisions have in recent decades targeted outlying areas of the increasingly multinucleated U.S. cities. These decisions have contributed to suburban congestion. As with earlier suburbanization, the preferences of average citizens have played a less important role than the capital investment decisions of industrialists, developers, and other investors in the recent shaping of suburban sprawl. For a number of reasons corporations have been moving outside the central cities. Between 1960 and 1980 two-thirds of all jobs created were located by companies in the suburbs; in the late 1980s nearly 60 percent of all metropolitan employment was located outside the central business district. The job location outside central cities stems from the decisions of the developers and employers who control the flow of capital from one place to another within and between urban areas. The share of total office space outside central cities has been rising sharply; from 25 percent in 1970, to 43 percent in 1980, to 57 percent in 1984. One reason for this suburbanization lies in the cost savings. Suburban office space typically costs $20 per square foot, compared with $45 or more in the central city.[41] Employers and developers also seek decentralized locations because of lower land costs for plants and warehouses, lower suburban taxes, and building codes that are frequently less restrictive. In addition, the earlier rounds of suburbanization brought many workers and their families to the suburbs; these workers are now an attraction for many corporations.

Mismatch between Jobs and Housing Many workers in suburban office parks and shopping centers cannot afford to live near their places of employment. For instance, at the Cumberland-Galleria office center northwest of Atlanta, employers cannot attract enough clerical office workers from the predominantly black central-city area because public transportation is lacking and because the housing nearby is too costly. As a result, the jobs are filled by people in less expensive suburbs living farther away. In Stamford, Connecticut, and other suburban areas of New York City, some fully employed workers have actually had to live in shelters for the homeless because they cannot afford homes or apartments where they work. For example, Charles Lark, a 25-year-old New Yorker who came to Stamford to work as a food handler at the Sheraton Hotel, reported that "jobs aren't the problem—housing is." Lark, who was sleeping at the West Main Street Shelter for the homeless, had plans to move to Brooklyn in order to find an apartment.[42]

John Mitovich, president of Connecticut's Southwestern Area Commerce and Industry Association, has observed that only a *fifth* of workers taking jobs in New York suburbs, where many big corporations are now based, can afford to live there. By the late 1980s families needed an annual income of $62,000 or more to live and work in a typical county there. As a result, local government and business officials actively advised job seekers not to come unless they expected to get substantial salaries. Not surprisingly, most suburbanized corporations would not have been able to sustain the recent pace of economic expansion without recruiting thousands of women, many already residing in the suburbs, into the work force for the first time.[43]

There is a similar housing problem in the outlying areas of West Coast cities. During the late 1980s in Walnut Creek, a growing suburb of San Francisco, the average new home cost nearly $200,000. Such a house normally required about $61,000 in annual household income to qualify for a mortgage. But the median yearly income of Walnut Creek's current residents was only $32,000. New families in that income range could no longer buy houses there.[44] The mismatch between jobs and affordable housing is characteristic of all regions. Moreover, as Cervero notes, "the overwhelming majority of suburban office developers feel no responsibility for building housing either on site or nearby; most believe the marketplace alone will respond to the housing needs of their tenants' workers."45

The traffic flow and congestion found in suburban areas is not only the product of corporate location of jobs outside the central cities but also the result of the mismatch between job sites and workers' housing. As a result of these conditions, suburb-to-suburb trips are the dominant commuting pattern today. According to a study by the Eno Foundation, 12.7 million people commute from a suburb to a central city each day, but almost twice that number—25 million—commute from one suburb to another. In the metropolitan areas of Boston, Pittsburgh, St. Louis, and Detroit, the suburbs' share of total commuting trips exceeds 60 percent. Several proposals to reduce the congestion have been offered. Some have suggested that, instead of sprawling, low-density settings, suburban developers could provide moderate-density, mixed-use facilities deemphasizing auto transport, thus allowing workers to shop or dine without using cars. Employers could reduce parking spaces and encourage ride sharing and van-pooling. Such restructuring would reduce suburban rush-hour traffic by an estimated 5 to 10 percent.46 Another common proposal is to build more roads. However, as noted earlier, more road construction often brings the vicious cycle of even greater congestion; and neither the local nor the federal governments are prepared today to tax to fund another massive round of highway construction.

Privatization of Road Development   This inability of governments, many in chronic fiscal crisis, to respond to all the subsidy needs of private development interests has led to some new private-public mechanisms to facilitate decentralized roadway development. Those who believe that more roadways are the answer have recently begun looking to developers and employers themselves to provide more of the highway funding. The mechanisms employed by local governments are called "impact fees" and "road-utility districts." Developers have become more willing to participate in such plans and to make payments for roads, because they recognize that access to their new development sites may not otherwise be provided. In the last decade impact fees have been assessed in more than a dozen states. For example, by the late 1980s developers with projects in Texas' four largest cities had paid nearly $500 million in right-of-way donations through "road-utility districts." The largest road-utility district has been formed in Pleasanton, near San Francisco. There more than $80 million has been collected for such infrastructure projects as cycling trails and freeway improvements.47

Moreover, the Westchester area of western Los Angeles boasts the most expensive impact fee program. There a one-time fee of $2,010 has been collected for each evening rush-hour auto trip generated by new commercial developments; the revenue was expected to cover $235 million in road improvements. Elsewhere in California nearly $180 million in financing was provided by developers for 50 separate suburban highway projects. For example, the developers of the Irvine Spectrum, a large MXD in central Orange County, agreed to pay the largest private contribution yet, $65 million, toward the construction of two new freeway interchanges, the reconstruction of three interchanges, and traffic control improvements.[48]

Even more dramatic has been the development since the 1980s of private development organizations whose purpose is the purchase of land for freeway construction. For example, in Houston one developer project is the Grand Parkway, an outer 100-plus-mile loop around Houston already under development. Houston developers and other land-interested actors expect that the already multinucleated metropolis will eventually have many decentralized communities many miles from downtown. Houston landowners and developers seeking to open up outlying land for development created the Grand Parkway Association, a private group that in 1984 secured state legislative approval for private organizations to accumulate land for highway development. The Grand Parkway Association has been successful in getting donations of right-of-way land from landowners for this mammoth beltway project; remarkably, they have also secured monetary donations to pay for private, not governmental, design and engineering work on the highway loop. The cost of this initial private developmental work has been estimated at $56 million; it is anticipated that the Texas Highway Department will take over the project and build the Grand Parkway with public funds. One Houston developer noted that "in 20 years almost every major freeway built within a metropolitan area will be done this way." Here is another private-public mechanism to continue the roadway construction that facilitates secondary-circuit property investments.[49]

Altering Commuting Plans Another solution to auto congestion that has received much media attention is the formation of Transportation Management Associations (TMAs). These private organizations relieve traffic problems through such techniques as promoting ride sharing and shift work. For instance, a TMA has been responsible for getting half of Atlantic Richfield's 2,000 employees in Los Angeles to participate in company-subsidized car pools. Beyond these efforts, a number of communities have attempted to enforce ordinances to reduce congestion. These include trip reduction ordinances, parking reduction ordinances, and growth moratoriums. The parking reduction ordinance approach has had little impact. The idea is to allow developers or employers to reduce building-code-required parking in return for commitment to ride sharing. However, in Los Angeles the option of taking a 40 percent reduction in code-required parking in exchange for the purchase of employee vans failed to attract a single employer in the first 2 years of the program. Trip reduction ordinances have been more successful. These ordinances mandate that employers reduce the percentage of solo auto trips to their sites. For example, largely in response to the rapid growth of the Hacienda Business Park, the California suburb of Pleasanton passed an ordinance in 1984 that required all employers with 50 or more workers to institute trip reduction programs in order to reduce peak-hour auto trips. By 1985, 33 of the city's 35 largest employers had met or exceeded the first-year target of a 15 percent reduction in peak-hour trips. The reduction was accomplished primarily through the introduction of flex-time work arrangements for employees.[50] We will discuss a third method of reducing suburban congestion, the growth moratoriums, in Chapter 10. All these strategies to reduce congestion demonstrate the social costs of an auto-centered system.

URBAN AND SUBURBAN SPACE

Structure of Space   Urban land use and urban architecture in the United States have been shaped, directly and indirectly, by automobile transportation. For example, in suburbia and in central cities there are many drive-in and drive-through establishments—banks, liquor stores, even churches. And in suburbia the low-density sprawl caters to automobiles and trucks, with acres and acres of macadam parking lots and connecting roads. The sprawl consumes much land when compared to high-density development. This consumption of land has been accelerated by the increase in suburban office parks and shopping centers. It is common practice to construct more parking spaces at business parks than required by local building codes to facilitate marketing of the projects; the typical office park averages 1.05 parking spaces per employee. Moreover, there is twice as much floor space per worker in suburban workplaces as in downtown settings; and there is more than 30 times as much land area per worker in suburban than in downtown office settings. Higher maintenance and energy consumption costs are also associated with low-density developments.[51]

In central-city areas high-rise parking garages dot the urban landscape. Central cities, especially in the South and West, are very auto oriented. Indeed, most downtown areas of central cities are "places to drive through, or to drive into in the morning and out of in the afternoon. Their architecture is that of a way station, not of a place to live."[52] One study found that 59 percent of downtown Los Angeles was devoted to streets, parking, and similar uses; for most major cities the proportions were 40 to 55 percent, with the highest figures in large Sunbelt cities. Automobiles have remade the built environments of our cities because of their requirements for so many streets, parking lots, garages, repair facilities, and new and used car businesses.[53]

This auto-centered built environment shapes and interrupts social life at home as well as in downtown business areas. Those residential streets with heavy traffic have been found to have much less social life than light-traffic streets. Wide streets busy with automobiles make it difficult for urbanites to visit with neighbors in front yards, for children to play outside, and for neighboring patterns to extend across streets. Moreover, residential streets are commonly 50 feet or less wide; but freeways can cut 300-foot-wide swaths of urban landscape. Sometimes these freeways have cut off or destroyed urban communities. For example, there is the story of the Fifth Ward area in northeast Houston; once a famous black community in the Sunbelt, the area was a major center for black entertainment, businesses, and churches. However, Houston's business elite decided to construct major highways through the community, starting in the 1940s. The result of this auto-centered construction was community deterioration. In a major restructuring of urban space two freeway systems created a cross pattern through the heart of the black community, separating sections once closely related and seriously disrupting community life and demolishing many homes and businesses.[54]

Another serious problem of an auto-centered society like the United States is that millions of people have no access to reliable automobiles. Indeed, during the period 1910–1930 a *majority* of Americans either could not afford or could not use, because of age or handicap, an automobile. This majority did not "choose" the auto freely as a liberating technology. And many suffered as their mass transit systems deteriorated. By 1980 the proportion without the means or the ability to use an automobile had dropped well below a majority, but the number was still about 35 million people over the age of 16. The low-income family, the handicapped, elderly households—these are the Americans who depend most heavily on public transportation. One Chicago study found that three-quarters of bus riders could not have made their trips by car; many of these riders were poor, elderly, and minority Americans. Minority workers tend to commute longer distances to work than white workers, and they depend more heavily on public transportation than do whites. Many of the automobiles owned by people in poorer groups are older, unsafe, or unreliable. Indeed, federal and state government commission reports have found that the lack of good public transportation was an important factor in the urban black riots of the 1960s and in the black community riots in Miami and a few other cities during the 1980s.[55]

REVIVING MASS TRANSIT?

Alternatives to Automobiles Why do many Americans continue to "prefer" the automobile? Some analysts argue that there is a fundamental human preference for freedom of movement. Others argue that this preference stems from the fact that "alternatives to the car are virtually nonexistent; that some very powerful economic interest groups have labored hard and long to keep it that way; and that the structural characteristics of the nation's economy work to prevent the kind of changes needed to develop viable transit alternatives."[56] A number of organizations have studied American attitudes on the automobile. One study financed by highway-building interests found that the general public favored improved public mass transit as well as highway systems. One question asked in this survey was: "The auto pollutes air, creates traffic, demolishes property, and kills people. Is the contribution the auto makes to our way of life worth this?"[57] Fifteen percent said no, and 85 percent said yes. This seems to confirm the argument that consumers prefer the heavy reliance on auto transportation. Yet in this same survey fully *half* of those who said yes also said that the auto was worth all this damage because it was the only convenient transportation available to most people. Thus the availability of more efficient and convenient types of surface transportation might alter the apparently favorable attitudes many Americans express toward automobiles.

Expanded mass transit is one alternative to automobiles. The importance of mass rail transit has long been recognized in many European countries, where pressures from the public have kept rail transit systems as major parts of urban and national transportation systems. Organized citizen movements in Europe have defined public transportation as a political, rather than a technical, issue. Governments in capitalistic countries such as West Germany, Great Britain, Sweden, and France have recognized that they do not have the economic resources to sustain a transport system primarily centered on cars and trucks.[58]

Automobiles are probably the least-efficient method of transportation for trips to work in larger cities. Public rail transit can carry far more passengers than a single lane of freeway, on a per-hour basis. A local subway train can carry 40,000 passengers per hour; this can be compared to the 2,625 passengers that can be carried by autos on one lane of an elevated highway per hour. Nonetheless, there is today a crisis in public mass transportation. Private investors move away from mass transit even when transit systems show modest profits. Until the early 1960s most bus systems in the United States were profitable. But, as had happened earlier with electric rail transit, private investors in bus systems decided to shift money away from less profitable systems, accelerating their decline. Moreover, in the United States public transportation is supported in regressive ways, with sales taxes, increased fares, or bonds backed by property taxes; this contrasts with Europe, where more progressive forms of tax support have been used to support mass transit. And the dominance of U.S. government transport policy by auto, truck, oil, and construction company interests has led to an antirail, antielectric bias in planning for future transportation needs. The United States does not now have the sophisticated electrical transit capabilities it once had. The few local government authorities that have added new electrical transit and subway systems, or repaired old ones, have usually had to go to Europe for the know-how, the engineers, the equipment, and the parts. Moreover, the number of commuters using mass transit has declined since 1960; by the late 1980s no more than 6 percent of trips to work were on mass transit, down from 12 percent in 1960. Part of this reduction has resulted from the previously discussed inter-suburban commuting patterns.[59]

Nonetheless, support for greatly improved mass transit does exist in the United States. Public opinion surveys indicate widespread support for using tax money to improve and expand public transportation. There have been numerous public protests over transit reductions in cities such as New York and Boston. A growing number of riders use transit systems in Portland and Baltimore. In New York, with 3.7 million riders daily, the share of commuters traveling into the city using transit systems is above 50 percent. In sprawling San Diego there has been a return to the use of trolley cars. According to the Mayor of San Diego, "everybody in San Diego loves the trolley. The only problem now...is we can't get them into the neighborhoods fast enough. They're a clean, efficient system, and they're cost-effective...it's not just the senior citizen and the low-income household, but it's the professionals that are using the trolley."[60]

Who Decides? One difficulty with mass transit decisions in the United States is the undemocratic nature of much of that decision making. For example, research by Allen Whitt on five major mass transit decisions made by California voters between 1962 and 1974 found the business elite there to be centrally involved in planning new mass transit systems for that state.[61] Corporate executives participated actively in the five transit campaigns and contributed money to them. Downtown business elites organized campaigns for public bonds to construct mass transit in San Francisco and Los Angeles. The Bay Area Rapid Transit District (BARTD), a rail system, is one example. The public construction and funding of this system were strongly supported by corporate executives with offices in densely populated San Francisco. The BARTD system was presented to citizens as a solution for transportation problems such as congestion. Yet Stephen Zwerling suggests that business promoters and governmental planners of BARTD saw it primarily in terms of its economic benefits for the downtown San Francisco business community, as "a tool by which the future growth of the region could be shaped."[62] As a result, there were major design flaws, including poor location of stations and expensive fares.

Moreover, in 1970 Proposition 18 was placed on the statewide California ballot; it would have allowed local governments to use a portion of the revenue derived from the gasoline tax for environmental and mass transit purposes. After extensive lobbying *against* Proposition 18 by auto-oil firms it was defeated in the general election. Numerous auto-oil firms contributed to the campaign against the proposition. Chevron and Shell donated, respectively, $75,000 and $50,000. Nonetheless, public sentiment was building for alternative transit systems, and in a subsequent election a more modest proposition, allowing a smaller percentage of the fuel tax money to be diverted to mass transit, was passed with little organized opposition from the auto-oil complex, which was willing in this situation to accept a token program because of the substantial citizen pressure.[63]

By the late 1980s the business and political leadership of at least 20 other U.S. cities, including Seattle, Dallas, Houston, and Los Angeles, were seriously examining the possibility of mass transit. Some urban developers, frustrated by city traffic congestion, were becoming interested in rail mass transit; an Urban Land Institute report noted that "many people [that is, developers] feel the private automobile cannot remain the primary mode of travel for the work trip."[64] The irrationality of a capitalist system that permitted the automobile to be featured at the center of a societal transport system is now evident even to many industrial and development capitalists.

CONCLUSION

In this chapter we have examined the growth and extension of an automobile- and truck-dominated transportation system from the early 1900s to the present. As we have seen, this transport system services very large corporations, small businesses, and the general public. However, the major decisions about the character, location, and development of transport services have usually been in the hands of small elites of business actors and their governmental allies. The auto and truck were placed at the center of the system without much democratic input. The choices of the citizens were limited as mass rail transit systems died under the poor management of private transit company executives and the intentional actions of the auto-oil-rubber complex to reduce this rail competition.

In the 1950s the new interstate highway system was designed by the executives from the auto-oil-rubber complex, but was substantially paid for by rank-and-file taxpayers. Government capital investments flowed into this secondary circuit of highway and road investments. Corporate industrialists and developers, together with allied political officials, made the important decisions shaping the public investments in a transportation system that features the automobile and the truck. This system has facilitated decentralized and multinucleated cities. In the chapters that follow we will examine the development projects that have followed, and been linked to, patterns of urban decentralization—business parks, shopping centers, and residential subdivisions.

NOTES

1. Clemens P. Work, Gordon Witkin, Lisa J. Moore, and Sharon Golden, "Jam Sessions," *U.S. News and World Report*, September 7, 1987, 20–27.
2. ABC News, *20/20*, "Bumper to Bumper Coast to Coast," ABC News, *20/20* Program Transcript for January 8, 1988, p. 6.
3. Alan Lupo, Frank Colcord, and Edmund P. Fowler, *Rites of Way* (Boston: Little, Brown, 1971), p. 9.
4. Scott L. Bottles, *Los Angeles and the Automobile: The Making of the Modern City* (Berkeley: University of California Press, 1987), p. 249.
5. Delbert A. Taebel and John V. Cornehls, *The Political Economy of Urban Transportation* (Port Washington, N.Y.: Kennikat Press, 1977), pp. 6–7.
6. Glenn Yago, *The Decline of Transit* (Cambridge: Cambridge University Press, 1984).
7. Ibid.
8. Charles W. Cheape, *Moving the Masses* (Cambridge, Mass.: Harvard University Press, 1980), p. 215.
9. Glenn Yago, "The Coming Crisis of U.S. Transportation," paper presented at the Conference on New Perspectives on Urban Political Economy, American University, Washington, D.C., May 1981, p. 9.
10. CBS News, *60 Minutes*, "Clang, Clang, Clang Went the Trolley!" *60 Minutes* Program Transcript, December 6, 1987, p. 11.
11. Ibid.
12. Bradford C. Snell, "American Ground Transport," in *The Urban Scene*, edited by Joe R. Feagin (New York: Random House, 1979), pp. 239–266.
13. Ibid., pp. 239–266.
14. Bottles, *Los Angeles and the Automobile: The Making of the Modern City*.
15. Yago, "The Coming Crisis of U.S. Transportation," p. 10.
16. Ibid., pp. 6–7.
17. Helen Leavitt, *Superhighway-Superhoax* (Garden City, N.Y.: Doubleday, 1970), p. 9.
18. Yago, *The Decline of Transit*, pp. 179–183.
19. Taebel and Cornehls, *The Political Economy of Urban Transportation*, pp. 55–60.
20. Ralph Gakenheimer, *Transportation Planning as a Response to Controversy* (Cambridge, Mass.: MIT Press, 1976), p. 11.
21. Robert Atwan, Donald McQuade, and John W. Wright, *Edsels, Luckies, and Frigidaires: Advertising and the American Way* (New York: Dell, 1979), p. 171.

22. Ibid., p. 183.
23. Ibid., p. 347.
24. Leavitt, *Superhighway-Superhoax*, pp. 34–36.
25. Quoted in ibid., p. 40.
26. Taebel and Cornehls, *The Political Economy of Urban Transportation*, p. 5. See also pp. 4–7.
27. Quoted in Robert Goodman, *After the Planners* (New York: Simon and Schuster, 1971), p. 69.
28. Quoted in Leavitt, *Superhighway-Superhoax*, p. 116.
29. Ibid., pp. 153–155.
30. Robert A. Caro, *The Power Broker* (New York: Alfred A. Knopf, 1974), pp. 837–839.
31. Ibid., p. 843.
32. Robert Cervero, "Unlocking Suburban Gridlock," *Journal of the American Planning Association* 52 (Autumn 1986): 400.
33. Yale Rabin, "Federal Urban Transportation Policy and the Highway Planning Process in Metropolitan Areas," *Annals of the American Academy of Political and Social Science* 451 (September 1980): 24.
34. Work et al., "Jam Sessions," p. 22.
35. Ibid., p. 21.
36. Alan Pisarski, "Commuting in America," U.S. Department of Transportation, Washington, D.C., U.S. Government Printing Office, 1987, cited in ibid, p. 22; Work et al., "Jam Sessions," p. 21.
37. National Council on Public Works Improvement, *The Nation's Public Works* (Washington, D.C.: U.S. Government Printing Office, 1986).
38. Elizabeth Kolbert, "$3 Billion in Road Bonds Is on New York's Ballot," *New York Times*, November 6, 1988, Sect. 1, p. 22.
39. Work et al., "Jam Sessions," pp. 22–24.
40. Henry Aubin, *City for Sale* (Toronto: James Lorimer, 1977), pp. 348–349; Work et al., "Jam Sessions," pp. 21–22.
41. R. Lindsey, "Fast-Growing Suburbs Act to Limit Development," *New York Times*, December 2, 1985, A12; Work et al., "Jam Sessions," p. 23.
42. Thomas J. Lueck, "New York Suburbs Offer Jobs but a Daunting Cost of Living," *New York Times*, August 30, 1986, 1.
43. Ibid., pp. 1, 5.
44. S. Maita, "Contra Costa Faces Anti-Growth Threat," *San Francisco Chronicle*, January 23, 1986, 30.
45. Cervero, "Unlocking Suburban Gridlock," p. 392.
46. "People Patterns: Studying Changes among Commuters," *Wall Street Journal*, December 18, 1987, 25; P. M. Fulton, "Changing Journey-to-Work Patterns: The Increasing Prevalence of Commuting within the Suburbs in Metropolitan Areas," paper presented at

the 65th annual meeting of the Transportation Board, Washington, D.C., cited in Cervero, "Unlocking Suburban Gridlock," p. 400.

47. Kenneth C. Orski, "The Private Challenge to Public Transportation," in *Urban Transit: Private Challenges to Public Transportation*, edited by C. Lave (San Francisco: Pacific Institute for Public Policy Research, 1985), p. 331; Work et al., "Jam Sessions," p. 26.

48. Cervero, "Unlocking Suburban Gridlock," p. 400.

49. Bob Sablatura, "The Great Grand Parkway Experiment," *Houston Business Journal*, November 17, 1986, 1A.

50. Work et al., "Jam Sessions," p. 26; City of Pleasanton, "TSM Compliance Report," Staff Report 12C, 1985, Pleasanton, Calif., cited in Cervero, "Unlocking Suburban Gridlock," pp. 402–404.

51. Cervero, "Unlocking Suburban Gridlock," pp. 380–391.

52. Taebel and Cornehls, *The Political Economy of Urban Transportation*, p. 121.

53. W. P. O'Mara and J. A. Casaza, *Office Development Handbook* (Washington, D.C.: Urban Land Institute, 1982); A. Lenny, "Canyon Corporate Center—From RVs to R&D: Transition to a Higher Use," *Urban Land* 43(4): 20–24, as cited in Cervero, "Unlocking Suburban Gridlock," p. 391; John B. Rae, *The Road and Car in American Life* (Cambridge, Mass.: MIT Press, 1971), p. 220.

54. Bill Minutaglio, "Houston's Baddest Street," *Houston Chronicle Magazine*, June 12, 1983, 1–15; see also Donald Appleyard, *Livable Streets* (Berkeley: University of California Press, 1981).

55. Taebel and Cornehls, *The Political Economy of Urban Transportation*, pp. 96–111.

56. Ibid., p. 60.

57. Cited in Leavitt, *Superhighway-Superhoax*, p. 186.

58. Peter J. Hovell, William H. Jones, and Alan J. Moran, *The Management of Urban Public Transport* (Lexington, Mass.: Lexington Books, 1975), pp. 6–10.

59. C. Conte, "The Explosive Growth of Suburbia Leads to Bumper-to-Bumper Blues," *Wall Street Journal*, April 16, 1985, 37; Leavitt, *Superhighway-Superhoax*, pp. 13–14; Richard A. Walker and David B. Large, "The Economics of Energy Extravagance," *Ecology Law Quarterly* 4 (1975): 974.

60. Yago, "The Coming Crisis of U.S. Transportation," pp. 13, 29–32; Work et al., "Jam Sessions," p. 23; CBS News, *60 Minutes* Transcript, pp. 12–13.

61. J. Allen Whitt, *Urban Elites and Mass Transportation* (Princeton: Princeton University Press, 1982), pp. 107–132.

62. Stephen Zwerling, *Mass Transit and the Politics of Technology* (New York: Praeger, 1974), p. 30. See also pp. 31–33.

63. Whitt, *Urban Elites and Mass Transportation*, pp. 107–132.

64. Urban Land Institute, *Industrial Development Handbook* (Washington, D.C.: Urban Land Institute, 1975), p. 221. See also p. 203.

7

SHOPPING CENTERS
AND BUSINESS PARKS
Decentralized Urban Growth

Long accustomed to spiffy returns and steady growth, real estate investors have been taking some lumps lately....Among the beacons in an otherwise gloomy landscape are regional shopping centers. Much of their good fortune derives from the limited supply of new malls....Analysts believe that the energy belt states are becoming saturated with malls, but they see plenty of potential in the Northeast. They consider Rouse Co., a publicly traded company famous for its harborside shopping plazas in New York City, Boston, and Baltimore, a great way to profit from mall mania.[1]

Along with a lot else in industry, industrial parks are heading for extinction. At least in name...Today's business-corporate-office park is almost certain to be located in a suburban community and near an interstate highway. And that, Mr. Beyard [senior research associate at the Urban Land Institute] points out, has given rise to a new urban problem. "You find corridors developing, lined with parks and shopping centers," he says. "It's totally unexpected and unplanned. Traffic approaches gridlock. No one political subdivision is in control. No one even knows what to call these places, except suburban activity centers."[2]

INTRODUCTION

The decentralization of American cities has been anchored by the movement of major workplace and shopping facilities to outlying areas. In the late 1970s the Massachusetts Court of Appeals granted a temporary injunction stopping construction of a 70-store mall in Hadley, one of several towns clustered in central Massachusetts. The mall was being built by the Pyramid Corporation on farmland near this town of 3,800 and was expected to bring thousands of cars onto the town's streets daily. Pyramid's representatives argued in public meetings that the new mall would be landscaped to create a "rural atmosphere." The mall would house numerous fast-food restaurants, dozens of other specialty chain stores, and large department stores. Supporters argued that the mall would bring jobs and prosperity with no significant negative side effects.[3]

Many local people saw the project differently and protests followed. One local activist explained: "Our town's selectmen and planning board told us there was nothing we could do to stop the mall. But we talked, we organized, we hired a lawyer, we held meetings, we raised funds, we went to court."[4] Local citizens' groups argued that the mall would have many social costs for the people and towns in the area, including increased traffic congestion and environmental damage. Organized citizens took their case to town meetings and argued against the facility. But they had to contend with the local growth coalition—business leaders and their political allies who pressed for more "economic growth" and "progress." And they had to contend with fatalism. Many local residents felt that the "big boys" would get their way, that these mammoth development projects were inevitable. Moreover, the Pyramid Corporation did have first-rate lawyers and public relations consultants. Pyramid conducted a campaign to win over local politicians and citizens. They took senior citizens' groups to dinner, made a contribution to the Little League, and offered land for new road expansion. And they succeeded; the mall was built. But the citizen protests were not in vain. One result was an increase in organized opposition to local development, and subsequent projects were opposed more successfully.

According to an analysis by Jay Neugeboren, the mall and related development projects did indeed bring many of the predicted community costs. Traffic snarls on roads near the shopping center intensified. And there were more traffic accidents. Crime increased. The town dump's capacity was pressed, and $300,000 in repairs on the sewage treatment plant became necessary as a result of the increased activity. Most ironic of all was the destruction of local downtown businesses by the mall. Business in the nearby downtown areas of Amherst and Northampton was off by at least 30 percent. Merchants at the other malls in Hadley conceded losing business.[5] The citizens of this urbanized area in Massachusetts had fought what has been called by some analysts the "malling of America," and in the short run they had lost. As the Hadley struggle indicates, large-scale urban development projects are not confined to central-city areas. They can also be found in suburbia and outlying smaller cities.

Two major types of nonresidential projects symbolize the decentralized urban geography of modern capitalism—large shopping centers and industrial or business parks. About half of all retail trade now takes place in shopping centers. Moreover, as we will document in the next chapter, this commercial and industrial decentralization has been critical in both fostering, and following, residential subdivisions in suburbia and in smaller cities beyond the suburban fringe of metropolitan areas.

MODERN SHOPPING CENTERS

Nothing seems to characterize the distinctive character of modern capitalist cities as does the large shopping center dominated by a handful of the largest retailing chains, sitting astride a government-funded highway, and surrounded by acres of parked automobiles. Many analysts see these centers of retail capitalism as new "village squares" in which much of the social and community life of America is now centered. Others are not so sure, suggesting that these concentrated retail centers may be the signals of deterioration in vital community and cultural aspects of American life.

Different Types of Shopping Centers A shopping center has been described by developers as an integrated set of buildings providing space for retail stores and for parking facilities, as a center owned and managed as one integrated unit. These shopping centers of varying sizes now dominate the shopping habits of U.S. consumers. In 1987 shopping centers generated more than $580 billion in retail sales, about 54 percent of the nation's total nonautomotive retail trade. There are several types of shopping centers, the smallest of which are known as "convenience" centers. These small developments are frequently constructed where a gas station once stood and usually have a few stores with little parking. Typical tenants include convenience stores, fast-food restaurants, dry cleaners, video stores, and hairdressers.[6]

A somewhat larger center is commonly called the "strip center." Strip centers, or "mini-malls," are street-oriented collections of a dozen or so stores similar to those found in convenience centers, assembled in a line, a U-shape, or an L-shape behind a parking area facing a street. They usually do not have a major chain store as an anchor. As one business editor noted, "malls get all the glory, but for every one built, hundreds of small neighborhood and strip centers are constructed and this is where the action has been lately."[7] Indeed, 85 percent of the 1,345 shopping projects built each year during the first half of the 1980s were these strip centers. La Mancha Development Company, a major developer, has built more than 300 in several states, principally California. The firm's president, Sam Bachner, has argued that the rapid growth in strip centers has been consumer driven; consumers began avoiding the larger shopping centers because "they had to go deep into the center, deep into a parking configuration."[8] Shopping at the strip center is more convenient. For developers the lure of strip centers has traditionally been the promise of annual investment returns as high as 15 percent, tax breaks, and cheap rents. In recent years, however, overbuilding has dampened economic returns and tax reform has denied developers an important incentive.

Then there are the larger shopping centers. Some are large community shopping centers ranging in size between 40,000 and 200,000 square feet; they typically have a supermarket anchor, specialty stores, and a drugstore. They are built around a large parking area. Even larger are the regional shopping centers, with a large leasing area, centered around one or more large full-line department stores. Piped-in music, plants arranged in neat rows, electronic games, fast-food restaurants, chain stores specializing in clothing and greeting cards, a long air-conditioned mall anchored at the ends by large department stores—this is the regional shopping mall, a landmark on many a suburban highway. Consider Paramus Park in the New Jersey suburbs near New York City. Completed in the mid-1970s, it has 276,000 square feet on 60 acres of land, three-quarters of which is parking and landscaped area. There are more than 100 mall tenants, including 2 major department stores. The Paramus Park mall was only one of two dozen shopping centers owned and managed by one major development corporation, the Rouse Company, in the late 1970s. Connecticut General Life Insurance Company was a primary financial partner in the project, which illustrates the point we made in Chapter 3 about the important role of insurance companies in channeling capital into secondary-circuit real estate projects. Note too that the prosperity of suburban New Jersey malls contrasts starkly with the decay in the once-bustling downtown areas of nearby New Jersey central cities.[9]

Superregional Malls   The superregional malls are very large regional centers with three to six major department stores, located in major growth centers along suburban highways. One example of a superregional shopping mall is Philadelphia's Franklin Mills, constructed by Western Development. This mall, the largest in the city's history, covers 325 acres and encompasses 1.75 million square feet of retail space, 7 major anchor stores, and 225 smaller tenants. The superregional center attracts people from far away and for longer periods of shopping. Citing Western's Potomac Mills retail complex in Washington, D.C., as a precedent, James D. Beste, Western Development's president, anticipates that a fifth of Franklin Mill's customers will come from more than 100 miles away, and he expects the average customer to stay in the center for more than 2 hours. Beste expects Franklin Mills to be "an intensive and long-term shopping experience."[10] Emphasizing the economic benefits for Philadelphia, Western Development executives underscored the creation of 2,000 temporary construction jobs and 5,000 permanent jobs, as well as $15 million annually in tax revenue. The real estate on which Western's center is constructed required rezoning by government officials as commercial space before the project could proceed. The rezoning was unanimously approved by the Philadelphia City Council in November 1986, but only after the mall corporation agreed to make $9 million in concessions to city needs, including $2 million to widen an interstate interchange, $1.6 million to help construct a senior citizens center, and a donation to community programs. These concessions by developers are, as we suggested in the Santa Monica case cited in Chapter 1 (also see Chapter 10), relatively new and suggest the growing political power of some local citizens' groups opposed to some (or all) aspects of large-scale mall developments.

Mall Developers Several powerful groups are involved in building and operating large shopping malls: developers, financial institutions, national chain stores, and smaller business tenants. Major shopping center developers typically locate the centers, sign up tenants, and secure the loans. In their public discussions developers often say that their shopping center developments are just a response to consumers; a developers' handbook says that "the shopping center exists in response to a consumer demand for retail goods and services."[11] This demand-side explanation, however, conceals the role of a variety of retailing, advertising, and development capitalists in shaping consumer demand; it also conceals the supply-side factors, discussed in Chapters 1 and 3, that channel surplus capital from all over the globe into these real estate projects.

The character of retail merchandising capitalism has profoundly changed over the last few decades. There were only a few large integrated shopping centers and malls before 1945; those that did exist often served rich communities, such as the River Oaks area in Houston. Most shopping was concentrated in downtown stores or scattered small businesses outside the downtown area. Relatively small neighborhood shopping centers increased rapidly in number after World War II, but not until the 1950s were large regional malls constructed around major department stores. Today these large chain stores anchor regional and superregional shopping centers. The increasingly dominant chain store executives, sometimes nudged by developers, made the decision to migrate from downtown areas for both demand-side and supply-side reasons. Consider the words of Don Fitch, vice-president of leasing for a Dallas company:

> *The way it often works is when we're talking to a Penney or Sears, they'll tell us they want to close a downtown store and open in a mall. Sometimes the developer even nudges the tenant by telling him the store he's got is old and decrepit and should be shuttered and replaced with a new store in a mall....*[12]

Since the 1950s the growth of retailing megacorporations and abandonment of downtown areas by the larger department stores has had a negative impact on the smaller businesses, as well as the general downtown atmosphere.

Concentration and Centralization An increasing concentration and centralization of capital has occurred in the commercial retailing industry over the last two decades. The concentration of capital can be seen in the growth in value of capital in the major retailing firms as a result of accumulation and the elimination of smaller and weaker firms. The centralization of capital can be seen in the fusion of different retailing corporations by mergers and acquisitions. Thus by the late 1980s much of the general merchandise business was controlled by the 10 largest chains; in order of total sales, these largest chain stores were Sears, J.C. Penney, Federated, May Department Store Company, Dayton Hudson, R.H. Macy, Montgomery Ward, Allied Stores, Carter Hawley Hale, and Batus. All had sales over $2.4 billion in 1986. Most of these corporations have played an important role in anchoring large-scale shopping center developments.[13]

An important event in the history of shopping centers was the mid-1950s opening in suburban Minneapolis of Southdale Center, one of the first enclosed malls featuring major department stores. It boasted a partially glass roof over a common space with a cafe, seating, fountains, and exhibitions. Thousands of malls have been built since then. An association, the International Council of Shopping Centers, has been formed, symbolizing both the importance and the integration of shopping center developers and other owners in postwar cities. In 1957 there were only 2,000 shopping centers in the United States, but by the 1970s the *Shopping Center Directory* listed nearly 19,000 shopping centers in the United States and more than 1,200 in Canada. That number had increased to more than 30,000 by the late 1980s. And most of these shopping centers are less than two decades old.[14]

Shopping center, especially mall, development has been dominated by a few large corporations. The largest mall developer, billionaire Edward DeBartolo, started in 1949. He invested heavily in suburban shopping centers; he became involved in large regional malls in the 1960s. By the late 1980s this "King of Malls" owned or controlled over 84 million square feet of space in shopping centers. DeBartolo's firm also owned nearly 8 million square feet of office space and had a sizable stake in hotels, condos, video game parlors, and undeveloped land surrounding existing malls. He has also become involved in attempts to buy major department store chains, including loans for Robert Campeau's purchase of Federated Stores. In 1988 his wealth was estimated at $1.4 billion.[15] Another example is Santa-Monica-based MaceRich, a developer and operator of 23 malls and 19 community shopping centers. Buying up existing malls, this firm added three regional malls and four community centers to its inventory of retail space in 1987 alone. As part of their $284 million investment, the company acquired Fresno's Fresno Fashion Fair, a 917,679-square-foot center; Ventura's Buenaventura Plaza, an 878,102-square-foot mall; and Huntington Beach's Huntington Center, a 969,313-square-foot retail center.[16]

Several of the richest Americans have become wealthy by constructing, owning, and managing shopping centers. The 1988 *Forbes* listing of the 400 richest Americans identified a number linked to shopping center investments. In addition to DeBartolo, the *Forbes* list included Melvin and

Herbert Simon, now worth $800 million. They formed Melvin Simon and Associates in 1960 to build shopping centers. Now the second-largest mall developer, Simon and Associates began with strip malls and moved into regional malls. By the late 1980s Simon and Associates owned over 56 million square feet of mall space and managed another 13 million. To cite another example, the brothers Richard E. and David H. Jacobs, together worth $740 million, constructed their first mall in Columbus in 1962; they have grown to be the fourth-largest mall firm, with more than 44 malls and 42 million square feet under their control. With a net worth of $600 million, developer-investor Jerry J. Moore began buying strip malls in 1966 and in the late 1980s controlled 152 shopping centers and 19 million square feet of mall space, mostly in Houston. Another wealthy shopping center developer, Frank Morgan, opened his first big shopping center in 1967 and in the late 1980s presided over 11 million square feet of shopping malls; he also controlled numerous Kansas City area banks. He and his partner, Sherman Dreisezun, have maintained their wealth, estimated at over $600 million, in family trusts and friends' names. Shopping mall investment and development has clearly been a major source of entrepreneurial wealth in the United States.[17]

As with other types of real estate investments, investments in decentralized shopping center projects in the secondary real estate circuit have oscillated over time. Capital has flowed back and forth between the Sunbelt and the Frostbelt, and from overseas into both regions. Since the early 1980s regional centers in certain southwestern cities have not been the choice investment opportunities they once were. One problem is that there are now few large metropolitan Sunbelt areas without numerous regional malls in key places. During the 1960s and 1970s the booming Sunbelt cities were the focus of much mall development, and there were commonplace discussions of moving investment from the declining Frostbelt cities. However, by the mid-1980s many Sunbelt cities were saturated with malls, and those in the energy belt were in serious recession, and shopping center analysts were calling the Northeast the area with "plenty of potential." According to a 1988 investors' advisory in *Fortune*, "among the beacons in an otherwise gloomy landscape are regional shopping centers" in the Northeast. *Fortune* also noted that industry analysts considered the strategy of the Rouse Company, a developer of harborside shopping centers, as "a great way to profit from mall mania."[18] And in addition to the movement of investment capital into large shopping centers in northeastern cities, there has been the previously cited increase in investments in strip centers in many cities across the country.

The "Science" of Center Location The business of locating, building, and operating shopping centers is sometimes referred to as a "science." Many developers pick locations years in advance along either actual or projected highways. Profitable shopping center developments may involve careful decisions about location. Developer analyses often look at consumer demand, including the income of people in the area to be served, and market control, especially competition from other shopping centers. According to developer theory about consumers, an average person will drive 1.5 miles for necessities such as food, 3 to 5 miles for other necessary items when range of selection is not important, and 8 or more miles when range of selection is important. Accessibility is also important. Regional malls are located near major highways, and smaller centers are often located on busy streets near residential subdivisions. If so desired, developers involved in residential subdivisions can help in the creation of a captive audience for their own shopping centers. Shopping center developers also examine supply-side factors such as land costs, governmental subsidies, loan and other capital availability, and their own interest in land speculation and ownership. One developers' handbook recommends that shopping center owners should own land adjacent to their shopping centers for future expansion.[19]

Even the positions of shops within malls are arranged in terms of suitability of location, compatibility with nearby shops, and crafty merchandising. Retail shops are located to maximize the enticement of consumers. The large anchoring department stores are usually located at a considerable distance from one another to maximize the exposure of consumers to small stores in between. In the development literature numerous technical terms are used to describe the logistics involved in locating malls, among them gross leasable area, parking index, convenience goods, and impulse goods. The last two terms refer to the types of products that are offered to customers. Developer handbooks suggest how centers should be arranged to manipulate customer expenditures. One such book suggests that "impulse goods have an indefinite trade area and are placed so as to get them into the customer flow created by other businesses or within a store where people are passing by on their way to find a definitely sought-for item."[20] Put simply, items that consumers do not seek should be placed where consumers will see them on the way to merchandise actually sought.

Money Machines: Rents and Profits Developers, lenders, and chain stores alike profit from shopping centers. The large department store chains cited previously earn a large proportion of their profits from stores in shopping centers. As noted above, recent decades have brought an increasing concentration and centralization of retail capital. The retail megacorporations have the economic power to dictate construction and leasing conditions to the shopping center developers, including such boons as lower rents for themselves. For consumers, however, the deterioration of stand-alone downtown stores and the concentration of retailing in the chain stores of shopping centers have often meant less variety in some consumer items, more product standardization, and much the same goods and services in every large shopping center across the country. This reduction in competition has brought higher prices.[21]

Retail shopping centers have been profitable investments for surplus capital in the domestic and foreign circuits of capital. Annual return on a capitalist's investment in many U.S. and Canadian shopping centers has ranged from 15 to 100 percent. Profits come both from rents and from selling the centers later on. American investors' income from a sale has until recently been taxed at the capital gains rates, which were for many years less than ordinary tax rates. The *Shopping Center Development Guide* has termed shopping centers "money machines."[22] In many cases the developer-owner manages the shopping center; in other cases a management company is hired. Management functions include rent collection, security, and sales promotion. Shopping center owners can make substantial profits on rents. In some cases the rents for stores in shopping centers include a percentage of the store's total sales, so that the owner of the shopping center not only gets a normal per-square-foot rent but also a percentage of the profits (called "overage" rent) of the profitable stores. Overage rent, to quote a real estate journal, is "a major reason why well conceived and carefully planned regional shopping centers have emerged as secure and profitable investments for long-term lenders and equity interest."[23]

The Power of Financing We noted in Chapter 3 that projects such as shopping centers and malls have been supported by loans from U.S. and foreign insurance firms, banks, and pension funds. By the 1980s the surplus capital in the hands of executives in these firms had increased substantially, to the point that they were investing more heavily in "trophy" real estate investments, such as regional shopping malls in major cities. In some cases the insurance firms have bought shopping centers. For example, in the late 1980s Metropolitan Life purchased several shopping malls in Chicago, Cincinnati, Orlando, and Bismarck for its own portfolio and for pension fund clients.

As with other development projects, lenders can exert control not only over the mortgage loans themselves but also over construction and day-to-day operation. There are several examples of the power of finance capital. If the majority of stores in a center are local businesses, lenders may provide only half as much as when most of the renters are national large chain stores. Some lenders have required three-quarters of mall space to be occupied by national retail chains, rather than independent businesses. Since the 1980s there have been more joint ventures by developers and lenders and more participation by financial institutions in actual ownership as a condition for making the loans. And some finance capitalists have operated as developers themselves, as in the Urbco, Inc., case cited in Chapter 3. This development arm of Connecticut Mutual Life Insurance Company developed 1 million square feet of office, shopping center, and residential space in the mid-1980s. Moreover, in recent years foreign banks and pension funds—European, Japanese, Mexican, and Middle Eastern—have had an increasingly important role in the financing and ownership of shopping malls. While new office towers are the international investors' property of choice, they have also invested in shopping malls. For example, Dutch real estate investor Rodamco and Canada's Trizec Corporation have placed major bets on U.S. shopping malls.[24]

Government Subsidies for Centers   Local governments have provided many services that make shopping malls possible. Part or all of the cost of sewerage, water, gas, and electric utility services for shopping centers is frequently paid for by local government bonds and funds. The Urban Land Institute has observed that "enlightened municipal planning bodies tend to look favorably on planned developments, such as shopping centers."[25] Typically, government officials are seen as "enlightened" decision makers only if they meet the utility and other service needs of developers. Urban developers have pressed for government-subsidized utility and other service districts for projects such as shopping centers. Yet, at the same time, these real estate decision makers have often criticized governmental regulations on housing and land matters and governmental decisions dealing with problems such as pollution, unemployment, and welfare. As we noted in Chapter 1, capitalists, and particularly real estate capitalists, generally have a laissez-faire view of government, preferring the state not to interfere in the "free market" economy as a general principle. However, this general principle is ignored when it comes to particular types of government subsidies for real estate development. Many local developers have sought aid for shopping centers, and government officials respond because centers are perceived as providing economic stability. One example of the active role that local officials have taken is the $80 million in general obligation bonds offered by the Bloomington, Minnesota, Port Authority to subsidize the Triple Five Corporation's construction of a huge shopping mall in that Minneapolis suburb. This governmental capital has been provided for land purchase and for utility and parking improvements.[26]

Because suburban sites for shopping centers have become harder to find, some developers have begun to reconsider building in central-city locations and redeveloping older shopping centers. As Chapter 5 suggests, downtown development has become more viable because of a returning population and employment base in selected major downtown areas, as well as renewed growth coalition activity and government assistance for developers in downtown areas.

PROTESTING AND DEFENDING DEVELOPMENT

Citizens' Protests Some citizens and social science researchers argue that shopping centers often have substantial negative effects. Several citizens' groups have protested, and even succeeded in slowing, mall development. For example, in Manassas, Virginia, builder John T. Hazel has proposed the construction of a 1.2-million-square-foot shopping mall, together with 1.7 million square feet of office space, on land that many believe is an unmarked graveyard of Union and Confederate soldiers. More than 3,000 Civil War preservationists gathered in the Manassas National Battlefield Park to protest the planned mall. As of late 1988, the actions of these citizens and sympathetic members of Congress had indefinitely delayed the construction of the proposed mall and related large-scale development.[27] Local citizens have also protested the smaller shopping centers that have proliferated in recent decades. Homeowners' groups, local merchants, and law-enforcement officials in southern California and elsewhere have worked to curtail shopping center projects. Shopping strips are "examples of urban blight," says Michael Woo, a Los Angeles City Council member. "They make our thoroughfares look like parking lots. They're built cheaply. They're ugly." In the late 1980s Woo's ordinance to limit their spread was approved by a Los Angeles City Council concerned with discouraging strip shopping developments.[28]

Shopping center protests in a number of North American cities have led to the creation of government regulations and commissions designed to study the problems created by shopping centers and malls. For example, cities in Ontario, Canada, have seen heated struggles emerge over mall development, with several shopping centers being delayed or vetoed by governmental officials under citizen pressure. In Fredericton, New Brunswick, a regional shopping mall was rejected by city officials and local voters after a long struggle. And the entire province of Prince Edward Island established a freeze on shopping center development, which was followed by a public study of such centers. Moreover, the Newfoundland Independent Business Association, formed in the early 1980s, pressed local governments for a freeze on mall development until new controls could be implemented. Interestingly, these *local* business leaders made radical demands. They included the suggestion that half the ownership of new shopping malls should be local, that half of all retail spaces should be reserved for local businesses, that local businesses should be charged the same rent per square foot as national chains, and that the chain stores should be specially taxed on mall profits. Remarkably, these demands came from local business people in the towns and cities. As one local merchant ironically put it, without these controls to protect small businesses, "you have the Marxist idea [being fulfilled]; the big boys squeeze out the little fellows, the rich get richer."[29]

The Developers' Defense   Shopping center developers have a different view. They and associated politicians commonly argue that center projects improve the local tax base and increase employment, that whole communities benefit, and that development implies increased tax revenues and general prosperity. Whether centers are far out in suburbia, or in closer-in older residential areas, they are defended with the same justifications. For example, a major controversy erupted in Denver, Colorado, over the rebuilding and redevelopment of an older shopping center a few miles from downtown. The Cherry Creek Shopping Center was originally built in the mid-1950s. The 600-acre Cherry Creek area includes not only this shopping center but also a large number of boutique shops and an exclusive residential section. One of the nation's largest shopping center developers was brought in by the owner of the mall to rebuild it into a huge multiple-use project with a regional mall, office buildings, a luxury hotel, and parking garages for thousands of cars.

However, 13 citizens' and downtown business groups protested this redevelopment. A University of Colorado study revealed that downtown businesses would lose millions in annual sales and their growth rate would decline substantially. Downtown business groups became concerned about this decline. Neighborhood groups expressed concern with the traffic problems an enlarged center would create and they raised questions about the destruction of the area's unique architecture. As with similar developments in other cities, a top executive representing the owner-developer of this project argued that there would be a tremendous benefit to the city in the form of sharply increased tax revenues from the center, which would "more than pay for all of the traffic improvements and other services needed to handle the increased density." His explicit statement was that "this is our neighborhood too" and that we "intend to preserve and protect it." The executives of the large national shopping center development corporations visualize themselves as friendly neighbors bringing great innovations and benefits to urban areas.[30]

Community Costs of Shopping Centers   Few city residents know how shopping center economics works. Small-business people in downtown areas typically know little about the process of suburban mall development, except that it costs them business. The construction of a large regional mall has often created serious trouble for downtown retail stores not far away. We have previously explained the consequences of the concentration and centralization of capital in retailing. The growing retail corporations are concentrating their business in shopping centers, centers that have increased the dominance of large corporations in local retail markets because smaller local businesses cannot gain access to the more or less closed center settings. A major consequence is the concentration of consumers' shopping in a decreasing number of areas. Another consequence is sameness.

Across the nation the architecture of shopping centers is standardized, in what some critics have called "upside-down ice cube trays, on a carpet of macadam."[31] The stark exteriors encourage people to gather inside rather than outside, and the absence of windows and the calculated variations in lighting, greenery, and physical layout enhance the probability of impulse buying.[32]

In the long run new development may not even bring the projected level of new governmental tax revenues; some taxes may be lost because older stores are abandoned as local businesses go bankrupt. Moreover, the new tax revenues are partially paid by the developer-owners and the new shopping center businesses. They, in turn, can usually pass their taxes along to local consumers in higher prices, lower wages, or both. And in some cases developers receive direct tax reductions. In addition, the argument articulated by the local growth coalitions—that shopping center development brings new jobs to local areas—is problematic. New construction jobs are short term, and many are filled by outsiders. Existing jobs are lost because local businesses go bankrupt. Introducing large new retail centers usually means, according to one study, that "once the new mall becomes firmly established, the number of retail jobs in the city will not be higher than the number there would be had the mall never been built."[33] Many shopping centers have been developed with the explicit intention of drawing business away from older facilities. One developers' handbook notes that "new shopping centers do not create new buying power; rather, they attract customers from existing districts or capture a portion of new purchasing power in a growing area."[34] In addition, malls owned by the giant national and international developers frequently channel profits away from communities into outside investments that do not benefit local consumers.

Large shopping centers can also bring environmental problems. Shopping centers depend heavily on cars and trucks. Two-thirds to three-quarters of a typical center's acreage is reserved for parking. In the development process it is not uncommon for acres of trees and natural drainage to be destroyed, thereby creating polluted water run-off problems. The operation of malls with large open spaces to heat and cool is wasteful of energy. In the last decade developers have become worried about the imposition of stringent environmental rules and traffic regulations as local communities realize the negative impact of shopping centers.

Too Much Shopping Space?   In recent years many U.S. cities have become "over-stored" in terms of the amount of shopping center retail space. The vacancy rate nationwide for smaller shopping centers rose from 9.9 percent in 1985 to an estimated 13 percent for 1988. In the late 1980s the president of the International Council of Shopping Centers summarized the state of his industry: "We don't have an overbuilt situation to the extent the office building industry has, but if we continue to mature...we will have a tendency to develop more intensely than we have in the past. We are particularly concerned about the smaller unanchored shopping centers where the majority of our unleased space is located."[35]

However, some in the industry have argued that there is no national problem of overbuilding. John Tuthill, president of Southmark Commercial Management's retail division and the manager of 114 properties, has argued that a few inexperienced developers built shopping centers in poor locations. And in the late 1980s Bob Johnson, executive vice-president of Leo Eisenberg, one of the major small-center developers, described center overbuilding as "a regional situation, not an overall problem."[36] According to this view, a few Sunbelt states such as Texas, Louisiana, Florida, and Oklahoma have experienced overbuilding because developers there constructed speculative real estate projects in anticipation of business growth that did not occur. In Atlanta, between 1964 and 1977, the general population increased 73 percent, yet the amount of shopping center space expanded by a remarkable 440 percent. And in metropolitan Houston, shopping center overbuilding has remained a persistent problem. A survey of 16 regional malls there found, even with rent concessions and other substantial incentives, an average occupancy rate of 93 percent. While this figure was a little low, it did not include the many strip centers that were partially or totally vacant; between 1986 and 1987 alone, nearly 100 of the smaller centers were forced to close because of foreclosure, a sharp increase from the previous year.[37]

The pressures created by the overdevelopment of shopping centers have sometimes led to internecine competition among otherwise cooperative real estate actors. Developers compete with one another to attract regional and national stores to their malls, even if that means killing off older shopping centers and local businesses. Developers and chain stores are often willing to absorb losses for a few years if they can drive out competitors and gain substantial monopoly control over local shopping markets in the long run. In addition, even the increase of store bankruptcies within shopping centers in the 1980s did not dampen the trend toward shopping center dominance of retail trade. Whereas the majority of centers in many cities saw at least one of their member stores go bankrupt in the 1980s, an estimated three-fifths of *all* new retail store square footage was still being provided in shopping malls during the decade.[38] The department store chains continue to spend billions annually adding and renovating millions of square feet of retail space. According to the trade publication *Chain Store Age Executive*, the top 25 retail chains were planning to increase their gross square footage by two-thirds of a billion square feet in 1987.[39]

SHOPPING CENTERS: MODERN VILLAGE SQUARES?

The Impact of Shopping Centers: The Question of Community   Some observers picture shopping malls as the new village squares, as facilities embodying the rich traditions of older-community gathering places. In the early 1980s Philip Brous, president of a large retail chain store company, viewed the modern enclosed shopping center as replacing

> *the candy store of our youth as the place for young people to go to congregate...young people like to go there and particularly to show up on Saturday and Sunday. They also like to go there all summer long when school is out....In suburbia, there are no downtowns. The youngsters (whom Bloomingdale's calls "the Saturday genera-tion") gravitate toward the enclosed shopping mall. They like nothing better than to arrive early on a Saturday morning and do some shopping, have lunch in one of the fast-food places, do some more shopping or meet friends, and then possibly go to the movies or to an ice skating rink if the mall has one.*[40]

Similarly, in 1988 a reporter for the *Wall Street Journal* observed in an analysis of consumer trends that "malls have become more than hubs of commerce: With most Main Streets and village greens relegated to the status of quaint relics, the malls have become places to hang out—to relieve loneliness, alienation or boredom."[41]

In their research social scientists have given mixed reviews to shop-ping centers. One urban ecologist has provided a favorable view of malls as "Main Street, Fifth Avenue and the community social and entertainment center—all wrapped in one."[42] In the shopping centers people can eat, drink, shop, play, and exercise. The vitality of centers is viewed as resulting from their alleged integration into community life. Other researchers have been more critical. Mark Baldassare, a University of California (Irvine) sociologist, has raised questions about civic identity in suburban life, noting that malls "provide what little civic identity exists in the sub-urbs....They are places to go—if not to meet people, then to see other people, to feel you are a part of things."[43] And social scientist Jerry Jacobs has argued that malls have both positive and negative functions. For many they provide an occasional shopping break from everyday life; for others they become a means of escape. Some, particularly some teenagers, be-come oriented to or obsessed with malls as places to be. Jacobs suggests that such use of malls for escapism can be unhealthy.[44] At the Hudson Valley Mall in Kingston, New York, like many others, as many as 500 teenagers can gather in a single evening. Many of these youth frequently spend $30 to $50 a weekend there. However, they are not welcomed; they have reportedly labeled the shopping center "Auschwitz Mall" for the rigorous handling of teenagers' "loitering" by the security guards.[45] Across the nation groups of teenagers are discouraged from gathering in shop-ping centers. Only a few malls have truly become social centers for adults. The Rimrock Mall in Billings, Montana, a regional development, has reportedly displaced the downtown area as a central gathering place for ranchers and other people coming to town on nights and weekends.[46]

Studies of modern shopping centers suggest they fall short of providing the kind of environment characteristic of traditional gathering places. In particular, traditional street life differs greatly from mall life. Commenting on this difference, architectural analyst James Sanders:

> *At its root, the essence of a suburban place (no matter what its location or how many cafes it boasts) is that it is conceptually a point in space, discontinuous from all else. People drive to it, park, use it, get back in their cars, and drive away. Those using the mall make a deliberate decision to do so; no one is "just passing through" to get somewhere else....A street by contrast...is also a connector between two or more other places. Some people may have made a special trip to use the street's facilities, but others are just passing through to get somewhere else. It is the combination of conscious and casual use of the street that makes for its complex web of interactions and possibilities. With no casual use, is it any wonder that a mall, despite its fountains, trees, and cafes, might somehow feel "artificial"?*[47]

We have here two different uses of space. In the mall case the use of space is conscious and oriented to buying and selling, to commodities. There are usually no other layers of social interaction. In contrast, traditional street life in neighborhoods combines shopping in small stores with a palimpsest layering of other uses of space, such as neighbors chatting and children playing.

Malls Are Private Property   A sign at one downtown office plaza prominently proclaims: "PRIVATE PROPERTY. CROSS AT THE RISK OF THE USER AND BY REVOCABLE PERMISSION ONLY." In one important sense, shopping centers, malls, and MXDs can never replace the older centers of urban social life, because unlike the old downtown areas and real village squares, shopping malls are as a rule private property. Owners can prohibit malls from being used for purposes with which they do not agree. Signs are posted indicating management control of the mall; community groups may be excluded or may have to pay rental fees; and leafleting and campaigning by political candidates may be prohibited.[48]

The federal courts have struggled with the question of shopping centers as private property. Initially, in a 1946 case, *Marsh v. Alabama*, the U.S. Supreme Court extended constitutional protection of civil liberties such as free speech to private property if the owners of that private property were taking on a public role. This "public function" reasoning was specifically applied to shopping center owners in a 1968 case, *Amalgamated Food Employees Union Local 590 v. Logan Valley Plaza, Inc.* In this decision, the Supreme Court concluded that the new shopping center should be seen as public space. However, this interpretation was jettisoned in the 1970s when conservative justices became dominant on the Supreme Court.[49]

In the late 1960s several young people went to a Portland, Oregon, shopping center and distributed antiwar leaflets to passersby. They were peacefully exercising their First Amendment right of free speech, but the center's management prohibited the distribution. A federal judge ruled in favor of the young people, arguing that the mall was "open to the general public" and was a public place because the management encouraged use of the facilities by groups such as the Salvation Army. The Ninth Circuit Court of Appeals upheld the rights of the young leafleters, but in 1972 the U.S. Supreme Court ruled in favor of the property rights of the owner. Similarly, in 1975 the Supreme Court decided in *Hudgens* v. *National Labor Relations Board* that the free speech of union picketers had no federal constitutional protection at a privately owned mall, in this case the North DeKalb Shopping Center in suburban Atlanta. Though the Supreme Court has maintained this position since the Hudgens decision, it has permitted individual states to protect freedom of speech on private property if that is consistent with their state constitutions. In light of a 1980 Supreme Court decision (*PruneYard Shopping Center* v. *Robbins*) five states have interpreted their state constitutions so as to protect freedom of speech on private property dedicated to public use.[50] Nonetheless, the majority of shopping malls still have the right to ban freedom of speech if they believe that to be in their interest.

Security is a major concern among the owners and managers of shopping centers. But "security" in their language refers not only to medical emergencies and shoplifters but also to community groups that "may create problems—picket lines, political rallies, panhandlers, noisy youth, vagrants, and street people," to quote a shopping center developers' handbook.[51] This developers' handbook goes on to say that owners and managers must weigh the rights of assembly and free speech against property and profit rights, with the latter being a major priority. One shopping center advertising manager has expressed the owners' perspective: "We don't try to duplicate the downtown community....We don't do anything unrelated to our main purpose, which is merchandising."[52]

Advocates for shopping centers may believe they are providing a new community, but their idea of community is distinctly commodified. Their ideas are based not on affectional ties but on commodity sales considerations. The central idea is to strive to reshape urban social life in a profit-oriented setting. And the fiscal crisis of the local and national governments, to which Americans historically have traditionally turned for the creation of parks and plazas, now means less public construction. As a result, city governments increasingly rely on private developers "for the creation of these new 'public' spaces, to the retailers, developers, and corporations who, for their own economic return, are creating them in record numbers, often as the centerpieces for larger office, shopping, or housing efforts."[53] Yet these are no longer true public plazas and parks, for they are privately controlled.

Co-opting the Local Community   Fearful of community protest against development, development handbooks encourage shopping center developers to introduce public uses into their projects. Because numerous communities have protested the construction of shopping malls, organizations of developers have sometimes sought to influence communities in subtle ways. An Urban Land Institute publication put it this way: "Community attitudes are demanding. They are apt to be fraught with political intrigue and occasional bad judgment....Because he is asking for a change, the developer must be able to overcome people's natural preference to keep things as they are."[54] Local residents are here depicted as conservative, as resisting an inevitable urban metamorphosis; it is the developers who rescue communities by bringing progressive changes to cities. Moreover, the National Association of Home Builders' *Shopping Center Development Guide* (published to assist developers in assembling shopping center projects) recommends that developers map out a campaign to pacify the surrounding community. For example, it suggests that they seek to share their large parking areas with a church, library, or other community facility to "make important allies."[55]

MOVING INDUSTRY OUT OF CITIES: INDUSTRIAL AND BUSINESS PARKS

Suburbanization of Investment and Employment   Suburban shopping centers are one anchor of real estate capitalism outside central cities. Another major anchor is the industrial, business, or office park. In the North and the South much capital investment since the 1960s has gone into suburban office and manufacturing facilities. By 1973 there was more employment in the suburbs of cities than in the central cities. During nonrecession years in the 1970s and 1980s the suburban rings of a wide variety of older and newer cities had faster-growing economies than did their central cities; these included the metropolitan areas of Philadelphia, New York, Denver, Houston, Dallas, Phoenix, and San Francisco.[56] So great has been the growth of some outlying areas that they have been called the "dynamic outer cities," "megacounties," and "booming urban villages." In spite of the image of residential villages, these outlying areas are often centered around business activity centers. In the late 1980s *Time* published a major story on these megacounties; that discussion covered Fairfax County, Virginia, across the Potomac from Washington, D.C.; Orange County, between San Diego and Los Angeles; Du Page County, just west of Chicago; Gwinnett County, northeast of Atlanta; and Johnson County, Kansas, near Kansas City. These counties have been characterized by growth not only in residential subdivisions, but also in employment in office and industrial developments. Unlike earlier suburbs these counties are not simply bedroom communities, but are more or less self-sufficient areas within multinucleated cities. As we noted in Chapter 4, there has been considerable office construction outside downtown areas since the 1970s. Many suburbanites now commute to work in their own or adjacent suburban counties.[57]

Planned Parks The U.S. Department of Commerce has defined a "planned industrial district" (industrial park) as a "tract of land which is subdivided and developed according to a comprehensive plan for the use of a community of industries, with streets, railroad tracks, and utilities installed before sites are sold to prospective occupants."[58] In effect, an industrial park is a packaged arrangement with its own zoning controls and regulations. Many corporate facilities are now situated in industrial parks. In Louisville, to take one case, most newer factories have been located in such parks; and many of these plants were relocated from the central business district.[59]

Initially, most facilities in the outlying industrial parks were for manufacturing plants, warehouses, and commercial distribution. But in recent years a growing number of parks include lighter industry, as well as office towers, shopping facilities, and occasionally recreational and government facilities. For example, the Los Angeles Industrial Center is a 549-acre industrial/business park that initially contained light manufacturing, research, warehousing, distribution, and commercial facilities. Its developer later added a motel and a bank and space for police and fire stations. One study of parks in the 1970s found that there were 700 *major* industrial/business parks averaging 300 acres each. Between 1960 and the mid-1980s, thousands of parks of varying sizes were built along suburban and other outlying roads.[60] A consulting firm specializing in these parks, Conway Data, Inc., of Atlanta, has divided them into three categories: basic, moderate, and advanced. The first refers to the heavy industrial park; the second type encompasses parks involved in light manufacturing, distribution, and warehousing; and the third category includes parks with offices, research and development, and associated manufacturing. By the late 1980s there were nearly 6,000 parks of all types consuming about 2 million acres of land. Conway has estimated that there will be 9,000 parks by the end of the century. No "advanced" parks were built prior to 1950. And the proportion of advanced parks grew from about 6 percent of all parks in the 1950s to 33 percent in 1985.[61]

Development of industrial/business parks is similar to development of residential suburbs. Private developers usually provide the land packaging, the internal roads and services, the government permits, and often the landscaping and building design. Space is leased out to commercial and manufacturing companies; the companies that locate in the industrial park may not own the land but instead pay a leasing fee to the owner. As with shopping centers and central-city development, major sources of financing for parks have been insurance companies, banks, real estate investment trusts, and foreign investors.[62]

Substantial profits have been made from industrial parks. The overall return on investments has been as much as 75 percent per year. During the 1970s and 1980s investment in proposed and existing parks was recommended by real estate advisers. Landauer Associates, an international real estate consulting firm in New York, called such parks "the best immediate real estate buy in 1985" and the "safest and most assured investment."[63] This consulting firm cited corporate flight to the less suburban locations as the main reason for the continued vitality of industrial/business parks as an investment.

Profiting from Park Location   The reasons given for the suburbanization of corporate locations are diverse; they have included the pleasant character of a low-density environment and the shift in the United States from a manufacturing to a service economy. The most important factors are linked to corporate needs. Park developers have specific requirements in mind when selecting locations attractive to potential corporate clients. One company that assists in this development has listed the following requirements for larger parks:

1. Select cities of 1 million or more people, with economic growth potential
2. Select large sites near expressway systems
3. Analyze population growth and composition in the area
4. Analyze industrial growth in the area, especially type of industries
5. Analyze community attitudes toward industry
6. Make sure gas, water, sewer, electric, and other facilities will be available at low rates[64]

Note here the concern of industrial and development corporations with highway access, the provision of cheap government services, and favorable community attitudes.

Conventional locational analysis usually emphasizes the lower costs attached to decentralized locations. Suburban industrial land, office space, and utilities are often cheaper than in the central city. And there is frequently a large supply of labor, including women who have been enticed to work outside the home. Some business analysts accent the lower labor costs and less unionization in many outlying areas. A study of Elk Grove Village in the Chicago area, a huge industrial park with many companies, found that the corporate executives there liked the suburban location because it was close to *their* homes. The title of an article in the *Atlantic* has underscored the main suburbanizing force: "How Business is Reshaping America."[65]

Governmental Support   A study of 157 industrial parks in the New York–New Jersey metropolitan area found that most were near an interchange of a limited-access highway. Since corporations have moved out of central cities, and often away from railroads, the suburban locations bring a heavier dependence on trucks, automobiles, and highways. Highway systems have developed hand in hand with industrial/business parks. Here again, the needs of corporations and the actions of government administrators regularly correspond. Park developers have sometimes acquired sites near projected highways years before the roads are laid and lobbied for the expansion of highways at public expense. In addition, developers and industrial corporations pressure local government officials to supply services, tax concessions, and cheap land for parks, and many government officials are eager to comply. They do so because, like the mainstream analysts Peterson and Downs cited in Chapter 1, they believe that all their constituents will benefit from economic growth. Local governments strive to obtain these parks for their districts and provide the local utility services and tax concessions that make the parks viable. But park location frequently affects a local community's basic services in ways the politicians did not anticipate. Providing new water and sewerage facilities and adequate streets for business parks can bring a sharp increase in expenditures by local governments, and in turn an increase in local property taxes.[66]

A new wrinkle in the governmental funding of business parks is the creation of "foreign trade zones" (FTZs), such as the Riverport project established in the Louisville, Kentucky, area. The importance of these foreign trade zones is that they allow corporations to store their manufactured goods there duty-free until they are shipped—in other words, to avoid taxation on their inventories until the goods are sold. Since Louisville established its FTZ, Toyota, General Electric, and Ford have all built facilities in the area. According to Riverport's president, the development is substantially government financed: "If you're going to have a first-class park development...it's got to involve public money....FTZ status has assumed a major importance in such parks. It's a virtual necessity."[67] He further argues that the FTZ status for industrial parks has become essential to their success. Here again we see governmental subsidies for private development.

CONCLUSION

When corporate America decentralized its shopping facilities, its industrial complexes, and its many office parks, it determined the shopping and work places for tens of millions of Americans. These deconcentrated investment patterns have created multinucleated cities. Only a few decades earlier, most urban Americans lived and worked in central cities. Cities were focused on downtown areas. There was little public discussion or debate about this process of relocating jobs and shopping; rank-and-file Americans were not directly consulted about the concentration and centralization of industries or the investments in the secondary circuit of real estate in outlying areas. Yet it is they who must often move and accommodate themselves to the decisions of the powerful investors. The dramatic expansion of suburban residential developments is linked directly to this decentralization of commerce and industry. We will now turn to an analysis of these residential suburbs.

NOTES

1. John J. Curran, "The Bright Jewels in Real Estate," *Fortune* 116 (Fall 1987): 24.
2. Donald B. Thompson, "The Lure of the Park," *Industry Week* 230 (September 15, 1986): 45–46.
3. Jay Neugeboren, "Mall Mania," *Mother Jones* 4 (May 1979): 21–24.
4. Ibid., p. 21.
5. Ibid., p. 31.
6. Ellen Graham, "The Pleasure Dome," *Wall Street Journal*, May 13, 1988, 5R.
7. Steven Bergsman, "Shopping Center Developers Are Learning That Small Is Beautiful," *Barrons*, February 3, 1986, 59.
8. Cited in ibid.
9. Urban Land Institute, *Shopping Center Development Handbook* (Washington, D.C.: Urban Land Institute, 1977), pp. 207–217. (Cited hereafter as Urban Land Institute, *Shopping Center*.)
10. "Ben Would Feel at Home at Franklin Mills: Super-Regional Center Ties Theme to 'Historicity' of Philadelphia Area," *Chain Store Age Executive* 63 (November 1987): 168–170.
11. Urban Land Institute, *Shopping Center*, p. 249.
12. Cited in "Some Developers Opt for Middle Markets," *Chain Store Age Executive* 63 (May 1987): 94.
13. David P. Schulz, "Stores' Annual Ranking," *Stores*, July 1987, 14, 24.
14. James Sanders, "Toward a Return of the Public Place: An American Survey," *Architectural Record* 173 (April 1985): 89; David J. Jefferson, "Mini-Mall Boom Fades as Developers Face Economic and Political Pressures," *Wall Street Journal*, June 25, 1987, 27.
15. "The Forbes Four Hundred," *Forbes* 142 (October 24, 1988): 160.
16. "Macerich Masters the Art of Acquisition," *Chain Store Age Executive* 63 (November 1987): 166.
17. "The Forbes Four Hundred," pp. 201, 216, 254.
18. John J. Curran, "The Bright Jewels in Real Estate," p. 24.

19. Curtis T. Bell, *Shopping Center Development Guide* (Washington, D.C.: National Association of Homebuilders, National Housing Center, n.d.), mimeographed, pp. 50–56; see also Urban Land Institute, *Shopping Center*, pp. 25–26.
20. Urban Land Institute, *Shopping Center*, p. 3. See also pp. 71–72.
21. Leonard Downie, *Mortgage on America* (New York: Praeger, 1974), pp. 102–104.
22. James Lorimer, *The Developers* (Toronto: James Lorimer, 1978), p. 215; Bell, *Shopping Center Development Guide*, pp. 56–57.
23. Edward J. Minskof "Mortgaging-out the Regional Mall," *Real Estate Review* 7 (Fall 1977): 38–40.
24. Andrew Marton, "The World's New Property Barons," *Institutional Investor* 21 (August 1987): 99; see also Bell, *Shopping Center Development Guide*, pp. 17–18; Urban Land Institute, *Shopping Center*, pp. 256–257.
25. Urban Land Institute, *Shopping Center*, p. 46.
26. Jacquelyn Bivins, "Change Is Still the Only Sure Thing," *Chain Store Age Executive*, August 1986, 52.
27. "Civil War Buffs Fight for Field," *Corpus Christi Caller-Times*, July 17, 1988, p. 3.
28. Jefferson, "Mini-Mall Boom Fades as Developers Face Economic and Political Pressures," p. 27.
29. Graeme Lang, "Shopping Centres: The Case Study of Corner Brook," in *After the Developers*, edited by James Lorimer and Carolyn MacGregor (Toronto: James Lorimer, 1981), pp. 58–59.
30. John Simms, "Creative Gambler Marches On," *Colorado Business*, June 15, 1981, 12–13; Jeff Smith, "Cherry Shopping Center to Cost Downtown," *Denver Business World*, June 7, 1982, 13–14.
31. Quoted in Neugeboren, "Mall Mania," p. 31.
32. William Applebaum and S. O. Kaylin, *Case Studies in Shopping Center Development* (New York: International Council on Shopping Centers, 1974), pp. 38–40, 70–71.
33. Lang, "Shopping Centres," p. 57. See also pp. 52–58.
34. Urban Land Institute, *Shopping Center*, p. 25.
35. "Forecast 1986: The Shopping Center Industry," *Buildings*, January 1986, 52.
36. "Overbuilding: A Real or Imagined Issue?" *Chain Store Age Executive* 63 (May 1987): 48.
37. Carl Hooper, "Occupancy Slipping at Malls," *Houston Post*, April 17, 1987, 1F.
38. Lang, "Shopping Centres," p. 55; "A Liferaft for Malls when a Tenant Sinks," *Business Week*, August 30, 1982, 30.
39. "Big Builders 1987," *Chain Store Age Executive* 63 (November 1987): 22.
40. Philip Brous, "The Chain Store Looks at the Future," in *Shopping Centers: U.S.A.*, edited by G. Sternlieb and J. W. Hughes (New Bruns-

wick, N.J.: Center for Urban Policy Research, Rutgers University, 1981), p. 247.

41. Graham, "The Pleasure Dome," p. 5R.
42. John D. Kasarda, "The Implications of Contemporary Redistribution Trends for National Urban Policy," *Social Science Quarterly* 61 (December 1980): 386.
43. Graham, "The Pleasure Dome," p. 5R.
44. Jerry Jacobs, *The Mall: An Attempted Escape from Everyday Life* (Prospect Heights, Ill.: Waveland, 1984), pp. 93–113.
45. Ellen Graham, "The Call of the Mall," *Wall Street Journal*, May 13, 1988, 7R.
46. Urban Land Institute, *Shopping Center*, p. 263.
47. Sanders, "Toward a Return of the Public Place," p. 89.
48. William H. Whyte, *The Social Life of Small Urban Spaces* (Washington, D.C.: Conversation Foundation, 1980), pp. 65–69.
49. The cases are, in order of listing, found at 326 U.S. 501 and 391 U.S. 308.
50. The last two cases are found at 424 U.S. 507 and 447 U.S. 74. We have drawn on the discussion in Sam Bass Warner, Jr., "The Liberal City," *Design Quarterly* 129 (Summer 1985): 18. See also "Shopping Centers: Property Rights versus Free Speech," *New York Times*, July 9, 1972, 53.
51. Urban Land Institute, *Downtown Development Handbook* (Washington, D.C.: Urban Land Institute, 1980), p. 131.
52. Quoted in Downie, *Mortgage on America*, p. 103.
53. Sanders, "Toward a Return of the Public Place," p. 87.
54. Urban Land Institute, *Shopping Center*, pp. 53–54.
55. Bell, *Shopping Center Development Guide*, p. 6; see also "News," *Buildings* 73 (September 1979): 30.
56. Peter O. Muller, "Are Cities Obsolete?" *The Sciences*, March/April 1986, 43–46.
57. George J. Church, "The Boom Towns," *Time*, June 15, 1987, 14–17.
58. Quoted in Urban Land Institute, *Industrial Development Handbook* (Washington, D.C.: Urban Land Institute, 1975), p. 4.
59. Urban Land Institute, *Downtown Development Handbook*, p. 10.
60. Urban Land Institute, *Industrial Development Handbook*, pp. 30–33.
61. Thompson, "The Lure of the Park," p. 46.
62. Urban Land Institute, *Industrial Development Handbook*, p. 159.
63. Richard Eisenberg, "Parking It in Parks," *Money*, July 1985, 173; see Lorimer, *The Developers*, p. 153.
64. R. John Griefen, "Creating an Industrial Park," *Lawyer's Title News*, May–June 1972 (Richmond, Va.: Lawyers Title Insurance Corporation), as cited in Urban Land Institute, *Industrial Development Handbook*, pp. 76–77.

65. Christopher B. Leinberge and Charles Lockwood, "How Business Is Reshaping America," *Atlantic*, October 1986, 43–52.
66. Urban Land Institute, *Industrial Development Handbook*, pp. 78–81; Lorimer, *The Developers*, pp. 154–155.
67. Quoted in Thompson, "The Lure of the Park," p. 49.

8

SUBURBS AND CENTRAL CITIES
Residential Housing Development

In 1963, the mortgage payments on a new home consumed only 19 percent of the median income of a man who worked year-round, full-time. In 1984, the mortgage payments on a new home absorbed 31 percent of the median income of a man who worked year-round, full-time. Most banks won't give a mortgage to a family that would have to spend 31 percent of its income on house payments.[1]

Three homes costing over $20 million are currently for sale in Bel-Air and Beverly Hills; $2 million will get you only a handyman's special in either. Some real estate agents catering to fast-lane clients have waiting lists of people willing to pay $2 million or more for houses they intend to tear down and replace with new ones.[2]

INTRODUCTION

Suburbs—no other residential areas of U.S. cities have received so much attention. Much-maligned suburbanites have been the butts of countless jokes and the centerpieces of many a fiction article in popular magazines. Supposedly, the suburbs have bred new types of Americans—lonely, bored, carbon copies of one another with similar houses, yards, and life-styles. Authors such as John Keats have fostered a distinctive image of suburbia: "For literally nothing down...you too can find a box of your own in one of the fresh-air slums we're building around the edges of American cities."[3] Other writers have emphasized conformity, mental illness, family chaos, and adultery in suburbia. Critics of this suburban image have pointed to its many flaws. Researchers have found that suburbanites are much like other city residents. They have no more psychological or family problems there than elsewhere. Nor is conformity limited to the suburbs. Although suburbanites do tend to be white, white-collar, and middle- to upper-income, even this homogenized character of the suburbs has been challenged by the large number of blue-collar families that have moved there.[4]

However, even the critics of the suburban myth have missed an essential point. Most discussions about suburban family life, housing styles, and conformity have suggested that it is the consumers, the residents of suburbia, who have produced the great decentralization waves in our cities. Implicit in the conventional view is the suggestion that suburbs are the spontaneous result of the housing demands of consumers expressed through a rational market system. Jack Lessinger conveys a typical view of the consumer as the lead actor in urban decentralization; as he describes it, "a new kind of real estate consumer is emerging" who prefers "the simple yet cosmopolitan lifestyle" found outside large central cities:

> *For most of this century, Americans migrated to the suburbs by the millions to preside as little kings and queens over their one-sixth acre domains. There, plumbers and steelworkers indulged themselves in a regal lifestyle that exceeded their parents' wildest expectations.*[5]

Absent from this rosy portrait is any mention of several other factors that have profoundly shaped U.S. suburbanization, including the investment and related decisions of industrialists, developers, financiers, realtors, land speculators, and government housing officials in connection with suburban migration and job creation. As we noted in an earlier chapter, in recent decades many employment opportunities have been created by corporate investments in outlying areas. Researchers Logan and Golden studied the transformation of central cities from industrial centers to administrative service centers and documented the loss of employment. Manufacturing employment grew 16 percent in the suburbs between 1958 and 1963, while dropping 6 percent in central cities. Between 1963 and 1977 central-city manufacturing employment fell by 700,000 in large metropolitan areas, while adjacent suburbs gained 1.1 million jobs. Central-city retail and wholesale employment fell by 100,000 while adjacent suburbs gained 1.8 million jobs.[6]

In a 1981 interview prominent suburban developer William J. Levitt accented the close ties between this decentralization of industries and suburban residential development:

> *But you can't build if you don't have an economic base. So you have to build and work in conjunction with industry, so that industry moves into the area, people move into it, and land is bought at a respectably low price.*[7]

An economic critical mass emerged in the suburbs during the 1970s; the regional and national headquarters of numerous large corporations moved to the suburbs, along with their manufacturing and warehouse facilities and supporting restaurants, hotels, and other specialized businesses. Capital from national and international sources flowed into secondary-circuit investments in the suburbs—with facilitating assistance from local and federal governments. Although many research studies and popular accounts portray consumers as the central actors in the dramatic evolution and sprawl of U.S. suburbs, there is substantial evidence that workers go where the jobs and housing are.[8]

HOUSING DEVELOPERS

A Master Developer: The Rise and Fall of William J. Levitt Developers and builders have worked closely with industrial corporations in building suburban America. The development of suburban subdivisions began in earnest after World War I, when a growing number of larger builders bought land on the edges of cities. Most early suburbs were modest in size. By 1938 there were 70,000 homebuilders, with most constructing only a few houses per year. However, the larger builders among them were influential in planning and government circles. The larger builders were becoming developers of large subdivisions. By the end of World War II, there was a severe housing shortage. Most homebuilders were still small local firms. Under the pressure of surplus capital and increased government aid for single-family homes, this soon changed. For example, studies of San Francisco have revealed that by 1949 half the new houses were being built by medium-sized and larger builders, the new subdivision developers; and the national pattern was similar. By the 1960s large developers were constructing from two-thirds to three-quarters of all new housing.[9]

Conventional urban analyses usually omit any discussion of the residential housing developers who plan, build, and, if necessary, destroy residential areas in a quest for market control and profits. No large-scale producer has had more influence on suburban development than William J. Levitt, builder of 140,000 houses in subdivisions around the globe; Levitt for a time was *the* model for other developers. By the 1950s three-quarters of local residential development in metropolitan areas was taking place in suburban areas; large residential developments were characteristic of this vigorous postwar expansion. And development corporations such as Levitt and Sons were producing large-scale subdivisions with standardized housing. On Long Island, for example, Levitt and Sons built houses, roads, and utilities in several large subdivisions. Levittowns were built on Long Island, New York, near Philadelphia, and in New Jersey. During World War II, Levitt and Sons built much military housing, pioneering in a mass production process that became its trademark in the postwar period.

After the war Levitt and Sons generated prefabrication and assembly techniques that enabled the company to build 150 houses per week. Levitt pulled together in one corporation all aspects of home manufacturing and marketing, from controlling the source of lumber to selling the finished house. Levitt and Sons arranged the houses' design to fit assembly-line construction techniques. Larger developers differ from smaller firms; they can buy materials in bulk directly from manufacturers, develop specialized work forces, and undertake major research analyses. They can also make better use of government programs. Thus Levitt and Sons had a working arrangement with key federal agencies administering housing loan programs, such as the new Federal Housing Administration (FHA) and the Veterans Administration (VA), which had just been established to provide federally insured mortgage loans for the thousands of houses being built (see discussion below). Without these governmental programs that protected lenders against the possibility of default on home loans by homebuyers, the Levittowns and similar decentralized subdivisions would not have been built, and thus consumers would not have migrated to sprawling suburbs. This fact underscores the general point accented by analysts such as David Harvey and Mark Gottdiener, who have described the role of governments in facilitating the flow of capital into the secondary circuit of urban real estate. U.S. bankers generally have not been willing to risk loans to middle-income Americans without the federal government protecting their investments.[10]

Levitt was not primarily concerned with building well-rounded and integrated communities, but was developing housing subdivision "showpieces." The first Levittown was all white. William Levitt told sociologist Herbert Gans that he feared the project would not sell if it were opened to blacks. For more than two decades Levitt was very successful. Profitability was the basic standard in designing the Levittowns; community-oriented features were, for the most part, acceptable if they enhanced profit.[11] By the 1970s, however, William Levitt's profit-and-loss situation had changed dramatically. He was no longer the model of the successful housing developer. His problems began in 1968 when he sold his New-York-based development company (then the nation's second largest) to the multinational corporation International Telephone and Telegraph Corporation (ITT) for $60 million of ITT stock. Over the next 5 years, Levitt used the ITT stock as collateral for bank loans. In that period the ITT securities declined in value from $60 per share to $15, and Levitt's banking partners demanded he cash in the stock to pay off the uncollateralized portions of the bank loans. Moreover, because of a 10-year clause in the contract prohibiting competition with ITT, Levitt was not able to renew his building activities, except in cities where ITT had no interest. In addition, Levitt invested $20 million in a Levittown development in Iran, but that project was taken over by the new Iranian government after the 1979 revolution.

When the aforementioned contract clause expired, Levitt announced plans for a new 10,000-house Levittown in Orlando, Florida. However, the Starrett Housing Corporation, which had bought the firm called Levitt and Sons from ITT, sued Levitt. The court prohibited Levitt from using the name "Levittown" for his new subdivisions. Undaunted, he went ahead with the project, renamed "Williamsburg," but ran into problems with environmental standards and poor workmanship. In 1981 he began yet another project, a 4,500-unit housing subdivision 60 miles from Orlando, but he again encountered major obstacles. His bank foreclosed on the undertaking in 1985. After the foreclosure, Levitt announced plans for a 26,000-house development known as Poinciana Park, but this project collapsed less than a year later when his partner, Old Court Savings and Loan, entered bankruptcy proceedings. On April 1, 1987, Levitt's interest in Poinciana Park reverted to Old Court Savings and Loan's receiver, and Levitt was given until June 1987 to put his personal estate up for sale.[12]

Levitt's life history illustrates the extraordinary range of real estate activities of the twentieth-century U.S. developer. Levitt was a real risk-taking entrepreneur who pioneered not only in the design and assembly-line production of suburban houses but also in the governmental financing of suburban house sales. But his case suggests too that some capitalist developers take on too much risk or become unable to adjust to the changing political and economic realities of an evolving real estate capitalism. In the late 1980s, 40 years after pioneering the first large suburban housing subdivisions, the 81-year-old William Levitt faced business and personal ruin.

Concentration and Centralization in Homebuilding We have discussed in earlier chapters how the larger builders, from 1910 forward, worked for concentration and centralization in the homebuilding industry by using the local and federal government regulations to displace smaller builders. Weiss describes two steps in the process of the rationalization and concentration of residential subdivision development.[13] In the first step, large builders worked with professional planners to secure public land-use planning and regulation. By the 1930s the larger homebuilders associated with the NAREB and other real estate organizations had found that land-use regulatory laws were not being administered in ways that provided the desired rationalization and stability. So the NAREB, together with other major finance and real estate associations, worked for the passage of the 1934 National Housing Act, which created the FHA. With a staff recruited from the private development sector, the FHA thereafter wrote regulations that not only buttressed the U.S. lending industry by insuring individual mortgages, but also standardized subdivision development nationwide, a process that gave greater market control to the larger developers who could afford to comply with detailed regulations. It is also important to note the organizations created by the residential developers. From the 1910s to the 1940s, the larger homebuilders organized themselves through the City Planning Committee and the Home Builders and Subdividers Division of the National Association of Real

Estate Boards (NAREB). The early land developers and residential subdividers were usually real estate brokers. In the 1940s two spin-off organizations, the National Association of Home Builders and the Community Builders' Council of the Urban Land Institute became the leading organizations of the residential builders.[14]

The centralization and concentration process has continued since the 1940s. In some cases major corporations not formerly involved in real estate, such as ITT, Boise Cascade, Alcoa, Exxon, and Penn Central, have become directly involved in building housing. Giant homebuilding firms, such as Levitt and Sons, have been acquired by multinational corporations such as ITT. In other cases the centralization and concentration have taken place within the housing industry. From the 1970s to the 1990s, there have been a number of bankruptcies, mergers, and acquisitions that have reduced competition. Large homebuilding corporations are today a major factor in residential housing, both single-family homes and apartments. Thus in the late 1980s the Ryland Corporation, number 6 on *Builder* magazine's Top 100 list of home and apartment builders in 1987 with 7,638 housing starts, expanded into California by buying the M.J. Brock Corporation. And the Miami-based Lenar Corporation, number 15 on *Builder* magazine's Top 100 list with 4,681 housing starts, bought Development Corporation of America, which ranked forty-fourth on the list. Also in 1987 the nation's largest single-family homebuilder was created as a result of the merger of Ryan Homes and NV Homes. The new company had 8,389 total apartment and single-family home starts in 1987 and grossed nearly $900 million. The merged company, NVRyan Homes, ranked number 3 among all home and apartment builders.[15]

However, far outstripping its nearest competitors, Trammell Crow Company was the nation's largest builder of apartment and single-family homes in the late 1980s. In 1987 the firm started 12,037 apartment and single-family housing units, nearly 3,000 more than second place Cardinal Industries, Inc. Trammell Crow then controlled assets of $14 billion in more than 200 cities.[16] Although homebuilding is one of the least oligopolistic areas of the real estate industry, and corporate rankings fluctuate as a result of the merger and acquisition activity, concentration and centralization of capital are increasing in the housing industry. By the late 1980s there were 93,000 companies that were building housing, with the top 100 firms controlling more than 16 percent of the market.[17]

Planned Unit Developments   Some new suburbs are supersuburbs that go by such names as "new towns" and "planned unit developments" (PUDs). Gulf, Exxon, Goodyear Tire and Rubber, Prudential, and other big corporations known for products other than housing have periodically become involved in these new towns. One of the largest, which we discussed briefly in Chapter 3, is The Woodlands, a multibillion development project on the northern edge of the Houston metropolis. Built by Woodlands Development Corporation, a subsidiary of a Texas oil company owned by George Mitchell, this PUD housed 13,000 residents and 200 businesses in the early 1980s. Public relations brochures for The Woodlands describe the development in this way: "The hometown idea is refreshingly simple. You'll sense it during your first visit here."[18] Mitchell's view of this "hometown" is broader than that of most developers. Mitchell has envisioned lower- and moderate-income housing (and minority residents) as being a part of the otherwise very affluent supersuburb. The Woodlands represents Mitchell's vision of how urban problems are to be solved, of a satellite city where poor and rich mingle in one planned development. This vision will not be fulfilled; the profit logic of capitalism is such that low- and moderate-income housing, in other than modest amounts, are practically beyond the pale, for they ordinarily generate too little profit. Mitchell is in reality creating yet another upper-middle-income suburb.

A significant feature of large-scale PUDs is the role of government subsidies. For example, federal government loan guarantees have been provided for $50 million in loans for The Woodlands subdivision. Government aid provides essential start-up support for such for-profit developments. In 1970 a "new communities" bill was passed by Congress, and the Department of Housing and Urban Development (HUD) opened a new agency providing guarantees to help developers obtain loans to build the "new communities." Direct federal aid for planning was granted. Hundreds of millions of dollars in loan guarantees have been provided by HUD to new town developers.

Most PUDs have been described in dramatic terms: "a city in the country—ecology in action" (Westlake, California) and "the next America" (Columbia, Maryland). But they are usually only expensive suburbs with more green space, but with the same problems, such as race and income segregation, faced by other suburbs. Substantial taxpayers' dollars have supported new town projects. Westlake, California, is a 12,000-acre area developed by the American-Hawaiian Steamship Company and Prudential. The Los Angeles area development has relied in part on a number of smaller builders, has shopping areas, and provides narrow greenbelt strips.[19] To take another example, during the 1980s two development companies put up Fox Valley Villages, a 4,000-plus-acre PUD 35 miles from Chicago's central business district. This planned development has various types of low- and high-density housing, its own shopping mall, corporate offices, schools, and recreational facilities. Both developments signal longer-term planning by developers seeking to organize "how people will not only live, but work and play."[20]

Exceptionally large private real estate developments are frequently justified, often by developers themselves, in terms of their presumed efficiency, diversity in terms of income, and protection of the environment;

smaller-scale development is viewed as disorganized and ugly by those who prefer larger developments. According to Richard Walker and Michael Heiman, the data do not generally support these contentions about large-scale development. Houses in large developments tend to be at least as expensive as those elsewhere, and little housing in the big suburban developments is provided for low- and moderate-income families. Generally speaking, the cost savings of such development seem to go into higher profits, not into lower-cost housing. Moreover, the new towns usually do not save transportation costs, because in most cases commuting distances are at least as great as those from conventional suburbs. With few exceptions the large PUDs are no more racially integrated than other suburban developments, and many have as serious environmental problems as conventional suburbs.[21]

CONSUMERS AND PRODUCERS

Consumers as Housing "Kings and Queens"   Conventional city planning and social science analyses view most suburban sprawl as unplanned and consumer driven. Suburban development is characterized as an explosion on the urban scene—the result of unknown or "invisible" hands. Suddenly farmland becomes large suburbs. A related image sees disorganized development as the result of consumer preferences. The traditional view is that "suburban development prevailed because the public demanded it, directed government to provide incentives for suburban production and consumption, and fueled a revolution in the residential construction industry."[22] Developers and powerful allied actors in the housing sphere publicly suggest that the choices of consumers are the primary cause of their development actions. Edward Eichler, a prominent builder, and his coauthor Marshall Kaplan, have argued that "the owner, trader, or developer of land has not shaped America; rather, his behavior has been a response to such forces as national policies, changes in technology, social and cultural factors, shifts in income distribution, or rises in total income." From this viewpoint developers are dependent on technological, consumer, and government forces.[23]

"Suburban sprawl" is a phrase that has become controversial among some social scientists. Some have suggested that the term is too critical, that the spreading out of residential subdivisions reflects the desires of consumers for detached single-family homes. They see attempts to provide housing at higher densities (for example, apartments) as being rejected by most households. Surveys of Americans are cited to indicate that 70 to 80 percent do in fact express a strong preference for owning a single-family home. Other surveys show that most Americans, wherever they now live, prefer living in small towns, rural areas, and suburbs to living in larger central cities. Thus, this argument goes, urban planners and other professionals should not force ordinary people to accept someone else's housing values.[24] Many urban analysts also see the suburbanization of cities as a manifestation of technological forces, an argument we explored in Chapter 1. Thus urban ecologist W. Parker Frisbie argues that "deconcentration of population and industry occurred as new technology led to assembly-line techniques (and thus increased single-story space requirements), as improvements in intramural transportation allowed easy accessibility to all parts of the city."[25]

Suburbia: The Powerful Decision Makers   These commonplace views assume that consumers "were free to choose among several residential alternatives, that their choices reflected real preferences and that their preferences were the independent factor in suburbanization."[26] Suburbs do offer escape from the city and, sometimes, better housing for the money. Given the lower cost of land there, more houses have been built on the suburban fringe than elsewhere. And many U.S. families do place great value on a detached single-family home. Only a modest proportion prefer to live in central cities. An opinion poll of 1,200 recent college graduates found that the ideal home for the majority was a three-bedroom house on a detached lot in a suburban community. Only 4 percent selected an apartment in the city as an ideal place to live.[27]

But what is missing in the conventional consumer-as-monarch view is a clear understanding of the organizational and institutional framework of modern real estate capitalism, within which consumer decisions about housing and suburbs are made. Little attention is focused on the producers of housing and their exchange-value interests and goals. Barry Checkoway suggests that the major decisions creating suburbia were in fact made "by large operators and powerful economic institutions supported by federal government programs and that ordinary consumers had little real choice in the basic pattern that resulted."[28]

Suburbanization has been shaped in fundamental ways by the profit-oriented decisions of the real estate investors and producers. This quest for profit has created or exaggerated the U.S. trend toward suburbanization. Since the 1920s suburbs have gradually come to be seen in the eyes of many capitalistic investors as safer secondary-circuit investments than housing in central cities, where utilities and housing are older, if not decaying, and where the population mix includes poor, elderly, and minority people who cannot pay much for housing. Moreover, when middle-income people in older central-city areas cannot get financing to improve their housing because banks will not make loans to them, they often *must* move to the suburbs, thus accelerating decentralization. When small central-city landlords cannot get the financing they need, or when they cut maintenance and squeeze out the most profit they can, rental housing in central areas deteriorates. When the federal government skews mortgage insurance programs toward suburban areas, such actions accelerate suburbanization; an individual homebuyer can get financing with greater ease for a suburban home than for a central city home. Suburban taxes may be lower, at least in the beginning, and basic services are often newer. Suburbia is more than the result of the American consumers' dream; it is the combined result of state- and investor-produced options and consumer choices.[29]

Together with their financial and political allies, developers make most of the fundamental decisions. Prospective homebuyers are given choices that are predetermined in large part. New houses in many subdivisions look so much alike that some critics suggest that there seems to be one master architect drawing the plans used by developers and builders across the country. Jeffrey Schrank argues that many developers and builders do not attempt "to offer a well-made product, honestly presented and clearly explained." Aggressive advertising of the product often signals some deception. Developments are given rustic names such as Briarwood, Normandy Village, Westwood Heights, Timberlake Estates, Riverview, and Woodlake, names typically bearing little relationship to the actual settings. "Most builders," Schrank notes, "work on the McDonald's principle—like a hamburger, housing is standardized and customers need to be convinced that the standard house is what they want."[30] In most subdivisions houses are built for anonymous buyers.

In short, suburban areas are the U.S. housing ideal not because they necessarily provide the best type of housing and living spaces for Americans, or because they resulted from the democratic input of consumers initially, but rather because they are the best available option developer-producers have provided. There are major alternatives to existing U.S. patterns of building residential housing far from downtown areas, such as closer-in developments of row houses and garden apartments built around recreational, small-business shopping, and child-care services and serviced by convenient mass transit, options that have not been pursued by most U.S. developers.[31]

Inflation and Declining Homeownership   Whether they live in suburbia or in central cities, typical U.S. families spend the largest share of their incomes on housing and related expenditures. Low- and moderate-income families commonly spend 30 to 70 percent of their incomes on rent, even though they occupy much of the worst housing available. In one analysis, for both renters and homeowners, about one-quarter of housing expenses went for taxes, one-quarter for utilities and overhead, and half to payments to the lender or landlord.[32]

Periodic inflation in housing costs has been a serious problem in the United States. In the first years after World War II, the price of homes went

Table 8.1 Average home prices: 1977 and 1987

Area Surveyed	1977	1987	Percent change
United States	$44,000	$ 95,000	+116
San Francisco	$72,000	$169,347	+135
Los Angeles	$65,000	$142,900	+120
New York	$48,500	$142,400	+194
Minneapolis	$47,250	$114,000	+141
Chicago	$50,900	$110,000	+116
Baltimore	$47,000	$106,500	+127
Milwaukee	$42,900	$ 76,400	+ 78
Houston	$46,900	$ 73,000	+ 56

up 15 to 18 percent. Recent inflation has been even more dramatic—from 56 to 194 percent between 1977 and 1987. Table 8.1 shows the price increases for *existing* homes over the past decade for selected cities.[33]

Most Americans do not understand the underlying causes of this 56 to 194 percent housing inflation. Neither governmental officials nor housing industry leaders have provided a candid explanation. Optimistic builders and developers have in recent years argued that community living in the future will not be much different from the recent past. The average family will still buy a home and enjoy a high standard of living. Yet this optimistic view is problematic. Today many Americans do not have a high standard of living and cannot find affordable homes or apartments. And among those who do enjoy homeownership, there are many who express anxiety about their children's housing. No longer do the majority expect their children's situations to be better than theirs. In a recent Harris survey of 1,200 homeowners nationwide, only 43 percent expected their children to live in better homes than theirs. Nearly 40 percent expected their children to live in similar homes, and 5 percent said that their offspring will live in worse circumstances. Even these estimations may be too optimistic. Many of their children will have a harder time because of the shortage of affordable housing, higher house prices, huge down payments, and difficulties in obtaining mortgage insurance.[34]

In the 1950s a history of the National Association of Real Estate Boards (now the National Association of Realtors) said that "for the first time in our history we have a situation in which the average young family, even the average newly married pair, can afford to own its own home."[35] This was an exaggeration for young families at the time. Today it is far off the mark. Consider, for example, that during the 1950s, about two-thirds of all U.S. families, young and old, could have afforded the average new house without spending more than a quarter of family income on the house. By 1970 the proportion had dropped to one-half; and by the early 1980s fewer than *one in ten* families could afford the average *new* house without spending more than a quarter of family income. As Leo Zickler, head of Oxford Development Corporation, has expressed it, "private industry as it's constituted cannot reach the bottom one-quarter of the [housing] market; it has difficulty reaching the bottom 50 percent."[36]

As a result, the proportion of family income going for housing-related expenses has been increasing to a third or more. Between 1968 and 1984 median house prices increased 40 percent faster than the income of those buying houses. By late in 1987 the median new house price had reached a record of $110,000, a 21 percent increase over the previous year. In the same period total personal income rose only 4 percent.[37] Not surprisingly, the actual rate of homeownership in the United States has declined, especially for younger families. In 1976 about 61 percent of those aged 30–34 owned their homes; by 1987 the figure had dropped to 53 percent. Moreover, in the early 1980s first-time homebuyers, who have usually accounted for 40 percent of home purchases in a typical year, purchased just 13 percent of the homes sold.[38] As one researcher noted about the younger families, "in many cases, if your family [parents] can't help with the down payment and closing costs, you can't buy."[39] By the late 1980s the proportion of Americans owning their homes was 64 percent, 2 percentage points lower than the 1980 figure.

Why the High Housing Cost?   Why is owning a home such an expensive undertaking? Some business analysts cite labor costs. Yet labor costs make up an estimated one-fifth of the total cost of new housing; this means that rising wages, and union wage contracts, are not likely to be responsible for the lion's share of inflation in costs. Another factor in higher prices, cited by some realtors and builders, is the homebuyers' insistence on features, such as more floor space, fireplaces, and air conditioning, that boost prices.[40] This argument is not compelling, because many homebuyers are not looking for such features. Moreover, between 1980 and 1983, when the median price of new homes rose 16 percent, the median floor space actually declined, as did the percentage with basements and garages.[41] Other analyses of rising housing costs have pointed to the impact of the 1986 Tax Reform Act. Thus Richard Peach has noted that while "mortgage interest and property taxes will remain deductible for homeowners, the value of those deductions will be significantly reduced, causing the after-tax cost of homeownership for both current and prospective homeowners to increase relative to the costs of other goods and services that households consume." Yet this law went into effect after much housing inflation had occurred.[42]

And then there is the familiar argument that government action is responsible for the rise in housing costs. One idea here is that builders are passing along the growing costs they incur for the sewer hookups, parks, roads, and schools that local governments used to subsidize. Sanford

Goodkin of the real estate consulting firm Peat Marwick/Goodkin has argued that "about 99 percent of the time, the builder passes those costs on to the home buyer."[43] The National Association of Home Builders (NAHB) is another group that sees rising housing costs substantially in terms of government regulation. However, even the research discussed in a NAHB bibliography suggests that governmental regulation adds only a *small* amount to home costs—and that the main causes of housing inflation are rising land costs, financing costs, and the cost of building materials. Slow-growth ordinances, such as those adopted by local governments in California and Maryland, often raise lot sizes and implement similar restrictions to limit the number of houses constructed. Yet this particular type of regulation is widely supported by affluent homeowning families, including builders' families, that live in the suburbs; it is not an arbitrary regulation imposed by distant government officials.[44] Moreover, while such slow-growth ordinances increase land prices by reducing the supply of house lots, they are as yet in effect for only a *few* residential communities.

Land Costs and Land Speculation   Housing prices include not only the costs of labor and materials, but also the profits of builders, developers, and other key real estate decision makers. One study of a Canadian suburb with modest $63,000 houses found that large land developers there were making $20,000 on every house lot sold, in addition to the normal profit from building and selling the house. In many U.S. areas the sharp price increases in suburban housing have come more from the rising land prices than from rising construction costs. Land prices rose twice as fast as inflation over the 1980s. In some fast-growing areas prime-quality land has been scarce at any price. For example, in Orange County, California, new one-eighth-acre lots have recently sold for $80,000—without the house! Land speculation, landbanking, and land development decisions by powerful private decision makers are important in increasing land, and thus housing, prices.[45]

Rising land prices lend themselves to speculation. Suburban speculators, sometimes including subdivisions of development companies, operate as a critical group of capitalists who often fill the ownership gap between agricultural and urban land. Pressure at the urban fringe eventually forces most agricultural users to sell out, sometimes directly to those wishing to develop the land and sometimes to speculators willing to hold the land for price rises. By A.D. 2000 perhaps 50 million acres of land will have been withdrawn from other uses for urban and suburban growth. On city fringes land will often go through the hands of a series of speculators before it becomes a housing subdivision or industrial site. In communities from California to New England, land operators have bought out farmers by offering thousands more an acre than the farmers paid for the land. Such sales push up the property taxes on surrounding farmlands not yet sold. Tax pressures, coupled with such factors as the water runoff and pollution of new development, eventually force the most obstinate farmer to sell out. As a result of such speculation, in many areas residential land prices have risen 200 to 400 percent faster than the price of housing.[46]

Land speculation is regarded in the conventional business literature as a positive bridging force—a brokerage operation between the farmer, the suburban developers, and the builders. But speculation has negative effects. Where large developers control a lot of land, small builders can have trouble buying lots. And such action has hastened the decline in the number of profitable smaller builders. Illegal and unethical activity is, according to researcher Leonard Downie, rife among speculators, allied developers, and their financiers; "land speculators push farmers off their land and employ deceit and bribery to rezone and subdivide it." Moreover, Bruce Lindeman argues that real estate speculation and landbanking *restrict* the supply of available land, forcing prices above what they would have been without speculative activity. Higher-than-necessary prices come in part from expensive, highly leveraged financial arrangements that land speculators get into, as well as from competition in the speculative process itself.[47]

Finance Capitalists and Housing Loans   Another major reason for the growing cost of suburban and other residential housing is the high interest rate charged by lending institutions to individual homeowners, builders, and developers, as well as the new loan arrangements lenders have put together to maintain their profitability. Generally speaking, with some market-rate oscillation, loans to developers, builders, and apartment owners have gotten much more expensive in real terms since 1970. The standard long-term, fixed-rate commercial or apartment mortgage became increasingly scarce during the 1980s. Lenders have moved to sharing with developers the equity and long-term gains from large development projects and are no longer content with fixed interest rates. Lenders have often replaced long-term loans and fixed interest rates with short-term loans and adjustable interest rates. Lenders pass along the costs of interest rate inflation to landlords and developers, who shift these costs to tenants and homebuyers. The way real estate is financed has changed in recent years as the finance capitalists have taken over a significant portion of the profits formerly reserved for developers.[48]

Homebuyers face changing requirements imposed by finance capitalists as well. Suburbanization has been sustained by a "mountain of debt." Residential housing has traditionally been bought with the aid of a 70 to 90 percent loan, which is paid back over 20 to 30 years. For the first years of the loan the house occupant's monthly payments are mostly interest paid to the lender; over 20 to 30 years several times the original amount of the loan is paid back. The mortgage lending industry has been dominated by commercial banks, mortgage companies, savings banks, and savings and loan associations, with some participation by insurance companies and retirement trust funds. However, the standard 20-to-30-year loan at a fixed interest rate had become rarer by the 1980s. An estimated three quarters of homes were being bought through financial arrangements other than the formerly typical fixed-interest-rate first mortgage.

Some New Loan Arrangements   Lenders have developed new loan arrangements. In the early 1980s Ryan Homes introduced a reduced-interest-rate loan that required the homeowner to give Ryan Homes one-third of the appreciation in value when the house was sold. Adjustable-rate mortgages (ARMs) have also became popular since 1980. These loans permit lenders to raise (or lower) interest rates over the life of a loan. By the late 1980s lenders such as Great Western Savings and Loan of Los Angeles and the Dime Savings Bank of New York had more than 90 percent of their multibillion dollar housing loan portfolio in ARMs with negative amortization. Negative amortization occurs when rising interest rates on adjustable-rate mortgages increase the interest owed, thereby (often substanially) enlarging loan balances for consumers. Another innovation in home mortgage financing is the "reduction-option loan," advertised as being cheaper than the fixed-rate mortgage. This loan carries a 30-year maturity, and allows the borrower to reduce the interest rate on the loan only once (between the start of the loan's second year and the end of the fifth year) if prevailing interest rates fall at least 2 percentage points in a year. More than 20 major lenders had introduced the mortgages by the late 1980s. A major drawback in these loans is the borrower's inability to take advantage of a gradual drop in interest rates.[49]

The ARMs and other variable rate mortgages entail great risks for homebuyers, because the arrangements assume *rising* real incomes. If a family does not get the expected wage and salary increases in the future, or if an illness should occur, they may well lose their homes. Defaults on home mortgages have reached record highs in recent years. During the 1980s the foreclosure rate on home mortgages increased dramatically, from 0.1 foreclosures per 1,000 mortgages in 1981 to 4.1 per 1,000 in the first quarter of 1985. In the third quarter of 1986 the Mortgage Bankers Association reported the highest foreclosure rate since they began keeping track in 1953. Similarly, the number of delinquencies (mortgage payments 30 days or more late) reached historic highs during much of the 1980s.[50]

GOVERNMENTS AND HOUSING

Advocating Houses: Government and the Real Estate Industry   Governments have cooperated with and subsidized the housing development industry. Many development costs are paid for by the general taxpayer; governments have provided land for the roads, sewers, and water lines required for suburbs. Directly after World War I, both the real estate industry and the federal government pressed for growth in single-family home construction. The U.S. Labor Department put up "own your home" posters from Maine to California with captions such as: "Own a Home for Your Children's Sake," "Thrift Puts Savings into a Home," and "Construction Now for a Greater and Still Happier America." Amplifying the government ads, in 1930 the president of the National Association of Real Estate Boards spoke out strongly for the development of more homes for middle America. Since Herbert Hoover, every U.S. president has pressed the idea of homeownership as a key to being a good citizen. In a time of impending depression Hoover advocated the idea that homeowners were loyal citizens. And Franklin Roosevelt's support for homeownership reflected his bias against multifamily dwellings; he felt every family should have its own detached home on its own piece of turf. After World War II, a large-scale government advertising campaign for homeownership began in earnest. Neither real estate developers nor government officials were willing to leave citizen housing choices to chance. Much new housing was channeled by developers, real estate organizations, and federal agencies to the growing suburbs.[51]

Government Assistance for Housing Development Government officials not only have cooperated in extolling the virtues of homeownership, but also have provided the subsidies for suburban development that powerful real estate decision makers have desired. Suburban developers have fundamentally altered the pattern of city expansion. The older pattern was for city governments to expand roads and services gradually into rural land on the edges of cities. Now developers' actions on the fringes can force a variety of government actions. Large developers package vast amounts of land, plan the suburbs, seek financing, and build multitudes of houses or sell lots to smaller builders and homeowners who build in the subdivisions. Developers in the United States and Canada, since the 1950s, have bought up great amounts of land. Developers who own the land along transportation routes, the freeways and the highways, shape the character of much suburban development. The interest of businesses in moving to locations outside the central cities and the availability of auto and truck transportation have spurred development of residential suburbs strung out along highway routes. If the subdivisions are already inside city boundaries, local governments must provide a multitude of services (for example, fire fighters and police) for the new residential areas. If outside the existing city, the new subdivisions may develop their own governments and their citizens may not pay taxes for the services in the central cities where they work or shop. And in some areas, the subdivisions will eventually be annexed by the cities, thereby putting demands on the central city government for service delivery.[52]

Federal Government Financial Assistance As early as 1913, the path-breaking Federal Reserve Act stabilized U.S. banking and commercial credit, but did nothing for expanding home loans. Direct financing for urban residential housing did not expand much until 1916, when nationally chartered banks were permitted to make some housing loans. The limited appeal of early loan plans to average customers could be seen in their terms: 1- year loans of 50 percent of property value. As a consequence, real estate leaders sought government intervention to protect home loans. A Senate investigation led by New York Senator William Calder, a Brooklyn builder and finance capitalist, looked into the shortage of mortgage money. The NAREB supported a Calder bill to create homebuilding loan banks. At the 1920 NAREB convention, emphasis was placed on tax law changes to encourage homebuilding and homebuying. The NAREB recommended to Congress that interest paid on mortgages be exempt from federal income taxes. Note that the idea for tax concessions did not come from housing consumers, but rather from the builders and real estate agents concerned with having more consumers buy their housing products.[53]

In the 1930s housing construction declined sharply; nearly a third of the unemployed workers in the United States were from construction-related industries. By 1931 real estate leaders were pressing President Hoover to set up a central mortgage bank to save the homebuilding industry. That conservative president put together a Conference on Home Building and Home Ownership, which called for federal government investment in public housing to be constructed by private firms and for government agencies to provide capital for lending corporations. By the early 1930s there were 5,000 bankrupt banks, and 7,000 other banks were in trouble. Soon government support for private banks was provided. The Federal Home Loan Bank Act (1932) established the Federal Home Loan Bank Board (FHLBB)—with savings and loan associations constituting most of the membership. The FHLBB was a backup capital source for savings and loan associations, which were to become the most important home mortgage lenders after World War II. This board has operated as a central bank for its member banks, making loans to them and accepting deposits from them, thereby helping to extend loans and maintain their profits. Funds have come from selling FHLBB securities to investors. Whenever the real estate lending industry has faced serious recessions, including the severe problems of the savings and loan associations in the 1980s, government officials have been asked to bail out, with government funds, ailing finance capital institutions.[54]

In the mid-1930s a conference of real estate people and bankers helped work out a plan for the federal government to create an agency to insure the loans of private lenders. Industry executives suggested that borrowers pay an insurance fee with their monthly payments to the lenders. Created by the aforementioned 1934 National Housing Act, the

FHA has provided insurance making possible long-term home loans with lower monthly payments than was previously possible. The FHA standards for mortgages, loan insurance, and determination of qualified buyers soon stabilized the mortgage market. FHA-insured mortgages could cover up to 90 percent of the cost of a house. The idea behind industry demand for government intervention was to increase the loan money available by protecting lenders; and this program did encourage developers and builders to expand their operations. Note that the FHA protects *lenders*, not homeowners, from going bankrupt because of home loan defaults. This type of government intervention was neither conceived nor approved by American voters; they undoubtedly would have rejected such a plan in favor of one protecting homebuyers as well. This governmental approach has permitted virtually risk-free loans by lenders and has shored up private profit making in the housing finance industry. Homebuyers and tenants benefit; but the first consideration has been to protect the interests of lenders, then to see how the needs of homebuyers can be met within that framework.[55]

Nathaniel Keith notes that the "clientele of FHA was primarily the large commercial banks, mortgage banks, insurance companies, building material suppliers, and private builders."[56] Large developers and builders, as seen in the Levitt and Sons example cited earlier, have been favored by these federal mortgage insurance programs; they have typically received credit more easily. The FHA loan insurance program and the similar Veteran's Administration program (provided for lenders to military veterans) have also contributed to the concentration and centralization of capital in the larger financial institutions, those that have been most able to meet government standards for loans. Large lenders have indirectly controlled the FHA system. Certain financial institutions have become citywide in scope, providing mortgages for suburban development and restricting loans for central-city housing rehabilitation. Moreover, for a long period FHA manuals discouraged loans to applicants in central cities, particularly in moderate-income and minority (for example, black) areas, thereby contributing to persisting racial segregation in U.S. cities and facilitating white suburbanization.[57]

Other State Financial Subsidies   Since the 1930s the federal government has provided many subsidies for building and banking interests. In the late 1930s the Federal National Mortgage Association (FNMA) was created as a secondary mortgage market for FHA and VA loans. FNMA helped stabilize the mortgage industry by buying up mortgages in times of recession in homebuilding and then selling them when times got better. This nationwide secondary market has made it possible for lenders to sell mortgages to secure new funds for investment. The FNMA was created with federal tax funds and instructed to buy mortgages. Additional capital has been secured by issuing interest-bearing notes bought up by wealthy investors. A government-sponsored private agency, FNMA was rechartered in 1954 as a reserve bank for all mortgages. Between 1938 and 1963 FNMA bought more than a million mortgages for $12.5 billion. Periodically, the FNMA has reinvigorated the mortgage industry. In the 1980s FNMA introduced new types of mortgage loans that reduced the initial loan payments for homebuyers. FNMA buys such mortgages from frontline lenders, and in this way makes more money available to finance capitalists for home loans. Other government-sponsored corporations such as the Federal Home Loan Mortgage Corporation have done the same.[58]

Because of federal intervention, finance capitalists can obtain more mortgage money to loan than would otherwise be possible. Abrams notes that "in short, the government now not only makes it possible for builders to embark on risky ventures with little or no cash but it underwrites risks in the mortgage business and provides liquidity to the lending institutions when they no longer want the paper."[59] Under pressure from the development and finance capitalists, the federal government assumed risks for private lenders. Abrams views government intervention in the 1930s as a program primarily to restore profitability to the banking and homebuilding industries. Protecting developers and lenders from risks may seem un-American from a "free enterprise" point of view, but private developers and lenders have been strong supporters of this interference in the market economy. Real estate organizations have lobbied for federal legislation. Although publicly owned and built housing has been seen as "socialistic," especially for the central cities, by business organizations (the NAREB, U.S. Chamber of Commerce, American Bankers Association), the same groups have lobbied for government intervention supporting suburban development. There is also the revolving-door phenomenon; many top officials in government housing agencies have routinely come from—and returned to—the private real estate sector.

The State and New Bankruptcies? Savings and loan ("thrift") associations have been central to the financing of home mortgages in the United States. Yet since 1980 they have become a major national problem. Many have gone bankrupt; many others are in such serious financial straits that organizations such as the U.S. League of Savings Associations and the National Association of Mutual Savings Banks have asked the federal government to bail them out with rescue plans costing taxpayers more than a hundred billion dollars. Savings and loan associations have gotten into trouble because their loans have traditionally been in long-term fixed-interest-rate mortgages. This approach was viable until the early 1980s when the federal government lifted the amount of interest banks and savings and loans could pay on deposits. Competition in offering higher rates of interest to depositors caused many financial institutions to pay higher interest rates to attract savings than they received on their fixed-rate mortgages. And the competition from other lenders increased. Thus the number of mortgage companies (members of the Mortgage Bankers Association) competing for homebuyers' business grew steadily, from 800 in 1978 to over 1,500 by the end of 1987. Mismanagement, including the actions of unscrupulous lenders using depositors' money to fund risky ventures, added to the strain. Finally, real estate values in the Southwest that accompanied the decline in oil prices in the 1980s worsened the situation for many of the thrifts. The number of savings and loan banks in financial trouble increased sharply in oil-recession states such as Texas. As a result, the supervising federal regulatory agency (the FHLBB) and its ancillary insurance agency, the Federal Savings and Loan Insurance Corporation (FSLIC), have had to aid or take over ailing thrifts, often merging the failing institutions with stronger banks.[60]

Nearly one-third of the nation's roughly 3,100 savings and loan institutions lost money in 1987—a total of $13.4 billion; and the thrift industry lost an additional $9.4 billion in the first 9 months of 1988. At that time there were still more than 430 savings and loan institutions open that were insolvent; their assets were not earning enough to cover their liabilities. The General Accounting Office of the federal government estimated in December 1988 that the government would have to spend $112 billion to rescue the entire system. Numerous failing savings and loan institutions have been liquidated, merged, or otherwise propped up. During 1988 alone, 222 insolvent savings and loan institutions were sold off by the FHLBB at a cost of $38.6 billion. The number of bailouts greatly exceeded the 48 closed in 1987 and approached the record of 277 set in 1938. Moreover, regulators and expert observers have repeatedly intimated that the pace of mergers and liquidations will increase, with more extensive action required in the next few years. Many expected the final government bailout of the poorly managed savings and loan institutions to exceed $200 billion.[61]

Some in the industry have speculated that the federal government's take-charge approach will eventually leave the thrift industry with only 500 large firms, another signal of concentration and centralization in the finance capital sector. Since 1980 approximately one-third of the thrift industry has vanished, mainly through mergers. And some observers have questioned whether these thrift institutions will be able to continue to play their central role in financing residential housing. Indeed, that central role already appears to be eroding. The thrifts' share of all U.S. home mortgages has fallen below 30 percent, and since 1960 these home mortgages have declined from 73 to about 50 percent of the thrifts' assets.[62]

Tax Subsidies for Homebuyers   The idea of income tax advantages for homeowners goes back to the Civil War emergency tax act, when mortgage interest and property taxes were made permissible deductions for certain taxes. This deduction became part of federal income tax laws in the twentieth century. But the homeowner deductions did not become important until the 1950s. By that time individual tax rates were rising, and the tax advantages of housing deductions were significantly increasing. Income tax deductions for interest and for property taxes helped to spur the boom in residential housing, particularly in the suburbs. These deductions are an indirect subsidy for builders and developers, because more people can buy homes if a large portion of their monthly payment is tax deductible. Without these income tax deductions, even more Americans would be renters. Recent tax law changes have not significantly altered this homeowners' advantage over renters, who *cannot* deduct rent on their income tax returns.[63]

All federal expenditures for moderate- and low-income housing assistance programs in the last 50 years—from public housing in the 1950s to today's variety of housing assistance programs—total less than the cost of housing-related income tax deductions for a single year in the 1980s alone. The federal government gives away more in homeowner tax deductions than it spends in all its direct housing programs. Tax losses from homeowner deductions have to be made up by other taxes, so these deductions can be regarded as "tax expenditures." Rolf Goetze has demonstrated that, of the $30.5 billion in direct and indirect tax subsidies that homeowners received in 1979, 64 percent ($19.6 billion) was in the form of deductions on their income tax forms. Subsidies for poor and moderate-income homeowners came to much less, only $9.2 billion. In addition, tax benefits disproportionately benefit higher-income families with more expensive homes.[64]

According to a housing study by Cushing Dolbeare, low- and middle-income residents are *not* the chief beneficiaries of housing assistance in this nation. In 1981 the average amount of federal housing expenditures was $10.40 a month for households earning less than $10,000 annually. However, the average household earning $50,000 or more a year was receiving $155.54 in assistance each month. Dolbeare's report indicates that one-quarter of all federal housing assistance went to the 7 percent of the households with incomes above $50,000, while only half that much went to the 25 percent of households with annual incomes below $10,000. This study asked, "Inasmuch as we're spending $33 billion for housing subsidies for the top fifth of the income distribution, shouldn't we spend at least half that much to meet the housing needs of the bottom fifth?"[65] A more recent study has confirmed that the U.S. tax structure still strongly favors individual homeownership over other types of housing tenure. A study of affluent households found that the homeowners among them spent $1,000 to $5,000 *less* on housing annually than households that rented. The primary reason for the difference was the homeowners' income tax deductions for mortgage interest and property tax payments.[6] Moreover, as we will show below, during the Reagan administration many housing assistance programs aimed at modest-income Americans were slashed, but the subsidies for the usually more affluent homeowners were mostly untouched.

SUBURBS: THE NEGATIVE SIDE

The Issue of Sprawl   Numerous critics have pointed to suburban sprawl, the hedgehopping pattern of decentralizing residential development, as a problem. In Chapter 6 we examined the early sprawl effects of real estate speculation by the owners of mass rail transit companies. According to Downie, business leaders in Los Angeles admit that the more recent sprawl development there has also been heavily shaped by a single-minded quest for private profit, that this sprawl pattern is part of the California land rush:

> *Buy a tract of vacant land, wait a short time for the population and roads to move toward it, subdivide it into lots for cheaply built single-family homes, and sell them to builders at prices that total several times the land's original cost—then take your profit and buy another, larger tract of land farther out to begin the process all over again.[67]*

By the 1970s and 1980s, with many Americans moving to California for jobs, the homes on most lots in the sprawling subdivisions were becoming increasingly expensive.

Some urban researchers and policy analysts have taken issue with the idea that suburban sprawl is problematical. For example, the previously discussed *Urban America in the Eighties* report argues that the physical landscape of older cities is technologically obsolete, that the new polycentered (sprawl) landscape better fits in with the modern technologies associated with an auto-centered transport system and modern communications. That report also asserts that the low-density suburban residential sprawl increases energy consumption by only 3 percent compared with higher-density construction. According to the report, suburbia even reduces the exposure of people to pollution, because people are spread out more and thus per capita exposure to pollution is less than it otherwise would be. And suburbanization, by means of a trickle-down process, has allegedly brought better housing to the central-city poor. The *Urban America* report is a thorough-going defense of what industrial and commercial corporations and suburban developers have created over the last several decades.[68] However, low-density sprawl has frequently generated, or been associated with, environmental, construction, energy, and segregation problems.

Environmental and Other Problems   In booming Orange County, California, the home of Disneyland, the last few decades have seen much agricultural and coastal land transformed by residential developers and construction companies into acres of houses and asphalt. Former tomato fields and citrus groves have had "will build to suit" and "land available" signs posted. Subdivisions once planned for a few thousand people now house a hundred thousand. Yet the developed area of northern Orange County has been described by the U.S. Army Corps of Engineers as the "worst flood hazard west of the Mississippi." An analysis by Wesley Marx highlighted the problem: "To look at a zoning map in Orange County today is to look at a guide to multiple disaster. Find a floodplain, an unstable hillside, or a fault zone, and chances are you will also find a building, an entire city, or at the very least a 'land available' sign."[69] Much of this area is a large floodplain for the Santa Ana River; normally a dry riverbed, the Santa Ana, fueled by rainstorms, flooded in 1969, with several fatalities. An earlier flood had taken 28 lives. Yet developers have continued to build subdivisions in the flood hazard area, which is artfully advertised as "Southern California's Fairest Valley! Beautiful! Busy! Bustling! Brimming!"

California law requires that natural hazards be reported to homebuyers, but one study found that these reports have often been written in technical language or have asserted that hazards such as flooding are beyond a particular report's scope. Many land developers regard laws regulating building in floodplain and similar land-use reforms as too radical. One advocate of such regulations reports that such controls have even been characterized by opponents as "Communistic." Such environmental hazards are not confined to California. For example, a civil engineering report for the National Association of Home Builders found that builders in Denver were constructing houses on land with serious soil problems. Swelling clay soils have cracked foundations and undermined houses in the metropolitan Denver area. Because of the housing boom there in the 1970s and early 1980s, construction expanded onto land once considered unsafe.[70]

Some critiques of suburbia have focused on the quality of construction and on energy consumption. Numerous subdivisions have been poorly constructed. Residents in suburbs across the nation have complained about cracked foundations, water seepage, leaning walls, faulty plumbing, and unbuilt community facilities. Natural environments (trees, water) are sometimes destroyed unnecessarily in a too-quick seeking of profit from development. Rising energy costs have made suburbs more expensive to sustain. In addition, suburban housing construction is not as energy efficient as it could be. A modest additional cost—for more insulation, double-pane windows, and so forth—could slash most utility bills in half.[71]

Ironically, recent reports have found that many suburban areas are facing many of the same ills as central cities. In places like Fairfax County, Virginia, near Washington, D.C., Orange County near Los Angeles, and the New Jersey and Connecticut suburbs near New York City, there are frequent and massive traffic jams. Huge and unsightly garbage landfills and public schools bursting at the seams are problems in affluent suburbs such as Gwinnett County near Atlanta. High commuting costs are a consequence of suburban living for those who still work in the downtown areas. For example, in recent decades many people who work in downtown New York have moved to the outlying suburbs to find affordable housing. Yet a recent study for the *New York Times* found that, when all taxes and commuting expenditures are figured in, the total cost of homeownership is about the same in the major suburbs as in the expensive areas of central New York.[72]

Racial Segregation: Suburbs and Central Cities   The decentralized suburbs with growing numbers of jobs are mostly white; this job and residential redistribution contributes to the racial polarization of metropolitan areas. As we have observed heretofore, the creation of better-paying jobs a long way from the central cities makes it difficult for many black and other minority Americans to have access to such employment. And there is a major problem for suburban whites as well. As Orfield has expressed it, the future white leaders who grow up in suburban enclaves will have "no skills in relating to or communicating with minorities."[73] The federal commission reporting on the black riots of the late 1960s warned that the United States was then resegregating itself into two "separate and un-equal" societies, a conclusion reiterated by a follow-up commission two decades later. The white suburban counties cited above are indicators of the persistence of these separate and unequal urban societies. A research study of housing patterns in 59 metropolitan areas in 1980 found that black Americans were still highly concentrated in central cities, where they were also highly segregated from whites. Even within suburban areas black segregation in relation to whites was found to be high, especially when compared to the residential situations of Hispanic and Asian Americans.[74]

Housing and employment discrimination directed against minority Americans is common in both central cities and suburbs. There have been a number of important research studies that sent a trained black auditor and a white auditor (of similar socioeconomic backgrounds) to realtors selling homes and to apartment rental agents. Studies done in Dallas, Boston, and Denver found differential treatment favoring the white audi-tors looking for housing, whether they presented themselves as looking for a home or looking for an apartment. In all studies whites were more likely to be shown, or told about, more housing units than blacks. In a 1980s Boston study the white auditors were invited to inspect 17 units on the average, 81 percent more than their black (matched) counterparts. Another Boston study found a similar pattern of discriminatory treatment for blacks, Hispanics, and Asian Americans. And a 1980s Denver study found extensive discrimination against Hispanic owners and black renters across the city, while Hispanic renters and black owners faced high levels of discrimination in certain areas of the city. In addition, these studies have found that some real estate agents reserve housing units to show to whites, and others for minorities. Whites are more likely to be encouraged to seek housing in suburban areas. A common pattern is for minorities to be shown advertised housing units, but not to be shown or told about other housing units that are available to whites. Highly segregated cities persist today decades after the 1968 Civil Rights Act banned discrimination in housing.[75]

Wasted Capital? Capital invested in the various aspects of suburban construction, some critics argue, means valuable resources wasted, because there are more important societal needs. A major problem for investors in this period of late capitalism is finding new investment opportunities so that the surplus capital in the primary and secondary capital circuits can be recirculated and enhanced. After World War II, the suburban built environments were a critical outlet for capital investment in housing, shopping centers, and credit arrangements. Suburbanization has been an expensive capital-absorbing expansion. One estimate is that all goods and services directly or indirectly tied to this suburban phenomenon, for many years, could be as close to half the total gross national product. In part, postwar crises in capital accumulation have been resolved by pumping surplus capital into the secondary circuit of suburban real estate. Research by J. Ullman and his associates has concluded that higher-density urban development would not have absorbed as much capital, in part because many consumer products (such as autos) would not have been as necessary.[76] Moreover, suburbanization is part of the individualized consumerism encouraged by U.S. business elites. According to Manuel Castells, very "important was the role of the single-family house in the suburbs as the perfect design for maximizing capitalist consumption. Every household has to be self-sufficient, from the refrigerator to the T.V."[77]

THE MYTH OF AN INNATE DESIRE FOR HOMEOWNERSHIP

Before World War II, most Americans were tenants; they did not own their own homes. Fifty-six percent were tenants in 1940. By 1950 this had dropped to 45 percent. And by the mid-1970s only a third of Americans were renters. However, as we have seen above, in the 1980s this trend was reversed; the proportion of Americans who are renters began to grow. The homeowning percentage is now declining. However, this has not lessened the desire of Americans for such housing tenure. In a Harris poll cited earlier, most college graduates interviewed said they would rather own a house than live in a rental unit of any kind.[78]

Cross-National Variation   Is there something in human nature that makes people want to own single-family homes? In exhaustive research on housing patterns in the urbanized industrial countries, Jim Kemeny has demonstrated the tremendous variation in housing preferences. Homeownership rates ranged from less than 35 percent of households in the prosperous capitalist countries of Sweden, West Germany, Switzerland, and the Netherlands to 64 percent in the United States and 69 percent in Australia. Clearly, there is not a universal human propensity for homeownership in capitalist countries. Countries with a high standard of living have both low *and* high rates of homeownership. In the low-homeownership countries renting is commonplace and respectable; people rent from public housing authorities, private rent-at-cost associations, and private landlords. There are also complex cooperative (joint) housing arrangements, which combine certain features of owning and renting.[79]

Homeownership is sustained by a variety of myths asserting its superiority over other types of housing tenure. Defenders assert that homeownership "satisfies a deep and natural desire."[80] In addition, various pro-homeowning studies have shown the tax and other advantages of owning a home in the United States. But what they really measure is the structural bias built into the U.S. housing system, which favors homeownership over other types of housing arrangements. U.S. homeowners receive *huge* governmental subsidies. And until recent tax law changes, private landlords have made high profits from governmental tax subsidies. Kemeny demonstrates that, without the massive tax subsidies for homeowners and for private landlords, an efficient (public or private nonprofit) rent-at-cost housing system would cost households *less* than the present system of homeownership. He also notes that homeownership locks owners into long-term indebtedness, favors the well-off over moderate-income households, and increases the costs of job and residential mobility. In a given society the housing preferences of the general public are substantially the consequence of the housing tenure systems that have historically become available; those preferences are not necessarily the cause of the existing housing systems. Kemeny sums up:

> It is hardly surprising, for example, that in a society where private landlords make super-profits, where access to cost-renting is stigmatized and severely restricted, and where homeownership is heavily subsidized there is likely to be a very strong preference for homeownership.[81]

Existing governmental subsidies and patterns of private capital investment substantially determine the dominant housing tenure system—and
thus the housing preferences—of many individuals and families.

Homeownership, Ideology, and Housing Classes An often-neglected function
of homeownership is the role it plays in keeping working people wedded
to the established social order. Sternlieb and Hughes have argued that the
"importance of housing" rests in the way it serves as "an essential tool
binding together the implicit social compact that gives coherence to an
America of enormously varied humanity." In their view, "home ownership glues people to the system."[82] In addition, Karen Taylor has summarized the view of a recent president of the Mortgage Bankers Association:
"When renters become home owners, their whole world changes...home
owners identify with the private-property system, they register to vote,
and they become better citizens in the strongest sense."[83]

The capitalists' advocacy of single-family homeownership is a key
part of the ideology of possessive individualism and helps it flourish. That
ideology frustrates attempts to build a social consciousness for cooperative and nonprofit housing developments. And it divides working-class
Americans into different, sometimes conflicting, housing groups. Some
British analysts of cities such as Peter Saunders and Ray Pahl have accented the central political importance of this distinction between homeowners and renters, two differentiated "housing classes" with different
political orientations.[84] Homeownership has long been an important mark
of social status in the United States, with renters occupying a relatively low
position. In this way working-class homeowners are divided from working-
class renters. Moreover, homeowners themselves have different mortgage
burdens, with some owing lenders a lot of money and others owing nothing
at all. This fragmented situation often makes the political organization of
working-class people with different housing situations very difficult.[85]

TENANTS AND RENTERS: CRITICAL HOUSING ISSUES

For tens of millions of Americans renting an apartment has been a major
alternative to buying a single-family home. In the 1980s the rising cost of
single-family homes was increasing the number of households destined
to spend most or all of their lives renting. In the central areas of New York
City most families are not homeowners; most now pay rent to someone
else. In a number of central cities renters are now a majority of the
households. Whether in the central cities or in suburbs, apartments are the
major alternatives for families unable to afford detached single-family
housing. Yet there are not enough apartments available at affordable rents.
As Gilderbloom and Appelbaum have expressed it in their recent book,
"one of the most serious domestic problems facing America today is the

ongoing and seemingly intractable crisis in rental housing."[86] Between 1970 and the mid-1980s, median rent tripled in the United States, although the incomes of renters did not rise so rapidly. And there was also a severe shortage of public housing. In the face of this housing crisis in the 1980s, the Reagan administration cut federal housing assistance programs for low- and moderate-income families by 85 percent.

Apartment Construction and Ownership   In recent years U.S. cities have varied in the levels of apartment construction and thus in vacancy rates. Oil-related cities such as Austin, Dallas, Houston, and Denver had many vacant apartments in the mid- to late-1980s. There were, however, numerous cities with low apartment vacancy rates, especially eastern cities and Chicago, Los Angeles, and San Francisco. One reason for the low vacancy rates in many cities was the reduction in rental construction in the 1980s.[87] Depending on the city and the time period, real estate investors, developers, and landlords blame the periodic shortages of multifamily apartment units on high interest rates, high construction costs, or government interference in the "free market" with such government regulations as rent control laws. Conventional housing theorists argue that housing prices and rents result from supply and demand factors. From this perspective the "marketplace" will provide enough affordable housing if governments simply leave it alone. But there is more to the rental crisis and affordable apartment shortage in cities than that. In their careful analysis Gilderbloom and Appelbaum demonstrate that there is no free market in rental housing: that there is in fact a concentration of rental housing ownership in the hands of a modest number of landlords and that the formal organizations and informal networks of landlords often work to reduce competition and increase rents. They also demonstrate that governmental regulations generally have a very small influence on housing construction and rents.[88] In addition, there is the factor of the cyclical availability of capital, from U.S. and foreign financial institutions, for housing construction.

Apartment complexes can be profitable for developers and landlords. Land that is shifted from low-density use (for example, older houses) to high-density use (for example, higher-rent apartments) can frequently be sold at an above-average profit. Developers may buy land zoned for low-rise housing cheaply, then have the land rezoned for high-rise buildings. A variety of tactics have been used to secure land for high-rise developments. One study reports that some developer representatives posed as homeowners and put motorcycle gangs in a few developer-owned houses to drive out nearby homeowners; some reportedly used arson to chase residents out of certain areas. In some cases the buildings go up and the developers make their profits and move on to other projects, leaving tenants and nearby residents to cope with the long-term problems high-rise buildings can bring.[89]

The development and operation of apartment buildings have frequently been very profitable. Because of special tax advantages provided by the government until the late 1980s, most apartment buildings produced both annual operating profits and long-term profits from inflation in the buildings' worth. Interest, taxes, and maintenance were tax deductible. When the building was later sold, the gain was taxed at less than half as much as income from wages. Investment corporations often put together a number of apartment buildings into a portfolio and then sold an interest in the portfolio to several wealthy investors. Tax breaks were a major incentive for investing in apartment buildings until the late 1980s. Wealthy individuals and companies around the globe have invested in apartment buildings for the affluent in many U.S. cities.[90]

A large proportion of the apartments and rental houses in a specific urban area is typically owned by a small landlord group. A study of ownership in Cambridge, Massachusetts, found that just 6 percent of the households owned 60 to 70 percent of the housing units. The study also found close connections among executives at local banks, which made most of Cambridge's real estate loans, local government officials, and property owners and developers. This powerful network promoted the construction of luxury apartments and commercial development by the city government rather than the needs—effective rent control and enforcement of housing codes—of the majority of citizens, the less affluent tenants. The local planning board and the zoning board were dominated by real estate people. Moreover, a late 1980s study in New York found that just 975 owners (4.7 percent of owners) owned 56 percent of the rent-stabilized units there. Nationwide, Gilderbloom and Appelbaum suggest, rental housing ownership is becoming increasingly concentrated, that is, controlled by a decreasing number of large owners who cooperate with one another in formal and informal associations to control rents and other aspects of rental housing.[91]

Tenant Dependency under Housing Capitalism   Those who rent in the United States commonly face problems. They usually find themselves in a very subordinate position. Real estate journals provide articles advising apartment managers and developers on how to "deal with delinquent rent payers." One article offers the following tips: "Rent to tenants with a history of paying on time....Assess charges if rent is late, Don't renew leases of tardy tenants, Tie resident manager's bonus to on-time rent collections." The same journal suggests that, if a tenant's rent is 10 days late, "the manager should take action to begin court eviction proceedings and follow-up with an attorney to ensure a speedy process."[92] Another example of strong landlord organization and group consciousness is the use of service firms offering computer databases containing the names of people who, for whatever reason, make late rent payments or are conspicuous in ways not related to their rental histories. Such firms compile lists of "high risk" tenants based on data gathered from eviction notices, court cases, and questionnaires sent to landlords. Such surveillance and invasion of the privacy of tenants have been described by some critics as "police state" tactics.[93]

For less-affluent renting households the rental situation is often precarious. Average rental payments captured a quarter of tenants' income in the mid-1970s. However, by the late 1980s the proportion had climbed dramatically to nearly 30 percent. In addition, 5 million households were spending more than 35 percent of their incomes on rent, and another 6 million were spending half or more. Because of escalating rents, millions of families were unable to find affordable apartments and were thus "rent poor." Average rental costs have risen faster than wages; between 1972 and 1986, while rents were rising, the median incomes of renters dropped from $18,000 to $15,300. And certain groups, such as younger and single-parent families, have been particularly hard hit by housing inflation. Many U.S. renters face an affordable housing crisis.[94]

Service Problems   Some owners of apartment complexes have reputations for not meeting tenants' needs for heating and the like. Slow decay is characteristic of many apartment complexes not built to last. Many people live in apartment zones with rapid growth-decay cycles. One such area near Dallas has been described this way: "Addison is so new and so sterile that it seems to be wrapped in cellophane, and yet many of its granddaddy apartments, built as long as seven or eight years ago, have already deteriorated into Sunbelt slums with rotting floors, sewage backups, leaky roofs, buckling pavement, mildew, roaches, and rats."[95] Maintenance can also be a regular problem for tenants. Both low- and high-rise apartment buildings are complex living environments requiring maintenance of public areas, such as grounds, stairways, and elevators. Larger complexes may use a building manager hired by the owner. If for any reason maintenance costs are resisted by owners, because of a desire for higher profits or in response to residents' support of rent control, the apartments and the public areas may deteriorate. Maintenance is particularly a problem when apartment complexes are developed by one company and then sold to another. The major incentives for owning apartment complexes are frequently short term, but the maintenance costs are a long-term commitment.[96]

Evictions and Rent Increases   Many tenants have been the victims of unexpected evictions. When owners see an opportunity to convert apartments into condominiums for sale, displacement often occurs, a phenomenon we discussed in Chapter 5. Similarly, when landlords can capitalize on temporary income-generating situations, such as a world's fair or an Olympics, some will evict even their long-term residents. Such landlords justify their actions with the free-market ideology: Property owners have the right to earn whatever they can from their property. For example, when Knoxville, Tennessee, hosted the 1982 World's Fair, at least 1,000 tenants were evicted by landlords so apartments could be offered at inflated prices to visitors. During that world's fair, some landlords raised the rent so high that existing tenants had to vacate. Thus, at the Bramblewood Two apartments, the rent advanced from $285 a month to $144 *a day* during the fair. Knoxville's vice mayor observed that "What this amounts to is our own people getting thrown out of their homes so somebody can make a quick buck off the fair."[97] A similar scenario unfolded as Vancouver prepared for the world's fair called Expo86. There, local hotels evicted hundreds of low-income tenants, most of whom were old-age pensioners; and rooms rented to the elderly at $220 a month were subsequently rented for as much as $85 a night to the world's fair tourists.[98]

Starving Public Housing   Unlike many British and other European cities, the United States has never had much housing that was constructed and subsidized directly by governments. The housing that has been built by governments in the United States generally has been reserved for those with modest incomes and the elderly. For the most part, suburban governments have kept public housing out of their communities, usually because of fear that the residents would not be white. From the beginning much public housing has been segregated in minority and moderate-income areas, built cheaply and with spartan characteristics, and, as Downie puts it, "given all the homeyness of prisons by government officials under constant pressure from real estate interests and homeowners who fear the alternatives."[99]

The U.S. Congress was motivated to pass the first Housing Act in 1937 because of two concerns: a high level of unemployment and a growing number of people who could not afford private housing. The federal government mandated that each community would have a local public housing agency (PHA) to oversee construction, management, and operation of public housing. But World War II intervened. After the war the 1949 Housing Act set the construction goal at 810,000 public housing units in the next decade or so. But persistent opposition from the real estate development industry, which labeled the program "socialistic" and feared that public units would compete with private construction, kept the number of public units smaller than the goal, and many fewer than the need. Since the 1930s the National Association of Real Estate Boards (NAREB), for example, has been a consistent and very successful opponent of public housing. As a concession to the real estate interests, public housing units have generally been reserved for low-income families. Construction has intentionally been kept at modest levels. Moreover, during the 1950s many middle-income families living in public housing were assisted by FHA and VA programs to move into privately constructed homes, thereby increasing the homogeneity of the remaining residents and decreasing middle-income support for government-constructed housing.

By 1961 there were still only half a million public housing units, well below the 1949 goal. New housing efforts were proposed during the Johnson administration in the 1960s. However, in spite of the fact that half a million families were on waiting lists for public housing in 1964, only 24,000 to 31,000 units were built each year between 1962 and 1966. Even in a city such as Boston, one with a relatively large number of public housing units, there was a waiting list of 8,000 families. And the situation was much worse in most Sunbelt cities. There was some acceleration in public housing construction in the late 1960s, but the numbers declined sharply in the mid-1970s. Construction has remained modest in most years since then.[100]

By the late 1980s there were still only 1.4 million publicly owned units housing more than 4 million persons. Who are these tenants? A major survey sent to PHAs by the National Association of Housing and Redevelopment Officials (NAHRO) was answered by 223 authorities managing 3,352 public housing developments. In the NAHRO public housing sample (which covered 1.7 million persons) minority Americans made up the majority; 60 percent were black, and 24 percent were Hispanic. The public housing population was also relatively young; 44 percent of tenants were 18 years or younger. The majority of families had resident children; 40 percent of the households were single elderly persons and single-parent families. Most were very poor; the average income for all households in public housing was a little more than $6,800. Although many depended on governmental assistance for income, earned income was the principal source of income for a quarter of the families. These latter tenants are the working poor, for whom a job does not guarantee an adequate standard of living. In addition, the NAHRO study found that there was considerable tenant participation in operating public housing. The surveyed PHAs employed nearly 6,300 residents, and more than 100 public housing residents sat on PHA boards and commissions. There is a severe shortage of public housing. In addition to those currently residing in public housing in the late 1980s, another 800,000 families had applied. Then there were only 17,000 vacant public housing units in the country; the ratio of demand to available supply has been about 46:1. The average wait for an available public housing unit is more than a year; and in about 1 in 10 cities the average wait is more than 3 years.[101]

Interestingly enough, most public housing developments are not of the high-rise variety often cited as a disastrous example of governmental intervention by conservative critics of housing programs for the poor. In fact, only 30 percent of public housing buildings are four or more stories high; another 40 percent of public housing consists of two- and three-story structures. And the remaining 30 percent is made up of single-story or scattered-site, single-family housing. As Matulef suggests, "the days of building huge, high-rise developments are over."[102] Publicly owned housing encompasses the apartments and houses that are the property of the U.S. government. There are also other governmental housing programs. Publicly *assisted* housing (both apartments and houses) for low- and moderate-income families differs from publicly owned housing in that the former is privately owned by landlords who receive assistance from government programs—including direct loans, interest rate subsidies, and rent subsidies—that have been developed since the 1960s. In exchange for governmental subsidies, private owners of publicly assisted units have often agreed to restrict rentals to low- and moderate-income tenants for 20 years. Most recent aid programs have funnelled aid through private landlords.

The Reagan Revolution: Cutting Back on Housing Aid   In the 1980s, with the advent of the Reagan administration, one with close ties to private real estate interests, the federal government's commitment to all forms of housing assistance to low- and moderate-income Americans waned. Federal money to finance construction was reduced from $4 billion in 1981 to only $400 million in 1987. In spite of considerable popular opposition, the Reagan administration gutted housing programs not only for the poor but also for lower-middle-income households. One careful analysis summarized the impact:

> *Federal housing programs have taken a beating from the Reagan revolution. The housing budget has been cut by more than three-quarters, from $30.2 billion to $7.8 billion. Reagan has all but eliminated the government's two largest programs for low-income apartment construction.*[103]

In addition, an attempt was made in the mid-1980s by the Reagan administration to sell off, to "privatize," public housing units. Like the conservative Margaret Thatcher administration in Great Britain, the Reagan administration launched this privatization effort with a demonstration program designed to sell 1,600 public units. However, this conservative program was not well received. Only 35 of more than 3,000 local PHAs applied to participate. The administration rigged the demonstration program to achieve the greatest success possible: three-quarters of the first 1,600 units offered for sale were newer single-family houses in pleasant neighborhoods. Moreover, the tenants selected in the privatization experiment had higher incomes than most of the public housing population, and the federal housing agency provided buyers with significant incentives, including specially reduced mortgages and down payments. The major problem with such a privatization effort is that it permanently decreases the supply of housing for low-income households. The director of one PHA explained the lack of interest about privatization among PHAs when he testified before a congressional hearing: "It is incumbent upon us to increase the number of rental units, not decrease them. Every unit placed in any homeownership program is no longer available to other low-income Americans."[104]

The Reagan administration also pushed for a housing vouchers program, a low-income subsidy program in which families rent wherever they can, at whatever price they can pay. By 1987 the administration's voucher demonstration projects were underway in 20 communities. Yet the voucher program has also been riddled with problems. Compared to other subsidy programs, it makes housing more costly for low-income families; tenants generally are required to pay more of their income for rent. One research study found that the average of 34 percent of income paid by voucher recipients for rent was 8 percent more a month than those helped by the Section 8 certificates program, an older government program subsidizing tenants by paying stipends to landlords. When vouchers were offered to low-income families in New York City, the majority were returned unused because the city did not have enough housing at affordable rents. Yet New York City alone has more than 200,000 applicants on the waiting list for public housing. The voucher program is flawed because it does nothing to increase directly the supply of low-rent housing and requires most tenants to devote an increasing share of income to rent.[105]

The lowered priority assigned to housing programs since the 1980s has brought a reduction in the number of public units being constructed. In 1984 the number of units in the inventory of PHAs was boosted by 20,000, because of money previously committed. However, in the following years the Reagan cuts began to take effect, and the number of constructed units decreased; by 1986 the number was cut to only 12,233 units. Moreover, as we noted in Chapter 5, the total stock of publicly *assisted* housing is likely to decline sharply in coming years as federal use restrictions made 20 years ago expire. According to a report by the General Accounting Office of the U.S. Congress, nearly 2 million low-income units could be lost by 1995. This means an even more serious housing affordability problem for the country's moderate-income families.[106]

THE EUROPEAN EXPERIENCE

Middle-Income Public Housing   In contrast to the U.S. situation, a significant proportion of *middle-income* families in numerous European cities live in cost-rental (nonprofit) housing, much of it being housing facilitated or subsidized by the government. In numerous British cities the proportion of families in public and nonprofit housing reaches or exceeds 40 percent of all families. The public housing stock constitutes one-third of the country's housing inventory. In contrast, public housing in the United States accounts for just *1.3 percent* of the nation's housing. Moreover, unlike the U.S. situation, British public housing residents represent a wide segment of the population. For example, only 29 percent of units have no earner (primarily those housing the elderly); two or more wage earners can be found in 40 percent of the British governmental housing units. In Britain less than a quarter of public housing consists of apartments, whereas most public housing units in the United States are apartments. And most British public housing is in better physical shape than that in the United States. Until the Thatcher government of the 1980s, British officials allocated sufficient funds for new construction and maintenance.[107]

In European countries there is generally no stigma attached to being a tenant in publicly subsidized housing. Dreier writes,

> *If there is a lesson to be learned from Europe, it is not to sell off public housing. The success of Europe's post-war housing experience is its insistence that the government help provide housing for the middle class as well as the poor....It enjoys widespread public support because it is not stigmatized as "poor people's housing" and is designed to resemble privately built housing. The only comparable American program is the 450,000 units of family housing constructed by the U.S. military.*[108]

A European Alternative to Single-Family Homes David Popenoe's comparative study of suburban development in Europe and the United States has led him to the conclusion that the United States is atypical, that sprawling low-density suburbanization is not an *inevitable* development in industrialized cities. The United States does not have much high-density suburban development; European cities do. Popenoe studied a large suburb of Stockholm, Sweden, called Vällingby, a residential area where people live in apartments, mostly three-story buildings with garden apartments spaced out around acres of public spaces such as parks. Emphasis there is given to pedestrian paths, although there are streets and parking lots. Each cluster of low-rise buildings is centered around a bustling town center. Facilitating access to all parts of the city, a subway links this suburb, inhabited by middle-income families, to other parts of Stockholm. Extensive retail, day-care, and recreational facilities are to be found in Vällingby, facilities in excess of those found in most U.S. suburbs.[109]

Popenoe also studied the U.S. suburb, Levittown, Pennsylvania. He found both communities to be family centered. Yet Vällingby has a better housing environment for women working outside the home because of its child-care facilities and also easier access to the rest of the city by mass transit. Leisure-time activities are generally more varied in Vällingby; there is less TV watching and more walking and interacting with children than in Levittown. Vällingby is a pedestrian-oriented suburb. Why the differences? One reason lies in the fact that Vällingby is built on publicly owned land; long-range governmental planning resulted in public ownership of 70 percent of Stockholm's suburban land within city boundaries.

This city control eliminated the costly impact of land speculators on suburban housing costs and made possible careful governmental planning—a first-rate transit system, many playgrounds and parks. Much building in the Swedish suburbs has been done by publicly owned development corporations similar to public utilities in the United States. Government involvement not only has made possible middle-income, higher-density housing environments with excellent facilities, but also has kept the rental costs below what they would have been if private speculators and developers had been the only groups involved in development and construction.[110]

CONCLUSION: AN AFFORDABLE HOUSING CRISIS

The housing crisis in the United States has often been blamed by business interests on governmental intrusion into the economy. Developers blame excessive governmental regulation for driving prices up. Developers and landlords blame rent-control laws for reducing new apartment construction. There is little evidence, however, that governmental regulations are the main problem in the U.S. housing crisis. The main problem is that decisions about investment flows into the secondary circuit of real estate, decisions which are shaped primarily by concerns for market share and profitability. Sometimes surplus capital is not available for housing projects. Much of the time, capital that is available does not flow to housing developments for low- and low-middle-income Americans. The United States contrasts with many European communities that have provided governmental capital in order to provide housing for low- and low-middle-income families.

Interestingly, growing economic pressures in the United States make the Swedish type of low-rise garden apartment buildings in multiple-amenity developments attractive alternatives to single-family homes even for middle-income Americans, because the cost of land, materials, and financing has put new homes out of sight for a growing number of families. We have noted how inflation has excluded many families from owning a decent home. Families buying homes are paying larger percentages of their incomes for housing, and the average square footage in new single-family homes is declining. Some families are buying smaller homes; others are buying into converted apartments sold as condominiums and other multifamily housing. Even housing developers are turning to multifamily housing projects. In some areas in Orange County, California, land sells for $300,000 to $400,000 an acre, making it necessary to put a dozen or more condominiums or similar housing units on an acre of land. In the mid-1980s one builder in Chicago has noted that "most builders in Chicago have given up on reasonably priced single-family houses and are building condos and townhouses." Smaller U.S. housing units may become much more commonplace in the future.[111]

Indeed, some critics of U.S. housing patterns have argued that higher-density housing may be more desirable in principle. Thus Hart and Radford have argued that single-family, detached housing provides more space than most families need and consumes unnecessarily vast amounts of raw materials and energy. They further suggest that low-density suburban housing often prevents a sense of community from emerging because of the greater physical separation and that such housing also reduces participation in local community organizations and activities by imposing a large burden of housing maintenance on homeowners.[112] In any event, the 1990s bring a continuation of the affordable housing crisis—a crisis likely to generate increasing citizen discontent.

NOTES

1. Cheryl Russell, "It's a Bum Rap, Lee," *American Demographics*, 8 (May 1986): 7.

2. Kenneth Labich, "Agony and Ecstasy in Family Castles," *Fortune* 114 (December 8, 1986): 42.

3. John Keats, *The Crack in the Picture Window* (Boston: Houghton Mifflin, 1956), as quoted in Herbert Gans, *The Levittowners* (New York: Random House, 1987), p. xvi.

4. Gans, *The Levittowners*, pp. xv–xxix; Larry H. Long, "Back to the Countryside and Back to the City in the Same Decade," in *Back to the City*, edited by Shirley B. Laska and Daphne Spain (New York: Pergamon, 1980), pp. 61–75.

5. Jack Lessinger, "The Emerging Region of Opportunity," *American Demographics* 9 (June 1987): 33–34.

6. John R. Logan and Reid M. Golden, "Suburbs and Satellites: Two Decades of Change," *American Sociological Review* 51 (June 1986): 430–431; see also Joe Schwartz, "On the Road Again," *American Demographics* 9 (April 1987): 40–41.

7. "Straight Talk from a Builder," *Housing* 59 (June 1981): 29.

8. William K. Stevens, "Beyond the Mall: Suburbs Evolving into Outer Cities," *New York Times*, November 8, 1987, E5.

9. S. J. Maisel, *Housebuilding in Transition* (Berkeley: University of California Press, 1953); J. P. Herzog, "Structural Changes in the Housebuilding Industry," in *The Dynamics of Large-Scale Housebuilding*, edited by Real Estate Research Program (Berkeley: University of California Press, 1963).

10. Gans, *The Levittowners*, pp. 5–13; Barry Checkoway, "Large Builders, Federal Housing Programmes, and Postwar Suburbanization," *International Journal of Urban and Regional Research* 4 (March 1980): 26–28; Mark Gottdiener, *Planned Sprawl* (Beverly Hills: Sage, 1977), p. 96.

11. Gans, *The Levittowners*, pp. 6, 5–13; Ruth Eckdish Knack, "The Once and Future Suburb," *Planning* 52 (July 1986): 8.

12. Lisa Gubernick, "Too Long at the Party," *Forbes*, May 4, 1987, 40.

13. Marc A. Weiss, *The Rise of the Community Builders: The American Real Estate Industry and Urban Land Planning* (New York: Columbia University Press, 1987).

14. Ibid., pp. 13–16.

15. "Acquisition Fever," *Builder*, February 1987, 42; David Landis, "Crow Tops in Nest Building," *USA Today*, April 28, 1988, 7B.

16. William G. Smith, "Debt-Defying," *Texas Business* 12 (May 1988): 44.

17. Penelope Lemov, "The 4th Annual Builder 100," *Builder*, May 1987, 179.

18. Woodlands Development Corporation fact sheet, in author's files; Woodlands Development Corporation, "The Woodlands," brochure in author's files.

19. Leonard Downie, *Mortgage on America* (New York: Praeger, 1974), pp. 154–172.

20. Richard A. Walker and Michael K. Heiman, "Quiet Revolution for Whom?" *Annals of the Association of American Geographers* 71 (March 1981): 80–81.

21. Ibid.

22. Checkoway, "Large Builders," p. 21.

23. Edward Eichler and Marshall Kaplan, *The Community Builders* (Berkeley: University of California Press, 1967), pp. 9–10.

24. A 1978 HUD survey is reported in Martin D. Abravanel and Paul K. Mancini, "Attitudinal and Demographic Constraints" in *Urban Revitalization* (Beverly Hills: Sage, 1980), pp. 29–31.

25. W. Parker Frisbie, "Urban Sociology in the United States," *American Behavioral Scientist* 24 (November–December 1980): 177–214.

26. Checkoway, "Large Builders," p. 37.

27. Barbara Mayer, "Dream Home in the Suburbs," *Springfield (Mo.) News-Leader*, January 3, 1988, 1c.

28. Checkoway, *Large Builders*, p. 22.

29. Richard A. Walker and David B. Large, "The Economics of Energy Extravagance," *Ecology Law Quarterly* 4 (1975): 963–985.

30. Jeffrey Schrank, *Snap, Crackle, and Popular Taste: The Illusion of Free Choice in America* (New York: Delta Books, 1977), pp. 122, 123.

31. James Lorimer, *The Developers* (Toronto: James Lorimer, 1978), p. 126.

32. Michael E. Stone, "Federal Housing Policy: A Political-Economic Analysis," in *Housing Urban America*, edited by Jon Pynoos, Robert Schafer, and Chester W. Hartman (Chicago: Aldine, 1973), pp. 434–427.

33. Cited in Ronnie Agnew, "Boomers Seek Quality in 2nd Homes," *Springfield (Mo.) News-Leader*, March 6, 1988, 1F; see also Richard

Eisenberg, "The New Vise on the Middle Class," *Money* 16 (September 1987): 48.

34. "Gloomy Tidings on Home Expectations," *Wall Street Journal*, December 9, 1987, 37.

35. Pearl Janet Davies, *Real Estate in American History* (Washington, D.C.: Public Affairs Press, 1958), p. 221.

36. Carol Anderson, "Builders Bemoan the Sorry State of Texas," *Builder* 10 (May 1987): 43.

37. Eisenberg, "The New Vise on the Middle Class," p. 48.

38. "The Politics of Homeownership," *Dollars and Sense* 114 (March 1986): 11.

39. Eisenberg, "The New Vise on the Middle Class," p. 49.

40. Ibid.

41. Phillip Longman, "The Mortgaged Generation," *Washington Monthly*, April 1986, 14.

42. Richard W. Peach, "A Permanent Decline in Homeownership?" *Mortgage Banking*, April 1987, 73.

43. Eisenberg, "The New Vise on the Middle Class," p. 49.

44. Carla Freeman, "Housing Costs: A Builder's Bibliography," prepared for Special Committee on Costs and Material Supply, National Association of Homebuilders, January 1981.

45. Eisenberg, "The New Vise on the Middle Class," p. 49.

46. Marion Clawson, *Suburban Land Conversion in the United States* (Baltimore: Johns Hopkins University Press, 1971), pp. 8–10; Bruce Lindeman, "Anatomy of Land Speculation," *Journal of the American Institute of Planners* 42 (April 1976): 142–152; Downie, *Mortgage on America*, p. 88.

47. Downie, *Mortgage on America*, p. 6; Lindeman, "Anatomy of Land Speculation," pp. 150–151. This section draws on Joe R. Feagin, "Urban Real Estate Speculation in the United States: Implications for Social Science and Urban Planning," *International Journal of Urban and Regional Research* 6 (March 1982): 35–60.

48. "News," *Buildings* 74 (April 1980): 16–17; Sy Nicholson, "Long Term Mortgages: R.I.P.," *Buildings* 74 (May 1980): 36.

49. "Fewer Negatives Spur Negative Amortization," *Wall Street Journal*, May 11, 1988, 21; "Reduction-Option Loan Gains Popularity," *Wall Street Journal*, January 26, 1988, 33.

50. "News," *Builder* 4 (February 1, 1981): 13; "Demise of a Dream," *Dollars and Sense* 112 (December 1985): 5–6; Carol Anderson, "Delinquencies Finally Fall Sharply," *Builder* 10 (February 1987): 42.

51. Davies, *Real Estate in American History*, pp. 138, 166; Mark I. Gelfand, *A Nation of Cities* (New York: Oxford University Press, 1975), p. 59; Peter Dreier, "Tenants as a Minority Group," unpublished manuscript, Tufts University, March, 1981, pp. 10–11.

52. Lorimer, *The Developers*, pp. 90–96.

53. Davies, *Real Estate in American History*, pp. 95, 140.
54. Robert Goodman, *After the Planners* (New York: Simon and Schuster, 1971), pp. 58–59.
55. Charles Abrams, *The City Is the Frontier* (New York: Harper and Row, 1967), p. 231.
56. Nathaniel S. Keith, *Politics and the Housing Crisis since 1930* (New York: Universe Books, 1973), p. 30.
57. Stone, "Federal Housing Policy," p. 430; Richard A. Walker, "A Theory of Suburbanization: Capitalism and Construction of Urban Space in the United States," in *Urbanization and Urban Planning in Capitalist Society*, edited by Michael Dear and Allen J. Scott (London: Methuen, 1981), pp. 404–405.
58. Abrams, *The City Is the Frontier*, p. 73; Stone, "Federal Housing Policy," pp. 423–433.
59. Abrams, *The City Is the Frontier*, p. 36; see also pp. 71–72; Goodman, *After the Planners*, p. 58; "How Safe Are Your Savings," *Newsweek*, March 15, 1982, 50–55.
60. Julie Stacey, "Lenders Woo Homebuyers," *USA Today*, May 23, 1988, 1B; Nathaniel C. Nash, "Thrifts Haven't Seen the End of Crisis Costs," *Corpus Christi Caller-Times*, June 19, 1988.
61. "S&L Cleanup Goes on Taxpayers' Bill," *USA Today*, September 6, 1988, 6B; Sarah Bartlett, "F.D.I.C. Is Supported as Sole Bank Insurer," *New York Times*, December 7, 1988, 36; "S & L Bailout Put at $112 Billion," *St. Louis Post Dispatch*, December 15, 1988, p. 11D; "S & L Failures to Reach 222 by Year's End," *St. Louis Post-Dispatch*, December 31, 1988, p1.
62. Robert E. Taylor, "Thrifts' Struggle Is Becoming Darwinian," *Wall Street Journal*, July 5, 1988, 6.
63. Downie, *Mortgage on America*, p. 53.
64. Cushing N. Dolbeare, National Low Income Housing Coalition, "The Need to Limit Homeowner Deductions," *Statement to Committee on Ways and Means, House of Representatives*, Washington, D.C., March 31, 1981, p. 8; Rolf Goetze, "The Housing Bubble," *Working Papers for a New Society* 8 (January–February 1981): 48–51.
65. "The Rich Reap Lion's Share of Federal Housing Aid," *Austin American Statesman*, April 8, 1985.
66. James M. Woodard, "Renting Is More Costly Than Owning, Study Finds," *Austin American Statesman*, October 1, 1986.
67. Downie, *Mortgage on America*, p. 10.
68. President's Commission, *Urban America in the Eighties*, pp. 32–37.
69. Wesley Marx, *Acts of God, Acts of Man* (New York: Coward, McCann, and Geohegan, 1977), pp. 108–114.
70. Ibid., p. 114; Jerry Ruhl, "Builders Suppress Soil Problem Study," *Rocky Mountain News*, March 6, 1980, 1, 68.

71. Henry Aubin, *City for Sale* (Toronto: James Lorimer, 1977), pp. 349–351.
72. Betsy Morris, "Shallow Roots," *Wall Street Journal*, March 27, 1987, 1, 6; Michael deCourcy Hinds, "Comparing Costs: City vs. the Suburbs," *New York Times*, May 24, 1987, 1, 4.
73. Quoted in George J. Church, "The Boom Towns," *Time*, June 15, 1987, 17.
74. Douglas S. Massey and Nancy A. Denton, "Suburbanization and Segregation in U.S. Metropolitan Areas," *American Journal of Sociology* 94 (November 1988): 592–625.
75. John Yinger, "Measuring Racial and Ethnic Discrimination with Fair Housing Audits: A Review of Existing Evidence and Research Methodology," HUD Conference on Fair Housing Testing, Washington, D.C., December 1984.
76. Walker, "A Theory of Suburbanization," p. 410; J. Ullman, ed., *The Suburban Economic Network* (New York: Praeger, 1977).
77. Manuel Castells, *The Urban Question* (Cambridge, Mass.: MIT Press, 1977), p. 388.
78. Mayer, "Dream Home in the Suburbs."
79. Jim Kemeny, *The Myth of Home-Ownership* (London: Routledge and Kegan Paul, 1981), pp. 8–46.
80. Quoted in ibid., p. 11.
81. Ibid., p. 63. See also pp. 8–46.
82. George Sternlieb and James W. Hughes, "Structuring the Future," *Society*, March/April 1984, 28.
83. Karen Cord Taylor, "Struggling to Support the American Dream," *American Banker*, October 26, 1986, 14.
84. Peter Saunders, *Urban Politics* (London: Hutchinson, 1979), pp. 66–73.
85. Ibid., pp. 63–64; J. A. Agnew, "Homeownership and the Capitalist Social Order," in *Urbanization and Urban Planning in Capitalist Society*, pp. 458–475.
86. John I. Gilderbloom and Richard Appelbaum, *Rethinking Rental Housing* (Philadelphia: Temple University Press, 1988), p. 3.
87. "Rental Housing Market Weakens Nationwide," *Buildings* 80 (November 1986): 32.
88. Gilderbloom and Appelbaum, *Rethinking Rental Housing*, pp. 9–12.
89. Jack Newfield and Paul Dubrul, *The Abuse of Power* (New York: Viking, 1971), pp. 113–120; Lorimer, *The Developers*, pp. 132–135.
90. Oscar Newman, *Community of Interest* (Garden City, N.Y.: Doubleday, 1980), pp. 101–118; Kaye Northcott, "In Ten Years They'll Be Slums," *Texas Monthly* 7 (November 1979): 163–265.
91. Gilderbloom and Appelbaum, *Rethinking Rental Housing*, pp. 57–60; also see John Mollenkopf and Jon Pynoos, "Boardwalk and Park Place: Property Ownership, Political Structure, and Housing Policy at the Local Level," in *Housing Urban America*, pp. 55–65.

92. "How to Deal with Delinquent Rent Payers," *Professional Builder* 50 (November 1985): 32.
93. "Landlord Intelligence," *Dollars and Sense* 110 (October 1985): 11.
94. Robert Kuttner, "Bad Housekeeping," *The New Republic* 198 (April 25, 1988): 22.
95. Northcott, "In Ten Years They'll Be Slums," p. 164.
96. Newman, *Community of Interest*, pp. 101–119.
97. Ernie Beazley, "World's Fair Deprives Some of Housing," *Wall Street Journal*, February 19, 1982, p. 31.
98. Jane O'Hara and Diane Luckow, "Evicting the Poor for Expo Visitors," *Maclean's*, April 7, 1986, 46.
99. Downie, *Mortgage on America*, p. 58.
100. Rachel G. Bratt, "Public Housing: The Controversy and Contribution," in *Critical Perspectives on Housing*, edited by Rachel G. Bratt, Chester Hartman, and Ann Meyerson (Philadelphia: Temple University Press, 1986), pp. 335–355; Joe R. Feagin, Charles Tilly, and Constance Williams, *Subsidizing the Poor* (Lexington, Mass.: D.C. Heath, 1972), pp. 40–55.
101. Mark L. Matulef, "This Is Public Housing," *Journal of Housing* 44 (1987): 176–179.
102. Ibid., p. 175.
103. "Shelter Skelter," *The New Republic*, May 11, 1987, 7.
104. Peter Dreier, "Private Project," *The New Republic*, August 4, 1986, 14.
105. Bill McCarthy, "Income Security Functions Lower Safety Net Further," *Nation's Cities Weekly*, February 10, 1986, 13; Michel McQueen, "Rents of HUD Housing Voucher Users Top Other Subsidy Plans, Study Finds," *New York Times*, July 9, 1987; "Freedom of Choice," *Time*, February 9, 1987, 23.
106. Cited in Carol Anderson and Marilyn Bart, "Where Will the Poor Live?" *Builder* 10 (January 1987): 151.
107. Dreier, "Private Project," p. 14.
108. Ibid., p. 15.
109. David Popenoe, *The Suburban Environment: Sweden and the United States* (Chicago: University of Chicago Press, 1977), pp. 61–63.
110. Ibid., pp. 29–43, 176–224.
111. Carol Anderson, "Coping with the Recession," *Builder* 4 (June 1, 1981): 18–19. The quotation is on p. 19.
112. Stephen Hart and Gail Radford, "Against Universal Homeownership," Letter to the Editor, *Dollars and Sense* 118 (July/August 1986): 2.

9

GOVERNMENTS AND THE URBAN DEVELOPMENT PROCESS

Partnerships between the public and private sector have produced exciting projects....The city of St. Louis' commitment to creating and nurturing these partnerships has been stimulated by a 1980 Census Bureau prediction that it would be a ghost town by 2015....The city has fought back with tax incentives, low prices, and a huge stock of vacant buildings which are attracting investors....Foundations, religious institutions, corporations and city hall have joined forces to change the city's image and attract investors to the community.[1]

INTRODUCTION

In recent years much discussion in the mass media has focused on the new public-private partnerships in cities from coast to coast, associations formed to deal with the problems of urban economic decline and development. The quote heading this chapter indicates the excitement one journalist found in St. Louis, one of central America's economically troubled cities. There the government officials have worked with corporate executives and others to try to boost and revitalize the city. This pattern has been repeated in cities from New York, to Cleveland, to San Francisco. Yet these public-private partnerships are by no means new. For many decades city, state, and federal government officials have worked with, and provided vital assistance to, private development interests.

An Older Partnership: Urban Renewal in San Francisco In the 1970s public relations releases extolled the virtues of a federal-government-assisted renewal project in central San Francisco: a "center city redevelopment to include a sports arena, 800-room hotel, office buildings, and parking for 4,000 cars...going up only a few blocks from the San Francisco Hilton."[2] The area at issue is a central-city district called South of Market, adjacent to San Francisco's downtown corporate complex. This was one in a series of federally subsidized redevelopment projects sought by the city's business elite. During and after World War II, San Francisco became a center for large multinational corporations, with headquarters buildings for such giants as Transamerica Corporation, Standard Oil of California, Crown Zellerbach, Bechtel Corporation, and the Bank of America. In 1946 the Bay Area Council (BAC) was created to coordinate corporate involvement in government decisions, including planning, transport, and regional development. Most of the 27 *Fortune* 500 firms have had top executives on the BAC; also included in the BAC were local newspaper and major West Coast bank executives. In 1955 business leaders in the BAC put together a committee of leading corporate executives to pressure the San Francisco Redevelopment Authority (SFRA), a local governmental agency, to pursue aggressively redevelopment and renewal in business-targeted areas of San Francisco.[3]

This business elite in turn created and funded a broader group, the San Francisco Planning and Urban Renewal Association, a coalition led by corporate executives; this private planning group was designed to generate widespread business interest in urban renewal. In the association's "Prologue for Action," the effects of the changes desired by this corporate business elite became transparent:

> If San Francisco decides to compete effectively with other cities for new "clean" industries and new corporate power, its population will move closer to "standard white Anglo-Saxon Protestant" characteristics. As automation increases, the need of unskilled labor will decrease. Economically and socially, the population will tend to range from lower middle-class through lower upper-class.[4]

Working with the SFRA and utilizing the newly available federal government urban renewal money, these corporate executives set out to accomplish business development objectives. Like other large renewal agencies, the SFRA was authorized to coordinate private and public developmental action. Carrying out its urban renewal plans with little democratic input, the SFRA relocated urban residents, bulldozed areas, and widely advertised its activities. Thus during the 1960s several large renewal projects were implemented, resulting in the displacement of 4,000 San Francisco families, mostly working-class blacks and Japanese-Americans. Governing in a major administrative and financial city, San Francisco officials have traditionally accepted the need for business growth and support facilities such as office buildings, convention centers, and hotels.[5]

In the later South of Market redevelopment project, another project of multinational corporate executives and local real estate operators, several thousand people, mostly retired workers, were forced out of their apartments and homes as buildings were razed to make room for new buildings. In the lexicon of downtown redevelopment, the common justification for pushing working-class residents, including the elderly, off their land is to allow it to be put to a "higher and better use." Justin Herman, then director of the city's Redevelopment Agency, put it this way: "This land is too valuable to permit poor people to park on it."[6] The South of Market project was approved by the San Francisco Board of Supervisors and went through a number of stages: from the issuing of a plan for the area in 1954 to resident displacement and building demolition in the late 1960s. Called Yerba Buena Center, the huge project in the South of Market area expanded the corporate business district to the south. Older structures were bulldozed, and new buildings, including a convention center, were constructed. Speculators and adjacent landowners gained from large-scale land clearance. Adjacent land was cleared and used for office buildings. Selling the redevelopment plan to the citizenry was somewhat difficult. Public acceptance for such governmental land clearance expenditures required the help of key opinion leaders and local newspapers. Editorially, San Francisco newspapers strongly supported the Yerba Buena development; news coverage generally buttressed the perspective of business leaders.

But the business and newspaper accounts left serious questions unanswered. For example, who were the thousands displaced to provide profits to a few corporations? South of Market had long been a retired workers' enclave. Before displacement most of the 4,000 residents of the area were single, older men living on modest pensions. Dozens of residential hotels, most in sound condition, provided them with low-rent housing. Moreover, the area was close to transportation and other service facilities that older citizens require. Some hotels needed rehabilitation, but the proposed massive clearance exceeded what was needed to improve the district. The area was not commodity space for sale; it was "home space," where single people could retire and find support and friendship networks.

As has often been the case with similar areas around the country, this area was often described by outsiders as a "skid row" or "transient area." These derogatory stereotypes were used in the mass media to stigmatize the retired workers and to persuade others in San Francisco to support business-oriented urban renewal. Initially, the retirees were conspicuously absent from the planning process. Nonetheless, area residents did eventually organize against the problems about to be visited on them. A tenants' group was formed that fought legal battles with renewal agencies over issues such as inadequate relocation plans and replacement housing for those displaced. They won a limited victory in the form of an agreement in which the SFRA agreed to construct several hundred low-rent housing units as part of Yerba Buena Center and more than a thousand low-rent units in other parts of the city. For virtually the first time in U.S. urban history, "exactions" were made from developers, and a policy of "linked development" was pioneered. A government redevelopment agency and developers had to make major *concessions* to a people's movement opposed to urban renewal efforts.[7]

GOVERNMENT ACTION IN THE CITIES

Is the Pluralist Perspective Adequate?   As we observed in Chapter 1, pluralist political analysis has dominated much analysis of local and federal governments. According to this perspective, city government officials respond to a variety of pressure groups; their decisions are the result of responding to multiple pressures from varying coalitions of individual voters, firms, and other citizen groups. Yet much pluralist analysis has neglected the economic decision makers. Analysts like Paul Peterson argue that government officials should work for the economic health of the city as a whole. In *City Limits,* Peterson has argued for a market theory of urban politics— that local officials should seek to enhance the general welfare and pursue growth in partnership with business leaders, growth benefitting all city residents.[8]

These "market" analysts of cities do not provide a critical analysis of capitalism and investment capital; they tend to view the fostering of private investment as maximizing the general welfare. They suggest that capitalist markets should not be restructured by governmental action. In contrast to this market-knows-best perspective, critical analysts note the overwhelming evidence that certain actors in urban politics and economics have considerably more power than others and that many urbanites do not benefit from market-oriented decisions. Moreover, as we have seen in the San Francisco case, the reality of government decisions is often much different from the optimistic pluralists' view of multiple-group pressure and the pursuit of the common welfare. Just as markets benefit powerful capitalist investors more than ordinary consumers, the urban political process has usually favored powerful business groups over ordinary voters. The research of social scientists such as Miliband and Domhoff has demonstrated that individual capitalists and their various organizations often have a disproportionate influence on local and national government decisions, including those on government subsidies. Moreover, in cases like San Francisco we see the importance of individual business decision makers, including the business executives in the powerful growth coalitions such as the BAC; and we also glimpse the significance of such political actors as entrepreneurial mayors, as well as such institutional arrangements as the federal government's urban renewal program.

DEVELOPERS, GROWTH COALITIONS, AND GOVERNMENTAL ASSISTANCE

Local Growth Coalitions and Government   Molotch has suggested that virtually all U.S. cities are dominated by a "small, parochial elite whose members have business or professional interests that are linked to local development and growth."⁹ This elite is usually centered around local developers, bankers, and industrialists interested in a city's economic growth, together with an array of supporting actors such as real estate agents and lawyers. In some cities most members of the growth coalition are local developers and other local business people, sometimes called "immobile capital," whereas in other cities the coalition has included business people in local firms and executives in multinational corporations, the latter sometimes called "mobile capital." Here we can underscore the governmental aspect of these growth coalitions. A city's growth coalition commonly links the business elite and local government officials in a quest for local growth. In recent years *public-private partnerships* have received a lot of media attention. But for more than a century, city growth coalitions have developed close working partnerships with supportive officials at all levels of government.

The business and political leaders in these coalitions have espoused a growth and development ideology. William Angel has underscored the importance of local "boosterism" in generating corporate development in cities. Cities, small and large, are intensively advertised by their growth coalitions as great places to do business. Local business-government alliances have been established to promote and retain local corporate investments. Approximately 15,000 cities, towns, counties, states, and other political jurisdictions have marketed themselves on a nationwide basis. In an effort to project the image of a "good business climate," boosters press for the expansion of government services and facilities necessary for business success, including highways, urban renewal, convention centers, and utilities. Local business leaders work hard to get such public investment capital in the hope that it will entice industrial corporations to their areas. They have developed an extensive array of relationships with government officials.[10]

Local politicians have sometimes played a key role, as political entrepreneurs, in developing partnerships with business officials for growth goals. There has been a resurgence of urban analysis accenting the role of governmental officials in fashioning modern cities. Analysts cited in Chapter 1, including Block, Mollenkopf, Gurr, and King, argue that city and national government officials have organizational interests of their own; they and the state agencies they control often compete vigorously with one another. Even more importantly, these political officials often develop new governmental policies ahead of articulated business demands. Many urban public-private partnerships have involved a central role for political entrepreneurs accented by Mollenkopf, who has argued that political officials "can bring together widely different, competing, and even conflicting political actors and interests by creating new governmental bases for exercising new powers."[11] The data we have examined in this book suggest that this argument is accurate for some cities at certain points

254   *Governments and the Urban Development Process*

in time. Particularly in cities with strong (for example, Democratic) political party organizations, politicians with little or no business experience have sometimes played a generating or coordinating role in revitalization efforts. However, as a rule, business elites have been the dominant partners in the public-private partnerships, especially in regard to economic and physical development issues.[12]

Government officials have been important members of the growth team. As we observed in Chapter 3, state and local officials have vigorously advertised the advantages of their respective business climates—lower taxes, lower wages, and government receptiveness to business. Molotch has argued that the organized effort to generate city growth is at the *center* of local government as a political force. Growth politics is part of the everyday politics that decides who gets what, and where, in cities. Local politicians have long worked to provide support for business-oriented growth, including aid for infrastructure, water, sewer, and utility projects.[13]

TRADITIONAL GOVERNMENTAL SUBSIDIES

Development Subsidies For decades government administrators concerned with local growth have provided much support for industrialists and real estate developers. Of central importance is a government-provided infrastructure: the roads and freeways, sewer and water systems, police and fire services, and tax and abatement programs. Whether they are building suburbs or shopping centers, developers and builders need city services. In an analysis of Milwaukee, Fleischmann examined the special utility assessments paid by residential developers in the 1950s. He found heavy use of governmental subsidies. For example, in 1954 the city government charged $3.00 per front foot on a residential housing block for storm and sanitary sewers. Through these assessments on residential developers, the city collected $322,000. However, the facilities actually cost the city $2 million. The general citizenry thus subsidized residential expansion and private profit making by homebuilders. The older neighborhoods of Milwaukee were in effect subsidizing the newer, outlying residential areas. Neighborhoods near the downtown area paid millions more in taxes than they got back in permanent utility improvements and operating appropriations.[14]

City governments have been good partners in providing business interests with many types of bond and tax subsidies. For instance, there are tax-exempt economic development bonds, sold to investors by city agencies and used to finance parking lots, garages, factories, office towers, and services for various private developments. These bonds reduce the taxes of well-off investors that purchase them, which diminishes the income of the U.S. Treasury. In this way, rank-and-file taxpayers pay for services and facilities required by urban developers and their corporate clients. This public-private partnership has provided government-assisted bond subsidies for profitable industrial corporations locating in cities, including Borg-Warner, Georgia Pacific, and U.S. Rubber.[15]

Another governmental subsidy frequently sought by real estate developers is the "special tax district." This subsidy involves the establishment of districts by local government authorities, usually for a singular purpose, such as constructing a water system. By using the special district, bonds can be issued at lower interest rates. Defenders of municipal and other special utility districts (called MUDs in some areas) insist that since the bonds are paid off over a long period of time, their use for subdivision utilities lowers the initial cost of housing in the area. There are tens of thousands of these districts, each with the ability to issue tax-exempt bonds. From the developers' point of view, the key advantage of these districts is that control over urban growth becomes ever more firmly entrenched in their hands—millions of taxpayer dollars are spent by real estate interests without those footing the bill having any voice in the matter. However, the bonds will have to be repaid, as well as the interest on the borrowed money; the total development cost, including interest, will usually be higher in the long run. In addition, the districts frequently create small sewer and water systems less efficient and more costly to maintain than larger regional systems.[16]

Local government officials have worked with business leaders to secure voter approval for a variety of projects. Bridges, highways, sewers, other utilities, and convention centers strongly desired by business interests, and dependent on local government bond issues, may appear desirable on the surface. And long-term bonds make them seem affordable. But because of the interest charges, private lenders will eventually be paid far more than they have loaned via bonds to local governments. Eventually, government-backed bonds must be paid out of a city's revenues or by securing additional loans. Commenting generally on bonds, Aubin has noted that "to be able to sell the bonds in the first place, and to be able to continue to sell new bonds in order to pay back those people who have bought the previous bonds (for this kind of debt is regenerating) the seller [e.g., city government] must jump through various hoops held by the underwriters."[17] The underwriters are usually banks. They actively assist government officials in planning debts and advertising bonds to investors. The underwriters' role is pivotal because they usually determine the interest rates a government must pay—based on how risky they gauge a particular city. Furthermore, they are in a position to deny municipalities money. Borrowing is necessary to finance government programs since property taxes are usually insufficient. Thus government officials must establish a cooperative rapport with private bankers, lest they risk being denied the financing needed to provide future municipal services.

OTHER TYPES OF PUBLIC-PRIVATE PARTNERSHIPS

An Early Partnership for Global Business Interests   The relationships between local governments and business interests have been extraordinarily complex and varied. Many public-private partnerships have involved arrangements encouraging specific, large development projects of investors and other business people. For example, during the 1950s David Rockefeller organized New York City leaders into the Downtown–Lower Manhattan Association, a major growth coalition. Rockefeller and his business associates were the force behind the World Trade Center, an office complex designed for large global corporations, and one that displaced residents and destroyed small businesses. With the support of the governors of New Jersey and New York, Rockefeller succeeded in persuading New York's Port Authority to construct the center. The Port Authority's role was a key one in the process because it had the ability to float tax-exempt governmental bonds and thus reduce the costs of the project with taxpayer subsidies. And the Port Authority had the power to condemn land for public use and to speed up the project by displacing existing occupants of the area faster than business leaders could displace them.[18]

A Private-Public Partnership   One major example of a local partnership that was neither publicly led nor publicly coordinated has emerged in Houston. Beginning in 1984, Houston's business leaders established the Houston Economic Development Council (HEDC) to work for economic diversification in this economically troubled city. The head of the new organization was the board chair of Century Development Corporation, then one of the 10 largest U.S. developers. The HEDC's leadership was initially drawn from the city's real-estate-oriented growth coalition—including bankers, developers, and newspaper editors. They developed a number of proposals for private and government efforts to bring new industries to the city. What makes the HEDC stand apart from other such organizations is that it is truly a *private*-public partnership. The HEDC as an organization was created under the auspices of private business leaders, yet has relied in part on local government funds to finance its activities. The HEDC can be distinguished from similar types of partnership arrangements in that a private organization was created first, and then public support was enlisted. Moreover, the leaders of the HEDC have gone to great lengths to restrict the governmental role to one of financial support. One of the HEDC's first presidents warned openly that if this Houston progrowth coalition accepted government support, they might have to be accountable to the citizenry and operate in a more public fashion.[19] The conservative progrowth coalitions in Sunbelt cities have not generally been formed by political entrepreneurs, but by business leaders, including those in Houston and Dallas.

Partnerships in Cincinnati and Louisville In other cities around the nation government officials have played a leading or coequal role with business leaders in luring industry and promoting local economic development. As Basile has noted, "public officials are now full partners in a wide variety of projects, from new city halls to major mixed-use development projects."[20] For example, an MXD project was unveiled in Cincinnati, with a luxury hotel and an office tower as its centerpieces. The project directly involved Cincinnati government leaders, who bought the land and leased it to the developer and owners, thereby subsidizing and enhancing private profit making. The city provided other developer subsidies as well, such as nearby street improvements, walkways, and landscaping. The economic and political decision makers there candidly view their project as lasting only a few decades, to be followed once again by bulldozing and redevelopment. Moreover, some city and county government leaders are becoming aggressive and entrepreneurial in their negotiations with developers, requiring a portion of the business profits in return for providing development subsidies for certain downtown projects. In one Louisville hotel project the city government was scheduled to get half the profits after the developer got a 15 percent return on his equity. The city government was also to get half of any appreciation in value of the property.[21]

Privatizing Public Projects A recent trend is for city government leaders to "privatize" the development of needed governmental facilities, from jails to city halls, by getting a private developer to build the public facility as part of a private development project. For instance, in the late 1980s in Fairfax County, the board of supervisors set up a public-private partnership, an agreement with private real estate developers, to build a new government complex. In exchange, the county government is giving the Charles E. Smith Companies and the Artery Organization, the private development partners, cash and land on which to build private projects, including more than a million square feet of office space and a 250-room hotel. Fairfax County will regain title to a little more than half the land granted in 75 years. County officials who defended the deal argued that they were taking land worth $4 million and by means of private development mechanisms turning it into an $83 million government center. But community groups cited the project as a giveaway, asserting that the local government could have received a larger return by maintaining ownership of land that will significantly appreciate in value. Local citizen critics also argued that the negative impact of the project on this highly urban county, in the form of additional density and traffic problems, was ignored in the county's negotiations with the large private developers.[22]

Similarly, the city officials in New Haven contracted with the private developers Olympia and York and Chase Enterprises to construct a city hall and library complex coupled to a private office building and parking facilities. The total project cost was forecast to be $88 million, with $70 million coming from private capital sources. Municipal bonds have been used to finance the city hall component, and the private developers received a subsidy for the private component in the form of a $15 million federal UDAG. Developers are finding these arrangements advantageous because governments are taking on some expensive front-end building expenses such as land costs, construction loans, and second mortgages. And some developers and their bankers now prefer this type of free-market interference because it transfers developmental risks that they have previously assumed onto ordinary taxpayers.[23]

Linkage: The New Developer Contributions   In recent years, as we have seen in earlier chapters and will detail more in Chapter 10, some local governments, especially in cities with economic prosperity, have pressed for greater contributions by developers to infrastructural facilities required for their private projects. By the mid- to late-1980s federal and state government contributions to public-works projects were no longer increasing. Taxpayer reluctance to subsidize development has also increased in many areas, particularly high-growth cities. As a result, some local governments have required significant developer contributions; these take the form of contributing land, making on-site or off-site utility improvements, and paying a variety of impact and development fees in order to proceed with private development projects. Some such fees are modest, while others, especially in California, Massachusetts, and New Jersey, have been substantial. One example of concessions is the MXD project being constructed in North Brunswick, New Jersey, by K. Hovnanian Companies, one of New Jersey's leading developers. On 189 acres of vacant land off Route 1 in the central part of the state, the $225 million multiple-use project will eventually include 1 million square feet of offices, retail space, a hotel, and condominiums. An increasingly common theme is revealed in the development of this MXD: the requirement of state and local governments that the Hovnanian Companies contribute cash for the provision of major improvements to nearby roads and highways. The ability of local governments to require developer contributions to the infrastructure usually provided by government is, however, limited. As we noted in Chapter 5, major concessions have been secured by local governments in growing areas.[24]

FEDERAL GOVERNMENT AID FOR GROWTH AND DEVELOPMENT

The 1949 Housing Act and Urban Renewal   The federal government has provided numerous subsidies to assist local governments in supporting growth, development, and redevelopment. We noted previously the federal urban renewal money in the San Francisco example with which we opened this chapter. The 1949 Housing Act not only authorized the construction of public housing units but also authorized a massive program of urban clearance and "renewal." The 1949 act envisioned the use of federal capital for "slum" clearance and the provision of decent low-rent housing for poor Americans by relying on free-market mechanisms. But this scenario did not transpire. As a candid report of the National Commission on Urban Problems characterized it, urban renewal became a "federally financed gimmick to provide relatively cheap land for a miscellany of profitable or prestigious enterprises."[25] And indeed, federal urban renewal programs have provided tremendous subsidies for private developers. Federal funds have been used to bulldoze large central-city areas considered "blighted," and the improved land has frequently been sold to developers for about a third of what it cost city governments to bulldoze. In this way, many central cities from Boston to San Francisco have been redeveloped since World War II. But heavy social costs have been exacted by government-assisted urban clearance and redevelopment. As the San Francisco case indicates, the majority of those forced out have been disproportionately poor or elderly. And only a small fraction of the new housing units built in renewal areas have had rents inexpensive enough for those who previously lived there to return. Far more housing has been *destroyed* by central-city redevelopment programs than has been built.[26]

Recent Redevelopment: CDBGs and UDAGs Since the 1970s government renewal and redevelopment programs have been reorganized, and their names have been changed, but the results have been similar. Originated during the Nixon administration and implemented under President Gerald Ford in 1974, the Community Development Block Grant (CDBG) program consolidated a number of federally subsidized renewal programs. Officially known as the Housing and Community Development Act, the legislation stipulated that every CDBG-subsidized activity satisfy one of three purposes: (1) to primarily benefit low- and moderate-income persons, (2) to eliminate urban "blight," and (3) to meet urgent local community needs. Every city with a population over 50,000 was to get a share of block grants based on its size, poverty population, and other demographic characteristics. Officially, the law establishing this program required that CDBGs "principally benefit" economically disadvantaged members of communities.[27] Some CDBG money has benefitted these target groups. For example, in a rural community south of Tucson, $100,000 in CDBG assistance was used to buy a special truck to deliver water to moderate-income residents; in Rockville, Maryland, the Manna Food Center, supported by $56,000 in CDBG funds, has provided food to poor families; and in 1986, $160,000 in CDBG funds were provided to Tampa's

Senior Home Improvement Program so that its members could fix leaky roofs, electrical systems, and plumbing.[28]

In the mid-1980s government officials claimed that 87 percent of the CDBG funds were spent for low- and moderate-income programs. However, the official figure is not consistent with government reports on Urban Development Action Grant (UDAG) projects, an important part of the CDBG program. More than one-third of all UDAG projects have involved manufacturing and related activities, and only 39 percent of the housing units built with UDAG assistance have been for lower-income families. The legislative mandate to serve low-income populations has frequently been undermined as local government officials attempt to entice developers to construct major private projects in their cities. The active encouragement of federal officials, particularly those serving in the Reagan administration, has been instrumental in subverting the program's original intent to help the poor.[29]

Between 1977 and 1987 the federal government spent $4.5 billion on nearly 3,000 UDAG projects in 1,180 cities. This variety of developer subsidies produced a ripple effect of more than $24 billion in private investment. While outward appearances suggest that the UDAGs have been a success story, an unanswered question is whether the private sector would have made these investments without special incentives. After all, many of these dollars have ended up going into profitable hotels, shopping centers, and similar projects in many cities.[30] For example, a total of $13 million in government subsidies was provided for the development of Baltimore's 500-room Hyatt Hotel in the early 1980s. Of that, $10 million came from a federal UDAG. According to an article in *Mortgage Banker*, the Hyatt project would not have been economically viable without the UDAG. This means that profit levels were higher because of governmental intervention. In the vernacular of bankers the situation is described this way: "In general, a real estate project showing a return on cost...of more than 12.5 percent in a normal...market is required. Our more sophisticated customers are now using return on cost as a key measure of viability early in the development process."[31] There is also the Detroit Poletown example cited in Chapter 5. In that case the General Motors plan to demolish 1,500 homes and 150 businesses to facilitate the construction of an automobile plant received generous government support, including a UDAG. In addition, Cleveland's city government received the largest number of UDAGs in 1987, many of which went to facilitate the development of a shopping center and office buildings.[32]

Thus in many cities local government officials, working with local growth coalitions, have channeled federal government money into a variety of revitalization programs aimed at reviving—from a business point of view—downtown areas and central cities. The original goals of decent housing and jobs for those living in poverty areas have not, for the most part, been realized; more often than not, government action in urban redevelopment projects has permanently displaced moderate-income working people from their neighborhoods and raised their cost of housing by forcing them to move elsewhere.[33]

FEDERAL AID IN CONTROLLING LAND USE

Private Support for Governmental Zoning Regulations Since the early decades of this century, national and local real estate investors and developers have been concerned with controlling "crazy mixes" of urban construction, land use, such as the commingling of industrial and residential building, and have been among the most influential supporters of zoning laws. These local statutes separate types of projects (for example, churches from massage parlors), regulate housing densities, and require case-by-case decisions on zoning variations. By 1920 nearly 90 percent of the country's largest 93 cities had zoning ordinances specifying which areas could be used for residential, commercial, and industrial purposes. And by 1937, more than 1,300 cities had zoning ordinances, and 517 had subdivision regulations. Real estate organizations lobbied for an extension of zoning regulations to encompass entire metropolitan areas and for city planning of roads, parks, and playgrounds. Zoning laws were declared constitutional by the U.S. Supreme Court in 1926. In a landmark case (*Village of Euclid (Ohio) et al.* v. *Ambler Realty Company*), the Supreme Court upheld the validity of comprehensive zoning. The decision specifically sanctioned zoning by small municipalities in metropolitan areas. It also legitimated the use of planning boards as a part of the zoning process.[34]

Why did many in the real estate industry support this type of local, state, and federal government regulation of land markets? It did represent, after all, a type of intervention that interfered with the right of owners to dispose of property as they saw fit. There are a number of reasons. We have discussed in previous chapters how the larger homebuilders favored zoning and other regulation of land and housing markets to bring stability to these markets and to enhance their own prosperity and control. Large homebuilders worked with professional planners and government officials to secure land-use planning and regulation. Private real estate organizations helped to secure local zoning laws and subdivision regulations. Many smaller subdividers and builders were indifferent to these regulations, or were openly hostile.[35] Although city planning in the United States began as a movement focused on refurbishing the downtowns of major cities, it soon spread to include governmental regulation of urban land use. The larger developers were concerned with developing the rings of residential areas "properly" and thus worked with the leading planning association (American City Planning Institute) to issue a joint statement that became the basis for the federal government's *A Standard City Planning and Enabling Act*. In this act the U.S. Department of Commerce recommended that state governments pass enabling legislation to facilitate city land-use planning and zoning regulation; the *Standard Act* became the basis of much local subdivision control and planning legislation.

Moreover, by the 1930s the larger developers associated with the NAREB and other development industry organizations had found that land-use regulatory laws were not being administered in ways that provided the desired standardization and stability. So the NAREB, together with other major finance and real estate associations, worked for the passage of the 1934 National Housing Act, which created the FHA. With a staff recruited from the private development sector, the FHA thereafter wrote regulations that not only buttressed the U.S. lending industry by insuring individual mortgages, but also standardized subdivision development nationwide with minimum requirements for streets, lots, and other subdivision services. This gave greater market control to the larger developers who could afford to comply with regulations; the FHA could prevent the development of subdivisions not meeting the new standards. This also provided leverage to get recalcitrant local officials to provide more comprehensive zoning desired by the big developers. Moreover, FHA was authorized by the law to insure rental housing, but because of the bias toward the larger developers of single-family housing the FHA provided mortgage insurance for few rental dwellings, thereby significantly contributing to the recurring housing crises for the large proportion of the U.S. population unable to afford home mortgages (see Chapter 8).

Real estate developers and builders often serve on, and greatly influence, the decisions of zoning boards. Rezoning a parcel of land can generate enormous profits for the owner, such as when an area is shifted from residential to commercial use. So it is not surprising that developers have supported zoning, or that they have attempted to dominate or influence zoning boards. Early support for such regulations and for deed restrictions came most forcefully from the largest real estate operators. John E. Burchard, a prominent architectural historian, once told a group of powerful developers that: "zoning can protect you against the small, inefficient entrepreneur. Zoning can protect the big fellow against the marauding of little guys who have nothing at all in mind."[36]

Questioning Variances   By the 1930s questions were being raised about numerous zoning variances being granted in many cities. Zoning variances had become marketable commodities; and powerful land speculators and developers could usually get around the zoning law. This problem has persisted since the 1930s. Bribery scandals have been common in the history of zoning; in recent decades there have been payoff scandals in New Jersey, California, New York, and Chicago. A study of the suburbs in

Suffolk County near New York City by Gottdiener supports the idea that local governments are heavily shaped by powerful business interests. His research indicates that some rezoning decisions were made in light of the political costs and gains confronting elected officials. Campaign contributions comprised one major category of rewards provided by developers, bankers, and other firms. Although payments were not made for every favorable zoning decision, such exchanges happened frequently enough to demonstrate that local zoning officials and other politicians were supporters of profit-making development.[37]

Further Rationalization of Large-Scale Development? Since the 1950s large corporations have increased pressure for further standardization and rationalization of land-use regulations and for zoning reform to permit higher-density, larger-scale development projects. Much public discussion concerning zoning reform has been led by planners who see zoning as too inflexible. But changes in the housing and development industry underlie this renewed discussion. Large-scale development interests have pressed for statewide zoning laws, so that regulations will be similar across a large geographical area. And they have pushed for streamlining of local land regulations. In contrast, smaller developers and builders have often not been vigorous supporters of these reforms because they operate more easily on a local basis.[38]

Because of the problem of diverse local land regulations, big business interests have worked through private planning groups such as the Regional Plan Association of New York, the BAC of San Francisco, the Committee for Economic Development, the Urban Land Institute, and the Real Estate Research Corporation to press for new planning laws. Particularly important have been reports sponsored by the Ford and Rockefeller Brothers foundations; these reports have argued that the patchwork quilt of local regulations should be transformed into a set of development controls operated by higher levels of *government*. The executives heading large corporations are not primarily seeking the common welfare in pursuing land regulation reform; they press for governmental regulations that serve their developmental interests.[39]

A major proposed piece of federal legislation was the National Land-Use Policy Act introduced by Arizona Representative Morris Udall and Washington Senator Henry Jackson in the 1960s and 1970s. While Senator Jackson claimed the bill would preserve the rights of local governments, it would have required that local government officials set up detailed land-planning requirements and agencies as a condition of eligibility. The bill was designed to provide a national land-planning policy. Interestingly, the land reformers have included not only environmentalists and civil rights advocates (who were seeking to get rid of local racial zoning), but also those representing the interests of big developers and major urban planners. Some large-scale development interests have worked for land-use reform, particularly major development and industrial companies (for example, Exxon's real estate subsidiary) that see centralized land-use policies as eliminating many local restrictions to real estate development.[40] In the mid-1970s, however, the reform bill was defeated in a close vote in the House of Representatives. Local business and government officials, small farmers, and local builders, as well as supportive local organizations, opposed the National Land-Use Policy Act. In his book *Keep Out*, Sidney Plotkin notes that the nationally oriented land development elite, which was pressing for the rationalization and standardization of real estate development across the United States, ran into the fact that few smaller developers and builders wanted such massive land use regulation changes.[41]

GOVERNMENT FISCAL CRISES IN CITIES

Development Subsidies and Public Services In the last two decades many cities, at first in the North and Midwest, then in the 1980s in the South, have faced serious government financial crises, with a few on the brink of bankruptcy. The costs of city services—highways and streets, fire and police services, city hospitals—have been rising rapidly in recent years, even while many services have been deteriorating in quality. Some conventional analysts have explained the problems of U.S. cities in terms of avaricious demands by unions, unnecessary city services, corruption, and inept government management. Although there is a kernel of truth to this interpretation, it overlooks broader trends in modern capitalism, including uneven capitalist investment and the use of state taxes and subsidies to facilitate profit making.

As noted in Chapter 2, the federal government periodically undermines the vitality of cities, particularly in the North, by exacting more tax revenue than it returns. The core dilemma of fiscally troubled cities is usually not a lack of money to finance government employees' wages and public services, but rather the unequal distribution of taxpayer funds that have been available. Substantial local and federal subsidies go to support the urban development projects of industrial corporations and developers. Neighborhood and public services suffer partly because government money is being funneled to development needs. In addition, corporate executives frequently move capital to areas where they can receive the greatest return. When corporations started heading for the Sunbelt in the 1960s and 1970s, they often left behind local governments with fewer people and industries from whom to extract taxes to fund essential city services. Many northern city governments were torn between the demands of powerful corporate capitalists for a favorable profit-making climate and the demands of municipal workers for an improved standard of living. Pressure escalated to reduce wages, corporate taxes, and city services, so that the costs of doing business could be reduced. Otherwise more corporations threatened to leave for the Sunbelt.[42]

The New York City Crisis Economic stagnation from 1972 through the early 1980s made it difficult for many cities outside the then-expanding Sunbelt to cope adequately without becoming heavily dependent on banking institutions. This dependence can be seen in New York City's financial crisis, which received wide public exposure in the mid-1970s. Because of sharply rising expenditures and a declining tax base, New York began to borrow heavily from banks. New York banking institutions, already in trouble because of shaky foreign loans, had a sizable proportion of their assets in New York City securities. If the local government failed, banking institutions might follow suit. In the spring of 1975, the city government reached the precarious financial position where it was neither able to meet its payrolls nor pay the interest on past loans. On the verge of bankruptcy, New York was bailed out by state and federal government assistance. The New York state government created the Municipal Assistance Corporation, which was empowered to sell securities to help cover the city's debts. When this strategy proved insufficient, the New York legislature took a more drastic step and established the Emergency Financial Control Board (EFCB).[43]

Composed of bankers and corporate capitalists, the EFCB became responsible for directly administering New York City finances, taking over from democratically elected officials. The government-created corporation was led by chief executives from such organizations as N.Y. Bell Telephone and American Airlines, as well as from banks. The board was supposed to balance the city's budget by 1978. Its authority had the appearance of putting the "fox in charge of the chicken coop," because banks held New York's municipal securities. Moreover, a new city government management office, staffed by corporate executives, was charged with supervising productivity for government agencies. In a speech to a conference of the National Municipal League in 1980, William Ellinghaus, president of AT & T, bragged about bringing fiscal responsibility to New York City by slashing city employment, controlling the wages of city workers, reducing services, and managing it more like a business. Moreover, he recommended that other cities follow his lead, employing the fiscal standards of investors and business managers to run their municipalities. He urged business executives to adopt a more activist role in government management.[44]

Within the context of a serious economic contraction, cities such as New York and Cleveland have been forced to work out agreements with financial capitalists to rearrange interest payments. But the cost was high—in terms of both new interest charges and in increased bankers' control over government expenditures. As a result, many cities have come under the management of what Mark Gelfand has called the "financial dictators."[45] Workers and their families have borne a disproportionate share of the burden for the financial salvation of cities. For example, in New York City, while taxes were being increased, services to residents were cut significantly. "Free tuition and open enrollment at the City University, library hours, sanitation pickups, city hospitals, day-care centers, the city work force—were cut back or eliminated."[46] City transit fares were raised 40 percent, city parks began to decay, and the streets became dirtier. Thousands of employees were laid off, and municipal unions were forced to give back millions in fringe benefits they had struggled to achieve in earlier years, to defer wage increases, and to accept the laying off of thousands of city employees. In short, banking and other corporate officials used New York's fiscal crisis to scare working people into accepting an austerity and sacrifice (for workers) plan as the main solution to the city's fiscal crisis.[47]

As one of the world capitals for multinational capitalism, New York City could not be abandoned to chronic fiscal crisis and overall governmental decline. While certain areas of the city such as the South Bronx have been allowed to deteriorate, the Manhattan district is too important to multinational capitalism to allow the city government to decline and decay. However, other central cities and their governments, North and South, have been allowed to decay. This has been the case in St. Louis, Newark, and Detroit, where local governmental revenues and local efforts at attracting new economic investment have been insufficient to reverse serious corporate disinvestment. At least since the mid-1970s, Detroit's city government has been in periodic financial trouble. The suburbanization and international restructuring of the automobile industry, including capital flight, brought high levels of unemployment, municipal worker layoffs, deteriorating governmental infrastructure, and rising public assistance costs. Central Detroit is not attractive to most investors, and the local business elite has tried to revitalize the city with a "corporate center" strategy. At the heart of this strategy was the new Renaissance Center (MXD) development, a massive hotel, office, and shopping complex constructed in the deteriorating downtown area. In order to build the center, its originator, Henry Ford II, solicited aid from 51 private real estate partners. But this effort to revitalize central Detroit has not been successful. The center lost money; and its major lenders were forced to trade $220 million in debt for a majority ownership share of the center. Old industrial Detroit has been abandoned, even while there has been new investment in Detroit's growing suburbs.[48]

Urban Revitalization and Worker Sacrifices   Many business leaders and their governmental allies believe that regional economic renaissance can be created, that troubled cities, whether in the Rustbelt or the Sunbelt, can recover economically. And the public-private partnerships mentioned above are at the heart of revitalization strategies. Much governmental aid is expected and delivered for redevelopment projects. Frequently, moreover, the prescription for accomplishing revival includes the requirement that workers in older industries and municipal governments accept the "good business climate." Like the citizens of many debt-ridden Third World countries, workers in selected cities must accept austerity—lower wages and benefits, weak unions, cuts in government services to ordinary citizens, reduced rates of taxation for corporations, and huge government subsidies to attract new corporations to economically distressed cities. This method of resuscitating cities by cooperating with capital implies significant rank-and-file sacrifices.[49]

Faced with severe problems of urban decline, the national governments in numerous western countries have taken some action to redevelop specific cities or specific areas within cities. As we noted in Chapter 2, one idea generated in the 1980s was the "urban enterprise zone." Like the free-trade zones in many underdeveloped countries, these are poverty-stricken areas where major governmental concessions such as tax-free production are made in order to attract capitalistic investors.[50] Initially, the Reagan administration saw no need for any urban policy. David Stockman, Reagan's first budget director, wanted to do away with most urban development grants and revenue-sharing programs. And the administration did in fact sharply reduce many urban aid programs. Indeed, President Reagan argued at one press conference that people living in troubled cities could vote with their feet: If they did not like their conditions, they could pick up and move to more prosperous cities. Reagan's approach emphasized reliance on unrestrained market mechanisms for solving problems. Eventually, however, pressure from urban mayors forced Reagan's advisers to back down and come up with a plan for distressed cities. And in 1982 the president's major approach to cities was put forward in the form of an "urban enterprise zone" proposal. The idea was to give huge tax cuts and other subsidy incentives to persuade corporations to locate factories and offices in inner-city areas. Otherwise, the Reagan urban policy was one of intentional neglect of city problems.[51]

A Chronic Service Crisis for Many Cities?   The years between 1964 and 1978 were golden years for local governments. There were numerous new federally subsidized programs to aid the cities and city residents, such as Medicaid and the CDBG program. In the 1970s, under President Richard Nixon's "new federalism," federal policy was oriented to giving local governments more control over local programs, with the federal government providing funding for this expansion of power in the form of revenue sharing. However, the rapid growth in local programs and local government expenditures was curtailed under the Carter and Reagan administrations. The Reagan philosophy was different from that of the "new federalism," for the Reagan administration expected city governments not only to control local programs but also to find funding from *local* sources of tax revenue. The problem is that many city governments have limited sources of tax revenue; they do not have the revenue-generating capacity of the federal government. In addition, because of their own problems, state governments have reduced their contributions to city programs as a percentage of local revenues. This has meant a chronic service crisis for many cities. City officials have frequently had to choose between major service cuts and substantial new local taxes. In a 1986 survey of 660 cities and towns, researchers found that the majority (56 percent) expected to have a budget deficit and had cut or stabilized growth in municipal employment. As one analyst has expressed the result of this conservative federal policy: "We are about to return to the days when city after city faced the reality of major service reductions or even bankruptcy. This is the implied intent of Reagan's policies: pit region against region and city against city."[52]

CONCLUSION

Until the 1930s the federal government generally took a laissez-faire (hands-off) approach to city problems. However, the enormous unemployment and housing problems of the Great Depression forced the federal government to expand its involvement with urban matters. Federal jobs and housing programs were central components of the aid programs to severely depressed cities. In addition, much federal aid during the Great Depression took the form of subsidizing ailing businesses, including banking and real estate corporations. In the decades to follow, this pattern of directly aiding business interests in cities would be expanded, not only in various urban renewal and redevelopment programs but also in a variety of other governmental subsidies for business interests. City and other municipal governments have become more numerous since the 1930s; many metropolitan areas are balkanized into many separate municipalities and counties. Greater Los Angeles, for example, today encompasses 5 county and 100 city governments, while greater Atlanta covers 7 county and 46 municipal governments. Such a complexity of governments throws barriers in the path of government officials seeking to respond to urban crises metropolitan in scope. And this profusion of local governments across the nation makes it easier for large industrial and development corporations seeking subsidies to play off one governmental entity against another for the best deals.

In this chapter we have reviewed the numerous ways in which governmental programs have been used to support a broad array of private industrial and real estate projects. We have seen how local growth coalitions have worked with local and federal government officials to bring industrial and physical development and redevelopment to cities. Peterson's argument that local government officials seek to enhance the general welfare and pursue growth benefitting all residents is not supported in our data. There are clearly winners and losers in the economic and real estate development games. Supported by the national business elite, local growth coalitions are usually centered around developers, bankers, and other business people interested in local growth. And these urban growth coalitions make important overtures to local government officials in their quest for growth. For more than a century coalitions have developed working relationships with officials at all levels of government; and many local coalitions have directly controlled local politics as well.

Public-private partnerships have received a lot of attention in the last decade or two. Some public-private partnerships have involved arrangements encouraging specific large development projects of investors and other business people. We saw the example of David Rockefeller's Downtown–Lower Manhattan Association working with a local governmental agency to construct two of the world's largest office towers. We also discussed the more recent trend for city government leaders to "privatize" the development of needed governmental facilities such as city halls by getting a private developer to build the public facility as part of a private development project, as in Fairfax County, Virginia. In the next chapter we will discuss the popular political coalitions that have emerged with conceptions of growth and development that differ substantially from the views of these public-private partnerships. Both in the suburbs and in the central cities, in cities from Boston and Burlington to San Francisco and Santa Monica, these progressive political movements have forced the implementation of new policy mechanisms, including those variously called "linked development," "exactions," "impact fees," and "in lieu fees." As Michael Peter Smith has pointed out, this linkage policy "has the potential to focus popular consciousness on the social costs of the 'public-private partnership' and the profit system itself."[53]

NOTES

1. Ruth Faith Santana, "St. Louis Leads Nation Again in Using Federal Tax Credits," *Nation's Cities Weekly* 9 (April 14, 1986): 4.
2. Chester W. Hartman, *Yerba Buena: Land Grab and Community Resistance in San Francisco* (San Francisco: Glide Publications, 1974), p. 13.
3. John Mollenkopf, *The Contested City* (Princeton: Princeton University Press, 1983), pp. 160–163.
4. Hartman, *Yerba Buena*, p. 43.
5. Ibid., pp. 48–50.
6. Ibid., p. 19.
7. Ibid., pp. 93–97.

8. Paul E. Peterson, *City Limits* (Chicago: University of Chicago Press, 1981).

9. Harvey Molotch, "Strategies and Constraints of Growth Elites," in *Business Elites and Urban Development*, edited by Scott Cummings (Albany: State University of New York Press, 1988), p. 25.

10. Joe R. Feagin and Robert E. Parker, "Economic Troubles and Local State Action: Some Texas Examples," in *Research in Politics and Society, Deindustrialization and the Restructuring of American Industry*, edited by Joyce Rothschild and Michael Wallace (Greenwich, Conn.: JAI Press, 1988), vol. 3, pp. 127–153; William D. Angel, "Beggars in Velvet Gowns," unpublished Ph.D. dissertation, University of Texas, 1977, p. 21.

11. Mollenkopf, *The Contested City*, p. 4.

12. The references can be found in the notes to Chapter 1.

13. Harvey Molotch, "The City as a Growth Machine," *American Journal of Sociology* 82 (September 1976): 313.

14. See Arnold Fleischmann and Joe R. Feagin, "The Politics of Growth-Oriented Urban Alliances," *Urban Affairs Quarterly* 23 (December 1987): 207–232.

15. Charles Abrams, *The City Is the Frontier* (New York: Harper and Row, 1967), pp. 221–227.

16. Ibid.; Rice Center Research and Development Corporation, *Houston Initiatives: Phase One Report* (Houston: Rice Center, 1981), pp. 13–14.

17. Henry Aubin, *City for Sale* (Toronto: James Lorimer, 1977), p. 373. See also pp. 372–374.

18. Jack Newfield and Paul Dubrul, *The Abuse of Power* (New York: Viking, 1977), pp. 88–96.

19. "City Leadership Presents Economic Development Plan," *Houston* 55 (July): 9–13; Feagin and Parker, "Economic Troubles and Local State Action: Some Texas Examples," pp. 141–146.

20. Ralph J. Basile, "The Changing Atmosphere for Dealmaking," *Nation's Cities Weekly*, October 6, 1986, 7.

21. "Cincinnati's Fountain Square South: From Historic to Commercial Asset," *Buildings* 76 (February 1982): 65; Robert Guenther, "Cities Getting Part of Profits," *Wall Street Journal*, September 29, 1982, sect. 2, p. 31; Arnold Fleischmann, "The Political Economy of Annexation and Urban Development," Ph.D. dissertation, University of Texas, Austin, Texas, forthcoming, 1983, chap. 3.

22. William Fulton, "The Profit Motive," *Planning*, October 1987, 6.

23. Urban Land Institute, *Development Trends* (Washington, D.C.: Urban Land Institute, 1987), p. 10.

24. Rachelle Garbarine, "Hovnanian Planning a Mixed-Use Project," *New York Times*, November 22, 1987, R12.

25. National Commission on Urban Problems, *Building the American City* (Washington, D.C.: U.S. Government Printing Office, 1968), p. 153.

26. Diana Klebanow, Franklin L. Jones, and Ira M. Leonard, Urban Legacy: *The Story of America's Cities* (New York: Mentor Books, 1977), pp. 351–353.
27. Reggie Todd, "The Case for Community Development Grants: The History and the Need," *Nation's Cities Weekly*, March 30, 1987, 1; Bill McCarthy, "CDBG: A Shining Past—A Clouded Future," *Nation's Cities Weekly*, February 24, 1986, 4.
28. Linda R. Woodhouse, "The Success Stories," *Nation's Cities Weekly*, March 30, 1987, 7; John Miller, "Bitter Medicine," *Dollars and Sense* 135 (April 1988): 8.
29. Bill McCarthy, "CDBG: A Shining Past—A Clouded Future," *Nation's Cities Weekly*, February 24, 1986, 4; Melvin J. Adams, "Who Needs UDAGs?" *Journal of Housing*, 43 (July/August 1986): 156.
30. David L. Aiken, "UDAG: 'An Effective and Proven Asset' in Aiding Cities," *Nation's Cities Weekly*, February 24, 1986, 5; James Kilpatrick, "Housing Bill Exceeds U.S. Responsibility," *St. Louis Post-Dispatch*, November 23, 1987, 3B.
31. Christopher W. Kurz, "Public/Private Leveraging of Urban Real Estate," *Mortgage Banker*, November 1980, 15.
32. Kilpatrick, "Housing Bill Exceeds U.S. Responsibility," p. 3B.
33. Mark I. Gelfand, *A Nation of Cities* (New York: Oxford University Press, 1975), pp. 112–114; Robert A. Beauregard, "The Redevelopment of the Advanced Capitalist City," paper presented at Conference on New Perspectives on Urban Political Economy, Washington, D.C., American University, May 1981, p. 8.
34. Pearl Janet Davies, *Real Estate in American History* (Washington, D.C.: Public Affairs Press, 1958), pp. 77–80, 146–147.
35. Marc A. Weiss, *The Rise of the Community Builders: The American Real Estate Industry and Urban Land Planning* (New York: Columbia University Press, 1987).
36. Quoted in Robert Goodman, *After the Planners* (New York: Simon and Schuster, 1971), p. 147; see also Davies, *Real Estate in American History*, p. 66.
37. Mark Gottdiener, *Planned Sprawl* (Beverly Hills: Sage, 1977), pp. 82–83.
38. Richard A. Walker and Michael K. Heiman, "Quiet Revolution for Whom?" *Annals of the Association of American Geographers* 71 (March 1981): 68; Richard E. Babcock, *The Zoning Game* (Madison, Wis.: University of Wisconsin Press, 1966), p. 139.
39. Walker and Heiman, "Quiet Revolution for Whom?," pp. 72–83.
40. Joe R. Feagin, "Arenas of Conflict: Zoning and Land-Use Reform in Critical Political-Economic Perspective," in *Euclid at Sixty: Both Past and Prologue*, edited by Charles M. Haar (Chicago: American Planning Association, 1989), pp. 73-100.
41. Sidney Plotkin, *Keep Out: The Struggle for Land Use Control* (Berkeley: University of California Press, 1987), pp. 185–200.

42. Traditional experts are quoted in "Urban Experts Advise, Castigate and Console the City on Its Problems," in *The Fiscal Crisis of American Cities*, edited by Roger E. Alcaly and David Mermelstein (New York: Vintage, 1977), pp. 6–9; also see Jacob Epstein, "The Last Days of New York," in *The Fiscal Crisis of American Cities*, pp. 61–62.

43. Kenneth Fox, "Cities and City Governments," in *U.S. Capitalism in Crisis*, edited by Bruce Steinberg et al. (New York: Union for Radical Political Economics, 1978), p. 179; Roger E. Alcaly and Helen Bodain, "New York's Fiscal Crisis and the Economy," in *The Fiscal Crisis of American Cities*, pp. 31–38; Ken Auletta, *The Streets Were Paved with Gold* (New York: Vintage, 1980), pp. 278–280.

44. William Ellinghaus, "Urban Management: A Businesslike Policy for City Planning," *Houston Business Journal*, November 24, 1980, 4.

45. Gelfand, *A Nation of Cities*, p. 51.

46. Auletta, *The Streets Were Paved with Gold*, p. 278.

47. Ibid., pp. 276–291.

48. Richard Child Hill and Joe R. Feagin, "Detroit and Houston: Two Cities in Global Perspective," in *The Capitalist City*, edited by Michael Peter Smith and Joe R. Feagin (Oxford: Basil Blackwell, 1987), pp. 155–169.

49. David Mermelstein, "Austerity, Planning and the Socialist Alternative," in *The Fiscal Crisis of American Cities*, p. 354.

50. Ted Robert Gurr and Desmond King, *The State and the City* (Chicago: University of Chicago Press, 1987), p. 101.

51. Timothy K. Barkenov, Daniel Rich, and Robert Warren, "The New Privatism, Federalism, and the Future of Urban Governance: National Urban Policy in the 1980s," *Journal of Urban Affairs* 3 (Fall 1981): 3.

52. Thomas R. Schwartz, "A New Urban Crisis in the Making," *Challenge*, September/October 1987, 41. The survey is cited on p. 40.

53. Michael Peter Smith, "The Uses of Linked Development Policies in U.S. Cities," in *Regenerating the Cities*, edited by Michael Parkinson, Dennis Judd, and Bernard Foley (Manchester: Manchester University Press, 1988), p. 108.

10

CITIZEN PROTEST
Democratizing Urban
Investment and Development

...the efforts of the group known as Santa Monicans for Renters' Rights (SMRR) had been hailed as the liberal answer to Reaganite populism by Mother Jones *and the* Village Voice *and ridiculed as "suburban radicalism" by the* Wall Street Journal. *Local public officials have been subjected to death threats and described as socialists or worse ("The People's Republic of Santa Monica") by landlords and conservatives.*[1]

INTRODUCTION

Two thousand riot police were summoned to evict tenants illegally "squatting" in eight houses. Without warning the police charge to disperse a crowd that had gathered outside the houses to protest the evictions. In the turmoil an 18-year-old tenant is killed by a bus. This incident is just one of many clashes between tenants and police in a city with a severe shortage of affordable rental housing, a city where the local government has a program of land clearance and redevelopment for officially defined "blighted" areas. In its wake that urban clearance program has brought about the destruction of many sound homes, numerous evictions, and replacement of older structures by more luxurious construction. The scenario described above unfolded in West Berlin during the 1980s. In that city the police, government officials, developers, and landowners were battling a cross section of young people who cannot find affordable housing. Numerous housing riots like this one have occurred in European cities.[2]

Can housing riots happen in the future in the United States? That question has been answered affirmatively by observers, such as those cited in Chapter 8, who point to the continuing U.S. housing crisis. During the 1980s housing construction has fallen behind the growth in new households. In the mid- to late-1980s there was an estimated shortfall of at least a half-million housing units each year in the United States. Those hit hardest have been low- and middle-income individuals and families seeking affordable housing for rent or for sale. To some extent, there has already been housing-related protest by some Americans. For example, the Miami, Florida, riots in May 1980 and December 1982 were in part precipitated by the affordable housing problems facing local black tenants in the Miami area. And about the same time that the previously mentioned West Berlin housing riot took place, a citizen's activist group (ACORN) helped several low-income minority families move into abandoned buildings in Philadelphia and Detroit. This "squatting" protest was strategically designed to pressure government officials to address the unavailability of affordable housing.[3] Such illegal squatting could become more commonplace, with middle-income whites joining in, if the U.S. housing crisis continues to worsen.

CITIZENS PROTESTING URBAN DEVELOPMENT AND REDEVELOPMENT

The land and property development interests, embodied in national organizations and local growth coalitions, include industrialists, developers, lenders, land speculators, and other powerful business interests, as well as allied politicians. These powerful groups have created and reconstructed our cities. These coalitions are oriented toward development and redevelopment projects, many of which have been subsidized by federal government assistance. Yet much development has been resisted and protested by citizens. Well-organized groups of workers and consumers can sometimes make a difference in patterns of urban development. This book opened with the dramatic example of well-organized workers and renters in Santa Monica, California, who threw out a developer-oriented city council and replaced it with a council seeking to restrict growth initiatives to projects which met at least some community needs. As we will recount below, these initiatives were still having a positive impact for Santa Monicans in the late 1980s.

In recent decades there have been many urban social struggles, encompassing class, race, and community-based movements. People's movements regularly force developers and government officials to make development concessions and to alter their plans. In Chapter 1 we cited mainstream urban social scientists, most of whom neglect urban struggles. In contrast, critical analysts, such as Castells and Fisher, have underscored the importance of group conflict in shaping city development. Indeed, in *The City and the Grassroots* Castells has called for refocusing urban analysis on this group conflict. Citizens' movements emerge in order to protect neighborhood and community spaces against the exchange-value goals of the industrial and development capitalists. Many urbanites struggle for a city organized around human, family, and neighborhood use-value concerns that go beyond exchange-value concerns of the development industry. Much critical analysis of cities focuses on the way in which households struggle to survive and maintain viable "family space" and thereby force a restructuring of the political priorities of business and political elites. In contrast to market-oriented analysts like Peterson, Berry, and Kasarda, the critical power-conflict scholars do not see "cities" as having a "common interest" in maximizing growth and development, but rather note the dramatic disagreement and conflict between class, race, and community groups over decisions about economic and physical development.[4]

Social Costs of Capitalist Development Many citizens' movements have targeted the negative consequences of unrestrained development in the hands of elites and growth coalitions. These costs, as we noted in Chapter 1, have not been a concern of mainstream urban theorists. The corporations recruited by urban growth interests have been a powerful force for urban social and physical transformation. Growth in capitalist cities hinges on the investment decisions made by these footloose controllers of capital. These points have been seen by mainstream analysts like Peterson and Kasarda. Yet, as we have demonstrated previously, the benefits of corporate-led growth are unevenly awarded, and there are usually substantial individual, family, and community costs. To quote from one recent Arizona analysis:

> *Private firms gain many benefits from urban growth, especially in the form of increased opportunity for new customers and higher profits....In particular, the principal beneficiaries of increasing city size and urban growth are those who possess monopoly advantage in the marketplace. Those who own fixed assets, such as land, receive a disproportionately large jump in value from the greater demand that accompanies urban growth....To individuals, many of the benefits not offset by costs diminish as growth continues. For example, while choices of housing, shopping and entertainment widen as a community grows from a small town into an urban area, a threshold frequently exists, beyond which additional benefits are minimal....To society as a whole, some of the benefits of growth, such as improvements to the infrastructure, are counterbalanced by costs, such as higher taxes and the higher cost of public services.[5]*

And there are *many* other individual, neighborhood, and community costs, not recognized here, such as environmental changes and pollution, congestion, and the destruction of elderly and minority neighborhoods.

"Social costs" under a capitalist system have been defined as the negative consequences of for-profit production and growth, as costs generated but not paid for by private corporations in the process of seeking profits, costs that are shifted onto outside individuals and communities. In U.S. society investment decisions are frequently made without a satisfactory accounting of the side effects and community consequences. Production and development costs are typically calculated at the microeconomic level of the individual industrial or development firm, with an eye on market share or profits, but such narrow accounting neglects costs displaced onto individuals and communities outside the firm. Some costs are related to the environment; towns, suburbs, and central cities grow and decline in physical environments with differential surface water flows, air patterns, rainfall, and soil characteristics. If environmental factors are ignored when profit-centered investment and production decisions are made, then the consequences of such decisions can be negative. The new critical urban analysts argue that many social costs result from the rapidity and unplanned character of private-investment-led growth. The rate of capital infusion into factory and office employment, and the consequent population growth, can accentuate the negative costs, including water pollution, traffic congestion, and displacement of existing residents. Industrial and development corporations create displacement, environmental, and other community problems because our system of urban capitalism and representative government gives them greater economic, ideological, political, and institutionalized power than it provides for rank-and-file citizens. The great inequality in income and resources accented by critical analysts makes it difficult for citizens to resist the locational, production, and development decisions of executives heading large firms.[6]

Government officials are often called upon, by citizens and capitalists, to deal with the costs of private industrial and development decisions. As we documented in previous chapters, however, many local government officials are typically allied with business-led growth coalitions—a point ignored or downplayed by mainstream theorists. The officials recruit corporations with tax abatements and other corporate subsidies. In this manner government officials have played a major role in suburban and downtown industrial and office development, providing roads, disrupting older neighborhoods, giving away publicly owned land, and displacing families to construct business-oriented projects such as convention centers. Nonetheless, local government officials are also confronted by demands from the citizenry to deal with many of the local neighborhood and community consequences of private (and public) development. Taking action to deal with community costs usually involves higher taxes. If government officials do not listen, or if they side with the industrialists and developers, aggressive citizen protest may erupt. The neighborhood and community costs of privately controlled growth and development are the underlying conditions for much urban protest.[7]

Protesting Highways Urban protest has targeted a variety of projects. Highway projects in such cities as Boston, New York, Philadelphia, and Washington have precipitated numerous urban protest movements. The thousands displaced by these projects have expressed dissent in various ways, including civil disobedience. Lawsuits have been filed, though in most cases the citizens have lost. For the most part, judges have ruled in favor of road construction. With only minor modifications, most highway projects have been permitted.

Yet in a few cities such as Boston citizen protest has periodically forced the cancellation of developer-supported highway construction or succeeded in having it delayed for significant periods. For instance, in the 1970s local and state governments in Massachusetts rejected commitments to certain long-planned expressways in the Boston area and redirected some $2 billion for mass transit projects. Community and neighborhood groups, as well as environmental groups, pushed for this moratorium and were satisfied with the decision. Meanwhile, business leaders were angered. A pivotal citizens' group was the Greater Boston Committee on the Transportation Crisis, a coalition of community groups opposed to expressways. An array of different types of people were included in the organization. For a time the chair was a local priest who earlier had helped organize protests against the expansion of the city's airport into East Boston neighborhoods. The citizens' federation argued that the proposed highways would benefit suburban developers and suburbanites at the expense of central-city residents, whose densely populated neighborhoods would be destroyed or cut apart by the expressways. Moreover, for many of the latter, car ownership was impractical—public transit was their most pressing need. In this Boston case citizen pressure was successful in defeating pro-highway development interests, at least for a time.[8]

Challenging High-Rise Construction New York City has recently provided several examples of citizen resistance to high-rise construction. A complicated example is New York's Columbus Center (Coliseum) site, one that Mortimer B. Zuckerman's Boston Properties has for some time tried to convert into mammoth skyscrapers. Still pending in the late 1980s, the proposed development is huge. As originally planned, the skyscrapers would have had more square footage than any project in midtown Manhattan—2.7 million square feet of office and retail space, including two towers rising more than 58 stories at a corner of Central Park. The large-scale project threatened to shade the city's famous park, affect wind patterns, and have a negative impact on air quality. When the shade and weather implications were realized by local residents, hundreds demonstrated against the project. Ed Linde, the president of Boston Properties, tried to counter project critics by arguing that "the issues raised about air and sunlight strike an emotional chord, but I don't think they're real."[9]

Citizen objections to the project included a concern with increased traffic congestion and with the fact that the proposed skyscraper architecture did not fit in with the existing neighborhoods. As one observer noted, "the tower by Moshe Safdie [the architect] was an arrogantly sculptured form, bearing little relationship to anything around it. Its abstraction seemed only to heighten the sense that this was a project imposed on New York City, not one that emerged out of any logical analysis of the city's needs."[10] In 1985 developers bidding on the site were told to build the most profitable project possible, in order to boost the revenues for the city government, which owned the land. Zuckerman's bid of $455 million and of $30 million more to renovate the Columbus Circle subway station was sufficient to beat out 15 other developers. However, a problem later emerged when Salomon Brothers, a coinvestor in and major tenant of the project, announced its withdrawal. As a result, and because of ongoing neighborhood agitation, Zuckerman's Boston Properties proposed a scaled-down version with a greater mix of offices, condominiums, and retail stores. In 1987 the firm renegotiated the bid to $357 million for the site, because the project's size would be scaled back by 15 percent. The land sale, if consummated, will be the biggest by far in the city's history.[11]

Criticizing the review process and the environmental impact statement, the Municipal Art Society of New York City initiated a lawsuit to block the sale. Acting Justice Edward H. Lehner of the state supreme court voided the original agreement with Zuckerman, finding that the city's practice of essentially selling zoning variances was flawed. Attempting to appease the persisting criticisms, on June 2, 1988, Boston Properties unveiled yet another proposal, one that featured shorter, thinner towers casting a smaller shadow on Central Park. To be considered by New York's Board of Estimate in 1989, the new proposal generated citizen criticism similar to earlier variants. Kent Barwick, the president of the Municipal Art Society, calls the revamped complex "largely a public relations event...they have returned with an unpopular project in new clothes."[12]

Another target of citizen opposition is developer Donald Trump's 150-story Television City office tower. If built, this would be the world's tallest building. Trump's plans for Television City also include 7,600 condos, the world's biggest shopping center, and 11 other huge skyscrapers. Undergoing public review in the late 1980s, the project has been vigorously opposed by local community groups concerned with great increases in the neighborhood's density. Estimates suggest the development would add 70,000 people to the neighborhood each day. And even New York's boosterish Mayor Ed Koch publicly labeled Trump as "greedy" for demanding $1 billion in governmental assistance for developing the site.[13]

Challenges to high-rise construction have also come in other cities. We have noted in Chapter 3 the various movements in San Francisco to control office towers. After much organization and voter protest, in 1986 San Franciscans passed a proposition restricting annual office construction to the small amount of 475,000 square feet. And a notable growth moratorium has been imposed in the San Francisco community of Walnut Creek. In response to a 500 percent increase in office space and the traffic it created during a 10-year span, voters in 1985 approved a ban on further development until every one of 75 congested intersections in the area falls below 85 percent of capacity.

Shopping Malls Shopping malls and industrial parks have also been targets of citizen opposition. There have been numerous attempts, and a few successes, by activist groups trying to stop mall developments. One attempt was in Burlington, Vermont, where local residents fought against a nearby mall proposed by a large corporation. Burlington's citizens voiced concern about the traffic congestion and the likely accelerated decline of the downtown area that the new mall would engender. And in Hadley, Massachusetts, as we discussed in Chapter 7, another citizens' group took on a national developer planning a mall for 35 acres of farmland there. This citizens' group slowed down the development of the mall but was unable to prevent it. Though they lost this battle, they were successful in winning a greater measure of public support. As a result, several proposed development projects were defeated and, more importantly, the idea of fighting developers was legitimized.[14] In addition, in Chapter 7 we observed that in the 1970s and 1980s several cities and towns in Canada have witnessed the emergence of citizens' movements to control the location of shopping centers, in part because of the internecine competition malls present to downtown areas. The residents of these North American cities have ousted numerous hard-line political supporters of unbridled urban development. This has led to a number of development control laws, including a moratorium on shopping malls on Prince Edward Island and freezes on development in the province of Ontario.[15]

There is also the case of the Uptown area in Chicago. At the heart of this northside area is a multiethnic community of black, white, Hispanic, and Native American (Indian) families—a logical target for corporate redevelopment. A developer proposed to transform this area into a large shopping center and residential complex with 100,000 square feet of shops and two high-rise office towers. Demolition of older buildings for this large-scale project was underway when a residents' organization filed a class action suit, *Avery* v. *Landrieu*, targeting the developer, the U.S. Department of Housing and Urban Development (HUD), and local government agencies. The suit was designed to lessen the impact of displacement on moderate-income residents and argued for "the existence of a historic conspiracy by which the city and private developers, acting in concert, fulfilled the demand for upper- and middle-income housing by the destruction of low cost housing in 'target areas.'"[16] The lawsuit contended that displacement would aggravate racial segregation by destroying one of the few integrated neighborhoods in Chicago.

After losing an attempt to have the judge dismiss the lawsuit, the developer agreed to important concessions sought by residents: (1) at least one-fifth of the new housing would be reserved for moderate-income families, with preference accorded to local residents; (2) affirmative action hiring programs would be implemented in the construction; (3) the total number of high-income apartments would be reduced; (4) a large grocery store would be built in place of planned specialty stores, with a majority of its employees drawn from the local community; and (5) damages would be paid to compensate tenants and for a legal defense fund. Negotiations were also carried out with HUD, the city of Chicago, and the Chicago Housing Authority to provide more than a thousand units of government-subsidized housing in the Uptown area.[17]

Protesting Urban Renewal and Land Speculation   Intense opposition to redevelopment and gentrification has been initiated by a variety of people's organizations in cities from San Francisco and Seattle to Boston. At the beginning of Chapter 9 we reviewed the organization of tenants in San Francisco's South of Market area; this tenants' group fought legal battles with urban renewal agencies over a major urban displacement project and won a limited victory—the construction of some low-rent housing elsewhere. Private developers had made concessions to a people's movement. Moreover, in Washington, D.C., the Capital East Community Organization and the Adams-Morgan Community Organization joined together to fight an urban renewal project and real estate speculation. In an attempt to stem the tide of speculative real estate development, these citizens' groups pressured the city council to pass a bill, the Real Estate Transaction Tax, that would restrict speculative buying and selling. For their part, developers and land speculators organized to resist what came to be known as the "Speculator's Bill." Calling it "socialism in our time," the real estate interests organized an effective lobby, and the bill that passed in 1978 was so diluted it allowed most developers and speculators to avoid paying the new taxes. In this case, community-based groups were only partially successful in bringing private land decisions under more democratic control.[18]

Another example of a resistance group formed to counter central-city speculation and gentrification is the St. Ambrose Housing Aid Center in Baltimore. Established in the mid-1970s, it set up a counseling service for neighborhoods faced with private real estate speculation and later became active in buying and repairing homes for sale to lower-income people on a nonprofit basis. And in the Queens Borough of New York City, residents were successful in having the City Planning Commission curb developers who had been replacing one- and two-family houses with multiple-family apartment dwellings. On Staten Island a major area of land was designated as environmentally sensitive and taken off development rolls after local residents objected to townhouses scheduled to be built there. Moreover, the head of the National Association of Neighborhoods has argued that government policies should require developers to relocate displaced individuals and families within their original neighborhoods. Such views signal the emergence of regional and national neighborhood associations that are not intimidated by real estate interests.[19]

Movements to Tax Corporations Capital flight and corporate location decisions create community costs the corporations ordinarily do not pay; downtown corporations are usually undertaxed compared to homeowners, renters, and small businesses. In a few cities grassroots organizations have sprung up, seeking to force corporations to pay more taxes. One such 1980s movement in San Francisco fought for a ballot proposal called Proposition M, which read:

> We, the people, declare that San Francisco must increase the taxes paid by its largest corporations. It is fundamentally unjust that large corporations, such as giant oil companies whose profits exceeded $1 trillion in the 1980s, pay a lower rate of taxes than the average wage earners; and that San Francisco's huge banks and insurance companies pay no local business taxes at all. We pay our share, and so should they.[20]

The proposition passed; it specifically required that the board of supervisors "increase taxes paid by its largest corporations." The electoral success, however, was met by court suits and by a failure of local government officials to enforce the proposition. City officials did, however, implement another, weaker, measure raising business taxes to 1.5 percent. In the end, then, popular pressure had increased taxes on San Francisco businesses, but modestly.

TENANTS' MOVEMENTS

Early Protests Tenants' organizations have increased in number and significance in the last few decades. Some have emerged to fight urban renewal and redevelopment. Others have been organized to deal with condominium development, rent gouging by landlords, and the protection of renters' rights. A barrier to organizing tenants is that they are seldom in an apartment complex long enough for long-term commitment. Acting as individuals, many tenants protest with their feet; they keep moving to find better apartments in need of less repair. Tenants may have to sue to get stubborn landlords to make repairs, and few are willing to do so. Although seldom recognized, the United States has witnessed a long history of tenants' movements.

In the case of New York City the organization of tenants into popular-based political movements goes back to at least the early 1900s. On April 1, 1904, for example, Jewish immigrants on the Lower East Side of New York City staged a rent strike. The successful strike prevented massive evictions, gained rent rollbacks for tenants, and secured longer-term leases. Following World War I, militant action was again adopted by renters as some 25,000 Jewish and Italian families in blue-collar neighborhoods joined together to form tenant leagues that were successful in obtaining concessions from governmental and private authorities, including antieviction laws, 6 years of rent control, and subsidies from private developers. During the Great Depression tenant activism emerged again. Organized by the Unemployed Councils, this movement involved both white ethnic groups and black citizens and featured a rent strike and eviction resistance actions. Initially this activism was suppressed by well-organized landlords and the police, but eventually it did lead to the formation of the Citywide Tenants League, which succeeded in establishing rent controls and a role for tenants in the administration of city housing programs.[21]

Who Protests? Since World War II, renters' movements have waxed and waned with changes in the U.S. economy. Tenants' movements have sprung up across the nation, protesting condominium conversions by developers, the lack of moderate-rent housing, and the ever-rising rents associated with the short supply of rental housing. A diverse variety of people, tactics, and locations have been involved in contemporary movements. Although young, low- and middle-income activists usually spring to mind when discussing renters' movements, these are not the only Americans who have protested. At a prestigious New York City apartment building, for instance, one-third of the high-income tenants, including lawyers, diplomats, and accountants, conducted a rent strike between 1987 and 1988 to protest lax security, air-conditioning failures, and inoperable elevators. The building's owner, to whom tenants pay $2,000 to $3,000 monthly, sued the affluent renters for protesting by withholding rent. Although rent strikes in luxury apartment buildings have been rare, they have become more common.[22]

As we have seen in the previously mentioned San Francisco example, protesting renters have included older Americans. Another San Francisco case has involved 170 tenants at the Alexander Residence, a hotel subsidized by HUD's Section 8 program. Early in 1986 the First Columbia Property Management Company, which operates several hotels in San Francisco's Tenderloin district, illegally raised its furniture rental rate. The tenants organized the Alexander Tenants Association, held protest meetings, consulted lawyers, and applied pressure to hotel management and HUD officials. After months of protest the group succeeded in rolling back rents and in getting rebates for overcharges. Frances Middleton, a former waitress and leader of the group commented:

> *I thought that when you're down like this, way below the poverty level, you're powerless. But I realized that you can make the big shots stand up and listen. It was amazing to me to learn that if you work together you can do something.*[23]

Tenant activists come from all walks of life.

Tenant Strategies: Using the Courts and Other Strategies The judicial system has been used by tenants, as can be seen in the cases of the luxury apartment tenants and the elderly renters. This tactic has supplemented the rent strike and other acts of civil disobedience. In New Jersey renters have successfully taken their grievances to the courts for resolution. One mid-1980s episode involved the tenants of an East Orange, New Jersey, apartment building. Affordable housing had been so hard to find in northern New Jersey that 11 tenants of this building remained in their $300-a-month rent-controlled apartments despite steadily deteriorating conditions. These tenants maintained their apartments even as they watched their ceilings fall down around them. The tenants believed these harmful conditions were directly connected to the desire of the building's landlords, whose net worth of $9 million was concentrated in New York City real estate, to displace the tenants in order to convert the building into upscale condominium units. The residents sued the owners, charging that they had hired thugs to take off their doors and cut off their water and heat to pressure them to move. In 1986 a jury agreed with the tenants and awarded them $138,000 in damages. This victory was broadened 2 years later when a New Jersey appellate court ruled, for the first time, that such extreme tenant cases constituted fraud under New Jersey's State Consumer Fraud Act.[24]

Another important legal struggle by tenants involved a governmental landlord. This *Wright* v. *City of Roanoke Redevelopment and Housing Authority* case was decided by the U.S. Supreme Court in 1987. This decision empowered tenants to challenge public housing authorities to comply with federal housing regulations. At issue was a 1969 addition to the 1937 Housing Act that limits the amount of rent that can be charged public housing tenants to a specific percentage of their incomes. In 1980 HUD issued regulations defining rent as including a reasonable amount for utility charges. A successful lawsuit was filed by a group of tenants after a Roanoke, Virginia, public housing authority imposed a surcharge for utility consumption that pushed the total charges for rent and utilities beyond HUD's maximum allowable percentage.[25]

A Variety of Tenant Organizations A major issue for tenants' movements since the mid-1970s has been "condomania," the extensive apartment conversion process in cities discussed in Chapter 5. By the early 1980s condominium conversions totaled hundreds of thousands of units in many cities, and tenants' groups were organizing politically to fight developers active in the conversion process. For example, the Seattle Displacement Coalition, composed of community groups, was organized to help tenants fight eviction and displacement, especially in situations involving condominium conversions. As a result of these struggles, legislation has been passed in two dozen states to protect tenants from condomania. Real estate interests have organized to fight such laws as intervening with the private production of housing. The solution, they argue, is to let the "laws of supply and demand" be "honestly observed without interference." Observing the laws of the market means that more conversions will take place, and that more moderate-income Americans will be displaced into unsuitable or unsafe housing.

Some tenants' groups have worked to assist low- and moderate-income renters with rodent infestation and other habitability problems. During the 1970s an important tenants' group known as the Bois d'Arc Patriots was formed in Dallas. After a lengthy period of landlord and tenant struggles over redevelopment projects, during which tenant organizers were threatened with shovels and guns, the tenants group gradually attracted more low-income members. Landlords were pressing the Dallas City Council to make *renters* responsible for rat and roach infestation. However, in a dramatic gesture the Patriots group caged several hundred rats from low-income homes and circulated pictures in wealthy parts of the city, together with leaflets explaining that the rats would be relocated to affluent neighborhoods if the landlord-sponsored infestation initiative passed. As a result, the Dallas City Council passed a very different ordinance making rat and roach infestation the responsibility of landlords. From these early campaigns emerged a larger renters' group—the East Dallas Tenants Alliance, which also took action to resist illegal evictions and gained some important victories against landlords in the Texas courts. The most basic of these was a "warranty of habitability"—a guarantee by the landlord that a rental unit was fit to live in. Several tenants' associations merged to form the East Dallas Neighborhood Association, a coalition that has worked successfully to lessen the negative impact of dislocation in the Dallas redevelopment programs.[26]

In New Jersey, the state with the most active renters' rights movements, organizations were initially created in the 1960s, and by 1970 the New Jersey Tenants' Organization (NJTO) had successfully organized 20,000 tenants to participate in 43 rent strikes. The strikes were generally effective in reducing rent levels and improving living conditions. The NJTO has been successful in part because it has sustained aggressive organizational and voter registration drives, which have led to the election of sympathetic politicians and the passage of rent control laws. The New

Jersey organizations have continued to be effective in recent years. In addition, by the early 1980s more than two dozen towns and cities in California had passed rent control laws under pressure from tenants' groups. In Berkeley, California, where more than 60 percent of the population rents, the Berkeley Citizens' Action Coalition held a majority of seats on city council positions in the 1980s. Responsive to their renter constituents, the council members passed rent control laws and restrictions on gentrification. And to the south, in West Hollywood, California, where 90 percent of the residents rent, the citizenry voted to incorporate the area and elected a progressive city council that implemented rent control regulations.[27]

Summarizing the national situation, Gilderbloom and Capek have noted that

> As a direct result of tenant organizing, roughly 130 cities and counties in the United States currently have some form of rent regulation. Most of these cities enacted controls in the early 1970s, including over 100 municipalities in New Jersey as well as cities and counties in Massachusetts, New York, Virginia, Maryland, Alaska, Connecticut, and California. Over half of all rental units in California, New York, Massachusetts and New Jersey are presently rent controlled. Altogether it is estimated that approximately ten percent of the nation's rental housing stock falls under some type of rent control.[28]

Statewide organizations for tenants now span the nation, from California, to Texas, to New York and Massachusetts. Housing issues have been a major focus of development-related class struggles in U.S. cities.

TRADITIONAL PLANNING AND ADVOCACY PLANNING

Reflecting on the public discontent over the current development and redevelopment of U.S. cities, some mainstream social service analysts believe that the answer lies in urban planners carrying out their duties more effectively. The reasoning is that the knowledge of planners and allied professionals can be used to manage and redress the problems of highways, displacement, malls, and condominiums more effectively. The neighborhood and community costs of urban growth and decline have long been regarded as amenable to change at the hands of professional planners. Yet, on the whole, planners and allied professionals have provided limited assistance to rank-and-file city residents facing problems associated with corporate-driven urban development.

Efficiency Planning Although urban planning originated in the "City Beautiful" plans prominent around the turn of this century, by the 1920s this urban planning had shifted its emphasis from aesthetic qualities to one of efficiency in the physical form of cities and to maintaining homogeneous land uses and the value of private property by means of the new governmental zoning we discussed previously. Moreover, after World War II, government urban renewal programs used professional planners and reinforced the planning emphasis on efficient business use of central-city space. Planning agency action has been a major example of governmental intervention designed, at least in theory, to cope with the costs of business growth. However, with their business-oriented, technical-expertise approach (cost-benefit analysis, modeling, systems analysis), many mainstream planners have actually operated as "expert" facilitators for the projects sought by developers and industrialists, and thus as "hired guns" who rarely respond in major ways to the social justice problems created by the profit-oriented city development they have helped to implement.[29] Influential planners have accented this technical expert-client approach to urban redesign, sometimes with an added emphasis on the role of educating clients on what constitutes "good" design. As a review of the urban planning profession has expressed it, planners have traditionally "lacked access to the decision-making process...have tended to avoid political conflict, have been technique-oriented rather than goal-oriented, and are facilitators rather than initiators."[30]

Robert Goodman has suggested that most urban planners today are "soft cops,"—experts who use what they view as "value-free" and "scientific" methods to shore up an urban social structure that is class-stratified, inegalitarian, and racially biased. In his view many practicing planners are so committed to building existing cities in traditional ways that they have become the instruments of powerful real estate actors who shape race and class inequality. City planners have frequently been called upon to assist in the implementation of business-oriented redevelopment programs, many of which have displaced large numbers of minority urbanites. Architects and urban planners play a role in providing technical rationalizations for projects whose character is principally determined by developers, builders, and lenders. This type of planning has led to congested complexes of high-rise buildings in downtown areas, many of which feature sunless streets and sterile workspaces. These buildings are not primarily viewed from the perspective of the needs of those who work in them or walk between them, or those displaced by them.[31]

Successful architects defend what they build and design in terms such as this: "As professionals, it seems that architects should try to make the best of the world *as it is*—before somebody else fouls it up even further."[32] Providing inhumane urban development with efficient architectural and planning tools fails to address its injustice. Many architects and planners speak of their buildings as "monuments" to business need. Less often do they see themselves as providing humane places in which ordinary people can live and prosper. For instance, in a major research study of a massive mall development in a southwestern city, McAdams found that the city's planners entered the development process in two ways—as private consultants for the developer and as staff planners for the city's planning commission. The first phase of development was completely hidden from the general public; behind a veil of secrecy, a hired-hand planner helped the developer prepare a profitable mall development proposal. When the city's planners saw the plan, several raised objections to its environmental impact. However, because of pressure to improve the business climate these planners squelched their misgivings and recommended approval of zoning changes with a plea that the applicant "continue to recognize" the environmental implications of the project.[33]

Planning in Great Britain Cities in many European countries such as Great Britain are subject to more urban planning in the public interest than most U.S. cities. Planners have often been more independent from immediate business interests. Even according to one critic of British planning there has not been as much piecemeal metropolitan expansion, and the peripheries of cities and adjacent agricultural land around British cities have not been gobbled up as rapidly as in the spread cities of the U.S. Sunbelt. Zoning of uses in British cities has reduced the number of polluted environments. And "Manhattan-type tower blocks" have not generally been allowed to submerge historic central cities.[34]

A recent research study comparing the cities of Houston and Aberdeen, Scotland, the oil capitals of the United States and Europe, found that the governmental planning system in Aberdeen has been much more comprehensive—it includes substantial economic planning—and considerably more interventionist than in Houston. Compared to Houston, the Aberdeen planning system has provided greater protection from the numerous negative costs of oil development and urban growth. The well-developed planning system in Aberdeen slowed down real estate development during the oil boom in the 1970s and early 1980s, in part because the process of obtaining permission for real estate development was often time consuming. Nonetheless, British planning critics have faulted the British planning system for not going far enough to protect the public interest, and for recent Conservative Party attempts to permit more "free market planning."[35]

Role of Advocacy Planners A minority of planners within the U.S. urban planning community have advocated and implemented more democratic and less business-oriented forms of urban planning. These people-oriented "advocacy planners" have given greater emphasis to the ideals of social justice in their professional activities. Advocacy planners are more likely to recognize and criticize the character of the power-privilege structure of the cities within which most planning takes place. In the 1960s some in this critical planning movement established the Planners for Equal Opportunity (PEO) to advance progressive planning ideals. A decade later the PEO, under the leadership of Chester Hartman and others, created an activist organization called the Planners Network, with a progressive statement of principles, which asserted that "planning should be a tool for allocating resources and developing the environment in order to eliminate the great inequality of wealth and power in our society."[36] In both its ideas and its activities, this contingent of the planning profession has explicitly criticized the undemocratic nature of most urban planning.

In 1965 Paul Davidoff, in an important article titled "Advocacy and Pluralism in Planning," argued that planners should be advocates for "plural plans," including those that stand in opposition to official governmental and business elite plans and policies. Today the planning philosophy expressed by Davidoff continues to be influential. Chester Hartman, a Fellow at the Institute for Policy Studies in Washington, D.C., has noted that Davidoff made it clear that "all planners are, in fact, advocates for some definition of interest—but not necessarily the public interest." And Anshel Melamed, the coordinator of urban studies at Montreal's Concordia University, has said that the important thing is that Davidoff called on planners to become "advocates for the powerless."[37]

Robert Goodman's 1971 book *After the Planners* was one of the first sustained attacks on mainstream planning in the United States. Goodman argues forcefully for advocacy planning, for a kind of city and architectural planning that works for the needs of minority and moderate-income Americans in the halls of government. Modern capitalism has co-opted most planners for its own purposes. For this reason, most planners' reforms involve cosmetic changes that make private projects more palatable to the public. From this perspective, even giving the poor modest support from traditional planning experts does not significantly increase their incomes or improve their access to affordable housing. A valid move toward more-democratic planning requires more than meek reforms and a modestly revised planning theory. It requires putting theory into practice in planner-aided efforts shaped by and for working-class city residents. Accordingly, advocacy planners have attempted to provide planning skills for the "have nots" in the urban revitalization process. For example, Chester Hartman helped provide assistance to urbanites in San Francisco's South of Market area, where the previously mentioned tenants' association successfully forced corporate executives, developers, and builders to revise their inhumane development plans. In this case the advocacy planner and the tenants' association came in too late to stop the massive urban renewal process, but they did force significant concessions to local residents as the project was built. And in other struggles in several cities advocacy planners have provided some informational resources and financial strategies for local residents attempting to fight the razing of neighborhoods and residential buildings by real estate developers.[38]

However, the editors of *Planning* magazine have recently argued that in the conservative political climate of the last decade advocacy planning has lost some steam:

> ...*many people seem to be afraid of taking an advocacy position. It's no longer fashionable to do so—if it ever was. Many of the manuscripts and queries we get at Planning are about getting a job in the private sector or how planners can encourage development. There's a tone of fear about losing your job or not getting a job.*[39]

The capitalist real estate actors have so consolidated their political power that advocacy planners are rarely tolerated, and thus have difficulty finding jobs.

THE NEED FOR PUBLIC BALANCE SHEETS: CONTROLLING DEVELOPMENT

Writing in *Scientific American* more than a decade ago, Edward T. Chase noted:

> *For all the glories of free markets, market prices simply don't reflect the social costs of bad planning, or no planning. These costs aren't in anyone's books and thus go unaccounted. The public interest is lost among competing narrower interests.*[40]

In recent years some leaders in urban political movements and allied advocacy planners have suggested new analytical tools for scrutinizing and measuring the social costs of private-sector development. One of their tools is the *public balance sheet*, a way of tallying up, as David Smith puts it, the "tangible, measurable, quantifiable costs being imposed on citizens individually and collectively by the actions of the private sector."[41] The social costs and social inefficiencies of market-oriented development under modern real estate capitalism take a variety of forms: the shortage of affordable rental housing, large numbers of people displaced by urban developments without suitable housing alternatives, chronic racial segregation, enhanced traffic congestion, air and water pollution, constrained choices for consumers because of developer decisions of housing, and taxpayer burdens from tax subsidies for developers. Progressive people's movements in cities have tried to measure and document these costs and to bring pressure on developers, bankers, and other investors to compensate the citizenry and their communities for the broader social costs that profit-driven urban development creates.

Calculating Social Costs Traditional urban economists and other mainstream social scientists usually see social costs as "externalities" for which private enterprise is not responsible because in a capitalist system these social costs are not recognized by, and priced through, the market system.

While some liberal social scientists grope along proposing piecemeal reforms for some social costs, they lack a comprehensive view of who is actually responsible for the costs and how the capitalist system of necessity must transfer many internal costs to outsiders. In reality, the social costs of privately controlled industrial and real estate development are *not* "external" to modern capitalism, but are as a rule an internal part of its everyday routine operation. Clearly, a company's accountants do not usually calculate most social and community costs on their internal budget sheets. As one astute observer has noted: "These costs don't show up on any firm's ledger; no accountant writes them down. They're not charged against the income the firm makes from selling its products and services."[42]

Yet *someone* pays the costs associated with corporate choices regarding location, development, pollution and redevelopment. Low- and moderate-income Americans shoulder the heaviest burdens. City residents pay in a variety of ways. We have noted the great range of social and community costs of industrial and real estate development in previous chapters. For example, there are the billions of dollars in pollution and congestion costs, as well as in tax concessions, tax abatements, and direct government subsidies for development. These expenditures and tax losses are mostly paid by taxpayers in general, less so by the corporations involved. For example, in recent redevelopment in Cleveland tax abatements mean less money for local schools and school children. Using the public-balance-sheet concept, however, one concludes that the substantial social costs should be *directly paid* for by those powerful real estate interests guiding urban development. Interestingly, recent studies have demonstrated that tax credits and tax-exempt bonds are not high on the list of most firms considering urban locations, because they are now available to industrial and development capitalists in *most* urban areas, so these special subsidies have only a mild effect on location and investment decisions. Expressed another way, the aggressive bidding by communities for industry typically only serves to improve the profit margins of private enterprises that probably would have located there anyway. The subsidies make development less expensive for industrial and development capitalists, wherever they go, and thus more expensive for taxpayers. Such subsidies are often not required to attract most firms seeking new locations.[43]

Note too that apologists for the present system of privately controlled profit making argue that industrial and development corporations have a right to spend their capital as they see fit—it is *their* money. However, much of what they spend is, in fact, *not* their money, but rather money loaned to them by banks, insurance companies, and pension funds—and much of this money ultimately comes from the savings of working people. These workers, however, usually do not participate in the decisions about how *their* savings are invested in development and other corporate projects. Moreover, the profits of corporations that are reinvested in new plants and industrial development in a particular city or in a city in another region or country also come, for the most part, from the hard work of employees and from the consumers who buy their products. Under careful scrutiny the worker-generated character of "private" profits becomes obvious. Much private capital is the general public's hard-earned money.[44]

Progressive strategies to deal with the problems of elite-led development take many forms. One suggestion is the elimination of some government subsidy abatement programs, which encourage the waste of publicly generated capital. For example, governmental taxing policies have encouraged the destruction of older but still serviceable buildings and their replacement with newer buildings. And the overbuilding of office towers and shopping centers has been encouraged by local, state, and federal governmental subsidies available to owners and developers. Moreover, in an unnecessary waste of U.S. resources, many industrial, commercial, and residential buildings are discarded before their time, as real estate cycles create patterns of development and redevelopment. Rewriting the governmental subsidy and tax laws to discourage rapid and unnecessary development would be one step in the direction of a less costly development process. Another possibility is the kind of "linkage" initiatives citizens' groups around the country have undertaken—pressing developers to abandon or revise major projects, forcing the construction of new housing for displaced families, forcing bankers to invest local savings for local housing needs, and generally pressuring development interests to pay for more of the community costs.

Forcing Developers to Meet Community Needs: Linkage in the Santa Monica Case "Linked development" is one citizen demand. A number of grassroots movements in the United States have succeeded in securing concessions from the developers and others in the development industry to pay for social costs they generate and to provide community benefits in return for building profit-making developments. Among the most successful in forcing such linkages have been the citizens of Santa Monica, California, a city of about 100,000 people near Los Angeles. By the late 1970s the economic boom in California had created a situation where rents were rising rapidly; in much of the Los Angeles area landlords were making handsome profits. Santa Monicans, many on fixed incomes, began to organize around the issue of rent control. In the late 1970s several groups came together in a coalition called the Santa Monicans for Renters Rights (SMRR), which worked vigorously for rent control and progressive change. Their first success came in 1979 with the passage of a rent control law setting up an elective five-member rent control board with substantial authority to control rents. After this victory SMRR worked to elect progressives to the city council. In the early 1980s Santa Monica's voters, most of whom are renters, elected a progressive city council dominated by SMRR candidates and committed to reshaping development and protecting the interests of local citizens. Many of these were the same people who had been considered conservative voters in earlier elections. This newly elected council crafted a distinctive urban growth policy that required major developer concessions to address community needs. The majority of the new council members were not beholden to developers, because they did not depend heavily on them for campaign contributions. Committed to rent control and to community control of development, the majority of the city council has fought the current U.S. development trend, which has consistently attended to developer needs and neglected the broader housing and community needs of the local population of renters and homeowners. To illustrate, one developer came to the Santa Monica council for permission to build a multistory office complex. The council agreed, but only after the developer committed himself to linking community needs to the project—to include an affirmative action hiring program, a public park, 30 units of low- and moderate-income housing, a large community room, and a day-care center.[45]

In addition, an agreement between the city of Santa Monica and another real estate firm specified that a significant portion of a proposed commercial-office project be constructed to house low- and moderate-income renters, including units for the elderly and families with children. Energy conservation features including solar water heating have also been specified for this project. And in another agreement with a real estate developer, Welton Becket Associates, the Santa Monica City Council reportedly reshaped a 900,000-square-foot commercial-office-hotel complex to include the following: 100 rental units in new (or existing) buildings for low- and moderate-income renters (including the aged and handicapped), 3 acres of landscaped park areas with athletic sports facilities, a day-care center, promotion of car-pooling, bicycling, flex-time arrangements to reduce traffic problems, energy conservation measures, job training programs, and a social services fee.[46]

Reviewing these Santa Monica proceedings, Dave Lindorff notes the progressive character of such negotiations between a city council and powerful developers. These agreements are rare because in big cities such as New York "developers routinely threaten to drop projects if the *city* doesn't give *them* something (usually a height exemption and a giant tax abatement)."[47] As we have documented throughout this book, the usual procedure is for city councils and other government officials to rush to the aid of developers with an assortment of subsidies and services. Traditionally city governments have not attempted to negotiate with developers about making contributions to community needs or concessions in regard to social costs. The basic idea of this innovative city council has been to have developers pay for some part of the problems they create, including the destruction of existing housing and increased social service expenditures. The policy of securing givebacks from developers has a dual significance. It not only expresses the way that planning in this city was changed in a progressive direction but also reveals that elected city officials were now being loyal to human-scale dimensions—to preserving existing housing and neighborhoods and, in particular, making the local governmental processes more open to democratic participation. Rather than being content with a city run by the business elite, which had long been in power in Santa Monica, the council began to make appointments of progressive professionals at city hall and to extend funding to neighborhood groups.

Recent Political Developments in Santa Monica Working against tremendous odds, this council's electoral support has persisted for nearly a decade. In 1984 the council lost its majority because of a campaign technicality; an incumbent council member failed to collect enough ballot signatures to be placed on the ballot. Also by 1984 the business community had reorganized; conservative progrowth advocates came together in support of a city council slate known as the All Santa Monica Coalition. As a result, between 1986 and 1988 the seven member city council was evenly divided, with three members representing SMRR, three aligned with conservative business opponents, and one independent. In 1988 SMRR presented the only formal slate of council candidates; most of the opposition candidates were supported by groups such as ACTION, a landlord group opposed to rent control. In the 1988 election, ACTION distributed a mailing cautioning voters about the possibility of a takeover by "radicals," and telling its readers they could kiss their "property rights goodby" if the progressives won a majority.[48]

Nonetheless, the progressive coalition regained majority control of the council in the 1988 election; two incumbent progressives were reelected along with two other SMRR-supported candidates. Working with citizens' groups, the city council also adopted a comprehensive zoning code widely seen as a victory for a slow-growth philosophy. The 418-page document was a belated response to the city's worsening traffic congestion and sewage facilities. The new code limits building heights, uses, and sizes; in some areas development project size will be reduced by a third. For some council members, the restrictions were too little and too late. Council member David Finkel has said that "this ordinance came after all the gigantic development projects, such as the Water Garden [office complex], were approved. It should have been drafted before the city was inundated with large commercial developments."[49] By the late 1980s several progressive council members had softened their antigrowth positions and broadened their programs to include the concerns of reaching homeowners, making it difficult for the business opposition to label them as "radicals." James Conn, a United Methodist minister and a member of the first SMRR- supported council, was the mayor between 1986 and 1988. Yet his Ocean Park church received large amounts of money from developers, and he cast votes in favor of several major developments. As a result, he was booed at the 1988 SMRR convention for voting against the interests of his original constituents.[50]

Recent debates have centered on the issue of forcing developers to make even more concessions linked to community and neighborhood needs. Citizens committed to slow growth have been critical of negotiations surrounding two large-scale projects—one (Colorado Place) being erected by the Southmark Pacific Corporation (a Pasadena real estate firm), and the other (the Water Garden) a joint venture of J.H. Snyder of Los Angeles and California Federal Savings & Loan Association. The developers of the $550 million Colorado Place MXD won most of the approval they needed for this major project in October 1987. A majority of the council made the decision to allow the development despite threats of a referendum from the city's slow-growth movement. The project's first phase, completed in 1984, included 500,000 square feet of office and retail space, together with a 45,000-square-foot indoor pavilion and restaurant center, a large parking area, and a day-care center. The pavilion is available to nonprofit community groups and has hosted more than a hundred community and cultural events annually. By the time this 12-year development is completed, Southmark will have paid more than $8 million for fees to be used for parks, affordable housing, and traffic improvements.[51]

Santa Monica's Water Garden development is another project that slow-growth groups wish had been required to make more concessions. The Water Garden, a 1.26-million-foot project with several six-story office buildings, broke ground in mid-1988. Like other Santa Monica projects, the developers of the Water Garden have been required to provide numerous linked amenities: $6.4 million for traffic improvement, on-site sewage treatment, a child-care center, security facilities, extensive landscaping with a 600-foot pond (to serve as a gathering spot), $7.2 million for low-income housing and parks, $300,000 for a homeless center, and $150,000 for an art program.[52]

According to the most vigorous slow-growth advocates, the progressive city council has not forced enough concessions. Nonetheless, the Santa Monica government demonstrates a robust democratic political process; it continues to be shaped by progressive planning principles and embodies much more democratic input than before grassroots organizing began. The city retains rent control laws, regulated by an *elected* rent control board, that are among the strongest in the United States. The city's diverse appearance and built environment reflect more democratic input than most cities. In addition, SMRR has persuaded business opponents to work with them to revitalize the city's oceanfront. Moreover, the Santa

Monica citizens' groups and government continue to embody a strong commitment to social service programs and neighborhood organizing. The ferment produced the Community Corporation, a *nonprofit* community development corporation involved in building affordable housing and finding innovative ways to integrate that housing into neighborhoods. SMRR and other citizens' groups have encouraged alternative, often smaller-scale development projects. One is the Kendall Project on the oceanfront—a small-scale, for-profit multipurpose facility, with retail tenants on the ground floor along with a small number of affordable housing units on the upper floor, as well as amenities for moderate-income groups. Given its waterfront location, "free market" conditions would have dictated that the Kendall Project would only have been available to the wealthy. In addition, SMRR and other citizens' groups have drawn attention to, and devised solutions for, pollution in Santa Monica Bay. Ironically, this social cost stems directly from the excessive amounts of sewage generated by Los Angeles' rapid economic and population growth.[53]

Many suburban and central-city governments confront the social problems associated with the process of mall, office, and luxury apartment construction that reduces affordable housing, puts new demands on city sewerage and other services, and overloads streets with new workers. The actions in Santa Monica suggest the effectiveness of linked development: Require developers to provide community services and affordable housing and to pay substantially for city services as a part of the negotiated agreement for desired business development.

Citizens Organizing for Change: Other Communities   Santa Monica citizens are not alone in pressing for progressive urban change. Earlier in the chapter we described examples of citizens' protest and court action against various types of development. Other citizen strategies have included electoral efforts such as these in Santa Monica, Detroit, Madison, Burlington, and Cleveland. In a variety of towns and cities over the last two decades citizens' groups have been successful in electing progressives to office—men and women centrally concerned about the social costs of real estate development and industrial decisions. Thus in 1977 the late Ken Cockrel was elected to the Detroit City Council; he and his associates developed a citywide political coalition (DARE), which put together proposals for the humane reindustrialization and reform of Detroit. The proposals were an attempt to offset the social costs of auto company decisions to disinvest in the area. At about the same time the democratic-socialist mayor of Madison, Wisconsin, Paul Soglin, set up a city-owned development corporation to provide assistance to cooperatives and worker-owned businesses that had experienced a common difficulty among progressive enterprises—obtaining financing from conventional private lenders.

In an important book, *The Progressive City,* Pierre Clavel documented the actions of progressive city governments in Cleveland, Hartford, Berkeley, Madison, Santa Monica, and Burlington. One of the most important of the urban progressives is Dennis Kucinich, who was the popular mayor of Cleveland in the late 1970s. Kucinich recognized the fallacies in the traditional approach of the business-oriented growth coalitions. He recognized that the cost of subsidizing corporations to invest in downtown areas through tax abatements and other subsidies far exceeded the "trickle down benefits" that would accrue to city residents, especially those who live in central city areas. Kucinich, an idealist progressive with roots in a Cleveland working class family, took on the local business elite. He blocked public subsidies for huge projects desired by, and primarily benefitting, Ohio corporations, and he temporarily killed the tax abatement program.

Kucinich was vigorously attacked by the business elite for his progressive stance. And in a struggle with local bankers he lost. Local bankers refused to roll over a small debt of the city's unless Kucinich would agree to sell the local publicly owned electric company, Muny Light, to a private utility with close connections to the private banks. When Kucinich refused, the banks let the city fall into bankruptcy and organized a well-financed political campaign to defeat him in his re-election bid. Today the business elite has rolled back many of the progressive Kucinich reforms and has built a media image of the "Comeback City." However, this recovery has largely involved conventional business-oriented development, with new construction downtown funded by huge tax abatements and subsidies and with central-city residents, a majority of whom are now black, benefitting little (especially in the long run) from this state-subsidized corporate development. There are new construction projects and new low-wage jobs, but the city is still faced with a deteriorating public infrastructure, including its public school system, and the consequences of major population loss over the last two decades. Indeed, in contrast to the media imagemakers articulating a view of a city in good shape, one black middle-class leader recently told the senior author in an interview that many in the black community in Cleveland were so oppressed and angry that she expected rioting there in the near future.

Moreover, in March, 1981, the voters of Vermont's largest city, Burlington, elected Bernie Sanders, a democratic-socialist as mayor. Sanders, in defeating a political veteran for the mayor's office, was backed by an electoral coalition comprised of homeowners, former antiwar activists, and moderate-income families. Sanders won by opposing large-scale real estate developments, which many voters felt would adversely affect the city's quality of life; and he attacked the ties between the previous mayor and business elite proposals for building shopping malls and condominium development projects, as well as a new highway through an older city neighborhood. In a 1982 election Sanders' coalition won a number of seats on the board of aldermen, an electoral victory demonstrating solid citizen support for Sanders' goal of a more democratic local government. Sanders reduced corruption in city government, put contracts out for competitive bidding, installed a cost-saving phone system, assessed higher building fees, and worked for greater citizen input in decision making. He met directly with city employee groups and helped establish a Neighborhood Planning Association to democratize the use of federal funds. After reelection in 1983, Sanders created under his authority a Community and Economic Development Office, which worked with developers and neighborhood groups on downtown projects sought by the business elite and also on small business and affordable housing projects desired by rank-and-file Burlington citizens. Sanders had worked out a compromise with business leaders that provided development, together with numerous programs meeting neighborhood needs.[54]

Linked Development Strategies Because of increasing citizen concerns over the costs of growth, local government officials across the country have shown interest in the linked development approach, in restrictions or limitations on development like those in Santa Monica. For example, in Boston in early 1983 city council member Bruce Bolling advocated a proposal that every office developer produce one unit of housing for every four prospective employees. It unanimously passed the city council, but was vetoed by then Mayor Kevin White. However, the veto brought debates over requiring developers to make linkage concessions; the 1983 mayoral primary featured candidates Ray Flynn and Mel King strongly supporting linkage development policies. Once in office, Flynn's populist administration approved nine downtown projects already in the pipeline, but with linkage fees paid by developers totaling $25 million. In addition, developers made "voluntary" contributions in the form of extra payments for housing, park restoration, and job training programs. Under pressure from local neighborhood groups, the local redevelopment authority approved in 1986 a strong linkage formula requiring developers to pay the city a $4.70 per square foot housing and job training fee, to be paid for over a seven-year period after the building permit is issued. The fees go into a Neighborhood Housing Trust, whose managing committee had as of 1989 channeled much of the money into the production or rehabilitation of low- and moderate-income housing in Boston. Boston's recent economic resurgence has made possible these linkage development exactions from local development interests.[55]

One survey of 452 communities found that most required developers to contribute at least a little land for public roads, to make some service provisions for development projects, or pay some (often modest) impact and development fees. Increasingly, city governments, particularly in economically prosperous areas, are requiring downtown developers to link the construction of low- and moderate-income housing to the receipt of governmental aid (for example, tax abatements and the use of eminent domain) for their commercial development projects. Similarly, contracts and agreements with developers have become more commonplace in cities with healthy private economies. One survey in the mid-1980s found that at least 154 local governments had adopted or were working on agreements designed to get developers to provide a broader range of facilities and other concessions to public needs.

A Conservative Court: Legal Problems for Linkage?   Developers and other real estate interests have reacted vigorously against these new linkage controls and legislated concessions. Some of the community struggles with developers have been evaluated by the U.S. Supreme Court. By the late 1980s the Supreme Court had a conservative majority mostly appointed by Republican presidents. In 1987 two Supreme Court rulings reaffirmed the right of developers and other major property owners to do as they wish with their urban property, despite the social costs involved. On June 9, 1987, the Supreme Court held that government officials may be liable for damages if their zoning regulations prevent landowners from using their property, even temporarily, as they wish, a decision justified by the court in terms of traditional property rights. Also in June the Supreme Court ruled that if governments attach linkage conditions to building permits unrelated to the purpose of the developments or to problems directly created by them, the result may be a "taking" of property for which government must compensate landowners. According to lawyers representing landowners and developers, the two rulings may force government officials in many cities to stop using building permits to exact support from developers for other community goals such as low-income housing, child care centers, and mass transit. The conservatives on the highest court have undermined progressive efforts by reasserting the right of property owners and developers to dispose of land as they see fit. Still, the struggle continues, and these court decisions are likely to be temporary setbacks for urban citizens' movements. Indeed, many community groups have continued to win concessions and linkages from developers since the 1987 decisions.[56]

CONCLUSION: REINVIGORATING DEMOCRACY IN URBAN SETTINGS

More democratic control over home and neighborhood spaces. More control over the quality of life in communities. More direct democratic input into housing development. More popular control over local developers and lenders. These are the goals of the many citizens' groups we have discussed throughout this book. People are demanding control over

investors and corporate executives who too callously abandon communities, and thereby create severe social costs for workers with deep-rooted
ties to particular places in the form of mortgages, schools, and community
centers. Capital flight from one city or region to another, or from the United
States to another country, has created harsh problems—for some areas
within most cities and for certain Frostbelt cities such as Youngstown and
Detroit and numerous Sunbelt cities such as Birmingham and New Orleans. Citizens' groups have fought back, demanding laws that require
firms to pay some of the community costs of this corporate flight and
capital disinvestment. Such "corporate flight" laws already exist in European capitalist countries, and, as noted in Chapter 2, implementing legislation requiring notice of plant closings has been introduced into the U.S.
Congress. Citizens' groups are also fighting back against the social costs
of urban development resulting from the secondary-circuit investments of
large development, retail, and industrial corporations. These grassroots
groups are attempting to control highway, urban redevelopment, mall,
and office developments. Sometimes victorious, often unsuccessful, these
movements demonstrate a persisting thirst for greater control over community life.

One central issue today is greater political participation; another is
economic democracy. We have documented throughout this book the role
of powerful industrialists and a variety of real estate actors in shaping
urban growth and decline. People's movements are pressing for more
input into corporate location real estate development decisions that shape
the cities in which they live. They are asking for bankers, industrial
executives, and developers to be less obsessed with profit and market
demands and more responsive to fundamental community needs. Progressive citizens' groups from New York to San Francisco are pressuring
elected government officials to be more active in representing all citizens'
interests, regardless of their wealth or political connections.

Since the Declaration of Independence the principle that people have
a right to democratic control over their governments has been clearly
etched in basic American documents. This right has often been corrupted
because small elites, such as the omnipresent business-oriented growth
coalitions, have disproportionately shaped private and government decisions on urban development, housing, and urban renewal. Citizens' movements targeting the social costs of urban development, and holding
politicians and private interests accountable for those costs, demonstrate
that the democratic impulse is alive in towns and cities across the United
States. For more than two centuries the democratic political ideal has
asserted that rank-and-file Americans can make better political and economic choices for themselves and their families than small unrepresenta-
tive elites. Many citizens' groups insist that this ideal needs to be put into
everyday practice at every level of U.S. government. Furthermore, some

have maintained that this same democratic ideal should be applied to the private economic sphere. Citizens across the nation have asked, "if better choices are made democratically than autocratically in the political sphere, why should the same logic not be applied to the economic sphere?" Democracy in decision making in the private sphere of industrial location, capital investments, and real estate development is being demanded by many community groups across the nation. Expansion of democracy into urban economic decision making—about what gets located, built, or redeveloped in cities—seems a logical extension of the political ideals expressed in the Declaration of Independence and in subsequent statements of American democracy. The scale of this extension of democracy will likely be determined by the present and future struggles between citizen and capitalist interests in U.S. cities from coast to coast.

NOTES

1. William Fulton, "On the Beach with the Progressives," *Planning*, January 1985, 4.
2. Tom Sutton, "The Divided City: Squatters and Cops Face off in Berlin," *In These Times* 5 (October 7–13, 1981): 7.
3. Jeanie Wylie, "Squatters Protest Housing Programs in U.S. Cities," *In These Times* 5 (October 7–13, 1981): 6.
4. See, for example, Clarence N. Stone, "The Study of the Politics of Urban Development," in *The Politics of Urban Development*, edited by Clarence N. Stone and Heywood T. Sanders (Lawrence: University Press of Kansas, 1987), pp. 8–10.
5. Tom R. Rex, "Businesses Enjoy Benefits; Individuals, Society Pay Costs," *Arizona Business* 34 (August 1987): 1–3.
6. Karl Kapp, *The Social Costs of Private Enterprise* (New York: Schocken Books, 1950), pp. 13–25; Barry Bluestone and Bennett Harrison, *The Deindustrialization of America* (New York: Basic Books, 1982), pp. 106–107.
7. This section draws in part on Joe R. Feagin, *Free Enterprise City: Houston in Political-Economic Perspective* (New Brunswick, N.J.: Rutgers University Press, 1988), pp. 39–42.
8. Ralph Gakenheimer, *Transportation Planning as a Response to Controversy* (Cambridge, Mass.: MIT Press, 1976), pp. 38–50; Allan K. Sloan, *Citizen Participation in Transportation Planning: The Boston Experience* (Cambridge, Mass.: Ballinger, 1974), pp. 60–72.
9. Roger Lowenstein, "Building That Would Shade Central Park Draws Quiet Civic Group into the Light," *Wall Street Journal*, September 25, 1987, p. 29; see also Thomas J. Lueck, "Coliseum Developer to Revise Plans," *New York Times*, December 5, 1987, p. 31;

and Richard Levine, "A Towers Plan Is Scaled Down for Manhattan," *New York Times*, June 3, 1988, p. 12.

10. Paul Goldberger, "Skyscraper for New York City Site Is Redesigned," *New York Times*, June 3, 1988, p. 12.
11. Levine, "A Towers Plan Is Scaled Down for Manhattan," *New York Times*, p. 12; Roger Lowenstein, "Zuckerman Faces Risks as Salomon Inc. Quits Big New York Development Plan," *New York Times*, December 7, 1987, 11.
12. Levine, "A Towers Plan Is Scaled Down for Manhattan," *New York Times*, p. 12.
13. James R. Norman and Marc Frons, "Donald Trump: What's Behind the Hype," *Business Week*, July 20, 1987, p. 98; Jane Gross, "2 Big West Side Projects Fuel Anti-Development Sentiment," *New York Times*, November 29, 1987, p. 1; James R. Norman, "Koch to Trump to Koch: Drop Dead," *Business Week*, July 20, 1987, p. 98.
14. Jay Neugeboren, "Mall Mania," *Mother Jones* 4 (May 1979): 21–30.
15. Michael C. Ircha, "Regulating Shopping Centers: Canadian and International Experience," in *After the Developers*, edited by James Lorimer and Carolyn MacGregor (Toronto: James Lorimer, 1981), pp. 70–73.
16. Chester W. Hartman, Dennis Keating, and Richard LeGates, *Displacement: How to Fight It* (Berkeley: National Housing Law Project, 1982), pp. 190–191.
17. Ibid., pp. 190–191.
18. Eileen Zeitz, *Private Urban Renewal* (Lexington, Mass.: Lexington Books, 1979), pp. 81–84; La Barbara Bowman, "Handbook Guides City Residents in Resisting Displacement," *Washington Post*, July 22, 1979, B4–B5.
19. Quoted in Robert Reinhold, "Reversal of Middle-Class Tide Sets Poor Adrift in Same Cities," *New York Times*, February 18, 1979, iv-5; George Grier and Eunice Grier, *Movers to the City* (Washington, D.C.: Washington Center for Metropolitan Studies, 1977), p. iv.
20. Marlene Dixon, Tony Platt, and Barbara Bishop, *A Case Study: Grassroots Politics in the 1980s* (San Francisco: Institute for the Study of Labor and Economic Crisis, 1982), title page.
21. Craig Charney, "Fighting the Good Fight—and Winning Sometimes," *Monthly Review* 39 (September 1987), 57–59.
22. Alan Finder, "Tenants Strike Beneath Their Rooftop Pool," *New York Times*, February 12, 1988, B1.
23. Barbara Goldoftas, "Organizing in a Gray Ghetto," *Dollars and Sense* 133 (January/February 1988): 18–19.
24. Michael Winerip, "11 Tenants Persevere and Win," *New York Times*, September 2, 1988, Y12.
25. Cynthia Pols, "Supreme Court Opens Way for Tenants to Challenge Housing Regs," *Nation's Cities Weekly*, February 2, 1987, 5.

26. John Fullinwider, "The Sunbelt Buckles," *Dollars and Sense* 84 (February 1983): 12–14.
27. Roger Neal, "News from the People's Republic of Berkeley," *Forbes* 136 (September 23, 1985): 62; Jonathan Tasini, "A City Born with Gay Rights on Its Mind," *Business Week*, February 11, 1985, 20A, 20D; Andrew Kopkind, "Once upon a Time in the West," *The Nation* (June 1, 1985): 671ff.
28. Cited in correspondence with Stella Capek, September 26, 1988.
29. Robert W. Burchell and James W. Hughes, "Introduction: Planning Theory in the 1980s—A Search for Future Directions," in *Planning Theory in the 1980s*, edited by R. W. Burchell and G. Sternlieb (New Brunswick, N.J.: Center for Urban Policy Research, Rutgers University, 1978), p. xx; see also Melvin M. Webber, "The Urban Place and Nonplace Urban Realm," *International Journal of Urban and Regional Research* 6 (March 1982): 35–59.
30. Burchell and Hughes, "Introduction," p. xxvi.
31. Robert Goodman, *After the Planners* (New York: Simon and Schuster, 1971), pp. 12–13.
32. Quoted in ibid., p. 96.
33. D. Claire McAdams, "Powerful Actors in Public Land Use Decision Making Processes," unpublished Ph.D. dissertation, University of Texas, 1979.
34. Peter Ambrose, *Whatever Happened to Planning?* (London: Methuen, 1986), p. 258.
35. Joe R. Feagin, "Growth Costs and Planning Responses in Oil Boomtowns: Houston and Aberdeen," *International Journal of Urban and Regional Research*, forthcoming, 1990.
36. Ruth Knack, "Where Have All the Radicals Gone?" *Planning* 51 (October 1985): 12–13.
37. Ibid., pp. 12–13.
38. Goodman, *After the Planners*, pp. 171–173; Chester W. Hartman, *Yerba Buena: Land Grab and Community Resistance in San Francisco* (Berkeley: Glide Publications, 1974).
39. Knack, "Where Have All the Radicals Gone," p. 17.
40. Quoted in Rodney E. Engelen, "Meeting the High Price of Transportation," *Planning*, February 1974, 13.
41. David Smith, *The Public Balance Sheet: A New Tool for Evaluating Economic Choices* (Washington, D.C.: Conference on Alternative State and Local Policies, 1979), p. 2.
42. Ibid., p. 3.
43. Ibid., pp. 4–5.
44. Ibid., p. 6.
45. Dave Lindorff, "About-Face in Santa Monica," *Village Voice*, December 2–8, 1981, 20.

46. This discussion is based on copies of development agreements between the City of Santa Monica, California, and H. J. Kendall Associates and Welton Becket Associates in senior author's files.
47. Lindorff, "*About-Face in Santa Monica*," p. 20. His italics.
48. William Fulton, "On the Beach with the Progressives," *Planning*, January 1985, 4; Tracy Wilkinson, "Fierce Santa Monica Race Could Return Liberal Control," *Los Angeles Times*, October 23, 1988, part 9, p. 2.
49. Michael Fisher, "Santa Monica Approves Zoning with Slow-Growth Slant," *Los Angeles Times*, July 31, 1988, 1
50. Tracy Wilkinson, "Fierce Santa Monica Race Could Return Liberal Control," *Los Angeles Times*, October 23, 1988, part 9, p. 2; Tracy Wilkinson, "Minister-Mayor Bows out Praising Tie That Binds," *Los Angeles Times*, November 13, 1988, part 8, p. 1.
51. Evelyn DeWolfe, "Colorado Place Reaches Midpoint in Construction," *Los Angeles Times*, February 7, 1988, part 8, 6–7,
52. Anonymous, "Project Makes a Splash," *Los Angeles Times*, February 28, 1988, part 8, 1, 8.
53. Sam Hall Kaplan, "Housing: The Good, Bad and Ugly," *Los Angeles Times*, February 14, 1988, part 8, p. 2.
54. On Kucinich, see Todd Swanstrom, *The Crisis of Growth Politics* (Philadelphia: Temple, 1985), pp. 7–8; on Sanders, see Fred Boyles, "Hizzoner the Socialist," *Boston Phoenix*, May 26, 1981, 2, 8. See also Pierre Clavel, *The Progressive City* (New Brunswick, N.J.: Rutgers University Press, 1986), pp. 169–182.
55. Peter Dreier and Bruce Ehrlich, "Downtown Development and Urban Reform: The Politics of Boston's Linkage Policy," unpublished paper, Boston, 1989; Urban Land Institute, *Development Trends* (Washington, D.C.: Urban Land Institute, 1987), pp. 14–17.
56. Stephen Wermiel, "Justices again Back Owners' Property Rights," *Wall Street Journal*, June 29, 1987, 54. See also Dan McLeister, "Developers See Victories for Private Property Rights," *Professional Builder* 52 (August 1987): 28, 32.

INDEX

Printed in the United States
200315BV00003B/71/A